DATE DUE

DE 19 '97		
MR 31 '98		
AP 23 '99		
MY 27 '99		
JE 9 '18		

DEMCO 38-296

Drummin'
Men

Drummin' Men

THE HEARTBEAT OF JAZZ
The Swing Years

Burt Korall

Foreword by Mel Tormé

SCHIRMER BOOKS
An Imprint of Simon & Schuster Macmillan
NEW YORK

Prentice Hall International
LONDON · MEXICO CITY · NEW DELHI · SINGAPORE · SYDNEY · TORONTO

Copyright © 1990 by Burt Korall

1633 Broadway
New York, NY 10019-6785

Library of Congress Catalog Card Number: 89-10918

Printed in the United States of America

printing number
  6 7 8 9 10

Library of Congress Cataloging-in-Publication Data

Korall, Burt.
    Drummin' men : the heartbeat of jazz, the swing
years / Burt Korall.
      p.   cm.
    Discography: p.
    Includes bibliographical references.
    ISBN 0-02-872000-8
    1. Percussionists—United States—Biography. 2. Jazz
musicians—United States—Biography. 3. Big
bands—United States. I. Title.
  ML399.K66 1990
  786.8'1654'092273—dc20
  [B]   89-10918
                                    CIP
                                    MN

For my wife Paula—the best there is; for my son Andy
and daughter Diana.
For Frances Preston, a special musical lady.
and
For Buddy Rich, a friend and a great talent, much missed.

Contents

Foreword

I must have been a pathetic sight, dressed in saddle shoes, corduroy pants, and leather jacket, my breath steaming in the December cold, my nose firmly pressed against the huge pane of glass, my eyes focused longingly on the irresistible clutter of drums, festooned with cymbals, temple blocks, and cowbells, featured at the front of the Lyon and Healy music store display window in Chicago.

With Europe on the brink of all-out war, with the Great Depression still doggedly nipping at the heels of the American public, and virtually everyone worried about the future, the main concerns in my fourteen-year-old head and heart and mind were a) deciding whether to opt for a set of Wm. F. Ludwig drums, the sort Ray Bauduc played with Bob Crosby's Bob Cats, or a gleaming group of white Marine Pearl Slingerlands, the choice of my two drumming heroes, Gene Krupa and Buddy Rich, and b) how to talk my financially-strapped family into pooling their meager resources and popping for a drum set for me for Christmas.

Drums—and drummers—were the epicenter of my universe in 1939. That particular year itself was probably the optimum twelve-month period in the entire history of the Swing Era. The Big Bands were in full bloom. Virtually every weekend, the great swing orchestras were appearing at the Chicago Theatre, the State-Lake or the Oriental, as well as the mecca for jitterbugs and music lovers, the Panther Room of the Hotel Sherman.

I would make it my business to take a big double-decker bus to the Loop and drink in the talents of my favorite drummers. Cliff Leeman with Charlie Barnet; Big Sid Catlett with Louis Armstrong's crew; Buddy Schutz with J. Dorsey and Buddy Rich with Artie Shaw. Those guys magnetized and mesmerized me. I had been a child performer from the age of four. I had sung in vaudeville and acted on the radio. At one point, my ambition was to be a movie star.

But ever since I had heard Chick Webb play "Liza," and then Ray Bauduc's stirring march-like beats on Bob Crosby's record of "South Rampart Street Parade," my goals had firmed up, my ambitions had crystalized. I wanted, more than anything in the world, to become a drumming, singing, arranging bandleader. That desire became obsessive, pervasive. I mean, for God's sake, what in the world could be more rewarding, more exciting or fulfilling than to be perched high atop a great swing band, behind a shimmering set of white pearl drums and shiny brass cymbals, while the pretty girls in the front row of the theater or ballroom regarded you with hero-worshipping eyes?

And so, all through 1939, I practiced on my rubber practice pad, attacked the inadequate school drums I was allowed to play in the Shakespeare Grammar School drum and bugle corps, and doodled bass-drum head designs on the cover of my three-ring loose-leaf notebook, when I should have been paying attention to my schoolwork. I leafed incessantly through my burgeoning collection of *Down Beat* magazines and drum catalogues, noting the cymbal arrangements of O'Neil Spencer (drummer with John Kirby's fine little octet), the radical tilt of Gene Krupa's snare drum, the oversize hi-hat cymbals used by Basie's Jo Jones (thirteen inch!!), and the elaborate caricature gracing the head of Chick Webb's Gretsch bass drum.

Things did not work out quite as I had planned. When my career took a turn in the direction of solo singing, I felt a real sense of loss, of unfulfilled desires. Yet plainly, by 1947, the bands had been relegated to a secondary position in the public's affection, and the Day of the Singer had arrived. Perhaps I followed the path of least resistance—I don't know. Or perhaps I realized two things: first, that the glorious, golden, irregular decade (1935–1945) known as the Swing Era had come and gone and that we would never see its like again musically, and second, that while someday, somehow, I might become good enough as a singer to be thought of as "the best," as long as there was a Buddy Rich living, breathing, and drumming, I would never ever be competitive with him. And so it went.

I have never quite gotten over my thwarted ambitions where drums are concerned. I still play them during my concerts and enjoy it. And I remember, with no small amount of nostalgia and regret, the repeated offers I got to occupy the drum chair in the bands of Stan Kenton, Tommy Dorsey, and even Gene Krupa. At that time in my life, two things got in the way: my vocal group, the Mel Tones, and the awareness of the coming end of the Swing Era.

This wonderful book is not only a long-delayed tribute to the great drummers of that period—it is a paean to the Swing Era itself: evocative, nostalgic, and bittersweet. I simply cannot think of anyone more qualified to have authored this work than Burt Korall.

Long a distinguished writer and observer of the music scene, particularly knowledgeable about jazz, and most importantly, blessed with the talent to make you see and feel what it was like to play drums with the famous name bands and be lucky enough to live through that shining time, Burt Korall has written a book for the ages, a superbly researched and realized memoir that will stand as the definitive work on the subject. I am going to stop writing this now, open Burt's engrossing book and read it once again. (This will make the fourth time!)

Then I'm going to haul out my old dog-eared *Down Beat*s and my equally well worn drum catalogues and have a rendezvous with The Past.

Mel Tormé

Preface

This book has been in the making most of my life. It had its beginnings in my grandmother's living room in front of the radio, the center of fascination that captured my generation. I sat there daily and welcomed the preponderance of jazz all over the dial. Jazz was popular music back in the 1930s; it served a function, being essentially dance music. It was the concern of the many, as rock is today. I felt like the ultimate beneficiary. Drums became my sound and music, a central concern. A love affair began.

Memories abound. There were Sunday afternoon broadcasts by the Basie band from the Savoy Ballroom and evening programs by Duke Ellington from various spots, notably New York's Cotton Club. I vividly recall the Artie Shaw band after it hit with "Begin the Beguine," and, of course, the Benny Goodman band. Its records, radio shows, and "remote" broadcasts from ballrooms, hotels, and clubs around the country caught my ear.

Because of the motivation provided by radio, I moved out into the real world, seeking music and drummers in the flesh. My father got things started by taking me to the Paramount Theater, the mecca for name bands in New York's Times Square area. The attraction: Gene Krupa and his orchestra. My uncle followed up with another trip to the famed theater; this time I saw and heard the Tommy Dorsey band with Buddy Rich at the drums. My connection with music suddenly turned into something intense. From then on, I encouraged members of my family and my friends to accompany me to theaters with stage shows.

I graduated to clubs and hotels, while continuing to haunt the presentation theaters. I moved around uptown and downtown New York City. I was bent on experiencing everyone. After Krupa and Rich, I focused my attention on a variety of drummers and bands: Jo Jones with Basie, Ray McKinley with Will Bradley, Sid Catlett with Louis Armstrong, Jimmy Crawford with Jimmie Lunceford, Moe Purtill with Glenn Miller, Sonny Greer with Duke Ellington, Ray Bauduc with Bob Crosby, Cliff Leeman with Charlie Barnet, and others.

When Phil Brown, my oldest friend, moved into my neighborhood, my affair with drums and music entered a key phase. He had been playing drums for a while. At fourteen, he knew a lot and already was deeply into things. His enthusiasm was contagious, and he passed on his knowledge in a very open manner. I had a lot to learn.

I was lucky enough to link up with a great teacher before my

fifteenth birthday. Allen Paley was suggested to me by Danny Burgauer of Manny's, the famed musical instrument shop on Manhattan's West 48th Street. The studying process began before I had a
drum set. I was taught on a rubber practice pad, set on a stand. I
played sitting down. Allen placed primary emphasis on performing
correctly. He explained the best way to hold the sticks and how tightly
to grip them, depending on the circumstances. He emphasized wrist
development, constantly illustrating how to turn them in a precise
yet relaxed manner. "If you hit the drum just right, you get a good
sound," he insisted.

Allen's chief means to excellence were drum rudiments, or strok-
ings, in all their variety. Practice was a must. An hour or two of
concentrated daily practice sometimes turned into three or four hours
as I endeavored to progress as quickly as possible. Allen also taught
his students *about* music—how to read and interpret it. When I got a
drum set (courtesy of my grandmother) after a year or so of study,
things really started falling into place.

Allen had been an excellent drummer at the brink of a great
career; illness, however, had prevented him from realizing his enormous potential. As a teacher, he was a task master yet very understanding. He became my friend and mentor and developed in me a
sense of dedication.

When I got to college, I faced a dilemma. My English composition teacher strongly suggested I become a writer. For several years—
through New York University and during my service stint with Armed
Forces Radio-Special Services—I continued to study and play drums
but became increasingly involved in writing and radio work. Discharged from the Army in December 1954, I first sought employment
in radio. Then quite suddenly I got a job as an editor-writer with
Metronome, a prestigious music magazine that was heavily into jazz.
A decision had been made for me. I would write *and* remain close to
the music and players I loved.

Drums were left behind as I grew as a writer and music business
executive. Instead of traveling with bands and playing with small
groups, I wrote feature articles and reviewed jazz, worked for a record
company (Decca-Coral-Brunswick), and then was hired by BMI. I've
worked at BMI as a public relations executive, magazine editor, and
special assignments director longer than seems possible. Through the
years, I also wrote for newspapers and magazines, and continue to do
so. I also collaborated on a book, "The Jazz Word."

It all has worked out right, despite the fact that I have seldom
played. Do I have twinges of regret because I left the playing arena
before truly testing my ability? Sometimes. But it seems I have been
guided by a caring deity.

As experience shaped me, the love affair initiated in my grandmother's living room grew, stabilized, became permanent. Most significantly, the feeling for music and drummers was put to constructive use. While learning from other writers, composers, and a wide variety of musicians, I gave something back, exercising a talent that had been all but unsuspected when drums were the dominant force in my life.

My work at BMI and a variety of assignments as a writer, critic, and columnist made possible one-to-one exposure to a number of drummers treated in this book. Krupa and Rich became close friends. Ray McKinley, Sonny Greer, Cliff Leeman and Jo Jones were interview subjects before and/or during the research for "Drummin' Men." Cozy Cole was my teacher for a brief period in the late 1940s. The others passed on before I had a chance to meet them.

When the idea for *Drummin' Men* emerged at a meeting with Ken Stuart, former editor-in-chief of Schirmer Books, a number of years ago, I jumped at it. What could be more perfect for me? At the outset, the book had far more scope. It went through several phases. First the book was going to be a series of profiles of all the great drummers. Then it was going to be a history, or a dictionary. My editor, Michael Sander, and I concluded that the book needed a sharp focus. We settled for the Swing Years and the drummers who came to the foreground during that key period. It couldn't have been more appropriate; after all, swing drummers had lit the torch of interest for me in the first place.

The book ended up being something of an oral history. In addition to first-hand observation and/or listening to recordings, what better way to get to know drummers and how they play than by talking to them? If that wasn't possible—and even if it was—there were other fertile sources of information: those who knew the drummers, taught them, worked with them, employed them. I found the people who were close to a drummer could supply a sense of dimension sometimes lacking in the subject's own comments about his life, personality, and performances.

In the process of researching this book, I listened to countless recordings, conducted over 200 interviews and spent a lot of time in libraries and research centers such as the Division of the New York Public Library at Lincoln Center and at the Institute of Jazz Studies at Rutgers University in Newark. The book's content has *everything* to do with my own personal judgment. I covered in depth the drummers I felt had heavily affected the music during the Swing Years; I gave the other important drummers less detailed attention.

I received much assistance from friends and associates. Space limitations prevent me from mentioning all who helped, but the key people must be credited.

Certainly *Drummin' Men* never could have been completed without the aid of my friend Dan Morgenstern, director of the Institute of Jazz Studies at Rutgers University, and his associates Ed Berger and Ron Welburn. I was given great encouragement by PEN, by my personal doctors, Dr. Nat Stockhamer and Dr. Arthur Lindner, and by my cousin Sandy Yorn. My gratitude goes also to Gene Krupa, Buddy Rich, Mel Tormé, Mel Lewis, Jo Jones, Phil Brown, Allen Paley, George Simon, Helen and Stanley Dance, Loren Schoenberg, Judy Spencer, Gary Giddins, David Baker, Stanley Kay, Ray McKinley, Artie Shaw, John Hammond, Sy Oliver, Doug Ramsey, Whitney Balliett, Ira Gitler, Andy Kirk, Chico Hamilton, Marian McPartland, Philly Joe Jones, Bob Haggart, Pee Wee Erwin, Chip Stern, Max Roach, Tony Williams, Bob Thompson, Jonah Jones, Manny Albam, Chubby Jackson, Roy Haynes, Joe Morello, Stan Levey, Illinois Jacquet, Jim Chapin, Lee Konitz, Rick Mattingly of *Modern Drummer* Magazine, Walter Wager, Lee Jeske, Elliot Horne, Jerry Heermans, John Simmen, Ellen and Ken Stein, Lennie DiMuzio of The Avedis Zildjian Company, Bill Simon, Kenny Washington, BMI's Dan Singer, Evelyn Buckstein, Gary Roth and Michael Palladino, transcriber Richard Mealey, Managing Editor Michael Sander, Editor-in-Chief Maribeth Payne, and notably assistant editor Fred Weiler with whom I worked closely to put *Drummin' Men* into its final form. And last but certainly not least, I offer my appreciation and love to my wife Paula for her support and advice and for typing the final draft of the book.

Burt Korall

Drummin'
Men

Introduction

A few musicians are special. They bring something fresh, new, and unusual to music.

Some of these very gifted people establish immediate contact with both the musically knowledgeable and the less informed. Powerful and appealing melodic, harmonic, and rhythmic elements within their playing and/or writing make this possible.

Pioneers like Louis Armstrong and Duke Ellington found receptive audiences soon after coming to Chicago and New York, respectively, in the 1920s. Both Armstrong and Ellington adeptly used the existing structure of the entertainment business to advance the cause of music. Their innovations, integrated within show-business presentations, were acceptable specifically because they didn't *seem* too radical to the majority of listeners. Ellington was particularly clever when it came to achieving a balance between art and show business.

Other ground breakers, more rebellious and alienated than Armstrong and Ellington, generally ignored the rules of "the business" and chose to allow their art—and their art only—to speak for them. Many of these "originals" were mystifying at first. Only a few critics and fans got to the heart of their ideas early in the game. More frequently than not, these independent, confounding creators were denounced by commentators, musicians (usually of an older generation), and a number of jazz devotees.

I remember vividly the difficulties encountered by Charlie Parker and Dizzy Gillespie in the 1940s, by Thelonious Monk in the 1940s and 1950s, by Ornette Coleman in the late 1950s and early 1960s, and by Cecil Taylor and John Coltrane at about the same time. Many people didn't want to deal with what they had to offer.

These innovators and others who modified the contours of jazz—i.e., Lester Young, Coleman Hawkins, Roy Eldridge, Jimmy Blanton, and Charlie Christian—each caused a revolution with their conception of how feelings should be communicated through music.

Eventually, a new musical language is understood and placed in perspective. Sometimes it takes an awfully long time. But it always happens.

Drummers have also made meaningful changes in jazz and heightened its expressiveness. By altering concepts of time and rhythm—sometimes radically—drummers enrich the music and make it more meaningful. Each decade, one or two more artists of vision come along and push music into the future.

1

Baby Dodds helped consolidate the discoveries of early drummers while adding significant concepts and inventions of his own. Other supremely talented drummers brought a sense of creativity and more than a little of themselves to the music.

Zutty Singleton, Buddy Rich, Gene Krupa, Dave Tough, Kenny Clarke, Max Roach, Art Blakey, Elvin Jones, Tony Williams, and certainly Chick Webb, the giant of the 1930s, modernized drumming, paralleling experimentation within jazz as a whole and anticipating what would happen in the years to come. They made possible continuing vitality and adventure in the rhythm section. Because of them and others, the drummer, that central source of pulsation and color, became increasingly important in jazz.

Memories—they come in flood. Those of us who were shaped by the 1930s cannot forget a variety of things: the economic distress, the art, the books, the music. . . .

As a small child during the period, I was balanced on the periphery of all that happened, protected by my youth and my family. Our most immediate response to the economic situation was rather typical. My mother and father and I moved into my grandmother's big house to pool resources. There were no luxuries, and few trips to the stores for clothes and shoes; family members—all of whom were working, fortunately—walked instead of taking trolleys or buses. I recall overhearing several conversations about neighboring families losing their houses, being put out of their apartments; much was said about loss and lack of jobs, and the need for money and a firm foundation.

But in our family group, surprisingly, there was not the despair you might expect. My family became even more tight-knit in the face of adversity; each member drew strength from the others. There was a sense of exhilaration about small things: trips to the ice cream store, en masse, good company, and good friends. Basic things gained in value, like a memorable baseball game, or a tasty meal inventively organized from very little.

There were the movies—the fantasy musicals, the gangster films, the romances that always came out okay. Movies were uncomplicated and escapist; they showed attractive people in situations that took the collective mind away from day-to-day tensions. The cost of a ticket was minimal—and look at what you got for the price of admission: a double feature, news, a cartoon, perhaps a serial. In large cities, the movie palaces had one picture less, but a marvelous plus: a stage show, a complete vaudeville presentation that my father loved. More about that later.

Only the "privileged" went to Broadway plays and musicals.

Unless your family belonged to an organization that bought tickets in bulk, which brought the price down, you had little chance of seeing the "proletariat" plays of Clifford Odets and Maxwell Anderson, or the Rodgers and Hart, Cole Porter, and Irving Berlin musicals.

But there were books. At the library, a person could be transported for free by the novels of Steinbeck, Hemingway, Dos Passos, James T. Farrell, Erskine Caldwell, and Thomas Wolfe. And there were the poets: Carl Sandburg, T.S. Eliot, Archibald MacLeish.

Books, magazines, and newspapers documented the emergence of fascism, the spread of socialism, and the advent of Hitler. But one subject dominated: the Depression and how various kinds of people responded to it and survived.

Of course there was the radio—imposing, generally large, and located in a key spot in the living room. The radio gave relief in the form of comedy by Jack Benny, Fred Allen, Eddie Cantor, and Burns and Allen; adventure with Doc, Reggie, and Jack on "I Love A Mystery," drama and crime on "Gang Busters," "The Green Hornet," and "The Shadow"; and romance and fantasy on the soaps: Who can forget "The Romance of Helen Trent"?

Sports really came alive on radio. The Joe Louis fights were pure and unrelenting in their intensity and beauty. The second contest with Germany's Max Schmeling in 1937, a prelude to World War II, was classic in its brevity and detail.

Music seemed everywhere. It was all over the radio dial. From early morning into the evening hours, programs supported by well-known sponsors featured leading singers and bands and top musical figures. Sustaining shows (without advertising) offered lesser-known singers and instrumental groups, some of them very promising. Frank Sinatra and Dinah Shore, among others, were showcased on such shows.

From the ballrooms, clubs, and hotel rooms around the country late at night came "remotes" by the big bands. The names of the glamorous sites are lodged in memory: the Glen Island Casino "at water's edge in New Rochelle, New York," Frank Dailey's Meadowbrook on the Pompton Turnpike in New Jersey, the Famous Door on New York's Swing Street (52nd Street), and, twenty blocks downtown, the Hotel Pennsylvania. In Chicago there was the Congress Hotel, the Grand Terrace, the Palmer House, and the Hotel Sherman; in Los Angeles, the Palomar Ballroom and the Hollywood Palladium. Other spots also come to mind: New York's Hotel Lincoln, the Trianon Ballroom in Chicago, Sweet's Ballroom in Oakland, New York's Roseland, and "The Home of Happy Feet," the Savoy Ballroom in Harlem. Radio announcers with cavernous voices clearly enunciated the band leader's name over applause, the band played its theme, and the fun would begin.

Benny Goodman and his orchestra, with Gene Krupa at the drums, lit the flame of interest and fanned it to a high level at mid-decade. The music was jazz. But it became known far and wide as *swing*, captivating the young and old. After a highly depressed five years (1930–35), when popular music declined, the situation began to improve. Goodman turned America on. Other great leaders—Duke Ellington, who heralded swing's coming with his 1932 anthem, "It Don't Mean A Thing If It Ain't Got That Swing," Artie Shaw, Tommy Dorsey, Count Basie, Chick Webb, Jimmie Lunceford, and Glenn Miller—completed the process.

Swing revived the music business. The recording industry reflected the trend: Ten million recordings were sold in 1933, at the very depth of the Depression, thirty-three million in 1938, and 127 million in 1941. The juke box business was up. Radio's revenues rose because of the new positive thrust of popular music. Veteran music historian Russ Sanjek, writing about the 1930s, noted:

> In one week in 1938, as sampled by the Federal Communications Commission, 51.6% of all programming, both sponsored and sustaining (without advertising), included popular and light music, and the variety programs that depended on both. Of 6,000 hours of live programs, the networks and their affiliates devoted 2,291 hours to popular music and variety, and only 325 hours to the full range of news programs, sports, flashes, news, crop, and weather reports.[1]

Because swing was exciting and a great money maker, clubs, theaters, ballrooms, and hotels increasingly opened their doors to large and small groups of jazz musicians. The best musicians got work in major cities. But whether the venue was a large city or small, or a town, village, or hamlet, the jazz virus spread and eventually reached epidemic proportions.

Its principal vehicle was the big band. A powerful, convincing, often sleek, multifunctional apparatus, the big band served people who would physically expend themselves dancing to hot items or romancing to slow numbers.

The big band was both social and musical, and it conveyed an almost tangible feeling of excitement. If you heard one at its best, particularly in the dramatic setting of a theater, you never forgot the experience.

New York was the place to do just that.

In the Broadway area, "within eight blocks were the Capitol, Roxy, Loew's (State), Paramount and Strand Theaters. You had your pick of the big bands," recalls dedicated fan Lans Lamont.

> If you were lucky enough to get in, you lived in the theater for days on end. Nothing today can recapture that pause when the film ended, the

last chords of the organ [all major Broadway presentation theaters had organs and organ players in those years] had reverberated through the theater, and then it came: [Benny] Goodman's clarinet lilting "Let's Dance" or Charlie Barnet's saxophone shouting out "Cherokee." You sat bolt upright, nudging your schoolmate and unconsciously beginning to pound your feet in rhythm. The stage lights burst aglow and out of the pit rose this marvelous ark filled with sixteen to twenty men, their gleaming golden instruments flashing in the spotlights that bathed the whole scene.

There was hardly time to catch your breath—the band was already pulsating with life, the front sax section filling the hall with sweet notes, the brass setting your ears afire, Buddy Rich or Jo Jones flailing their snares, tom-toms and cymbals, a row of trombonists executing precision drill, Charlie Shavers or Cootie Williams piercing the rafters with a pure paroxysm of trumpet joy.[2]

Indeed, joy was what it was all about. The big band could be exultant or quietly delightful; it covered all the bases. The leader and key sidemen were stars who became as much a part of your life as the music itself. The big name leaders and players of the time were to the 1930s what the Beatles, the Rolling Stones, and Michael Jackson were to later decades of the future.

You had to be there.

"The universal language of man isn't music. It's rhythm. That's the one thing that people all over the world understand. The drum. The beat: boom, boom, boom. The person who sits behind the drum set gives us the foundation, the heartbeat of jazz."

—CHICO HAMILTON

"The drum is the first instrument. And the drummer is the key—the heartbeat of jazz."

—JO JONES

"Drums were there at the beginning. They have served us well. A common bond, a means of communication, they are the motor in the jazz machine. Drums and drummers provide the pulse, much of the life and excitement, the heartbeat of jazz."

—CARL HAVERLIN

Chick Webb
(1907-1939)

"He represented true hipness. His playing was original, different, completely his own."

—BUDDY RICH

Chick Webb, trying out a cymbal at the Avedis Zildjian Company factory in Massachusetts, circa 1938. Photo provided by The Avedis Zildjian Company.

Chick Webb turned things upside down in the Depression-ridden 1930s. He was the guy everyone went to hear and to watch. A truly dramatic figure, he deeply influenced musicians and excited fans. He surprised both and made them *feel*.

His sweeping talent made the impossible possible. Opening the door to a new place in drumming, he made use of previously undiscovered or disregarded techniques, bringing into focus ways and means to make the instrument a telling source of strength and graphic comment.

He redefined ideas concerning rhythm and syncopation. He brought rudimentary/military drumming into a highly compatible relationship with straight-ahead, swinging jazz. With the help of his great instincts, he made playing with a big band—his primary vehicle—a craft filled with artful subtleties. Calling on his unusual facility, and combining it with a super talent, Webb moved jazz drumming along as no one had before him. He created an entirely new view of what drums were all about in a jazz context.

Very simply, Webb—this computer with a heart and soul the size of Manhattan—was a genius.

"His beat demanded action, (his) drumming was capable of persuading members of the Women's Christian Temperance Union to lose some of their inhibitions or of making the Guy Lombardo band swing."

—*BARRY ULANOV*[1]

"He represented true hipness. His playing was original, different, completely his own."

—*BUDDY RICH*

"I found direction when I first heard Chick. He changed everything around for me, not long after I came to New York. Why? He thought in an original way and knew exactly what to do, particularly in a big band. He had style! *But there was so much beyond style. Chick had drive and ingenuity and magnetism that drew drummers by the dozens to where he was working. All of us in that 'learnin' groove' in the 1930s were enlightened by him."*

—*GENE KRUPA*

"Chick Webb was the boss. The man was touched by God."

—BEVERLY PEER

"Chick Webb does everything there is to be done to a drum and does it beautifully and sometimes he plays with such stupifying technique that he leaves you in a punch drunk stupor and ecstatically bewildered as this sentence has wound up to be."[2]

—DAVE TOUGH

"He came to New York very young. And he was so good they put him in bands. He was just ahead of everyone."[3]

—TEDDY MCRAE

"I don't speak of Chick Webb, the drummer, I speak of Chick Webb, the epitome."[4]

—JO JONES

"He was a powerhouse, an elemental force. . . . The big thing I remember about Chick was the sense of controlled abandon that permeated his playing."

—ARTIE SHAW

"There were great drummers in those times. But they weren't in the same league as Chick Webb. Compared to him, they were society drummers. You know what I mean?"

—DOC CHEATHAM

"I looked up to Chick as a great, great person. His reputation preceded him. When I finally heard him play, he scared the life out of me."

—CLIFF LEEMAN

"You never thought anything except that he was a heck of a drummer and nobody played nearly as well. And that was all there was to it."

—DICK VANCE

"The records keep Chick's enormous talent a secret. They only suggest what he could do. I saw and heard him live night after night and it was never less than exhilarating. He felt such happiness

when he played and transmitted a spark to the players. The man was inspiring."

—*VAN ALEXANDER*

MEMORIES

Chick Webb passed from the scene when I was in the fourth grade, but he lives in my memory. I initially became fascinated with Webb because I had heard so much about him. Musicians and fans who had seen him in person couldn't forget what he had done; they spoke of Webb frequently and with special reverence. Their descriptions of the little drummer were colorful, often precise and detailed. My picture of Webb became increasingly clear. His records and transcriptions help sharpen the image. Though they don't reveal him in his true glory—essentially because of technological difficulties in the recording—they provide enough evidence for this listener to draw key conclusions. Webb was "the man" on drums in the 1930s. No other drummer of the period played with such flair, facility, and imagination. He brought jazz drumming to a new level of adventure and maturity. I'm sorry I never had the privilege of experiencing him live on his own turf in Harlem.

Chick Webb's love affair with drums and rhythm began at age three. It progressively grew in intensity and terminated only with his death. Because the little drummer responded so strongly to music and brought so much of himself to it, the need to play would always be there.

It was a night-and-day concern he shared with several of his contemporaries. With them, playing often displaced such basic necessities as eating and sleeping.

ROY ELDRIDGE: We never seemed to get tired. There always was enough energy for blowing, no matter what time it was. It wasn't unusual to get a call about a session in the middle of the night. Many a time I'd get out of bed, get dressed, and go out again. "Pres" [Lester Young] and Jo Jones and I got around a lot when the Basie band first came to Chicago. It seemed like I never put the horn away.

EDDIE BAREFIELD: Chick played all the time until he died. He never had to lay around and just do the thing on weekends. And that goes for all the musicians back in those days. Everyone was always on the go. When we weren't on the job, we were moving around whatever town it happened to be, looking for action. Each place had its good players and the sense of challenge always was there. Guys from that period, like Chick, Roy, Jo, Pres, Ben [Webster] learned from experience—the best teacher.

Chick Webb's competitiveness and enthusiasm were obvious as a youngster. "Little Chick" played on pots and pans, garbage cans, marble stoops, and iron porch railings in his native Baltimore, long before he earned enough money by selling newspapers (reportedly $103) to buy a secondhand set of drums.

Webb's family encouraged him to play drums in the hope it would strengthen him. He had grown increasingly frail following a tragic accident early in life. He had been accidentally dropped on his back, and several vertebrae were smashed. Because of this, Webb never grew to full size; he was rendered a hunchback and suffered a great deal of pain throughout his life. Drums gave him an interest and a means to build up his body.

RICHARD GEHMAN: Not much is known about his father; his grandfather, a porter in a downtown Baltimore shoe store, was the dominant influence in his life, for his mother moved back into her father's house when the boy was very small.

    The other kids called him Chick because of his size, and the name stuck. . . . At nine he had to go to work to help support the family. . . . By the time he was twelve he had his drums; he banged away at them for hours in the front room of his grandfather's house, and once or twice the police came. Presently he worked out a series of drum solos that got him work as a featured attraction with local jazz bands.[5]

STANLEY DANCE: Trick drumming came naturally to him, and passersby rewarded him generously when he performed on the streets. From there he graduated to weekend gigs with little bands. His first regular job was with the Jazzola Band that worked the excursion boats on Chesapeake Bay. Here he began a lifelong friendship with guitarist John Trueheart, who was his senior by three or four years. In times ahead, they shared prosperity and hardship together, and were never separated except by illness.[6]

Webb and Truehart moved to New York in 1924. They roomed together in Harlem, the center of everything for the black player. Harlem was a mixing bowl, inhabited by the great, the near great, and those on lower rungs of the ladder. Moving in fast company with other enthusiastic young musicians, including Duke Ellington, Sonny

Greer, Coleman Hawkins, and Bobby Stark, seventeen-year-old Webb learned the folkways of the New York scene.

It was a bit of a scuffle getting started. New York makes great demands on young musicians. Big-time, established players need proof that a new kid deserves to be in their company. The proof came in jam sessions, generally held after hours in clubs or apartments uptown. Sometimes there were audiences comprised of other musicians and jazz devotees. Often these contests of musical prowess were just a matter of a couple of players getting together and playing what they couldn't on the job with few witnesses, if any, to document the session other than the musicians themselves.

Webb made the session scene and filled in for other drummers on jobs with bands large and small, whenever possible. Musicians came to trust and admire him. Trumpeter Bobby Stark, who later played in the Chick Webb Band, recommended Webb for his first steady New York gig with Edgar Dowell's band.

When the band was to audition for a club job, Webb showed up, just in case he was needed. The regular drummer got lost in the subway, and Stark persuaded Dowell to allow Webb to play. He filled the gap laudably. In fact, the club owner said he would hire the band only if Webb were part of the package.

For a brief period, Webb was flush, making $50 a week. And because living was reasonable in Harlem, he sent most of his salary home to Baltimore. After the band broke up, the drummer had a somewhat easier time making it than he had before.

RICHARD GEHMAN: People never stopped marveling that the small, contorted man could make so much noise—and noise that made brilliant musical sense—with his drums. Other drummers went to watch him whenever he played a one-nighter with a pickup band. The word would spread that Chick would be on the stand, and those who weren't working would assemble.[7]

Duke Ellington, Webb's most vociferous champion, arranged the drummer's first engagement as a leader at Manhattan's Black Bottom Club in 1926. Heading a group that included saxophonist Johnny Hodges, Stark, Trueheart, and pianist Don Kirkpatrick, Webb worked there for five months before moving on to the Paddock Club under the Earl Carroll Theater on 50th Street. Tenor saxophonist Elmer Williams and a trombonist known as "Slats" were added for the stand at the Paddock, which burned down not long after the Webb band opened. Though the drummer had no real desire to be a leader—Hodges had to exert pressure and convince him—he never looked back. His band grew in size—from a quintet to an octet to ten then 13 pieces—and became more and more potent through the 1930s.

Webb had little room in his life for anything but music. "Music comes first," he often declared. When he wasn't playing, he thought and talked about music and how it should be played. He constantly mulled over the drummer's role in the band and what could be done to make the drummer more of a contributing factor in the music he loved.

Although he had no interest at first in being a leader, Webb grew into the job, gradually accepting the added pressure and responsibility. He in fact became quite intense about his ambitions for the band. Webb wanted two things that are not usually compatible: musicality and success, and that led to more than the usual share of problems.

HELEN OAKLEY DANCE.   For months on end the group endured starvation regimens. Relying on occasional gigs to pay the rent, they would hole up in one room and refuse to separate. Chick set an example, turning down jobs that called for changing the band. He tried to hire and hold the finest musicians he could get; most of the best instrumentalists of the day worked with him at one time or another.[8]

Webb was totally loyal to friends and those musically associated with him. He helped trumpeter Cootie Williams, who worked for him briefly and lived with him for a period. The drummer was close to Johnny Hodges. Webb also had a key relationship with trumpeter Mario Bauza: He brought Bauza into the band, and every night after work, he showed the young Cuban musician how to play his music. Few leaders would have done that for a sideman.

Though he had a strong sense of self, Webb was highly receptive to the needs of others. Musicians in and out of the band were given credit and respect for their accomplishments. Drummers he admired, such as Ray Bauduc, Krupa, and Dave Tough, were treated warmly and with deference. Webb didn't bad-mouth people. He was optimistic and had an engaging flair for the humorous.

HELEN OAKLEY DANCE: Whenever I think of Chick I always smile. Picture a bunch of musicians hanging around on the sidewalk near the Rhythm Club, uptown. Everyone seems to be engrossed and listening intently. Nine times out of ten, in the '30s, Chick was in the middle of it. Until you got up close, you didn't know what was going on. But when you arrived in the center of things, there he was hanging onto someone's lapels or poking his long finger at one or another of the guys and telling the tallest stories—boasting and everything. But he spoke with such humor that no one took offense. His dedication was so obvious and sincere that it only endeared him to everyone.

His most typical comment: "Ain't nobody gonna cut me or my band!"

Business apparently wasn't the drummer's strong point. But few black artists were allowed to handle business matters during that time. In a segregated America, the black musician, performer/or actor had to have a powerful, knowledgeable white person to handle his affairs.

It was up and down for Webb—with and without the guidance of bookers and agents. More than once, Webb took a wrong turn. For example, after successfully playing for dancers in New York ballrooms, he tried vaudeville, terminating a long-term successful engagement at Rose Danceland at 125th Street and Seventh Avenue in order to take the tour. It was a disaster. The band was out of work for a while, and the owners of Rose Danceland were bitter over the loss they took when the Webb band suddenly left the ballroom.

But Webb slowly put the pieces back together as the 1920s became the 1930s. The band played the Cotton Club uptown and the Strand Roof, Roseland, and later the Casino De Paris downtown. The drummer and his men toured with the show "Hot Chocolates;" they performed in theaters and made records with Louis Armstrong. And they began making records on their own: "Dog Bottom" (Brunswick, 1929), "Jungle Mama" (Brunswick, 1929), "Heebie Jeebies" (Vocalion 1931), and "Soft and Sweet" (Vocalion, 1931).

Harlem's Savoy Ballroom became the center of Webb's activities, particularly after he signed a management contract with Moe Gale, booker, personal manager, and stockholder in the Savoy. But the climb to prominence was slow and difficult. The band's recipe was not commercial enough to allow for the Webb organization to establish a strong link with a large audience.

The musical elements were all there. Webb and his charging ensemble impressed with boiling performances at the Savoy and other spots. In band battles with King Oliver, Fletcher Henderson, and Fess Williams, among others, the Webb crew won hands down. Moving through imaginative "head" arrangements—these were worked out by members of a band, memorized, and seldom written down—with enviable elan and pulsation, Webb and his family of players became the talk of Harlem.

Harlem was hot back then, and the Savoy provided a lot of the heat. Musicians, jazz fans, dancers, and the curious gathered there.

The music shouted and whispered, pulsated and throbbed. Its message was easy to grasp; it spoke boldly of good times.

At the heart of all this was Chick Webb. So much a part of the Savoy ambiance, the drummer, his musicians and later singer Ella Fitzgerald helped make the place a magnet.

Otis Ferguson, the stylish and perceptive writer who died during World War II, gives us a pretty good description of the Savoy: It was

a respectable place . . . no barrelhouse, no basement creep joint. . . . Inside, up the wide flight of stairs, the hall must be seventy-five yards long by twenty-five wide; the ceiling and lights low. . . . When the band gets pretty well into it, the whole enclosure, with all its people, beats like a drum and rises in steady time, like a ground swell. . . .

The dance floor is a hopeless mass of flying ankles, swirls, stomps, really beautiful dancing. . . . Everybody immensely busy, sweating, full of spirits.

It is a strange sort of atmosphere. You cannot see everything at once but you can feel everything at once, a sort of unifying outflow of energy, you can almost see it burn. Its focal point is around the stand of rough and well-splintered wood, . . . and the drum spiked to the floor and the string bass fixed in a socket and the big pianos with the keyboards worn like flights of old wooden stairs. . . .[9]

Allen Paley, an exceptionally promising young drummer in the late 1930s, who gave up playing in 1940 because of illness, has particularly vivid memories of Webb. A New Yorker, he made the scene at Harlem's Savoy Ballroom several times a week whenever the little drummer was the attraction. The band blasted, making the stand (60 feet, from end to end, with room for four bands) vibrate. Webb, a whirlwind, totally captivated him.

ALLEN PALEY: Chick was a god. What he did was totally unbelievable. His huge fourteen-inch by twenty-eight-inch bass drum obscured him. The guy was so small and, in some ways, fragile looking. He couldn't have been more than four feet tall. I wondered: How is he going to reach his cymbals, tom-toms, and the bass drum? But it was no problem for him. He had strong wrists, long arms, huge hands, long fingers and legs. Only his torso was short and relatively undeveloped. Sitting up high, he'd lean over the set and hit or softly touch the various drums, cymbals, and other accessories almost without moving. Sometimes he'd stand up and play.

Chick had great energy and power, even though he was chronically ill. He would sit back and hock those drums and come up with exciting and unusual sounds and rhythms. Every night I would be amazed at what I saw and heard.

I got to know him. He was quiet, shy, except behind the drums. Much of the time between sets, he would stay by himself.

His illness and deformity—Chick was a hunchback—didn't affect his playing. All he knew is that when he heard music he played. He couldn't read a thing. Untrained, he learned by playing, listening, and allowing his great talent to grow.

The man was one of a kind. There won't be another like him again. I've heard an awful lot of drummers. But he was the best natural player I ever came across. Fast, clean, flawless, he played like a machine gun ... but with enormous feeling and understanding of what the band was trying to do. It was almost barbaric the way he drove that band. He'd hold the sticks—7As, very thin—by the butt and use them just like whips.

Music was a part of him. He was original; he had ability and technique, an ear and taste. He had it all. Every drummer in town came to the Savoy, at one time or another, to pick up on him. None of us really knew what the hell he was doing because it was just too fast the way he cut it.

When he played a break, it was here and gone. You couldn't get hold of it. But the way he tied in the band—oh, you had to be there! The breaks could become quite complicated. Yet everything fit—each piece. His comments worked as drum patterns and as *music*. And they seemed almost custom made. Chick created with the sense of perfection you associate with a master cabinet maker. You know, I never heard him play a bad break or solo.

What he did was the beginning of the bebop thing. Instead of putting together a bunch of beats on the tom-toms, as many of the jazz drummers were doing in those years, he functioned in a more musical way, using drums to create rhythm and *melody*. Chick was the forerunner of what we began hearing on a broad scale five and ten years later.

He used to play off the cowbell a lot. He'd break things up, developing ideas off the cowbell, the cymbals, the tom-toms. The way he cut the thing up, using the snare as his basic instrument, it would get so disjointed many of us would shake our heads, knowing we could never fully unravel what he played. But for all their "mystery," his performances had logic to them.

When I think of him—and I often do—the word "explosive" comes to mind. He released energy in an almost violent way. His work in support of the band was so strong and aggressive; his solos—they were fantastically syncopated explosions.

The best of the drummers who came to the Savoy to sit in couldn't compare with Chick. Big Sid Catlett? Nothing next to the little man. Krupa? He was a salesman; he played a lot of beats. If Krupa lived four lifetimes, he couldn't play drum breaks the way Chick did.

So many years later, my memories of Chick and the Savoy remain quite clear. The thunder of Chick's drums and the shuffling and wild stepping of the dancers—the pictures and sounds from those nights uptown—are with me. Chick was a phenomenal drummer who played with his band in a historical spot, to a great audience, during a memorable time for jazz.

ARTIE SHAW: In 1929, not long after I arrived in New York, I found my way to Harlem. I was just a kid—nineteen years old. Of course Harlem in those days wasn't what it is now. It was sort of a playground for white folks. Because I was a reader even then and excited by writers who spoke of Harlem in their books and articles, it seemed the place to go and get to know.

It was great for players interested in jazz, particularly white musicians. White guys in New York had few jazz outlets. We were limited to dance and show bands like those headed by Vincent Lopez and Paul Specht. If you wanted to stretch your muscles, musically, your only option was Harlem and its clubs, ballrooms, and after-hour spots.

One night—oh, it must have been 'round midnight—I was walking up Lenox, near 140th Street, on my way to Pod and Jerry's to play with Willie "The Lion" Smith, the great pianist. I heard this band really blowing! What a surprise! There were no bands around town like that. The only band that came close in that period was the one led by Fletcher Henderson.

I just had to go into the place where all this great music was being made. I bought a ticket and went up the stairs. As I moved into the Savoy Ballroom, the music hit me head on. It didn't take me long to find out it was Chick Webb's band. I selected a spot near the drums. And things got even better. God, the sound Chick got out of those drums. What he did almost blew me away. He performed with such power and originality. You know, Chick so completely captured my attention, musically, I didn't realize he was so small and a hunchback until he stood up after the first set!

Unlike most people, Chick realized that drums are a *musical* instrument. He knew that unless drums are treated in a musical way, they're terrible, a burden to the other players.

Like my great friend Davey Tough, Chick tuned his drums beautifully. And he had great taste and ears. He must have *heard* really well because what he played was extremely apropos to what was going on. He seemed to *sense* so much.

Besides that, Chick was very forceful, propulsive. He literally lifted that band. When it cut loose, he was behind every phrase, like a charioteer driving horses. Offstage you would never suspect he could become so highly charged. Chick was a quietly friendly, affable, thoroughly unpretentious person.

I realize he had no training. But that can be very good. Not being tied down to formal techniques can free you. If you learn by playing on the job, there is no necessity of divesting yourself of various preconceptions that come with study. It's the same in jazz with any instrument.

What I'm trying to say is that not studying can be a positive thing in some cases. It depends on how much drive and need a person has. If we're talking about someone with the kind of motivation that Chick obviously had, there is no necessity for study. It can be an impediment for people who *really* want to play.

Looking back, I don't feel anybody during that period could hold a candle to Chick. Every drummer who heard him had to go away saying, "Hey, wait a minute. All I've heard up to now is a bunch of nonsense!" No question about it. Chick was unique, alone in his day. The guy was a force of nature. He came at you! His bass drum shots at the Savoy—I can feel them vibrating in my upper chest and abdomen right now.

It was a tremendous experience for me, digging Chick when I was so young. Later we became good friends and played together. There was a jam session that's affixed in my memory. Chick, Duke and I got it going.

Not only was Chick a great player and a gentle, giving person, he was ambitious for himself, his band and black people in general. I remember when my band was taking form in Boston in 1938, he was playing in that city at a dine-and-dance place called Levaggi's. Now and then he would come by and listen to the band. During one of the rehearsals, he sat very quietly in the dimly-lit cellar, chewing gum, obviously deep in thought. When we got finished, he came over to me and said:

"You know somethin', man? Some day I'm gonna be walkin' up the street one way and you gonna be comin' down the other way, and we gonna pass each other and I'm gonna say, 'Hello, best white band in the worl' ' and you gonna say, 'Hello, best colored band in the worl' '—you know that?"

And he gravely shook hands with me on that statement, almost as if we were entering into a solemn pact—and in a way, I suppose we actually were.[10]

ANDY KIRK: My band worked opposite Chick at the Savoy several times. That was the only place to get to the heart of what he did.

I'd often stand out on the floor after my set and watch him. During an evening, he'd get some wonderful things going with the dancers. He could translate into percussive terms what they were doing out there. He caught everything the dancers did, tricks and all. It was like a show in itself.

And he'd swing that band! Everything was definite, every accent. The whole band was him, really. Being a sickly little fellow, I don't know where he got the energy. But he played boldly. All his strength was in his music.

DOC CHEATHAM: Chick's band had the right style that suited the dancers at the Savoy. His tempos were right for them—not too fast or too slow. Remember, those lindy hoppers had a lot to do with the bands that succeeded at that place. Who was booked and who stayed on depended on them.

JERVIS ANDERSON: Webb's group played what came to be called "the Savoy tempo." In its relationship to what the dancers did on the floor, it bore a resemblance to the bands of the Southwest. Duke Ellington later remarked that Webb's "command of his audiences" sprang from his "communication with the dancers"—and what their feet were doing.[11]

BUDDY RICH: Until the mid-1930s, I had never been any place where jazz was played. I was in another world, a world called show business that really had nothing to do with music. I lived in Brooklyn with my family when I was becoming involved with jazz. One Wednesday night in '35, a bunch of my friends took me to the Apollo Theater on 125th Street in Harlem for the amateur night thing. That was the first time I dug Chick Webb.

He was the total experience on drums. He played everything well. A little later, about the time I joined Joe Marsala at the Hickory House in 1937, I went up to the Savoy to check him out again. What I remember most distinctly was that he was different and individual—not like Cozy Cole or Jimmy Crawford or any of the other cats. Even his set was different. He had cymbals on those gooseneck holders, the trap table, a special seat and pedals made specifically for him because he was so small.

Chick was hell on the up-tempos. He kept the time firm and exciting, tapping out an even 4/4 on the bass drum. That was *something* in the 1930s. Most of the guys downtown could hardly make two beats to the bar; they were into the Chicago style—Dixieland.

Chick set an example. He was hip, sharp, swinging. You know, only about a half-dozen of the top drummers since then, including today's so-called "great" drummers, have anything resembling what he had. If he were alive now, I think most drummers would be running around trying to figure out why they decided to play drums. That's how good he was!

As a soloist, Chick had no equal at that time. He would play four- and eight-bar breaks that made great sense. And he could stretch out, too, and say things that remained with you. It's difficult to describe his style and exactly what he did. One thing is certain, though; he was a marvelous, big-band, swing drummer. Gene [Krupa] got to the heart of the matter when he said, after the Goodman-Webb band battle at the Savoy in '37, "I've never been cut by a better man."

But Chick wasn't perfect. Though fast and terribly talented, he didn't have a stable, well-rounded technique. He was like a pitcher who can throw a ball 100 miles an hour but doesn't have the discipline to win all the time. Chick's dexterity and speed didn't work for him as well as they might have. They didn't always take him where he wanted to go.

A drummer as natural and gifted as Chick should have been able to exercise a bit more control over what he played.

Webb began to diversify his music in the mid and late 1930s. He bought arrangements from a variety of key writers and traded charts with other bands. It was a struggle; he had to take money out of his meager salary. First he used the arrangements of Benny Carter and Don Redman; later he hired Charlie Dixon, Van Alexander, Dick Vance, Kenneth Anderson, and other arrangers to give his band a sense of distinction.

Composer-arranger Edgar Sampson was crucial to creating an image for the band. His riffy concoctions, well-suited to the band's rhythmic focus, blended the written with the improvised in a natural, often provocative manner. His melodious originals, notably "Stompin' at the Savoy" and "Don't Be That Way," brought Webb special recognition, but only became Swing Era anthems after Benny Goodman recorded them (in 1936 and 1938, respectively).

Although Webb arrangers enhanced the band's musical impact, they generally failed to generate mass interest in the organization. But the drummer, who was a hard worker and a great showman, reached out to people while playing compositions and arrangements that he found satisfying and that featured him to advantage.

MARIO BAUZA: Chick was the musician's band leader—not exactly a leader who was *that* concerned about the public. He cared more about how *he* thought the music should be played. I don't think there has been anyone who had a better idea how to put together an orchestra and how to play arrangements than Chick. He had a conception of his own about rhythm and interpreting charts.

He kept saying, "I want the best band. I've got to go to the top!" And he did everything he could to make it. Sometimes he didn't have room rent because he had to pay arrangers—the top guys—to write for him. He was hurt, too, because every time he developed a player, the other leaders would take him away. They were able to pay more money.[12]

BILLY TAYLOR: Chick and Sid Catlett and Jo Jones had something important in common. They all were great showmen. These guys came up when the drummer and everybody, for that matter, had to hold his own spot. If you had a spot in a show in a theater or club and you didn't get as much applause as the juggler, singer, or shake dancer, then you lost that feature. Somebody else got it. It was a fight for survival.

That's why drummers threw sticks and did all kinds of show biz things, while they tried to play in a marvelous musical manner. What you have to understand is that musicians had certain problems during the '20s and '30s. They wanted to really play. But they had to do it in a way that attracted attention. Chick was in the forefront because he knew exactly how to deal with that situation.

Webb in action made quite a picture. When swinging hard, he brought the entire drum set into play as he proceeded, moving his sticks or brushes across, around, up, and down the hills and valleys of the set. He choked cymbals, teased sound out of them, or hit them full; he played time and variations on the pulse on his snare, high-hat, cymbals, tom-toms, cowbell, temple blocks (often behind piano solos), and, of course, on the bass drum. He had facility to burn; fast strokes, with diversified accents, most often were played to forward the cause of the beat.

His set was interesting and unusual in some ways. Built specifically for him by Gretsch-Gladstone, it was a console-type kit that moved on wheels, which made it easy to handle. A trap table, including temple blocks, was set right in the center, across a large twenty-eight-inch bass drum. Surrounding the table were his snare with wooden rims, made by Billy Gladstone, the great concert drummer, a nine-by-thirteen-inch tom-tom on the bass drum, and another tom-tom—sixteen-by-sixteen-inch—on the floor. His Zildjian cymbals—a large one on the right, a smaller one on the left—were hung on hoop hangers from gooseneck stands attached to the bass drum. On the far right, he had a large Chinese cymbal on a stand on the floor or attached to the bass drum, depending on what set he used. His high-hat cymbals weren't too large—twelve inches at most. Most drummers didn't use big high-hats back then.

SAM WOODING: Chick was the last of a line of drummers who developed after World War I. People wanted excitement. Drummers had to thrill people with something. So they got all kinds of new things to beat on and came up with new ideas. The more sensational they were, the better. Chick was in a good position. He had the freedom to do what he wanted on drums because it was *his* band!

Webb provided flashes of color and created a well-defined rhythmic concept. His breaks and solos flowed; they exploded like small arms fire and cannons. What they lacked in diversity and subtlety, they made up for with thunderous, force-of-nature creativity.

At the heart of every Webb performance was his work on the bass drum. It tied everything together, giving the band a strong time feeling, a sense of character, and solidity. Webb brought into play supportive bass drum accents to uplift the band; its individual sections and soloists at crucial spots in each score. He also filled holes in his arrangements with ideas that paired bass drum patterns with what he played with his hands. Generally, Webb made more advantageous use of the bass drum, and *all* his drums and cymbals, than his contemporaries. He pushed drums ahead to new functions.

Webb established outlines for more highly coordinated performances, combining bass drum ideas with what was played by the right and left hands. Nineteen forties modernists, such as Kenny Clarke—a prime mover—and Max Roach, further developed what Webb and a few others suggested in their work. They changed thinking regarding drums. In the process, the drummer became a more wide-ranging player. And it all stemmed, at least partially, from Chick Webb's increasingly flexible approach to the bass drum and drums as a whole.

ROY ELDRIDGE: Chick and most of the really good drummers in the 1930s used to tune their bass drum to a G on the bass fiddle. They *controlled* the bass drum and what they played blended with the *bass*. The guitarist played "four," too. Right? Everything was going in the same direction. It was a good, swinging feeling. Hey, did you know that Chick was the first guy I ever heard who dropped bombs, the way the boppers did later on?

Webb played assertively, loudly, filling ballrooms, clubs, and theaters with his sound. Secure in the realization that big band swing was a *drummer's* music, he performed with great drive. While most other stick-wielders lacked the confidence and capacity to inspire a band, Webb knew what had to be done.

But being a great black musician with a fine band did not add up to a whole lot. Until he discovered Ella Fitzgerald during an Apollo Theater amateur-night contest in 1934, Chick Webb was merely a moderately successful attraction. Not too many people outside the inner circle of the music business knew who he was. Only after he took the orphan singer into his home, became her legal guardian, and made her a key part of his presentations in person and on record, did his situation begin to change.

However, some people close to Webb felt a singer was inappropriate for Webb's band, particularly at a time when instrumental jazz was beginning to enjoy such success with the advent of Benny Goodman and his band.

HELEN OAKLEY DANCE: Chick had been totally immersed in the *band*. And the guys stood behind him 100%. But after he got Ella, it was different, because his point-of-view had changed. He began to see there could be a commercial future for the band.

No doubt he adored the way she sang. Pre-Ella, there was no one on that level. Chick knew exactly what he had. But I regretted the change because it meant that the band and Chick had to take a back seat. I hated for that to happen.

Others also had reservations about what Webb was doing.

JOHN HAMMOND: In 1931, Chick had a band with Jimmy Harrison, Benny Carter, Benny Morton, John Trueheart, and other real top-notchers. It was one of the great bands of its day. And I think Chick would admit that it would have given his present [1937] bunch more than a run for its money. All I hope is that Chick does some soul-searching and gives to himself and to his public a band that will conform to his own standards and one that makes no compromises for expediency's sake.[13]

There were, however, plusses for Webb in featuring Ella. Her hits with Webb, particularly "A Tisket, A Tasket," which was on the Hit Parade for eighteen weeks in 1938, opened many a door. The band got more radio exposure and received bookings it couldn't have had without Ella's nationwide success.

Webb now worked in New York at the Park Central *downtown* (a real break-through for a black band), the Loew's State and Paramount theaters *downtown*, Levaggi's in Boston, which never before had booked a black band, and other venues previously closed to him.

The hiring of Ella Fitzgerald was quite justified. Without her, it is unlikely the Webb band would have become so widely known and successful. Ella was the link that Webb had needed to make contact with the mass audience. Had he lived longer, Webb could have had it both ways. Because his singer was so well-liked and had established common ground with audiences around the country, Webb would have had the freedom to experiment with the band, having a crowd-pleasing singer as insurance. With Ella, he had that kind of acceptance.

Webb never really gave up the dream of having a truly top band. *Down Beat*, in its February 1938 issue, noted:

> Chick is now definitely reaping the fruits of success. His popularity has become so great on Broadway, that he was brought back recently to repeat his engagement at Loew's State Theatre within three weeks of the time of the original booking. He is drawing record crowds on the road and breaking records in theaters. It is common knowledge that in viewing his success, Duke Ellington and Cab Calloway are forced to take notice. Chick is planning on spending all his time and efforts on the band until he can feel it is one of the finest dance organizations in the country. He returned to the Savoy Ballroom the early part of December, and is relinquishing lucrative bookings on the road simply in order that he may have the opportunity to improve the band to the greatest possible extent.[14]

DAVE DEXTER: I caught up with Chick and Ella and the band when they were just starting to make it—in the summer of 1937. They came out to play at Fairyland Park in Kansas City.

I was working with the old *Kansas City Journal* and had reviewed several of Chick's Decca records, some featuring Ella, like "A Little Bit Later On." He had a good, clean band that drew crowds. Ella was well on her way to becoming an "attraction." She helped fill the places where the band played.

Funny thing, though: the Webb band never sounded really *black*. Here was one of the greatest drummers of all time, a black artist leading a black band featuring a black singer. And the music lacked the black characteristics found in the bands of Ellington, Basie, Lunceford, Earl Hines. It was the charts, mostly. And the kind of playing Chick demanded—the precision, the in-tune ensembles and section work.

As a player, Chick was a *bitch*. No question about it. I remember him mostly for his cymbal work. The way he *whacked* those cymbals. No one could play them better. He knew how to use them for a variety of effects and for sheer swing. The man had undeniable power.

His power at the drums stemmed from a variety of things. Not the least of these was the kind of man he was.

He dealt courageously with chronic illness and pain resulting from tuberculosis of the spine and other ailments, developing an attitude that allowed him to move easily from day to day. Webb accepted his problems, but never the limitations that went with them.

His motivation to perform at the top level and his need to be *somebody*—both were a direct response to an innate sense of ambition. But down deep, his approach to life stemmed from the things that dogged him: illness, pain, and blackness. He had to overcome!

While he could control his adjustment to illness and pain, he had no control over being black, and society's attitudes to blackness. Black artists in the 1920s and 1930s had no options; they had to go along with policy. Black musicians and entertainers didn't take any kind of major stand or overtly revolt about *anything*. If the "nigger" decided to make his feelings known, destruction of a career followed. The white man was in the driver's seat.

Webb made the best of a bad situation. He did whatever he could to progress, but between his illness and the trials of the music business, the burden was heavy. You wouldn't have known it if you were in his company, though.

VAN ALEXANDER: Chick was a kind, sweet man who went out of his way to be good to people. His musicians loved him and were very protective of him.

RICHARD GEHMAN: Everyone remembers his all but saintly disposition; he never spoke sharply and always appeared cheerful, even when the pain was blazing away inside him.[15]

HELEN OAKLEY DANCE: Self-pity was completely foreign to him, and he was endowed with a zest for life and a sharp wit that compensated for much that nature had neglected to provide.[16]

STANLEY DANCE: Everyone loved Chick. I remember when I first visited New York in 1937, he took Helen and me out one night after he got through at the Savoy. We went to the Brittwood, a club where guys went to jam. It was a small place. I think Lips Page was playing there. I do remember there were three trombonists blowing that night: Dicky Wells, Sandy Williams, and Fernando Arbello. Suddenly an argument arose involving these three guys. I don't know what it was about, but Arbello drew a knife. Chick thrust himself in the midst of the thing and stopped the quarrel. He was a go-between, a man of respect, particularly in Harlem. If that wasn't convincing enough, a small incident, following a stop at Smalls' Paradise for drinks and more talk, made the point. On the way home in Chick's chauffeur-driven car, we stopped for a light at a main Harlem intersection. The policeman immediately recognized Chick and came over for a chat. The cop was very warm. Chick enjoyed enormous popularity. You know, he was sort of Mayor of Harlem.

MILT HINTON: Chick was a nice little cat, so absorbed in the music, so happy to have a band. He constantly talked about the things the band played and how it went about playing them. I remember he stopped me so many times at 40th Street and Broadway. He'd generally say, "Hey Milt, we just got a new arrangement!" As we walked up the street, he'd sing the whole chart to me. He'd explain: "The trumpets and trombones do this: the saxes play that. Taft (Jordan) and Sandy (Williams) have solos. The rhythm sounds like this. And then I come in." He'd then go into detail about what he played and have a bunch of compliments for the guys. That's what Chick Webb was like. Real friendly and enthusiastic. And how he loved that band!

CLIFF LEEMAN: I knew Chick quite well for a four-to-five-month period in 1938. The Artie Shaw band was based in Boston, our headquarters—the Roseland State Ballroom in town. We were playing there and other places in New England; Cy and Charlie Shribman booked the dates. Billie Holiday was with us. Chick and his band were working at Levaggi's, a posh dine-and-dance spot not too far away.

Ella Fitzgerald, who was tight with Billie, used to come over and listen to us perform. And we returned the compliment and jumped over to dig Chick and Ella. Artie was very impressed with Chick and what he did. He really liked the way he established the rhythmic feel of a tune, playing time on this big ride cymbal right at the start, before the band came in. Artie suggested it would be a good idea for me. And we got it on record. Remember "Back Bay Shuffle?" I played time on a Chinese cymbal for four bars, at the beginning, before the band stormed in.

Chick was a lovely, dedicated person. Drums were his whole life. After Ella and Artie asked him to spend some time with me, he did. The guy never stinted; he gave me his full attention. Often he got so involved explaining and making suggestions that he had to be pulled back to his own job.

I was a kid, twenty-one or twenty-two. Chick seemed so much older and wiser than most people. I guess I felt that way because I admired him so. Because I didn't want to be too much of a bother and barrage him with questions, I tried to figure out a lot on my own. I made a point of watching everything he did on the bandstand and tried to analyze what he played and why.

Chick was very specific about certain things. "When the brass is bright, you step it right up there; stay on top of the beat and play loud with the section," he said. "When the saxes are cool and laid back, you come down and play with *them*." He felt the time should be firm, but at the same time, a bit flexible. "Move with the sections," he suggested.

He emphasized, by example, the importance of dynamics in a big band. Moving from loud to very soft and vice-versa, he'd always be authoritative while supporting the band. No matter what the level of volume, Chick kept things swinging. He established a lively pulse and a variety of feelings. But he always let the music guide him. I'll never forget how effective he was when he made the change from explosive loudness to triple pianissimo. The extreme change of color was *something*!

Tuning drums was another thing he talked about a lot. Chick worked on his drums all the time. Like most of the great players of the time, he tuned his drums in a highly intelligent manner, so as to get different sonorities from various parts of the set.

His bass drum work set an example for all other drummers. He played the big drum *open*. By that I mean he didn't resort to padding to muffle it and make it easier to control. To further enhance its full, warm sound, he used tympani heads on both sides of the drum. He allowed the drum to naturally resonate. He had great control of his right foot, which was very strong and flexible. Chick could perform miracles with his foot, achieving great speed and various levels of sound.

What do I remember most distinctly about Chick? His solos. When he got going, he often was just a blur. His hands and foot went a mile a minute. Jesus Christ, it was amazing what he'd do in a solo.

He played the shucks out of a show as well. I saw him so many times at the Apollo. Without being able to read music, he managed to catch everything the comics did and underline all the key spots in dance routines. His instincts were almost infallible.

Some nights when sleep doesn't come easily, I think about Chick. I can see him on the bandstand, playing for all he's worth. I can hear him talking to me. He had a great impact on my life. He was so helpful when I needed guidance.

JO JONES: There are a lot of things that he told me to do and told me I *must* do that I have never forgotten.

He said, "Don't lose your naturalness; be yourself. . . . You don't have to do *this* because somebody's doing something like *that*. You just go on and you develop what you develop."

When everybody else would be going to after-hours spots, I would be with Mr. Webb. He would be talking, but I would be listening. He'd show me and then come . . . and check me out.

This man taught me something that I had almost forgotten. He taught me *how important* the drum was.[17]

The last five years of Webb's dramatic life were the most vivid and important of all. He achieved a number of his goals. As an artist, he became far more influential. His band was among the most popular in America. His singer shot to the top.

His studio records for Decca and live recordings during this period were the most revealing of his career. Though not well recorded by today's standards, they do indicate his capabilities and at least partially clarify what the people who heard him in person talk about.

Webb was an innovator in reshaping big band drumming and

Chick Webb sits in with the Bob Crosby band during a stage show at a New York presentation theater in the late 1930s. That's guitarist Nappy Lamare on the left and Bob Crosby on the right.   Photo provided by The Avedis Zildjian Company.

reordering priorities for drummers. His recordings show that he was responsible for a variety of techniques and an approach to music that others, like Buddy Rich, Kenny Clarke, and Max Roach ultimately refined and worked out completely. More than that, Webb's creativity altered the general view of the fellow behind the drums and cymbals in the back of the bandstand. Webb was crucial to making the drummer more of a factor in music.

DICK VANCE: Drummers today play so many things that Chick introduced. He was the first guy I ever heard use the "push beat." What I mean is he played connective fills in certain open spaces in an arrangement and brought the band in strongly. He also pioneered when it came to backing important sectional and ensemble passages.

DOC CHEATHAM: Chick was a marvelous player of breaks and figures with the trumpets. I was in his section; I know how great it felt. He added impact to ensembles, too, by backing them in core spots in an arrangement. Nobody did that until he came on the scene. Before Chick, drummers were essentially time-keepers—from New Orleans days all the way into the late 1920s when he began to be noticed. He was the first one to get away from the old concept and move into a more expressive way of playing.

With Webb's recordings, adjectives like "ferocious," "imperious," "hot and swinging," "fast," and "authoritative" keep cropping up. This was not a shy, retiring player. A thundering, enveloping quality permeates his Decca (now MCA) and live-broadcast recordings.

The latter reveal a Webb who plays exactly as he feels. Free of the strictures of the recording studio, he performs loudly, strongly, with great energy and lack of inhibition. The buoyant feel of the band and his strong bass drum rhythm—Webb's prime source of time—make many of the numbers on these recorded broadcasts rhythmically fascinating.

On "Wild Irish Rose" (First Time Records, 1939), we get an excellent idea of his solo style. The time is hammered into your consciousness. During solos, his ideas roll out, unimpeded; patterns build and reinforce one another. Single and double strokes mingle, creating a barrage of colors.

Only Webb's ability to create shapes and statements with a bit of breathing space seems undeveloped. Using the entire drum set, he spews out one comment after another—many of which overlap. He is almost encumbered by the enormity of his own talent and all that occurs to him during a solo. Various meters, other than the one he is working within, suggest themselves. He plays little figures with and against the band. Different but consistently interesting kinds of tension result.

Why the tendency to clutter? His solos were so full-to-bursting because he literally could not stop creating. What drummers like Gene Krupa, Allen Paley, Buddy Rich, Johnny Blowers, and Jim Chapin, among others, heard at the Savoy is best described as "otherworldly." "Even on records," Chapin says, "you're not sure what he played. The accents are so various; there's so much."

But the solos were only a part of it. There was Webb, the showman, who brought the audience to him by engaging in a variety of maneuvers, including raising his hands and arms while performing to get attention. Sometimes it all could be quite puzzling.

BILLY TAYLOR: At a place in Washington, D.C., I had a Chick Webb "experience" worth passing on. During a number, all this marvelous stuff was coming from the drums. But his hands were up in the air, far from the drums, most of the time. Yet I heard solid, musical playing. It didn't seem possible.

BEVERLY PEER: One night in Lincoln, Nebraska, proves a point. It was Chick the people out there in the middle of the country wanted to see and hear. They dug Ella and she had a whole lot of fans. But Chick was the one who broke it up. He held audiences spellbound with his drum solos and little tricks. It was hell when Chick started to perform.

At the Savoy, there would be crowds of white and black people looking up at him. If he was feeling good, man, he'd really whip things up. Everybody would stop dancing, even at the far end of the ballroom, and watch this cat go crazy.

Sometimes he'd get into breaks or solos and go so far out, you'd wonder, "How is he going to get out of this?" But no matter how complicated it got, or how long the solo was, he'd come full circle and bring the band in at the right time. The cats in the band were as thrilled by him as the audience.

And Chick didn't hog the spotlight. He'd let a guy go if he was wailing. This made the band a very personal thing; everyone could live. Woody Herman was like that, too. All his bands had a family feeling.

But when Chick got going, he was a sight to see. It was beautiful to watch him—the way his hands and arms flew so gracefully through the air.

One of the things that really sticks with me is the way he'd let you know when to come in after one of his long solos. He'd turn around and say, "Watch it!" Then he'd box the cadence in. He'd paraphrase an idea in such a way as to give you an unmistakable cue.

DICKY WELLS: I remember playing a week with Chick once when Big Green was ill. It was at Lafayette Theatre in Harlem. All the bands used to go in there. Well, I was down front and the people were applauding and I was bowing and thinking it pretty nice, when something struck me to turn around, and there was Chick really breaking the joint up. He could break up a show any time he wanted. He'd start hunching his shoulders, and throwing sticks, and really playing![18]

Most important, Webb knew his basic job. He kept good time, providing a stable foundation for the band, while adding a kind of rhythmic sophistication that was most unusual for the time. By blending improvisation and planning, and by considering the design of the arrangement and its component parts, he more fully integrated the drummer into the overall performance. By emphasizing crucial sections of the score, and by underlining punctuations and devoting himself to the interior movement of the band, Webb shaped the music and brought to it a sense of light and shade.

There are many Webbs on record. The tasty Webb can be found on "Sugar Foot Stomp," (First Time, 1937), which concludes with a crafty triplet idea. For the persuasive Webb, who uplifts his players and forces them to *perform*, try "One O'Clock Jump" (First Time) from a 1939 remote broadcast. For the inventive, swinging Webb, listen to "Who Ya Hunchin," (Decca, 1938), which is highlighted by a surging, four-bar break toward the close, during which Webb manipulates rhythm and syncopation in an unexpected manner.

Then there's the classic rendering of the Benny Carter chart of "Liza" (Decca, 1938). A well-balanced piece in a medium tempo, it features some of Webb's best work on record. From the twenty-four bar opening solo through various eight, four, and two-bar breaks, he demonstrates space, heat, and musicality.

On "Liza," Webb serves the band particularly well, providing supportive figures and bass drum "shots" to swing things along. Balance and a sense of control are the hallmarks of the recording. Only once does he briefly lose hold of things; his chops fail and he bunches up some triplets, affecting the solo flow. But more than most of his commercially released records, "Liza" has the feeling of a "live" offering. The band responds in a relaxed way to the material and Webb gives the pulse a crackling reality.

ALVIN STOLLER: Chick's sound and the spirit of his playing on "Liza" caught my ear immediately. Somewhat unique for its time, the recording had a great influence on me. I loved Chick's feeling.

JOE NEWMAN: Chick Webb's "Liza" got to me when I was a young, aspiring musician in New Orleans. I must explain: for a while, before the trumpet caught hold of my imagination, I played drums. My father brought me a set and I had a lesson or two. After I heard Chick live—that was it, man. I used to sneak into beer gardens—they call them bars now—and slip nickels into the juke box and listen to "Liza." I was just in awe of Chick's technique and the way he used it. I loved the emotion in his playing.

MEL TORMÉ: Chick knew just when to stop. Listen to his first solo on "Liza." You'll get an idea of what I mean. He makes his point and pauses; then he starts again and further develops his ideas and builds through the 24 bars. It's like a horn player's statement. That's what I love about it.

To move more deeply to the heart of Webb's art, listen to "Harlem Congo," (Decca, 1937). A Harry White original arranged by Charlie Dixon, it embodies the inner drive that characterized Webb's efforts on a good night. The band is tight and together; the theme passes from one section to another, while the man at the drums stokes the fire. This fast opus keeps developing through solos and a call-and-response battle between brass and reeds. It culminates in a fast and furious climactic Webb solo that lacks only the definitive shaping and open space that would allow his ideas to be better understood.

Webb's last years were paradoxical. Success and accomplishment mingled with pain and rapidly deteriorating health. He was heard increasingly on radio in late-night broadcasts from around the country. He and the band performed on sustaining network shows from New York, such as the weekly "Good Time Society." His records sold well; his bookings were steady and enviable for a black band. As *The New York Times* noted at the time of his death, his "fame grew in proportion to the sweep of swing music across America."

But he continued to view his position as something that had to be earned, over and over again. He never stopped rehearsing the band and bringing in new material. The men who worked with the band clearly recall the rehearsals, and how very intense Webb was about what had to be done.

DICK VANCE: Chick knew what he wanted in arrangements. Especially on the swing things, he was very positive and exact, very emphatic about what had to be in the charts. Some people feel that Ella's success affected Chick's need to be musical. Don't you believe it. Sure we had commercial things—records that people liked. We played them frequently. But they just helped Chick to buy stuff that was good.

He was a very appreciative man. If you worked hard as a player or writer and gave him what he needed, he let you know he was pleased. I got a kick out of him. He'd hum riffs to me that I'd written. It was his way of showing how much he liked something. I really got a lot of pleasure out of working for him.

During rehearsals, he'd stand out in front of the band when we were running down a new chart. All we had to do is play it a few times and he had it. When he finally sat in, it was just like he could read.

BEVERLY PEER: He would take everything in at rehearsals, standing in front of the band or over to the side. Before long, he could tell you where every lick was supposed to happen in the new charts we were playing and just how the arrangement should sound. Once he got the thing in his mind, he never forgot *any* of it.

He worked out the approach to each number at rehearsal and got further into the chart every time he played it. After a while, it seemed as if he wrote the arrangement.

The reason he sounded so good and made the band shine was his time. He kept good time. His foundation was either a strong four beats to the bar or a melodic 2/4 played on the bass drum. He was melodic yet positive. All I had to do to get the rhythm together was to stay where I was in time. Soon we'd blend. I had a big tone, even as a youngster; that was helpful. And Chick had a feeling for time. He was awfully easy to play with and he swung with such strength.

Webb became increasingly concerned with his music and band during those last years. He seemed to sense that a lot had to be accomplished before the last chorus. Despite the fatigue and pain, he accepted a tiring schedule of theater, ballroom, and club dates in New York and on the road.

ILLINOIS JACQUET: Not long before he died, Chick Webb came to Houston. I was with the Milt Larkin band and we were working that night. I felt I had to go and see and hear him. Something told me it would be my last chance. I asked Milt to let me out. And he understood.

As I was making my way into the place where Chick was appearing, the band exploded into "Bugle Call Rag." It stopped me in my tracks. Despite his illness, which really was getting to him, Chick had to have two valets keep the drums from leaving him. He played with such strength and fire that the spurs holding the bass drum to the floor did little good. It seemed nothing could hold him back.

It was a blessing to be there. If I had missed the opportunity, there would have been a gap in my life. Chick was the greatest of all drummers—a musician who had what only God can give. He was built for the drums. You follow me? The way his body conformed to the drums—it was God's work, God's gift. Chick may not have had all the breaks in life. But the Lord has a way of evening things up.

Webb rarely took a breather. He didn't want to be known as sickly, so he would keep going. His loyalty to his musicians also made it impossible for him to ease up. Every challenge from other band leaders was accepted. There were at least three band battles—all at the Savoy—that brought him nationwide publicity. The most important of these, with Benny Goodman on May 11, 1937, was one of the key jazz events of the 1930s.

TAFT JORDAN: The Webb-Benny Goodman battle of music. . . . You never heard such playing. Chick and Gene Krupa really went at it. Before the night was over, Gene stood up on Benny's stand and bowed to Chick, as if to say, "You're the King." No one on earth could have taken it away from Chick that night. This band battle was one of my greatest musical thrills. Chick had his own way of doing things, his own style. And that night he did everything right.

ROY ELDRIDGE: Everybody was waiting to see what happened between Chick and Gene. Gene worked hard and played good; he even broke one of his drum heads. But he couldn't do anything with Chick. The little man was mean, baby. He was mean!

LIONEL HAMPTON: How Chick played those high-hats that night! He got that big chopping sound. Yeah!

BEVERLY PEER: It was strictly a band against a man. Benny wanted the best stand—the one on the 141st Street side. He was well prepared and knew what he had to do. The place opened at four in the afternoon. People started coming in at six. A guy named Scrippy played the first two sets for Chick. Those sets were like blood. We had a couple of guys in the band; we called them the corn section. All the cats went in training. Nobody was drinking whiskey. We were in good shape for all the sets. So Benny never got a chance to really get it together. The night was fantastic. At one point, the floor was shaking in the Savoy.

MARIO BAUZA: When we came to work that night, Chick said: "Fellows, I don't have to tell you this is the biggest thing that's going to happen to us. Tonight we got to make history. Our future depends on tonight. So I don't want any excuses. I don't want nobody drunk. I don't want nobody to miss; anybody do any little thing wrong, don't look for me to give you notice. Just pack and go home because this is my life!"[19]

The headline in *Down Beat* was "Call Out Riot Squad to Handle Mob at Goodman-Webb Battle." All-time Savoy attendance records were broken. More than 4,000 got into the ballroom and 5,000 were turned away. Because the crowds were so large and enthusiastic, the Savoy management had to call the riot squad, the fire department, reserves, and mounted police to keep the people in check. In the area surrounding the Savoy, traffic was held up for hours. The crowds outside the Savoy did not disperse until well after midnight.

"The climax and thrill of the evening," says Helen Oakley Dance, "was provided by Chick Webb who, in answer to requests, followed Benny with Benny's own hit number, 'Jam Session,' and blew the roof off the house with it."

Metronome, like *Down Beat* and the capacity audience on hand that night, gave the decision to Chick Webb. The word around town was that the drummer had given all he had. Other fine performances were to follow, but none of them came close to that spring evening in 1937 when Krupa and the Goodman gang came to Harlem, Webb's turf, to cross swords with the little dynamo and his colleagues.

It is interesting to note that a week earlier, Webb and Co. played against the Tommy Dorsey band at the same site. Dorsey's men said, "Come on, Chick. Show us some stuff." And Chick smiled and responded, "No, I'm waiting." As Dorsey's publicist, the late Jack Egan, told me, "Chick was playing possum. When Benny and the guys came to the Savoy, he showed them exactly what he had."

The other two big battles took place with Ellington, two months before the Goodman encounter, and with Basie on January 16, 1938. Both drew heavy crowds. Both were memorable.

SANDY WILLIAMS: We had the reputation of running out any band which came to the Savoy. But not Duke's. When we opened we broke up the house. Then he started, and he'd go from one tune right into another. The whole room was swinging right along with him. I looked and saw Chick sneaking into the office.

"I can't take it," he said. "This is the first time we've ever really been washed out."

You're right Boss Man, I said. They're laying it on us tonight! In fact, they outswung and out-everythinged us.[20]

TEDDY MCRAE: I think five windows broke in the Savoy that night. So much weight going up and down, you know. Everybody jumping on the same beat.

It really was a terrific battle. Chick said, "We're gonna work hard. The place is full." Someone said, "You all ain't gonna make no more money. Just play." Chick wouldn't hear of it: "No one gonna come here and lay down. Everyone has to work. You're up here in my nest!"

Before the battle started, Webb spied Sonny Greer setting up and tuning his battery of instruments. He leaned over to McRae and asked, "What is he tuning up for? I'm gonna kill him before he gets started."

TEDDY MCRAE: And he did.[21]

DICK VANCE: Chick had us make special arrangements for the band battles. Each one would be tailored for a certain band and a particular time in the evening. "I want one of those bullets!" That's what he would say.

The Basie battle also has a story behind it.

HELEN OAKLEY DANCE: I was doing publicity for Chick and wanted to do something that really was newsworthy. I laid one on. First of all, that battle between Benny and Chick: it was sensational. Of course, it was a foregone conclusion in a way because no matter what Benny had up his sleeve, and no matter how hard Gene worked, they really didn't have a chance against Chick in his home territory. He knew that in front.

But after that, I felt Chick had given the go-ahead to Ella. She really *dominated*. The band played a smaller role and its character was changing. I used to argue about it with Chick all the time. But he was committed to go his own way.

I thought if I did something that brought the situation to the public's attention, it would sting him. You know, he hated to be downed in any way. And I thought if I could get to him, things might get a little better.

So I arranged the battle of music between Basie and Chick. The presumption was that we had faith that Chick would hold his own the way he always did at the Savoy. But I knew perfectly well that he wouldn't because, after all, Basie had the greatest swing band around and nothing could stop him from swinging *anybody* out of the place. That's just what happened. Webb was mad as anything and the whole band felt the same way.

I believe I got fired. Or Chick threatened to fire me. I've forgotten. Everyone thought what I had done was unforgivable. But I thought of it as just a way of making my point. And it was.

Chick Webb at the Paramount Theater in New York City shortly before his passing.   Courtesy of the Institute of Jazz Studies at Rutgers University.

But regardless of how Helen felt, Webb continued to follow his own master plan. Unfortunately he couldn't bring it to completion. His health worsened. It got to a point shortly before he died where he had to have other drummers—Sid Catlett, Jesse Price, and Bill Beason—fill in for him. At the Paramount Theater, he didn't have the strength to walk off the bandstand himself and had to be carried by his valet and bodyguard Joe Saunders.

HELEN OAKLEY DANCE: TB of the spine was a terminal illness. But he was brave. He hated to confess that anything was wrong and never complained. He was frightened of hospitals; he figured, like a lot of people, that if he went in he might never come out. He was being overcome by pain and all that went with the disease. Many times after a show or a set, he would pass out. Hemorrhoids, a terrible case, made things even more difficult. He'd bleed profusely and lose tremendous amounts of blood. But game as anything, he would never quit.

His concern was for others. He would take Teddy McRae aside and ask him to look out for Ella and the band if anything happened. He warned his friend not to allow the band to mess up. Even as the chorus was coming to a close, he remained the perfectionist.

On June 16, 1939, the band, with Bill Beason on drums, was in Montgomery playing a one-nighter when the word came to Webb's musicians that their leader had passed away.

HELEN OAKLEY DANCE: He was at death's door for two or three days in Johns Hopkins Hospital in Baltimore and was resisting it bravely until, at the end, he knew he had to go. It was just astonishing. There he was propped up on his pillows and he suddenly said, "I'm sorry, but I gotta go." And he died then and there.

The band was last to know. It played several sets at a ballroom in the Alabama city to a strangely quiet audience.

TEDDY MCRAE: Taft Jordan said, "What's wrong with those people out there? They don't like the band or something?" The road manager called Taft inside the office. And that's the way we found out. We had been traveling all day long. We came straight off the road right into the ballroom—right into the man's place. He knew it. Everybody in town knew it. The story was on the radio all over the country. But we had no idea.

We returned the next day—June 17—to Baltimore for the funeral. People came from all over. I remember the body was laid out in his home on the first floor. It was a three-story house. People kept coming through the little parlor and moving out into the street.

The funeral was one of the largest ever held in Baltimore. People lined the rooftops and filled the streets. You couldn't get near the church.

An amazing thing happened—what I call a shower of blessing. Before they brought the body out of Waters AME Church, it rained like cats and dogs. And just about two or three minutes before the funeral was over, it stopped. I don't know where the rain came from. It had been a hot, sunny day. The crowds of people didn't move. Before you knew it, the sun was shining again.[22]

VAN ALEXANDER: I couldn't believe the number of people that were on the streets and rooftops of Baltimore the day of Chick's funeral. You couldn't move. And it was so hot! I drove in from New York. It was impossible to get to the church without help from the police. They moved me through the crowds. That sad occasion left me with so many memories—kids and grown-ups sitting on top of trolley cars, Ella singing "My Buddy" in the church, Teddy McRae playing a tenor solo. So many famous musicians and entertainers were there to say goodbye.

Duke Ellington, Cab Calloway, Jimmie Lunceford, and Gene Krupa were honorary pallbearers. Fletcher Henderson, Benny Carter, and Al Cooper served as pallbearers for their friend. The drummer's death was anticipated, but extremely saddening to the music community all the same. Gene Krupa, who was appearing at the Hippodrome in Baltimore, paid tribute to the man he so admired. The lights were lowered onstage; the band played taps in memory of the dynamic drummer. Krupa said, "It isn't fair. Chick scuffled for years to get the breaks. And just when he hit his prime he had to go."

The passing of Webb at 32 was a difficult thing to face for all who cared about him. Of course it was unfair. But more important, his life was a comment on inner strength and perseverance. He played a seemingly empty hand into a full house and won.

Gene Krupa
(1909-1973)

"Gene had showmanship and a great technique and musical taste, too. He was an excellent musician; he studied hard, and he had a great feeling for jazz. He was a real classy fellow."

—BENNY GOODMAN[1]

Gene Krupa in the glory days with Benny Goodman.   Otto F. Hess/
George T. Simon Collection.

The 1930s in many ways belonged to Gene Krupa. The most visible of the decade's drummers, he had a major effect on his colleagues, whether they admitted it or not. The Krupa "look," his ideas and techniques and showmanship, even the physical setup of his drums and cymbals, were dominant during that now-distant time.

Krupa brought high-level discipline and energy and a whole array of new challenges to drumming. Having assimilated the New Orleans ways and means of Baby Dodds, he combined elements of the Dodds style with the innovative, driving, highly instinctive big band mode of expression of Chick Webb, the premier drummer of the period, and emerged with a manner of doing things that helped set the tone for drummers for almost ten years. Only with the advent of modern jazz in the mid-1940s did the drummer and other gifted percussionists, like Buddy Rich, Dave Tough, Ray McKinley, Cozy Cole, and even the unusually "contemporary" Jo Jones and Sid Catlett, find themselves being gradually eclipsed by a new wave of drummers led by Kenny Clarke and Max Roach.

In the 1930s, while defining and formalizing a traditional swing vocabulary for drums, Krupa moved the drummer into the foreground. A technically advanced, exciting player, he had a lot to do with making the drum solo not only acceptable but musically and commercially viable. He was the key to the transformation of a much maligned craft into an art. Drumming became respectable because of him.

Krupa was a great salesman and showman. "I'm a child of vaudeville," he once told me, adding, "The first thing you have to do is get their attention." Some critics misunderstood his intentions. Expressiveness was his primary concern, the showmanship merely was a means of holding the audience until his musicality became apparent to those who came to see and hear him play.

Krupa had a profound effect on his fans. As attractive as a matinee idol, this graceful yet powerful performer was not aloof like Goodman, or businesslike in the Miller manner, or sophisticated like Duke Ellington. Krupa met you on your own level. An affable, gentle man, he made you part of his music.

Krupa loved music deeply and lived his passion through his drums. Drums consumed him; he often said that sticks were seldom out of his hands during waking hours when he first began to play, or later, when he studied with Sanford "Gus" Moeller. Krupa always made that extra effort to play better, more easily, and more creatively.

"Gene Krupa was so full of life. And he sure loved to swing."

—ROY ELDRIDGE

"He was a polite, good man. Fairly private. But you could bring him out of his shell now and then. He wasn't the man you saw onstage. I guess he saved his energy and a fund of feelings for when he played."

—CHRIS GRIFFIN

"Gene was the epitome of what you expect in a drummer. The guy was beautiful-looking. . . . And when he played solos in his own particular, easily identifiable style, people would come out of the woodwork. He had something. I guess you call it charisma."

—HENRY ADLER

"People had never before seen and heard a drummer play the way Gene did. He was the miracle drummer boy when I joined Benny Goodman. A professional who always did his job, Gene Krupa made people believe in what he did."

—LIONEL HAMPTON

"He had a sense of the dramatic that was absolutely unprecedented in jazz."

—JOHN HAMMOND

"Krupa the drummer is difficult to isolate from Krupa the showman."[2]

—WHITNEY BALLIETT

"A lot of times it seems that he might have been sacrificing drumming for showmanship. People didn't realize what a powerful, wonderful drummer Gene was because he was a showman. Another point that was missed—his being a showman was just as natural for him as being a drummer."

—BUD FREEMAN

"With the coming of Krupa, it was slam, bam, alacazam, with the rim shots exploding like Roman candles in the skies of the mid-thirties."[3]

—GEORGE FRAZIER

"I always felt that Gene was like Benny Goodman; he had this dogged determination to branch out and explore all aspects of music and his instrument."

—MEL TORMÉ

"He had a unique feel, a groove, a hell of a groove when he played.

—STEVE GADD

"I learned to be a student from Gene. There wasn't a time when he turned me away. If I knocked on his door, he was there. If I had any sort of problem he'd say: 'Come on in; let's work it out.' He had a special quality as a person and as a performer. My wife Pearl put her finger right on it. She said: 'If you assembled all the great drummers on a stage, you would inevitably turn to him. He was like a magnet.' "

—LOUIE BELLSON

"To all of us 'cats' from the '30s, '40s and even the '50s who sat in corner drug stores, playing fast runs with our straws on soda fountain marble tops, or who tapped a hip beat with our pencils on wooden classroom desks, he remains our hero."[4]

—JOHN LISSNER

"Gene Krupa did for drummers what Walter Hagen did for professional golfers—took them out of a backup role and made them far more important than they might have been."

—RAY MCKINLEY

"Things wouldn't be the way they are if he hadn't been around."

—BUDDY RICH

MEMORIES

Saturdays were special. They belonged to my father and me. One Saturday stands out. I was eleven and filled with a sense of anticipation. We were on an outing in New York City.

After a tasty lunch at Roth's, a Broadway delicatessen, we ambled leisurely through the theater district, discussing the attractions at the various presentation theaters. The Paramount Theater came into view. The marquee read: "GENE KRUPA AND HIS ORCHESTRA—ON STAGE." Approaching the ticket booth, I noticed a large, glossy "glamour" picture of a handsome young drummer. Dressed in a well-pressed tuxedo, he was seated behind a glittering set of white-pearl, chromium-plated drums and gleaming, well buffed cymbals. He was smiling, seemingly in possession of some secret knowledge. Upon closer examination of the picture I realized the man had a look of assurance and rightness, even in this somewhat artificial, show-biz pose.

"Gene Krupa, That Ace Drummer Man," the caption read. At the time, he meant relatively little to me. My father said, on the way to the large theater, that I was in for a treat. The drummer in the picture had played with Benny Goodman. That was recommendation enough for him. Even in his business—the diamond business—that had little or no connection with entertainment, he had heard a lot about Goodman.

The year was 1941. Teetering on the brink of war, hopeful but, by today's standards, naive, Americans looked with great affection on the big bands and their leaders. They offered a bit of fantasy mingled with optimism on radio and records, in the great theaters and cavernous ballrooms. They seemed larger than life, almost heroic.

In the dark of the Paramount Theater that afternoon, the direction of my life changed. When the spotlight found Krupa for the first time as his band played his theme, something delicious turned in me. After an up-tempo number and one of his specialities—I think it was "Blue Rhythm Fantasy"—I was never the same again. His flashing hands and rhythmic fire, the crackling explosiveness, the beauty and clarity of his performance did their work. Like many youngsters of my generation, I was converted by the drummer man's mastery and showmanship.

When Gene and I became friends early in the 1960s, I told him about my "experience." He simply smiled. Looking over at me from a large, comfortable chair in the den of his Yonkers, N.Y., home, he said: "I felt the same way about Baby Dodds and Chick Webb. I'm glad I gave you something. That's what playing is all about."

GENE KRUPA: Chicago is where it all started for me. I was born there on January 15, 1909, the ninth child in a family of seven boys and two girls. We lived in a rather poor neighborhood. My father died pretty early. Mama was a milliner; she had her own store. And she was determined to bring the kids up right.

   None of my brothers or sisters were musical, at least not to a professional degree. My brother Pete worked at this small music shop, Brown Music Company, on the south side of town. His specialty was repairing wind-up phonographs. He got me this job as a chore boy at the store. I dusted pianos and phonographs, ran errands, washed windows. On busy days, they let me sell records, piano rolls, things like that. I was about eleven at the time.

Contrary to a myth disseminated by ill-informed publicists, Krupa didn't turn to drums because of any special attraction. He just wanted to play an instrument because the music bug had taken hold. Ultimately he bought a rag-tag Japanese set for $16, from his earnings at the music store, because "drums were the cheapest item in the wholesale catalogue."

The youngster was completely fascinated by the instrument. But it wasn't easy to find people to play with.

KRUPA: Guys in my neighborhood were busy causing havoc, having gang wars. Mostly it would have to be a girl to play piano. Once in a while you'd find some guys who were into music. There were a few little bands in school that I got to hear at socials and tea dances, generally on Thursdays. I'd watch the drummers and pick up what I could. After a bit, I got to make music with some of these fellows and substitute at the dances and socials. I joined the American Musicians Association, one of the two unions in town. AMA members got the jobs that paid less and were on the rough side. But generally these players had a talent for jazz. I led a busy life for a kid, going to school weekdays, playing, and trying not to allow one to interfere with the other.

School in many ways was a trial. Krupa had difficulty keeping up with the work because of the number of nights that he played. Frequently he fell asleep in classes at St. Bridget and Immaculate Conception, the parochial schools he attended. The teachers expressed frustration with the situation; his mother indicated she was a bit disappointed with her son. The genial young man made an attempt to satisfy his family and teachers, while still following his own inclinations. It soon became clear to him that this was impossible.

KRUPA: In 1924, hoping to please Mama, I studied at a prep seminary, St. Joseph's College in Rensselaer, Indiana. I guess she hoped I would be a priest. I gave it a good try. But the desire for music was just too strong. I'll say one thing about the experience: I learned more during that one year than in the three years at Bowen High School. [Mama] said, "I can understand what music means to you. I want you to do what you want to do. But I want you to have an education, too."

While attending St. Joseph's for part of 1924 and 1925, Gene found a guide and inspiration there in Father Ildefonse Rapp, professor of music.

KRUPA: Father Rapp taught me the appreciation of all music. He was a wonderful trumpet player but strictly legit. But he was marvelously relaxed and cool about all music including jazz. "There are only two kinds of music," he would say, "good and bad."[5]

There was another person who had a major influence on young Krupa. The two met at one of the Saturday AMA meetings. Both were looking for work.

KRUPA: His name was Al Silverman. He could play some drums, I tell you. And he knew and talked about drummers who even to him were legends: Baby Dodds, George Wettling and Dave Tough. These were big-timers; they played in dance halls and nightclubs in various parts of the city. Al was older; he got around and took me along. I can't tell you how exciting it was. I got to hear both Tough and Wettling. Davey was with the Wolverines, a wonderful band that featured Bix. Bix Beiderbecke! We caught George at a theater; he was working with Husk O'Hare, "The Genial Gentleman of the Air." I couldn't have been more than fifteen.

Krupa's involvement with music deepened as he heard, came to know, and played with accomplished artists. His friends prodded the drummer to join "The Fed," the American Federation of Musicians. They felt affiliation with that union would enhance his work horizons and provide more opportunities to be associated with the better players. The time, they felt, was right. Krupa gave every indication of having a natural talent for the instrument and communication. He brought these abilities into play during a most intense apprenticeship.

KRUPA: I remember one gig I used to play on Saturday nights. It was at Wagner Hall, a place not too far from where I was born, right in the heart of a tough section on the South Side called "The Bush," around St. Michael's Parish.
    Alfie Gale, the clarinetist, was the leader. We played from eight o'clock to midnight. Every week without fail, come 11 P.M., a fight would break out and last through closing time, with a short pause to let me—and the other musicians—out of the place. When I was about to take my drums down from the stage, one of the gang leaders would give a shrill whistle and the battle tem-

porarily came to a halt. Then, a path was cleared for me. It was sort of a tribute; I had become something of a favorite there. As soon as we got clear, the fight resumed. Things could get pretty rough in that neighborhood if you ruffled anybody's feathers.

Krupa took the suggestion of his pals and became a member of the "Fed." The test for entry into the union—"Make a roll, kid"—was simple indeed. Krupa paid his fifty bucks and got his card. Before long he was working jobbing dates in and around Chicago with commercial bands like The Hoosier Bellhops and Ed Mulaney's Red Jackets. The drummer played country clubs, dance halls, saloons. The music was questionable but he viewed it merely as a means to an end. On these jobs, Krupa met several young white jazzmen including Frank Teschmaker, Bud Freeman, Bud Jacobson, Eddie Condon, and Milt "Mezz" Mezzrow. He looked up to them; they were trying to come up with something original based on what the leading New Orleans black jazzmen were doing. Krupa patterned himself after drummer Dave Tough, an intellectually alert person with leadership qualities. Tough not only played well; he gave every indication of knowing literally everything there was to know about jazz.

KRUPA:　Though only a year older than I, Dave was very experienced and knowledgeable. One afternoon he approached me at the "Fed" and said, "I hear you play pretty nice." Bashful, I answered, "Thanks. Can I hear *you* sometime?" You know, the usual things a kid would say to a guy with a "name." Dave nodded and made a suggestion, "If you think I can play, you ought to hear Baby Dodds at Kelly's Stable."

He took me to hear the great man, who was appearing with his brother Johnny Dodds' band, which also included Natty Dominique (cornet) and Charlie Alexander (piano). We also heard Tubby Hall drum with Carroll Dickerson at the Sunset. Louis Armstrong was the big cat in that band. Then up at The Nest, we picked up on clarinetist Jimmie Noone's group with Zutty Singleton on drums. I learned a lot from Zutty but it was Baby who *killed* me.

I remember all the guys in the Dodds band wore white barber coats. Those instinctive musicians connected with the people whether they were into the intricacies and subtleties of music or not. Baby was the band's central strength; the way he used the drums, the rims, the cymbals was just marvelous. He developed ideas and built excitement through a tune, playing mostly on the snare drum in a somewhat military fashion. He was both a source of pulsation and musical color. Right before going to the cymbal for the rideout, Baby would move into this press roll, dragging the sticks across the snare drum. Man, the place *rocked*!

I kept coming back to dig Baby, always showing my appreciation for the extremely musical things he was doing. It wasn't long before he sensed we had common ground for friendship. Our relationship lasted until his death. He was one of my main inspirations.

MAX KAMINSKY: The way Gene kept time on the cymbals, moved his head, and bent over when the music began swinging hard reminded me of Zutty Singleton. Zutty must have made a deep impression on my old friend.

BUD FREEMAN: Gene was very strongly drawn to a guy in Chicago few people knew about. His name: Don Carter. Don was one of the first drummers to chew gum and use dramatic facial expressions and head motions as elements of showmanship. Gene flipped over everything he did and was profoundly affected by him. A very important drummer on the Chicago scene when Gene was coming up, Don was smooth, technically accomplished, and exciting. I was there and saw it all. And of course Gene and I discussed it.

Almost from the outset it was clear to Krupa that the gifted black drummers set the pace. There were a few white stick-wielders with ability and excellent jazz instincts, like Tough, Wettling, and Don Carter. But the black players were his primary teachers.

From them came a seemingly endless flow of ideas and energy. They played with an unusual sense of freedom. With enviable cool, these canny gentlemen of rhythm gave lessons merely by *playing*. Not only did the great ones know how to lay down the "time," but they had a natural flair for adorning the beat, bringing to it expressive subtleties that both supported and inspired their colleagues.

Just exactly how did they go about all this? By reaching into the jazz and blues tradition to which they had more immediate access than anyone else. In a most imaginative manner, they mingled the sound and rhythmic qualities of the comparatively primitive drum set: snare drum, bass drum, one or two mounted cymbals, a woodblock, perhaps a Chinese tom-tom tuned by punching holes in it. To the dancing pulse, the drummers added unexpected colors and other surprises—a sweep here, a roll there, a tick, a whack, or cymbal pattern down the line—to help the music breathe, define its rhythm, and come alive.

The black pioneers, Dodds and Singleton and other drummers simultaneously developing in New Orleans, the East, and Southwest

(A.G. Godley, for one), indicated that drums were special and deserved to be treated in a very particular way. Via careful tuning of the kit, experimentation with drum rudiments (that stem from the military tradition—i.e., drum and fife corps and marching bands—and go back to the 15th century), instinct, and a sense of creativity stirred by the music itself, these drummers uncovered the instrument's wideranging tonal, rhythmic, and technical possibilities. They insisted, as did Jo Jones all of his professional life, that drums should be *played*, even caressed, but never *banged*.

This group of players sought respect for drummers, which was lacking in and out of the music community. It was common before the advent of Krupa and other accomplished percussionists to describe the drummer as less than a real musician. "How many in your band, Charlie?" "Twelve musicians and a drummer." That's how it was.

Though it might not have seemed so to the superficial observer, the influential black drummers took their work very seriously. The flamboyant nature of the entertainment business during the 1920s and 1930s and the emphasis placed on showmanship could obscure the fact that these were dedicated musicians. Playing well was a night-and-day concern, a central commitment.

In the 1920s, young Gene Krupa was completely immersed in what he once described as "the learning groove." He was interested in every type of listening and playing experience. Intense academic study would come a bit later. At this time he looked to those he respected for tips and advice.

MEZZ MEZZROW: More than anything, it was the Negro's sense of time and rhythm that fascinated us. I would sit there with Gene for hours, just beating out rhythms of Zutty Singleton and Johnny Wells until my hands swole double. I'd show him the secret Dave Tough had dug, that there was a . . . pattern of harmony to be followed and that what seemed like a steady beat was really a sequence of different sounds accented at the right intervals with just the correct amount of vibrations coming from the snare and bass so the other musicians who were improvising got the foundation to carry on and be more inventive. . . . I showed Gene how to keep the bass and snare in tune, and to get cymbals that ring in tune and were pitched in certain keys. . . . [6]

Krupa became intimately involved with a bunch of jazz-mad, white Chicagoans around his own age. Today, almost seventy years later, their coming together is seen as crucial to the progression of jazz. The Austin High Gang and other like-thinking emerging musicians in the area evolved what is now known as the Chicago style.

KRUPA: We were deeply affected by what the black musicians around town were doing, particularly Louis Armstrong. And out of all that came the Chicago way of doing things.

Actually, the way it all happened for me—Davey [Tough] was sort of restless; he wanted to write and so he went to Europe. Jimmy McPartland, Bud Freeman, Eddie Condon, Frank Teschmaker, Jim Lanigan, Joe Sullivan, Mezzrow—guys from Austin High and a few other fellows—had some work. They shopped around for a drummer. Someone recommended me; I believe it was Bud. And I got to play with them. It was great, like dessert, exchanging ideas with Tesch, Condon, Bud, and the rest after so many nights with commercial bands.

Our desire to be together more frequently resulted in marvelous after-hour sessions at the Three Deuces, a club across the street from the Chicago Theater. All the Chicago jazz people and musicians passing through came in to blow. Bix Beiderbecke, who was with Jean Goldkette and later went with Paul Whiteman, made it a habit. My future employer, Benny Goodman, also performed at several of the sessions. He was with Ben Pollack at the time.

But of all the players who jammed at the Deuces—I guess it was in 1927—Teschmaker was our favorite. We thought he was superior to Bix, so much more of a technician.

JIMMY MCPARTLAND: All of us were very ambitious; we wanted to *really* play. Like Gene, we were completely wrapped up in jazz and the desire to improve. People say the Chicago guys expanded on the New Orleans style and added something significant. What we did was take it from two-beat into four beat. It was simple as that.

RAY MCKINLEY: I met Gene at about this time. I was working with the Beasley Smith band out of Nashville at Lake Pawpaw in Michigan and Gene had a job with the Joe Kayser band from Chicago a half mile away. We used to get together and talk. He was very promising and just a kid, you know. I'll confess he was a better drummer than I was at the time. As for later on—I don't think so.

Krupa's close association with the Austin High Gang—also known as the West Side Mob—cemented his position in Chicago musical circles.

KRUPA: My first big break in Chicago came while I was working in Indiana at Violet Down's, a "black and tan" place with a colored revue and a line of about sixteen girls. Musically, it was a pretty good job. I dug playing jazz and backing the girls. But we weren't getting paid. And I was being pressured at home to get a *normal* job, to do better at school.

One day I got this call from Leo Shukin, a trumpet player who later became a writer in Hollywood. He said he was putting a band together, including guys like Teschmaker, Mezzrow, trombonist Floyd O'Brien, and pianist Joe Sullivan for the Rendezvous, a club in downtown Chicago. He had been hearing about me—probably from Tesch—and suggested I rehearse with the band. I went in one afternoon and played. He liked what he heard and hired me. I was absolutely thrilled.

I went to work that night in Indiana and told the bosses about what had happened. They all but dismissed it. "You don't want that job," they said, snickering more than a little about my great opportunity. I was broken-hearted. I called Leo and told him these guys wouldn't let me out. He quietly asked for the top man's name. The next night when I arrived at the Indiana gig, the boss handed me three weeks back pay and patted me on the back, benevolently, and said, "Gene, God bless you, son. We'll see you. We know you're going to be an enormous success."

Shukin had called his uncle Johnny Fogerty, a big man around Chicago who knew how to throw his weight around. Johnny got on the phone with the Indiana bossman and made it clear that if his request concerning my release was not granted, people would be hurt. Simple as that.

More and more people came to realize that the Chicagoans were on to something. To bring the music to records was the next logical step.

KRUPA: Our biggest champion was singer Red McKenzie who, with his Mound City Blues Blowers, had made it big in vaudeville. He fell in love with us and, being a big shot, used his influence to arrange some record dates with Tommy Rockwell. The label: Okeh. If I remember correctly, it was some time in December of 1927. Billed as McKenzie and Condon's Chicagoans, McPartland, Freeman, Teschmaker, Sullivan, Condon, Lanigan, and I made four sides—"China Boy," "Sugar," "Nobody's Sweetheart," and "Liza." The recordings made an enormous impression on musicians through the country, particularly in New York. The Dorseys, Red Nichols, Bix, Vic Berton, and fellows like that really were surprised. They felt we had moved the music one step ahead by modernizing New Orleans ideas and techniques and adding touches of our own.

Krupa came to the sessions with his complete drum set—one of the first times this had been done. Rockwell was convinced the recording equipment couldn't handle a complete set; most drummers used only a snare and cymbals. Red McKenzie, on hand but not a participant, persuaded Rockwell to give it a try, saying that if things went wrong, "I'll take the rap." Needless to say, everything worked out.

EDDIE CONDON: The nights and years of playing in cellars and saloons and ballrooms, of practicing separately and together, of listening to Louis and Joe Oliver and Jimmy Noone and Leon Rappolo, of losing sleep and breathing bad air and drinking licorice gin, paid off. We were together and apart at the same time, tying up a package with six different strings. Krupa's drums went through us like a triple bourbon.[7]

RICHARD HADLOCK: The biggest surprise was Krupa, an unknown whose . . . drum work on these sessions rocked the New York jazz cliques, and ultimately unseated Vic Berton as their chief percussionist. Krupa's intense study of Dodds, Singleton, and Tough, along with his natural energy and superb sense of time, placed him, as of the last days of 1927, in the front rank of drummers.

Most of the music was freely improvised in a small band style that stemmed from the New Orleans Rhythm Kings, various Beiderbecke recording groups, the Dodds brothers combination, Jimmy Noone, and inevitably, a number of semicommercial units around Chicago in which the gang had played over the years.

Hadlock also noted that the Eastern jazz establishment was particularly fascinated by two devices used on the four sides made during the December 1927 McKenzie-Condon Chicagoan sessions for Okeh (three of these—"Liza," "China Boy," and "Nobody's Sweetheart"—appear on Columbia's *The Sound of Chicago*, Volume II). One was the *explosion*, "a sudden flare preceding each repetition of the initial melodic statement in a conventional song structure," Hadlock explained. The other device was the shuffle rhythm, "a staccato, heavily-accented eighth-note pattern usually applied to the bridge or release of a song. These and other simple but effective methods of increasing and releasing tensions came largely from the mind of Dave Tough, who, more than any other single musician, translated New Orleans musical ideas into the jazz language of the Chicagoans."[8]

Krupa was particularly proud of his "traditional" playing. It reached back to New Orleans and his respect for players like Dodds and Singleton while emphasizing pulsation and the colors essential to various basic elements of the drum set. On several occasions, he told me that it was the aspect of his performance that had a real sense of authenticity and ultimate value. He found the traditional playing immensely effective later on when he was competitively involved with Buddy Rich: "It would bail me out when Buddy was about to wash me away during many Jazz at the Philharmonic concerts in the 1950s."

Indeed, the McKenzie-Condon Chicagoans recordings and others made in the next few years with Red Nichols and Fats Waller, among others, had about them an almost tangible excitement. Krupa was a mass of organized enthusiasm; he interacted with the other players, providing the pulse and rhythmic counterpoint, using drums, cymbals, rims. He had assimilated the lessons of Dodds and Singleton, but brought to their style more than a little of himself.

JOHN HAMMOND: He was into a new concept of drumming on those McKenzie-Condon Chicagoan records. Gene was rock solid and swinging. Really extraordinary. When I got the records at prep school, I felt he was the best drummer I had heard up until that time. He had something fine going in the Chicago years. Later on when he joined Benny Goodman and became so insanely popular, he would occasionally lose his concentration or get too excited. His "time" wouldn't always be reliable.

Because of the success of the McKenzie-Condon recordings, the Chicagoans felt it was time for them to mount an attack on New York. Singer Bee Palmer provided the opportunity. A major star in clubs and vaudeville who stylistically resembled another leading singer of the period, Helen Morgan, she signed to play an engagement at one of Manhattan's smart supper clubs. She asked Krupa and his friends— Teschmaker, Condon, Freeman, Joe Sullivan—to back her. The drummer quit a lucrative job with Eddie Neibauer's Seattle Harmony Kings. McPartland was contacted in New York. A meeting of the clan was arranged. The guys left Chicago, thinking the Apple would be carved up among them.

KRUPA: Things didn't work out. The top men at the club thought Bee was great but that we were ruining it for her. So there we were in the big town with few prospects. We went into a bit of a panic. How to pay the rent at the Cumberland Hotel where we all lived? The Dorseys, Bix, and others who respected us threw a bit of work our way and kept us eating.

I recorded with Tesch, Condon, and Sullivan during the summer of '28. Red McKenzie talked to Miff Mole and Red Nichols and persuaded them to use us on another recording session. We cut "Shim-Me-Sha-Wabble" and "One Step to Heaven" ["Windy City Stomp"] under Miff's name. Red was on cornet; Miff, trombone; Tesch, clarinet; Joe Sullivan, piano. Condon played banjo and I was on drums. At about this time, Sullivan, Jack Teagarden, Benny Goodman, and I started going uptown to Harlem to hear what was happening. It took up the slack when we weren't working and made for great kicks. We would go from one place to another, sitting in where we could. We had learned a good deal, listening to and hanging out with black players. Making the rounds in Harlem helped further our education.

Because of his mother's illness, Krupa returned to Chicago in the latter part of 1928. He worked at the Golden Pumpkin with Thelma Terry and her Playboys in the company of the two Buds—Jacobson and Freeman—and Floyd O'Brien and made what some critics feel is a rather significant recording: "Craze-ology"/"Can't Help Lovin' Dat Man," on Okeh Records (reissued on Columbia's *The Sound of Chicago*, Volume II). The band was Bud Freeman's, and featured four horns and rhythm, with Red McKenzie on vocals. The record summed up what the Chicagoans had learned in New York.

KRUPA: When I returned to New York, I joined Red Nichols' band. We went into the Hollywood Restaurant on Broadway to back a Nils T. Granlund [NTG] Revue and to play dance music. Our primary job was to "cut" the show and give the line of forty or fifty girls the musical stimulation they needed. It was a good band, thirteen strong; clarinetist-saxophonist Pee Wee Russell, Sullivan, and Glenn Miller were among my associates on this job. Glenn was doubling down the street as a member of the Paramount Theater house band.

I remember they had a Samoan number in the show. I got together a hot tom-tom routine; NTG and the girls went crazy. The way I used the tom-tom *made* the number. And people around town said, "We don't know what the kid is doing but he's sure playing that show!"

My first major success in New York had *everything* to do with the Chicago drum style. Unlike the New Yorkers, we Chicagoans were raw, more primitive, on the black side. The top white players in town like Vic Berton, Chauncey Morehouse, and George Beebe played mostly on the cymbals, doing little tricks underneath them and things like that. We moved the beat along on the drums—snare, tom-toms, bass drum. As time passed, however, an interesting thing began happening. Exchange of ideas became increasingly common. Black drummers uptown and guys downtown found things in our playing that they could use. And we learned ever so much from them. I was affected by a variety of influences and people; my style started to show signs of change.

While evolving conceptually and stylistically with increasing speed, Krupa continued to make records and accept important jobs.

Playing in the pit bands of two Broadway musicals was a major step forward. The first musical, the George and Ira Gershwin and George S. Kaufman collaboration *Strike Up the Band*, employed jazzmen hand-picked by Gershwin, including Red Nichols, Benny Goodman, Glenn Miller, Jack Teagarden, Jack Jenney, Babe Russin, and the drummer. The show, a satirical attack on war, opened at the Times Square Theater on January 14, 1930, and ran 191 performances.

For Krupa, the show was quite memorable. It provided an opportunity for him to show what he had learned in his travels through Harlem. At rehearsals, Krupa added a "hip" touch to "I Got A Crush On You"; he introduced Gershwin to the "freeze beat," something he had first come across in a Cotton Club show starring Duke Ellington, his orchestra, and the Cotton Club dancers.

This is what happened: The now-standard Gershwin song breezed along. At certain prearranged points, the band, dancers, singers, and actors "froze" for a bar or two. The pauses simultaneously offered the unexpected and focused the audience's attention on the stage. The little gimmick stopped the show every night of the run and made Krupa a Gershwin favorite. The composer insisted that he be in the pit for his next musical, *Girl Crazy*.

KRUPA: Recognition from a man of that stature was great for the ego. I was really flattered that he felt I brought something significant to his music.

MAX KAMINSKY: Gerswhin was crazy about his playing, and no wonder, because Gene was the first white drummer in a Broadway pit band who could swing the beat so that chorus girls could kick in time.[9]

The closing of *Girl Crazy* in 1931 after 272 performances found Krupa at an important juncture of his career. He had come to realize that good, instinctive playing was not enough, at least for him. It was clear that if Glenn Miller hadn't been in the pit of both shows, he might not have been able to make things work as well as they did.

KRUPA: I couldn't tell a quarter note from an eighth note and Glenn knew it. So every time we got a new thing to do, I'd pass my part up to Glenn who'd hum it for me a few times until I got it in my head. The conductor of the orchestra never caught on.[10]

It was time for some serious thinking about direction and the future. The natural ability, the enthusiasm and intensity were apparent. Recordings with Red Nichols, Muggsy Spanier (the Chicago Rhythm Kings), Miff Mole, and others represented a mingling of the good and bad, the creative and the wasteful that would identify Krupa's playing throughout his career. The balance, though, was in his favor.

Krupa had an immense feeling for jazz, despite a tendency to be a bit overbearing. He played little fills—as on "There'll Be Some Changes Made" with the Chicago Rhythm Kings (Brunswick-Vocalion, 1928)—that grew directly from the music and fit perfectly. He had the ability to make music move, bringing to it and his fellow musicians an uplifting, engaging feeling. Very simply, Krupa swung.

The Krupa influence was not only apparent at home but abroad as well. His recordings shaped the ideas of British drummers in particular. Veteran drummer and jazz journalist Harry Francis remembers that the Red Nichols recording of "After You've Gone" (English Brunswick, 1930) had a Krupa four-bar break: "One of the most exciting ever . . . that was to redirect the work of many British drummers."[11]

Interest in Krupa increased. His adaptability made possible some movie work on Long Island and many calls for jazz and commercial jobs. But this was not enough for him. He wanted to know a lot more and play better.

KRUPA: Music was absolutely everything to me then. Nothing existed but a set of drums. I made up my mind to excel as a "legit" drummer, while also trying to deepen my knowledge and understanding of jazz. Sanford "Gus" Moeller became my teacher. He taught the "up and down stroke" method of playing the twenty-six drum rudiments. It was his feeling that you've got to keep your hands and arms moving, rather than emphasizing just wrist action and flexibility. The whole secret of the universe is motion, he said. You don't hold your hand in the ready position until it's time to hit the drum. It has to be doing something.

ALLEN PALEY: Moeller, who had played at the Metropolitan Opera House and with the Seventh Regiment Army Band at the Armory on Park Avenue, understood the instrument as well as a surgeon does the human body. His system, which you had to modify in order to play sitting down—he generally stood—was a matter of three strokes that you brought together in a smooth flow. The tap stroke from the wrist; the up stroke and the down stroke for leverage. When I went to Moeller, Gene warned me not to allow Moeller's method to overpower me; it originally was fashioned for parade and concert drummers. To play with dance and jazz bands, you had to modify what Moeller taught and proceed from there. That's what Gene did and it worked. He took the best of Moeller, the strength, the grace, elegance, and continuity and applied it in a jazz sense.

KRUPA: I practiced on the rubber pad, six, seven, eight hours a day, after a while inventing my own variations on the rudiments. I wanted to make them work in jazz as well as they did in legit music. The possibilities were there and as time passed I sensed great progress. My work with Moeller made possible more graceful playing, better control and freedom to be myself no matter what kind of music I had to interpret.

     The involvement with the ins and outs of legit drumming became so intense that whenever I hit a town during a tour, I would try to meet with the top teacher and exchange ideas with him. In Boston, it was George Lawrence Stone; in Pittsburgh, Bill Hammond; further up in the New England area, Burns Moore. I had a pretty fair reputation, even in the early 1930s, and also a great 'in' because I was a Moeller student. These teachers would see me just to argue, if nothing else.

All the while Krupa's education in Harlem was continuing. He played and listened and learned. Krupa took all he could from each experience and filtered out what was best for him.

When Krupa discovered Chick Webb, it changed his life. Like most ambitious drummers of the time, he became obsessed with Webb. "He spent every possible free moment uptown at the Savoy and other places where Webb and his band played," Allen Paley said. "I know because I was at the same places night after night trying to unravel what the little man was doing. What Gene did was take many of the techniques 'downtown,' so to speak."

KRUPA: When I heard Chick for the first time at the Dunbar Palace uptown he gave me an entirely different picture of jazz drums. I had admired Baby and Zutty; Cuba Austin, the drummer with McKinney's Cotton Pickers, had flash and some good ideas. But Chick taught me more than anyone. I learned practically *everything* from him.

Before digging Chick, I was on the small-band kick, Chicago style, the offshoot of the New Orleans-Dixieland idea. Chick brought out a more modern tip. To begin with, he was a terrific high-hat man. Indeed he was one of the first I ever heard use a high-hat. He worked those cymbals with great facility and freedom and taste. The sound he got from his drums was marvelous. His playing, so clean and fast and technical, had the kind of drive that is impossible to describe if you weren't there to feel it. The records don't do him justice. Chick was the guy who made big band playing an art, a great craft. He introduced so many things. He showed us, by example, how to back sections, how to shade for the ensemble, how to play for soloists, how to structure drum solos and make breaks count. Talk about fast: he and the band played "Clap Hands Here Comes Charlie" at a tempo that was out of sight. Up tempos never seemed a scuffle for him; he dealt with them without any strain; everything seemed to come out and what he played fit. Chick did everything by instinct; he was thoroughly natural. I'll never forget him.

Many nights in Harlem, I had the good fortune to sit in with Chick's band. I played Luis Russell's band as well; he was at the Saratoga Club. The band featured guys like Red Allen, the great trumpeter, trombonist J.C. Higginbotham, clarinetist Omer Simeon, Paul Barbarin was the drummer—he had a beautiful simplicity about his playing. I got to play with Louis at Connie's Inn and even had a gig, some time in 1929, with Mezz, Tommy and Jimmy Dorsey, Joe Sullivan, Max Kaminsky, Bud Freeman, and Bix at the Renaissance Ballroom. The Renaissance was great on Sundays. A band with Zutty Singleton on drums was the feature. A kid used to hang around the band and occasionally sing a chorus or two. It was Cab Calloway.

What else do I remember? George Stafford was frightening drummers by the dozen with the Charlie Johnson band at Smalls' Paradise. What a show drummer! Ellington, a musician with a rare sense of the dramatic, dominated the scene at the Cotton Club. His sidekick Sonny Greer set an example for all the drummers in town. He had the shiniest and sharpest set around. A veritable battery—drums, cymbals, cowbells, gongs, vibraphone, it really looked terrific on the Cotton Club stage and added a bit more glamour to the Ellington image.

The jazz musician "lived" uptown but made his *living* downtown—generally with commercial bands. He viewed the uptown-downtown situation as an opportunity to round himself out as a percussionist. After *Girl Crazy* closed, the drummer went with Irving

Aaronson and his Commanders, a very businesslike yet entertaining big band that specialized in playing hotels and theaters.

KRUPA: I stayed with the Commanders for a year, until 1932. Then I joined singer Russ Colombo's band, which had been put together by Benny Goodman. Good people were hired—Jimmy McPartland, Harry Goodman, Jimmy Lord, Bo Ashford, Joe Sullivan. We worked a lot in and around New York. Many theater dates. I learned a great deal; you not only had to play drums in a theater but chimes, vibraphone, and timpani as well.

I recorded with Colombo—some romantic stuff: "You Call It Madness, I Call It Love," "Street of Dreams," that type of thing. [Both were recorded for Victor; the latter in November 1932; the former before Krupa actually joined the band, in September, 1931.] Russ was easygoing, a good person to work for. But Benny made things a bit difficult on occasion.

Romance made the Colombo band and broke it up. We suddenly got two weeks pay at the Shubert Theater in Cincinnati and were told it was all over. Russ had to hurry out to Reno and settle some personal problems with a lady. He found the problem *so* pressing he had to set us adrift.

BOB HAGGART: I heard Gene quite often in the early 1930s. My first time at New York's Roseland, I caught him with Sam Lanin—the Dorsey Brothers and Pee Wee Russell were in the band. A little later, I heard him with the Colombo band at the Park Central Roof. He was quite young and I was younger—fifteen years old. I was very impressed; he really had something in those days. His "sensational" style, though not exactly to my taste, communicated strongly with audiences. Though I generally prefer a more subtle approach to playing, Gene consistently made his point.

JIM CHAPIN: Everything that Gene played he meant. He was committed to what he played. The acting, the motion, were a part of him. Even when he played the simplest thing, it was dramatic and had a particular *sound*. The man was a theatrical player. Emotion and theatricality were linked in his case. Without showmanship, it didn't have the same intensity. Even with your eyes closed you could tell if he was performing with feeling or if the whole thing was done deadpan.

KRUPA: Right after the Colombo band folded, Paul Mertz of the Horace Heidt organization came along and hired the entire band. We played the new Roxy, a New York theater that later became the Center Theater and featured ice shows. There was no real music in the Heidt library. He concerned himself almost entirely with gimmicks and tricks. The saver was the percussion section— a mallet man (vibes and xylophone) and two drummers—Vic Berton and myself.

Before the crucial move into the Benny Goodman band in 1934, Krupa continued to move from band to band. He worked with Mal Hallett, a great showman, who made a point of hiring excellent musicians and playing good music. Krupa's associates in the Hallett band included saxophonist Toots Mondello, trombonists Jack Teagarden and Jack Jenney, pianist Frankie Carle, and arranger Spud Murphy who, according to Gene, was the first arranger to write for five saxophones. Then he joined the Buddy Rogers band.

PEE WEE ERWIN: Gene and I became friends in 1934 when we were members of the Buddy Rogers Orchestra. Buddy was a movie star who had bought the Joe Haynes band, out of the midwest, intact. I came with the package.

We used to do unbelievably commercial things in the Rogers band. For example we were given flashlights and during the stage shows the band did a routine with the lights, spelling out ROOSEVELT and NRA. The routine would conclude with a spotlight falling on an American flag on the side of the stage. A behind-the-scenes electric fan kept the flag fluttering. Buddy even had a boy from the CCC—the Civilian Conservation Corps—on his shows to sing "Home On The Range" and "Wagon Wheels." If all this weren't enough, Buddy played every instrument in the band *badly*. Every night he climaxed his show with an instrument-changing routine. It was unfortunate that things were so commercial; we could have done a lot better. There were some really good players in the band. Besides Gene, I remember trombonist Ward Silloway and clarinetist Johnny Mince.

KRUPA: Buddy didn't know what to do with what he had going for him. The band had tremendous possibilities. But as far as Buddy was concerned, for something to be good, it had to *sell*. When Benny became such an enormous success with the kind of music the Rogers band could have played, only then did he concede that he had all the components for a great musical breakthrough in his own backyard.

Things went from bad to worse in the Rogers band. Absolutely nothing was happening, musically. Only the after-hour jam sessions kept me going. I was really ready for a band like Goodman's when John Hammond came out from New York to make me an offer at the Sherman Hotel in Chicago.

I may have had some reservations about working for Benny at first. But John made a good case for my taking the job. I would only have to rehearse and play the 'Let's Dance' broadcasts on Saturdays. There would be time for extra jobs and study. And the pay wasn't bad either. But what really did it for me, to be truthful, was hearing the Goodman band on the air. It was thrilling! I came to New York in December 1934 and replaced Stan King.

JOHN HAMMOND: The guys from McCann-Erickson, the ad agency [involved with the "Let's Dance" program], thought he [Krupa] was so wonderful they insisted he set up in front with the rest of the rhythm section behind him. They thought Gene would help sell the band, and they were right. He was a showman.[12]

But it went beyond showmanship and even chemistry. Simply, Krupa was the right man for the job. He had developed a style that was consonant with the Goodman style. Both were focused on pulsation, swing. Having smoothed out the pulse to a fluid four, tapped out vigorously on the bass drum, he used that as a basis and addressed the arrangements—by Deane Kincaide, Jimmy Mundy, Fletcher Henderson, etc.—in a manner that strikingly merged drum rudiments and jazz syncopation, and academic and more informal techniques. He made a strong case for swinging and intensive, continuing study.

Krupa struck a balance between instinct, the roots of jazz, and a scientific approach to drumming. The language came directly from Chick Webb. But Krupa formalized, simplified, and clarified it. Krupa thrust the drum set into the foreground, making it not only a source of rhythm but of musicality and color as well. Before Krupa, only the great black drummers had so powerfully mingled these key elements.

And yes, Krupa knew how to sell. He looked terrific as he moved around the set, twirling sticks and acting out his solos with bodily and facial expressions. He built his playing on a musical foundation, but made sure that he and the music made an impression. He became an undeniable glamour figure in a sweat-drenched formal suit, the handsome "deb's delight"—as Life once tabbed him—who often transcended his leader in popularity. To a nation coming out of a Depression, Gene Krupa was new and exciting. To the musical community, he was a flamboyant figure, perhaps not as subtle as he might have been, but a musician, indeed.

KRUPA: The music we played in the Goodman band almost immediately took hold among New York musicians. Our rehearsals at NBC were standing room. Even the fellows in the Kel Murray and Xavier Cugat bands, who appeared with us on the "Let's Dance" program, turned out. Murray's drummer, Harry Stittman, a wonderful guy and a marvelous musician, was more cynical that most about me and Benny's music. Manny Klein and Benny Baker, who played trumpet with Murray, were excited about the band and thought I made quite a difference.

They kept talking me up to Harry and finally persuaded him to come by Studio 8H at NBC and give a listen. During our first break, Harry went out in the hall with Manny and Benny on his tail. They were anxious to find out how he felt. Harry pulled no punches. "What's he got?" he said. "A lot of rhythm. That's all!" What we were doing was nothing to him. He had to be sold, just like Buddy Rogers. When we began making it with the public, he loosened up a bit and his attitude began to change.

Great success for the Goodman band, following a disappointing stand at New York's Hotel Roosevelt and equally dismal appearances around the country, became a reality during an August to October 1935 engagement at the Palomar Ballroom in Los Angeles. The "Let's Dance" broadcasts had ignited great interest in BG swing on the West Coast. Dancers and listeners turned out in progressively larger numbers as the BG gang moved around the country. By March of 1937, when the band played its record-breaking, history-making stand at New York's Paramount Theater, Goodman was the rage and in the process of making an indelible mark on the popular music of the period.

Krupa, Pee Wee Erwin, Harry James, Vido Musso, Teddy Wilson and the irrepressible Lionel Hampton in the small groups, Jess Stacy, Ziggy Elman, Toots Mondello, Hymie Schertzer, Murray McEachern, and Chris Griffin were among the key players who brought character to this disciplined, unrelentingly swinging music that Goodman played so marvelously.

It was the Goodman band's overall effect, however, that made such a difference. It defined a view of music formerly restricted to the black ghettos, for the edification of the nation at large. A flood of feeling was unleashed, particularly among young people, the band's primary audience. The band's pulsating performances brought them to the brink of a pleasant, free-flowing form of madness. From 1934 to 1938, Krupa was in the catbird seat—at the music's center. But for all his accomplishments, the drummer felt his work was far from done.

PEE WEE ERWIN: Gene was the hardest-working musician I've ever known. He had an insatiable curiosity. I mean he wanted to meet and exchange ideas with everyone who played the instrument.

He'd do *anything* to enhance his technical ability and musical understanding.

The man practiced all day long. No exaggeration. I played a lot of theaters with him. Most of the time he didn't even go out. He'd come in for the first show and his wife Ethel would bring him his meals. He'd break for the shows but that was it.

Gene was a natural drummer. Had he never studied he still would have done well. He had that inner something, an instinct for the instrument. He was a *player* long before he became a technical wizard.

I've long had a theory about Gene. He developed a tremendous amount of power by studying and practicing constantly. And it affected the character of his playing. You had to play *with* him rather than his adapting to and playing with the band.

He performed particularly well in one circumstance. It was the second time I worked with Benny; we were at the Congress Hotel in Chicago, the Urban Room. I was playing lead trumpet and didn't have to play over Gene; he kept things down because of where we were performing and the nature of the job. We had to provide music for dancing and dining. It was a sheer delight; he played so well because he had to exercise unusual control. That's the reason I enjoyed it so much. I didn't have to play loud; my instrument could vibrate the way it should. And the band came together and blended.

Earlier, at the Palomar, it wasn't uncomfortable to play with Gene because he used his power only in his solos. But by the time the band got to the Madhattan Room of the Hotel Pennsylvania about a year later—with Harry James and Ziggy [Elman] in the trumpet section—it was gangbusters all the time. The band never really *blended* again.

HYMIE SCHERTZER: A lot of what we did in the Goodman band was ad lib, so everyone had a hand in developing the style. The band had a wonderful feeling about it. We had 14 men who all had the same conception of music. The band was so finely tuned it was like a fine watch. Gene gave the band a drive, and after a while he really started to become a crowd puller. So Benny began giving him longer and longer solos. . . . Gene's solos had great visual appeal. The crowd saw someone knocking his brains out and they loved it.[13]

The Goodman Victor records and recorded broadcasts on Columbia tell a story of Krupa's increasing strength and confidence; they bring into focus the chances he took and his admirable facility; they also reveal his tendency to showboat and occasionally rush tempo. But he did push the band and inspire it. He brought fire, grace, and elegance to the trio and quartet performances. And he undeniably added *juice* to all that was played. For example: On "Roll 'Em," Mary Lou Williams' boogie classic, he builds to a great climax, playing triplet rolls (Victor, 1937). Also, Jimmy Mundy's "Swingtime in the Rockies" (Victor, 1936), Fletcher Henderson's "I Found A New Baby" (Victor, 1936), and small-group numbers like "I'm A Ding Dong Daddy from Dumas" (Victor, 1937), "Benny Sent Me," and "Killer Diller" (Columbia, 1937)—all these recordings, made from 1936 to 1938, reveal a drummer very much in tune with his surroundings, taking the music as far as he can.

JOHN HAMMOND: Gene kept wonderful time in the trio with Teddy [Wilson]. Teddy was so light and delicate and so was Gene. And don't forget, in the trio Gene played brushes for the most part. He also played well in the quartet. Marvelous!

LIONEL HAMPTON: Gene used to tune his bass drum to Teddy's low F on the piano. It made the BG Quartet sound as if we had a bass.[14]

BUDDY RICH: You talk to people today and they say, "Did you hear so-and-so? He's the best small-band drummer of all. Did you hear so-and-so? Best big-band drummer around." I hate that kind of thing. If you're a drummer, you should be able to play in any style with any sort of band. Versatility is the key. One of the reasons Gene was so great was that he could do it all: blow the band out, come down front and play with a trio or quartet, then involve himself in a solo feature.

No big deal. He knew that if you played with three or four guys, you kept things down and used brushes. You didn't step on the pedal; you played the pedal. You were subtle behind what was going on. Then after exercising great control, bringing into play restraint and delicacy, he could turn around and perform like a monster on "Sing, Sing, Sing." That's a drummer!

BENNY GOODMAN: Gene . . . so conscientious and so concerned. He got mad at me if the band didn't play well. Whatever we played, and I didn't care what it was he did, sounded pretty good to me, then (and still sounds good) now. I still listen to those records, and if you can find fault with them you're a better man than I am. Not me, I love them. Gene had excitement. If he gained a little speed, so what? Better than sitting on your ass just getting by.[15]

Krupa's great influence even extended to equipment. He established a basic drum and cymbal set-up that many drummers adopted:

snare drum, bass drum, tom-tom mounted on the left side of the bass drum, and a larger tom-tom on the floor, at the drummer's right; ten- to twelve-inch high hats, thirteen-inch crash cymbal on the left on a stand, an eight-inch splash and fourteen-inch time/crash cymbal (both mounted on the bass drum), and a sixteen-inch crash on a stand, at the drummer's right. Krupa had a lot to do with the development and popularization of tom-toms tuneable on both sides. He also was responsible for the introduction of pearl finishes on drums (most sets had been painted black or white duco).

Still another innovation was a heraldic shield on the front of the bass drum (on the left) with his initials inside; the band leader's initials were used on the right side of the bass drum in bold, large lettering. The trend to initials and lettering rapidly displaced funny painted scenes on the front of bass drums.

At the apex of his popularity, Goodman took his band to the Savoy Ballroom in Harlem to do battle with the Chick Webb ensemble. The May 4, 1937, encounter was a historic one.

ROY ELDRIDGE: Chick played so much drums that night. Gene kept tryin'; I remember he broke a drum head. Ain't nothin' he could have taken out that night. Boy, that little cat was somethin'!

LOUIE BELLSON: Gene always said that every time he had to play opposite Chick at the Savoy, there was hell to pay. "Oh boy, I'm in for it tonight. He's going to snow me under again," he would say. And for a big guy like him to admit that. Wow! He was honest; he put it right where it was.

Life was a dizzying rush for Krupa after the record-breaking engagement with Goodman at the Paramount in 1937. He had success and all that went with it. As those who knew him well at this time attest, he did a pretty good job of handling the pressure; he was a gentleman with no time who had time for almost everyone.

MEL TORMÉ: I was a raging fan of Gene Krupa's. How did I become involved? The records and seeing and hearing him in person, certainly. But there was more to it than that. A sense of identification. We came from the same area in Chicago—the South Side.

I was so into the Krupa thing as a kid that I used to walk by what I believe was a Krupa family grocery, just to see the name on the green awning—LYKE and KRUPA. It was five blocks from my house.

I initially heard Gene play with the Buddy Rogers band at the College Inn in Chicago shortly before he joined Goodman. I believe I was twelve or thirteen when I met him. He was very sweet, self-effacing; he had no phony kind of *hauteur* about his playing. And as you know, he was so encouraging to other drummers. Down the line when I felt I had a little entrée—I guess it was in the mid-1940s—I'd go backstage to see him at the Paramount in New York. He was kind enough to show me some really difficult exercises and patterns.

MEL LEWIS: I first heard Gene in 1934 or '35, right after he joined Goodman. My father, who was a drummer, took me to what they call the Cinderella Ball in Buffalo, my hometown. He was the union delegate for that night. I was five or six years old. I didn't meet Gene then, but I got to see and hear him. And you know it just ruined me. From then on, that's what I wanted.

A little bit later, after we had met, we cemented a relationship. I became his man in Buffalo. Every time he was in the area, I was there. I used to get on a bike and ride to wherever he was playing and return home early in the morning; sometimes it was twenty to twenty-five miles each way. Nothing was too much trouble.

Occasionally he took me on the band bus if the band worked a distance from Buffalo. He'd call my mother and assure her, "the kid will be alright. I'll take care of him." I helped the band boy and things like that.

It's funny. I watched him, knew him, loved everything he did, and yet I never tried to play like him. What affected me most was his musicality. I heard something in his playing I had never heard before.

Though Gene was an academic player, he was easy to understand; that's why I think so many of the old musicians liked him. You know he kept taking lessons, but never got *too* technical when he went out to play. He always sort of stuck to his own way. I think he studied in order to become more musical rather than just technically proficient. Simplicity, getting to the musical core, was his thing—though it might not have seemed so when you first heard him.

KRUPA: With Benny, it seemed we were always doing something: rehearsals, jobs, traveling. Personal life became a jumble. We were making pictures, doing radio, making records. Sleep was a rarity. It seemed we were playing all the time, sometimes doubling and tripling jobs. At one point, we were doing the Camel radio show, the Paramount Theater, and the Hotel Pennsylvania all at once. I guess one of the reasons the band got so good was because we never stopped playing.

In addition to the hard work, inconvenience, and constant movement, Benny was a demanding guy in those days. If he took it into his mind to rehearse when you were about to hit the sack, that was it. He could drive you to the edge with his need for perfection. At record dates, many times our first or second takes had fire and freshness. But Benny often kept us going over and over things until the life was all but beaten out of them. You can't calculatedly touch off things; it has to be spontaneous. I've always favored the improvisational feel over perfect execution of the mechanics.

Though he was certainly a task master, I never lost respect for Benny, musically. Oh, we got into some beefs—you're bound to do that. I think Benny respected the fact that I was always ready to work very hard—I never dodged anything. I was always there—never missed a gig.

As years go by, you look at things differently and whatever animosities there were are forgotten. You forgive the unforgiveable. You put things behind you.

Talking about Benny brings back so many things. One time when I was sick, I happened to be going through a jewelry box. There must have been four or five thousand dollars worth of jewelry that he sent me over the years—tie clasps from Cartier's, a lovely watch, and gold chains and cuff links. Benny is not the most generous person in the world, if you know what I mean, so I thought I'd write the guy a note, telling him how much I appreciated his thoughtfulness. No one will probably ever see these lovely things; I'm not a jewelry cat anymore. But I thought it was important enough to mention.

Musically I got a lot from him. There was a certain empathy. A connection between us. Benny and I set each other off. Something magical often happened when we played together. He fed me, I fed him; the excitement built. Working with "the old man" always was a deeply musical experience.

We would take fire at the most unusual times. I remember one occasion, after not having played with him for a number of years, doing a New Year's Eve party somewhere. There were a lot of important people around, like Martin Block and Perry Como. The trio was there. It was just one of those things. Everything worked.

There are some days when those drums feel right to you and you can't do anything wrong; everything fits and life is beautiful. Other times you break your can; you use all your cunning, slyness, and cuteness and nothing works. It stinks; it sounds horrible.

Benny and I had so many of the good times. What a wonderful feeling when it's happening. No one says anything; you just sit there and you're happy all of a sudden. Everything is beautiful.

The difference between the special performances and all the others? Heaven and hell.

The rapport between Goodman and Krupa deteriorated markedly during the drummer's last months with the band. Krupa's enormous popularity had something to do with it; so did the increasingly extroverted and self-involved nature of his playing. The constant demand for drum solos from fans annoyed the highly disciplined leader, who wanted his band to be a reflection of himself and less of a vehicle for individual sidemen.

With the enormous success in late 1937 of the two-sided, twelve-inch 78 RPM Victor recording of the Jimmy Mundy arrangement of "Sing, Sing, Sing," Krupa took hold as never before. This ever-evolving, collective improvisation was a tour-de-force for Krupa.

KRUPA: When Mundy first brought the chart to rehearsal, it was a vocal feature for Helen Ward. Then the thing began to change. Mundy suggested I play a four-bar intro. When we ran it down, I felt tom-toms would work best on the opening. Benny liked what I did and after we played a while, suggested that I stretch it out and cue the guys when I was ready for the band to come in. Then there were additions and elongations in the middle section. Benny said we got such a good musical groove going that he soon cut the vocal out.

Every night "Sing, Sing" became more diversified. The band never played it the same twice. It turned into a jam session for us. We all got a chance to blow. I'd do a few little things and pull Harry [James] in first, then maybe Vido [Musso] and Jess [Stacy]. By this time, we were moving right along. Then the collective improvisations started. One of the sections would create a riff or theme, repeat and embellish it. Another section would work with it. "Sing, Sing, Sing" grew and developed. Each time we played it, the thing seemed to get livelier, longer, and more exciting.

"Sing, Sing, Sing" on recording was somewhat more contained and certainly shorter than in performance. But the record captured enough of the freedom and abandon that blew audiences away, and it made Krupa a star.

MILT GABLER: "Sing, Sing, Sing" changed things. After Gene's great success with that recording, drums became an important part of every jazz presentation. The drummer got more attention and worked harder, particularly at concerts and sessions. While the other players paused for a drink and some conversation, or maybe a breath of air with a lady, the guy at the drums did his best to put together showmanlike and musical elements in the inevitable long solo toward the end of an afternoon or evening of blowing. One of the few guys who had little or no use for solos was Dave Tough.

The Goodman Carnegie Hall concert in January, 1938 was a climactic piece of business for Krupa and Goodman, and pointed to the end of a truly major relationship.

JOHN HAMMOND: Contrary to what many think, Gene was not at his best during the Carnegie Hall concert. Benny took a new hard look at him that night. Suddenly he came to the conclusion that the way he was playing disrupted the whole structure of the band. The band had become too tight and tense, too precise. Benny wanted more subtlety within the time feeling—something he felt Gene no longer was capable of bringing to the band.

Hammond and Goodman were not the only ones who sensed what was happening to Krupa's playing, and how much attention he was getting because of his exaggerated showmanship. Francis D. Perkins, reviewing the Carnegie Hall concert for the *New York Herald Tribune*, noted:

The foremost contributor to [the visual aspect of the concert] was Mr. Gene Krupa, the group's super expert percussionist, whose gestures and facial expressions proved unusually engrossing for those near enough to note them in detail, and suggested he had talents as an actor as well as an instrumentalist.[16]

D. RUSSELL CONNOR and WARREN W. HICKS: On Friday, February 26, Benny and the band began a one-week engagement at the Earle Theater in Philadelphia. At the end of it, on March 3, Gene Krupa quit unceremoniously.

It was sad to see Benny and Gene feuding openly on stage those last few days. The audience helped widen the breach at every show; having waited impatiently through a simpering film titled "Swing It, Professor," starring Pinky Tomlin, they screamed for Gene to take off as soon as the curtain went up.

Gene, perched high on his drummer's throne downstage nodded toward Benny, gestured as if to break his sticks, pantomimed,

"He won't let me." Groans and hoots came from the crowd. . . .
Benny . . . left no doubt in anyone's mind as to his reaction to the
crowd's clamor for Krupa. A rupture was inevitable.

Krupa's leaving . . . changed the character of the Goodman
juggernaut; never again was it what it had been. For a period the
band floundered; then Dave Tough came in to regroup Benny's
men into a solid, more loosely swinging band.[17]

The trade, national, and international press treated the Krupa-
Goodman split as front-page news. The two had helped popularize an
exciting form of music and manner of performance, bringing to both
unusual fire and professionalism. With them, the cult of swing had
been born. The press reacted in a totally appropriate manner.

KRUPA: Managers had been after me for some time. Most of the major
sidemen—Bunny Berigan, Bob Chester, Glenn Miller—had been
approached. Big bands were big business then. I happened to be
ready to hear what the managers were talking about. Ego certainly entered into it. Why be a clerk when you can own your own
store?

Success practically was assured from the start. I had bookings for almost a year, a record contract with Brunswick. My
band made its debut at the Steel Pier in Atlantic City on Easter
Sunday, April 16, 1938.

GEORGE SIMON: About four thousand neighborhood and visiting cats
scratched and clawed for points of vantage in the Marine Ballroom of Atlantic City's Steel Pier. . . . The way the feline herd
received, reacted to and withstood the powerful onslaught of
Krupa's quadruple "f" [forte; loud] musical attacks left little
doubt that Gene is now entrenched at the helm of a swing outfit
that's bound to be recognized shortly as one of the most potent
catnip to be fed to the purring public that generally passes as
America's swing contingent. . . . Throughout the evening the kids
and kittens shagged, trucked, jumped up and down and down
and up, and often yelled and screamed at the series of solid killer-
dillers.[18]

Seldom, added Simon a bit later, had any band started off so well.

KRUPA: As the leader of my own band, at last I had the freedom to
fully present my ideas and to project the Krupa personality
through music. Arrangements by Mundy and Chappie Willett—he
wrote for Chick, too—helped us achieve identity. People always

said they could tell it was the Krupa band on the radio. In person, there was no doubt who led the band; each of the music stands had my medallion prominently displayed and a tom-tom mounted on it.

Krupa's snare drum sound was central to the character of his work. Crisp, clean, with a suggestion of echo, it enhanced the excitement of his performances. While playing "time" or patterns across the set, Krupa also established engaging relationships between the bass drum and the other drums, and between the cymbals and the drums. He used rudiments in a natural, swinging, often original way.

JOHN MCDONOUGH: Krupa's was a very special sound and it didn't occur by chance. He would strike the drum head and rim in such a way that the stick carried the impact from the rim down to the tip of the stick and transmitted it to the head, which then acted like an amplifier. Then—and this is the key—he would get the stick away from the head immediately so that it didn't kill the vibrations. Leave the stick on the drum an instant too long, he used to say, and you lose that echo that lingers after that shot and gives it its musical quality.[19]

The musical drama the drummer brought to his vehicles, such as "Wire Brush Stomp" (Brunswick, 1938), "Blue Rhythm Fantasy" (Okeh, 1940), and particularly "Who" (Okeh, 1940), where he developed multiple climaxes via potent use of press rolls, further imprinted Krupa on the public consciousness.

His band reflected the leader's awareness of the multi-currents within popular and concert music. There was evidence in the Krupa library of the influence of Goodman, Basie, Ellington ("The Sergeant Was Shy" [Okeh, 1940]) and Lunceford ("Full Dress Hop" [Okeh, 1940]). (Both recordings have been reissued on *That Drummer's Band* in the Epic Encore series.) There are also indications of the drummer's interest in "legit" music. Lenny Hambro, the saxophonist who played in the Krupa band on several occasions, remembers that his audition in 1942 included playing "American Bolero," a piece written in 5/4 time, quite adventurous for that period. (A version of "American Bolero," arranged by George Williams, turned up twenty years later on a Krupa Verve album titled *Percussion King*.)

Admittedly there was material in the Krupa book that could easily be dismissed: how about "All Dressed Up Spic and Spanish" (Columbia, 1939)? Clearly, Krupa wanted to blend musicality with entertainment.

During this phase of his career, Krupa had good players and singers to help him provide *jazz entertainment*. Among them: his Goodman buddy, tenor saxophonist Vido Musso; Sam Donahue, a highly distinctive tenor man, with more than a suggestion of Lester Young in his playing; scat singer and "chitlin" trombonist Leo Watson, one of the great jazz originals; left-handed trumpeter Corky Cornelius, among the first high-note specialists; and the attractive singer Irene Daye, a great crowd-pleaser, according to Krupa.

KRUPA: At the beginning, I went a bit overboard playing a drum solo at the drop of a hat. One night, old man Sullivan who ran the Steel Pier in Atlantic City took me aside. The band couldn't have been too old; we had seventy arrangements and sixty-nine of them featured me. "Gene," he said, "you're a good kid and a hard worker and everything, but even the Super Chief stops once in a while. Rest yourself. Don't take so many solos. My ears are hurting." I kept that in mind. And from that time on, the spotlight was shared. My singers and players got more of a chance. Of course I had to satisfy the demand of the fans. But I never overindulged myself after that first year.

A publicity still of "That Ace Drummer Man" taken after he had formed his own band in 1938. Courtesy of Modern Drummer Publications, Inc.

It was my change of direction and the coming into the fold of Roy Eldridge and Anita O'Day in 1941 that really put the band over. I'm sure many people came to see me. But after Roy and Anita had been in the band a while, and we had gigantic records like "Let Me Off Uptown" [Okeh, 1941], "After You've Gone" [Okeh, 1941], "Rockin' Chair" [Okeh, 1941], "That's What You Think" [Columbia, 1942], "Knock Me A Kiss" [Columbia, 1942], and some others, things really cooked for us [all these recordings appear on Columbia's box set *Drummin' Man / Gene Krupa*].

Roy, one of jazz's greatest trumpeters, had been a favorite of mine for years and years. We were friends and had made some records together. But I never thought he'd be interested in playing with the band. An established star, he had his own combo at the Three Deuces in Chicago. One night, much to my surprise, he said he would like to join the band. He felt he could do some good things with us. Really, I couldn't have been more delighted. Roy became our spark plug. Every time he played it was like a light going on in a dark room.

I came across Anita at the Three Deuces. I heard her with Roy and with the Max Miller group. Instantly I felt she was a rare person with a special talent and an enormous natural feeling for jazz.

The addition of Eldridge and O'Day made the Krupa band hot in more ways than one. Krupa responded to the prodding and pushing of these two gifted people by playing in a more direct and decisive manner. The best of his recordings reveal fire, inspiration, and consistency on a level equal to his more memorable performances with Goodman. All one has to do is listen to "Let Me Off Uptown," "After You've Gone," and "Massachusetts" to discern the difference in Krupa and the band. On "Massachusetts" (Okeh, 1942), the band hits hard, crackling in spots; O'Day phrases and swings in such a convincing manner that one is swept along. Krupa offers a memorable contribution—a stirring four-bar break at about midpoint, which he numbered among his best short solos. Single strokes with varying accents mingle with faster groups of three, four, or five strokes (called ruffs) in a simple, flowing statement that grows directly from the material. The improvisatory, musical quality of the break gives it special impact.

Krupa trumpeter Graham Young remembers vividly at least one incident after Eldridge joined the band:

Gene suffered occasionally from what some of the guys called "leaderitis," i.e., he would stand in front of the band while one of the trumpeters played drums—even me! A few days later after Roy joined, Gene said, 'Hey, Jazz, play some drums.' I guess he'd forgotten that Roy played drums before he took up trumpet. Anyhow, Roy started the band swinging like it hadn't for months! The look on Gene's face was really something! He realized what had been lacking and from that moment started playing real rhythm again.[20]

ROY ELDRIDGE: Until that time, colored musicians generally worked with a white band as separate attractions. That was how I worked with Gene at first; I wasn't treated as a full member of the band. But very soon I started sharing Shorty Sherock's book and, when he left the band, I took over. It killed me to be accepted as a regular member of the band. . . . All the guys were nice and Gene was especially wonderful.

   If Gene and I felt good, we could really make the music *happen*! Sometimes, because we traveled so much, we might be down and just play. But when we stretched out, man, it was something else. I loved playing with the cat.[21]

The feeling Eldridge and Krupa had for each other extended beyond the bandstand. *Down Beat* reported that Krupa "used his fists to subdue the operator of a restaurant here [York, Pa.] who refused Roy Eldridge admittance."[22] The band was playing a one-nighter at the Valencia Ballroom. The restaurant owner made "ungentlemanly" remarks about Eldridge and asked him to leave. The drummer took offense; he was taken to jail, fined $10, and released.

Eldridge took more than a little abuse being a star member of the Krupa organization. Not from his colleagues or Krupa. Not on the bandstand. But just living and traveling with a *white* band. Krupa was color-blind, but the country at large wasn't.

ANITA O'DAY: Gene didn't pay as much money as Glenn Miller and a few others, but being with his band was more fun because he was as excited about what he was doing as the most inexperienced cat in the aggregation. . . . After I joined Krupa I was out there every day to learn something from every job. I was always happy no matter what the working conditions were because I was performing my song styling. That was my life. Whatever else I did, music was my mission. . . . Although Gene took a lot of solos— and the crowd expected it—he left room for other people to shine. For a while his band became one of the swingingest, best bands of the time.[23]

All was as good as it could get for Gene Krupa. A top attraction, a world jazz figure, he had everything he wanted: a big band he was proud of, money, recognition, the opportunity to continue learning about drums and music. Then, early in 1943, the roof fell in.

KRUPA: I was arrested in San Francisco for the possession of marijuana. The way it came about was quite simple. My valet, a very
efficient but overbearing fellow, had gotten his draft notice. In
those days, I was the glamour boy—fifteen camel hair coats, three
trunks of clothes on the road—sort of the poor man's Buddy Rich.
I had just about all the material things.

We were closing at the Hollywood Palladium, prior to going
to San Francisco to play the Golden Gate Theater. My valet
wanted to get me a parting present. He shopped around L.A. and
finally decided on grass. Apparently he had a rough time buying
it and shot off his mouth a little. "This is for the greatest guy in
the world—Gene Krupa," he said. Someone heard and fingered
me for the narco police.

The valet showed up at my hotel in San Francisco with his
purchase. He said it was the only thing he didn't think I had and
shoved the stuff into the pocket of one of my coats. To tell the
truth, I liked booze so well by this time that I didn't think much
about the tea until the police showed up at the theater looking for
it. I got on the phone with my *new* valet at the hotel, knowing
they would go there next. I told him to send out my laundry and
to throw out the cigarettes he would find in my coat down the
toilet. But the kid put the stuff in his pocket and the cops nailed
him on the way out of the hotel. And I was arrested.

Anyway, there it was. The original plea was possession,
which is a misdemeanor. I made the mistake of hiring Jake Erlich, the best attorney in San Francisco, the guy who defended
Billie Holiday. He and the district attorney were enemies. The
D.A. was out to get Jake, it seemed, more so than me.

I became a target. The case was discussed in every paper
across the country. Some writers had me responsible for the
country's increasing juvenile delinquency problem, the coming
to popularity of zoot suits and long chains, anything and everything. Jake entered a guilty plea; it was his understanding that I
would pay a fine and that would be the end of it. I flew across the
country from Rhode Island, which I didn't have to do, and suddenly I found myself in jail doing a ninety-day stretch at One
Dunbar Lane in San Francisco.

Not long after that, I had to go on trial again, this time on
two counts, the second being contributing to the delinquency of
a minor. My new valet was a minor. We lost the felony case and
made a motion for appeal. This meant I had to remain incarcer-
ated until the appeal came up, or until the judge saw fit to let me
go. After 84 days, I got out.

I already had served the sentence for the misdemeanor. Out

on bail, still convicted of the felony, waiting on the appeal, I went back to New York and stayed around home in Yonkers. I began studying some harmony, arranging, tympani, and piano.

JACK EGAN: When he came out of jail, Ethel, his ex-wife, was the only one waiting for him. Everybody had deserted him. The band was gone; much of his money had been spent. No one was breaking his door down to put him to work.

Typical hypocrisy of the music business: as long as you're in a good position, everyone loves you. As soon as things start to come apart, it's as if you have the plague.

This was America in 1943; the word "marijuana" had some fearful implications for the average person. Its use was far from common. The country was electrified by the Krupa arrest.

When the news broke regarding the extent of Krupa's problems, *Down Beat* noted:

> "Frank Dailey, owner of the Meadowbrook [in Cedar Grove, N.J.] where the Krupa band was working, went to the AFM [American Federation of Musicians] in an attempt to have his contract cancelled, while other reports had the Paramount Theater, where Gene is booked to follow Harry James, equally anxious to sever connections with him. It was only when Dailey was assured that the drummer had pleaded not guilty that the dine-and-dance owner relaxed and allowed the band to complete its stay."[24]

If you are lucky, some friends and associates come to your aid. Benny Goodman extended a hand to Krupa.

KRUPA: One day, Benny called me. He had been one of the few guys who visited me in jail. I knew he had something definite in mind. "I don't live too far away; we're in upper Westchester. Drive up and bring your drums," he said. "I want to hear how you're playing." Guitarist Allen Reuss, a colleague from the old days, was there and we jammed. Of course this was a come-on. Benny was at the New Yorker Hotel and he wanted me to come back with him.

I took the job, grateful for the chance. I dug the band and playing for the ice show. In December 1943, almost two months to the day after I cast my lot with the "old man," I quietly joined Tommy Dorsey. My last date with Benny was at the U.S. Naval Academy at Annapolis. Dorsey insisted that I see how it would go for me in theaters.

We opened at the Paramount. The audiences had absolutely no idea I would appear. We were a little apprehensive about what might happen. The worrying was unnecessary. When the people saw me, I got the greatest standing ovation of my life. It lasted several minutes and I have to admit I broke down. At this show, and all that followed, I gave a rather flowery speech about Tommy and my fans and meant every word.

MEL LEWIS: My mother brought me to New York. It was Christmastime. Gene had just gotten out of jail. I went over to the Paramount where he was appearing. You remember how strict they used to be. But I got backstage. The doorman called upstairs and said, "There's some little kid here who wants to see you." And I could hear Gene's voice; he asked who it was? I yelled, "Red from Buffalo." He used to call me Red because I had bright red hair and a lot of freckles. "Come on up," he answered. When I arrived upstairs, there were a few guys standing around; reporters were constantly on the scene. Gene looked sharp in his camel hair coat and freshly pressed suit. You know what I did? I threw my arms around him. I wasn't very big at fourteen; I guess I reached his waist. "I don't believe anything they said about you." That's what I said. And he just held me close. I think I touched him.

KRUPA: I was with the Dorsey band in San Antonio when I received word from California that my felony conviction had been reversed.

The District Court in San Francisco handed down its ruling on May 31. A 2-1 decision upheld Erlich's contention that Krupa was being held in double jeopardy, and should be freed.

KRUPA: Boy, was I a happy kid! I booked the Capitol Theater in New York for a new band I intended to put together. I gave Tommy notice and expressed my appreciation to him for all he had done.
    But in no way was I the same guy as the Gene Krupa of 1942. The whole experience—the arrest, the court trials, jail, disappointments with people, the terrible waiting—had changed me.
    I didn't feel guilty. But the shock of the entire thing straightened me up. I returned to religion and many other things that were important to me before I became a so-called big shot. Certainly I wanted no connection whatever with drugs of any sort. I had taken a realistic look at narcotics and jazz and what happened to people who got hooked. About that time hard drugs were taking hold on the jazz scene. If it weren't for the bust, I might not have realized how truly destructive the hard drug thing was.

Though the case continued to come up over the years, and most people never took time to determine what *really* happened, Krupa overcame his anger and developed a philosophical attitude about the case. It continued, however, to have a deleterious effect: he lost certain kinds of work because of his connection with "dope."

BOBBY SCOTT: In the year or so I worked and traveled with him, occasionally taking meals with him, we spoke of his hitch two or three times at most. And always it was wrenched up out of his memory. It was not the recollection of the bars on the windows and the isolation but the shame of it that troubled him . . .

He remembered arriving in prison. "This one guard took me to the laundry, where I'd been assigned to work. He and I stood there before all the prisoners and he said, 'I've got a guest for you fellas. The great Gene Krupa.' Well, not one of the men cracked a smile. Then he gives me a big smile, don'cha see, and says, 'The first guy that gives him any help . . . gets solitary. You understand me?' Well . . . the minute he walks out, all of them gather around me, shaking my hand, and one of them, a spokesman, says: 'What is it we can do to help you, Mr. Krupa?''

He chuckled, remembering that moment of friendship. The prisoners knew he had been railroaded. They made sure his drumming hands never touched lye or disinfectants. . . .[25]

People in the media said that Krupa didn't have a chance of regaining his great popularity after all the negative commentary in the press and on radio. But the drummer came back all the way. His fans remained loyal.

Renewed involvement in music, and the challenge of leading a new orchestra with a ten-piece string section, brought Krupa a renewed sense of adventure and excitement. A direct result of the drummer's fascination with the Tommy Dorsey string section, Gene Krupa and "The Band That Swings With Strings" opened up a variety of musical possibilities for him. But the large, sometimes unwieldy orchestra simply didn't have the flexibility he needed. Following a successful ten-week debut engagement at New York's Capitol Theater in 1944, the orchestra increasingly proved an inadequate vehicle for its leader and a financial burden. When Krupa returned to New York from California about a year later, after completing *George White's Scandals* for RKO Radio Pictures, he made some radical changes. He opened at the Astor Roof with a streamlined "modern" band, sans strings, which initiated a key phase of his career.

KRUPA: I was attracted by the new jazz. After listening to Dizzy [Gillespie] and Bird [Charlie Parker] for a while, I began to hear music differently. It wasn't too long before I made a commitment to this music. I hired Gerry Mulligan. An original arranger who was deeply involved with what was happening, he brought in a number of excellent charts, including "Disc Jockey Jump," which not only were well-received but established the fact that we were serious about going in another direction. My other arrangers: George Williams, Neal Hefti and Eddie Finckel—he wrote "Leave Us Leap" [Columbia, 1945], our big comeback hit with the strings band—further defined our intentions. These were exciting, up-to-date guys. I let them go; only occasionally did I edit their scores or shelve what I felt wouldn't work.

My old friend Mal Hallett was a key source of talent for our venture into modernism. He sent me tenor saxophonist Buddy Wise, trumpeter Don Fagerquist, and trombonist Dick Taylor, the nucleus of this contemporary band. Young Red Rodney, a terrifically talented trumpeter, alto saxophonist Charlie Kennedy, and Charlie Ventura, our star tenor man, also helped shape the concepts of the organization.

I worked for a sense of balance, so the people who came to hear us wouldn't be completely turned around. We recorded ballad material showcasing Buddy Stewart—in my opinion the best ballad singer of all time. The mellow quality of his voice on things like "Along the Navajo Trail" [Columbia, 1945] and "I Don't Want To Be Loved" [Columbia, 1945] helped establish him. Buddy had admirable jazz talent as well. Remember Budd Johnson's "What's This?" [Columbia, 1945]? Dave Lambert and Buddy broke some new ground when it came to scat singing on that record. We had some major success with the novelty "Chickery Chick" [Columbia, 1945] and two other things Anita did when she returned to the band: "Boogie Blues" and "Opus 1" [both Columbia, 1945].

Everything was working again. The band sounded wonderful—clean, beautiful, together. We were into adventurous, meaningful music and managed to make it commercially at the same time. The guys in the band kept pushing me to stay on the ball, to keep learning. And I encouraged them to do whatever they felt was musically valuable. I showcased the heavy players. We had a good thing going.

This edition of the Krupa band (1945–1949) was clearly his most exploratory of all. Because of the band's commitment to modern jazz and his need to play the new style in a relevant manner, Krupa listened closely to young bop drummers. Progressively, he made adjustments in his performances and ultimately played in an "acceptable" manner in the contemporary idiom, though he had some reservations.

Krupa viewed drums differently than his younger colleagues. Drummers of the bop generation were endeavoring to free the instrument, make it more contributory, the equal of the melody instruments in the small and big band. They focused on the beat and color values; they played more, filling openings during a performance with "bombs" or comments. Krupa didn't feel natural doing these things.

Nor did he favor moving the center of pulsation from the snare drum, bass drum, and high-hat to the ride cymbals, using the bass drum in a sparing manner. Krupa didn't quite know when and how to play accents or bombs on the bass drum. He had difficulty bringing a sense of the melodic to his playing, which was just one of the things modernists such as Kenny Clarke, Max Roach, Stan Levey, Art Blakey, and Shelly Manne, among others, were doing. For Krupa, drums were strictly a *rhythm* instrument, and making changes in the character of drums was not easy for him. In short, he and his performances revealed an ambivalence concerning the modern style.

A swing drummer essentially wedded to the snare drum, Krupa was most comfortable in a swing groove, playing as many a swing drummer would, using the snare and bass drums and the high-hat as his basic tools. All one has to do is review his records of the period (1945–1949)—try "Lover" (Columbia, 1945)—and his position becomes clear.

Krupa did try to move ahead. Records he cut over the next few years, extending into the 1950s, make a case for his awareness and use of contemporary ideas. They also strongly suggest that he could not get away from his roots as a musician and completely alter his drumming style to fit in with the younger players; too much of his musical development and musical life occurred before bop.

MEL LEWIS: I watched him change in 1945 and '46 when he was trying to play bebop. At first he didn't seem to really know what to do. But he soon caught on. His bass drumming became lighter—not a hell of a lot, but a little. He started playing time on ride cymbals and dropping bombs, usually on the beat. But on the right beats. On "4" and "3"; not on "1" so much. He'd *listen*. That was the important thing.

He reached a midpoint between swing and bebop and made what he did work. When you think about how good he sounded playing light press rolls over 4/4 rhythm behind a bebopper like Charlie Kennedy, you realize that, my God, he brought two worlds together at a point where it wasn't obnoxious. It didn't sound dumb; it still was okay. And the guys in the band loved him for it; they forgave him for some of the old-time tricks he was laying on them and accepted him.

Gene met the young guys more than half way. He had the band's book written modern. He went out to listen to young drummers. Gene was not one of those guys who said only what he did was right. Sure he believed in himself, but the man wasn't an egomaniac.

Musically, Gene was open. He always was trying to learn. As far as I'm concerned, that's wonderful. He didn't sit around talking about the old days all the time. He wanted to go out and play and see what was happening, *now*.

RED RODNEY: Gene Krupa. Beautiful man. Beloved man.

For him to even try to make changes and become more modern showed what a great and thoroughly unprejudiced person he was. He knew how to handle men. He knew how to get the best out of you. Gene paid everybody as much as he could. He made you feel good about coming to work at night. You were working with somebody you liked. I remember that.

Years later when I saw him, I was messed up. He was saddened—I could see that. But he didn't try to lecture me; he tried to be helpful and, more important, asked, "Is there anything I can do for you?" I felt I had disappointed him in every way—not living up to my potential as a person or musician. He thought I had talent and ability to do a lot better than I was doing. He treated me as one of his children. Naturally he was saddened. I wish he was alive today to see everything is all right.

GERRY MULLIGAN: I was very young when I worked for him. And he was very good to me. You know, he introduced me to the music of Maurice Ravel. He always liked to take a record player with him on the road. He loved Ravel and Delius, too.

The last time I saw him was in 1973 at the Ravinia Festival, not too long before he died. I was waiting around for him to arrive. When he got there, he saw me and immediately came over. "Oh Gerry," he said, "I'm sorry, man, but all your music burned up." His house had just been badly damaged by fire. I had a hard time not breaking down when he put his arm around me and told me that. I knew he had leukemia and they were giving him lots of transfusions to sustain him. Even then, his thoughts were for other people.

KRUPA: Until about 1949, I enjoyed myself. I turned George Williams on to some of the colorful classical composers—Mussorgsky, Rimsky-Korsakof, Ravel, Stravinsky, among others—and suggested he develop some scores for the band on their themes. Out of this came Sibelius's "Valse Triste" [Columbia, 1946], "Fire-bird Suite," and Kabalevsky's "The Galloping Comedians" [Columbia, 1949], "Daphne and Chloe." . . . I got into fun things; I even did a softshoe with Anita on the Paramount stage to one of our hit tunes, "(Did You Ever Get) That Feeling in the Moonlight?" [Columbia, 1945].

Then the situation began to deteriorate rapidly. Several of my key men left for jobs in studios, with other bands, or formed their own groups. The replacements didn't fill the bill. Many of these young cats had promise but were into the heroin thing. I soon got tired of playing cop every night. After an appendicitis attack and an operation on the road, probably brought on by aggravation, I gave the band two weeks' notice and it was over.

A combination of things put an end to Krupa's career as a band leader in 1951. Bands had sharply declined in popularity. Popular music was in flux. But above all else, he had become deeply angry about the chaos that hard drugs had brought to his band. There was a bust in Detroit, another in Wheeling, West Virginia.

LENNY HAMBRO: Gene was furious when the thing happened in Wheeling. He told Ira Mangel, the manager: "Get them out of here! All three of them. I don't want them on the band. No two weeks' notice. Don't pay them anything. Just have them leave!"

DON FAGERQUIST: He was just trying to make a clean living, but the police would never leave him alone. If some pusher got arrested three states away he would say, "Gene Krupa gave it to me," and Gene would have to take two or three nights off to answer the charges. It must have been degrading for someone in his position.[26]

The years separating the close of Krupa's career as a band leader and his death from leukemia on October 16, 1973 at sixty-four lacked the continuity and the sense of growth that so typified the other stages of his musical life. He had evolved steadily until, in the 1950s, it became apparent that the drummer, though still able to play well, no longer was moving ahead. He had become a mainstream figure whose capacity to remain *au courant* was diminishing no matter how hard he tried to keep up. Krupa, the prototypical student, had made modifications as drumming continued to change. But the truth of the matter is that jazz is essentially a young man's pursuit, particularly for drummers.

Though Krupa dealt with both aging and the stylistic changes with constant study and an entirely flexible musical attitude, it was a losing battle. He was becoming more and more of an "attraction" who made people remember. Krupa found himself something of an anachronism in early middle age. Still admired by fans worldwide and loved by his colleagues, still capable of doing surprising, inventive things within his own style, he was sufficiently mature to accept—if not completely—the fact that music had moved beyond his capacity to remain on the cutting edge.

KRUPA: Norman Granz had been after me since 1945. That year, as the "Chicago Flash," I did that now-famous Los Angeles concert at Philharmonic Auditorium. It resulted in Granz's first and enormously successful *Jazz At the Philharmonic* album. Anyway, he really put on the pressure after I broke up the big band. As it happened, the time was right. After a short rest, I joined Norman's troupe [1951]. I never was sorry; it worked out extremely well. I was in great company—Oscar [Peterson], Ella [Fitzgerald], "Pres" [Lester Young], Flip [Phillips], Illinois Jacquet, Roy [Eldridge], Willie Smith, Hank Jones, Bill Harris, Jo Jones, Buddy Rich. People of that caliber.

The tour took us around this country, to Europe and Japan. Always we traveled first cabin; Norman didn't stint. We played two concerts a night. And it was real relaxed. We were competitive and wanted to do well. But it didn't get beyond that. I was spoiled during the JATP years [1951–1957]. The lack of pressure and the friendly atmosphere on and offstage made a great difference in how we felt. I certainly didn't miss the band. It was as if a weight had been lifted from me. It was a good period, all in all.

ROY ELDRIDGE: A lot of fun things happened during the JATP tours. I remember one thing in particular. Gene and I used to laugh about this. But it wasn't funny when it was happening.

We used to heckle each other when we were traveling. I'd go to sleep and he'd wake me; I'd wait until he began to snooze and I'd wake *him*. Well, we were flying to Norman, Oklahoma, for a date at the college there. Because we were having a pretty rough trip, we declared a truce. We weren't going to bother one another. Anyway, I was hitting it pretty good and Gene gives me the elbow: "Hey Jazz, you better wake up!" I said, "I thought you weren't going to start. . . ." He was real serious: "You better wake up, man; I think the plane's on fire." Half-awake, I thought it was just a put-on. Then he pointed out the plane's window to the wing: "Look!" he insisted. Sure enough, there was a little fire going on out there.

About that time, Ray Brown and Whitey Mitchell came running down the aisle with their basses. They wanted them in the back of the plane in case we crashed. Flip Phillips or Bill Harris— one of the two—started whistling "The High and the Mighty." Buddy Rich got salty. Then we gathered together, shook hands and said it had been nice doing the tour and all that. We really didn't think we were going to make it. But obviously we did. We landed in Garden City, Kansas, with just one engine. Yeah, I remember that.

JACK EGAN: One scene during the JATP years comes immediately to mind—opening night at the Band Box, right next to Birdland on Broadway. As usual, the crowd pleaser was the drum battle between Gene and Buddy Rich. During the first show, Buddy played like a whirlwind. He was so damn fast and creative, all Gene could do was play some cute things on his little cymbal for fun and contrast. I went back to see Gene after the show. He said, "Holy jeez, Buddy, take it easy out there, will you? I'm an old man!" Everyone in the dressing room broke up. Buddy smiled and pointed out, "There was this chick in the audience I was trying to impress."

Speed had been Krupa's calling card in the 1930s and 1940s. But as he got older, the inevitable happened. His reflexes were affected and he began to slow down a bit. Like a wily old fireball pitcher, he saved his best for the right spots; increasingly he used his head—not just energy and facility—to make his point. Krupa's musicality surfaced more in the latter portions of his career. He literally was forced to be imaginative.

Frustration about his diminished capacity was only partially apparent—and only to those who truly knew him. He talked very little about it, only opening up when already quite ill, two or three years before his death. By that time, it was impossible to reach a consistently good playing level. He spoke of failure and began to mistrust his talent.

HENRY ADLER: As far as I'm concerned, Gene had more talent than anyone including Buddy Rich. He was fantastic but frustrated. He had so much to say but couldn't get it out. I don't think he used his muscles properly. I didn't like the way he moved. Too much unnecessary motion.

Let me explain something. You have guys like Buddy, Louie

A smiling Krupa at the Band Box in New York City in 1956.   Charles Stewart.

Bellson. These guys are like good wine. The older they become,
the better they play. If a drummer moves correctly, he keeps
improving. If your machine works right, you keep playing well.
Simple as that.

Make no mistake, Gene was no slouch. But his talent re-
quired more than he had. Sure, his solos were phenomenal; his
taste and the things he did were great. But he was capable of
more. He just didn't have the chops to do them.

Krupa assumed the role of elder statesman of the drums, and quietly continued to offer the best of himself to music and other players. The role of sage fit him perfectly. He seemed to know just what to do and say in a variety of situations. Appearances in *The Glenn Miller Story*, *The Benny Goodman Story*, and a rather unfortunate film about his life, *The Gene Krupa Story*, revived interest in him throughout the world. He worked where and when he was disposed to do so with all-star units or with his own groups. He recorded with top players, generally in jam session circumstances, or under his own name with ensembles of various dimensions, ranging from trios to big bands.

In 1960 it all came to a screeching halt when he had a heart attack. While recovering, Krupa worried little about the illness or the possibility of death, only whether he could play again. Before long, he was back on track, working with his quartet, recording, and appearing on television in interviews and guest shots on music shows.

In 1967—another pause. This time it was emphysema.

KRUPA: I didn't do much except play with my kids, practice, take lessons, read, watch TV, and coach my local baseball team in Yonkers. I talked about permanent retirement; it was my feeling I couldn't play well anymore. But then, with the help of Jim Chapin and other friends, I began to work a bit again, pacing myself carefully.

JIM CHAPIN: He had been sick with a variety of things. This time it was emphysema. He was going crazy up in Yonkers [his home]. One day he called and asked me to come and teach him. He said he wanted to get more deeply into independence and find out how my hands worked. I told him it all was just an extension of Moeller. He laughed: "Then he knew more when he taught you than when he taught me!" From October of 1968 to May of the following year, I traveled to his home each week and gave him a lesson. He responded marvelously well. I believe I helped him do some things he wanted to do. And so did Joe Morello, who also taught him briefly. Musicians who had known him for years commented on the change and it gave him a lift.

Krupa suffered a great deal of pain from ruptured spinal discs. His divorce from Pat Bowler, his second wife, and separation from his two adopted children, Marygrace and Gene Jr., were not easy to tolerate or accept.

But make no mistake, it wasn't all unhappiness for the drummer man during the last years. He played between halves on TV's *Na-*

tional Game of the Week, with 90,000 people in the stands and millions watching and listening to him on TV. He spoke to young people, his subject narcotics. At home and abroad, this immediately identifiable figure made appearances for the Slingerland Drum Company. He worked for charitable causes. And he tried to remain current.

KRUPA: That's important! You don't have to like everything new out there. But you have to know about it. All through my life, I've listened and adapted, making changes when I thought they were right and necessary. I continue to do so, even at this late date.

Gene Krupa left life in October 1973 with the music community hungry for more. His final concerts with the Benny Goodman Quartet (Goodman, Wilson, Hampton, plus Slam Stewart on bass) at Carnegie Hall and the Ravinia Festival outside Chicago were memorable. Despite being weakened by leukemia, Krupa played well and linked up with capacity audiences. Inspired by his colleagues and the circumstances, he found the strength to acquit himself as only he could when the music and the musicians were right and spoke to him in a very personal way. Of course the performances were not vintage 1936–1938 Krupa, by any means. But they were the sort that remain in mind. At the very least, they were musical and courageous—tributes to a man who loved music and drums with the intensity one generally reserves for another person.

With the Goodman concerts and a live album, *Jazz At the New School*, made in April 1972 at New York's New School for Social Research (Chiaroscuro label) Krupa said goodbye. Appearing on the LP with a group of colleagues that made him comfortable and tapped his resources, the drummer very ably combined his Chicago stylistic foundation with a number of things he had learned along the way. He achieved a level of performance that had eluded him in the final years.

His great friend Eddie Condon, guitarist and host on this occasion, spoke in his typically offhand manner, but with special feeling, pointing pridefully "to some impostor here named Krupa on drums." The other players—cornetist Wild Bill Davison, clarinetist Kenny Davern, and pianist Dick Wellstood—joined Condon in filling the room with positive feelings and allowed Krupa the freedom to be himself.

Krupa's playing on this recording, though characteristic and most identifiable, goes beyond individuality. The drummer sums himself up for us; he consolidates his image for the last time on record. He leaves behind a vivid memory—of swing, charm, facility, and *authority*. Krupa creates an ambiance that is his alone, while offering a highly positive coda to a career spanning over five decades.

Ray McKinley
(1910-)

"His approach is very individual. He uses his technique in the best way possible. It just *works* within the music. And you can't figure out what the hell he did!"

—*BOB HAGGART*

"The music on the 16" by 16" tom-tom indicates a recording session," notes McKinley. The site: Majestic Records' Studio in New York City. The year: 1946. Courtesy of Ray McKinley.

Neither as flamboyant as Gene Krupa, nor a technical wizard like Buddy Rich, Ray McKinley has built his reputation on less obvious aspects of the craft. McKinley tends to be subtle and suggestive. A rhythm *presence* rather than an unrelenting force, he is aggressive only when the music calls for it. McKinley also has great humor; he brings the light touch to music more frequently than many of his colleagues. Sometimes he tickles you to a point where you laugh out loud.

His effectiveness stems from masterful and highly creative time-keeping and a deep sense of the musical. Few in the profession have his flair for color and ability to freshen material in totally unexpected ways. But McKinley is not *sensational*, in the most obvious sense of the word. He is, above all, highly supportive of his musical associates, a trait for which other performers and critics admire him greatly. The public probably doesn't fully grasp his importance as a keeper of the flame on drums.

McKinley is generally considered a singer of rhythm and novelty songs first, then a band leader, and finally a drummer. Most of his fans regard him primarily as an *entertainer*. McKinley has done little to dispel his image as a multiple threat.

It is drumming, however, that best reveals who and what he is. Rhythm is basic to everything he does. Key recordings with the Dorsey Brothers and with Jimmy Dorsey in the 1930s, with Will Bradley and the Glenn Miller Army Air Force Band in the first half of the 1940s, and with his own bands and groups since then, tell his story well. These recordings parallel McKinley's live performances in their ease, command, and natural swing.

There are some grounds for dispute with McKinley on only one issue: his position on modern jazz. He has never taken it very seriously, and has chosen to remain a combination two-beat and straight-ahead four-beat swing drummer.

It would have been interesting to hear McKinley bringing his talent to bear on the new music of the 1940s and subsequent decades. He has often indicated a capacity for change. After all, he gave visionary composer-arranger Eddie Sauter the opportunity to create much of the library for his post World War II band. And he did update his ideas and drum style, making it possible to validly interpret, rhythmically, Sauter's modern scores.

One thing is certain: McKinley never has been a musical hypocrite. Like many of his colleagues, McKinley points out that to change radically, just for the sake of being up-to-date, is not only difficult but unnatural. The turnaround, he believes, can negatively affect performance and ultimately play havoc on a player's security and sense of identity.

"In the spring of 1934 I heard a new band play the best organized swing I'd heard up to that time by a white group. It was a sleeper. Nobody had heard much about the Dorsey Brothers, but a few of us musicians went to hear it at Nuttings-on-the-Charles, near Boston, and were knocked for several loops. Being a drummer in those days, I was especially impressed with a dead-panned guy who kept the most marvelous time I'd heard yet, and who got a beaut of a tone from his drums. He was Ray McKinley."

—GEORGE SIMON[1]

"Any chap that can swing with a band the way he does is OK with us."

—DOWN BEAT, JANUARY, 1935[2]

"Mac makes the drum set into a truly 'musical' instrument. He always is subtle, charming and executes well without being too technical."

—CLIFF LEEMAN

"We were together for a while in the Jimmy Dorsey band in the late 1930s. Ray could be a little caustic and impatient in his dealings with people. But I'll tell you one thing: musically, he didn't screw around. He was a very sincere musician. I liked that. He took care of business. Most players did back then. Musicians weren't quite as cynical as they are now."

—JIMMY MAXWELL

"I really enjoyed playing with Mac in the Glenn Miller Army Air Force Band during the war. Our rhythm section was something: Trigger (Alpert) on bass, Mel Powell on piano, me on guitar, and Mac. I'll tell you something about McKinley. Being a Texan, he's a slow talker. At rehearsals, by the time he explained something, it was midnight."

—CARMEN MASTREN

"He's a very solid footman. McKinley knows just how to use the bass drum. One of the top guys, he never really has gotten the recognition he deserves."

—JIM CHAPIN

"McKinley is very sensitive to the beat, very concerned about swinging. He approaches everything with that in mind. No matter how commercial or far out the music is, he wants it to have that 'feel.' He likes to 'cook.' "

—LOU STEIN

"Mac could have been a good all-around modern *drummer if he had allowed himself to be concerned with that type of playing. He is much better than most musicians realize."*

—MUNDELL LOWE

"Mac makes it a pleasure for the player. You never have any doubt about the 'time.' He locks it in from beginning to end. You can make book on it. He plays for *the other musicians . . . and so* naturally. *That's why he's one of my favorites."*

—LENNY HAMBRO

"One thing you all probably don't know; he's nuts about fried ham and bananas."[3]

—GENE KRUPA

MEMORIES

One afternoon early in 1944, a friend and I went into New York City to catch the Glenn Miller Army Air Force Band. We had been hearing the band on its weekly I Sustain the Wings *coast-to-coast NBC broadcasts. Fascinated by its enormous, enveloping sound, its discipline, and great array of talent, we somehow managed to get tickets for a broadcast.*

Until that day at the Vanderbilt Theater on 48th Street, Ray McKinley was merely a picture in Metronome *or* Down Beat *and an attractive sound on records. I liked his playing and singing, particularly with the boogie woogie extravaganza he co-led with Will Bradley in the early 1940s. In fact, the Bradley hit, "Celery Stalks At Midnight" (Columbia, 1940), was the first recording I ever bought.*

Gene Krupa, Buddy Rich, and Jo Jones had gotten to me first; I was completely enthralled by them. Their technical ability and showmanship fascinated me. Flash not being his high card, McKinley was not so immediately impressive to this neophyte drummer.

Like many youngsters, I hadn't yet dug beneath the surface. I appreciated my idols for many of the wrong reasons.

That afternoon, however, I got a lesson in pure percussion. McKinley held Miller's forty-piece orchestra in the palm of his hand and inspired the members of the ensemble in a way that was hard to deny. His "time" and taste were indisputable. He focused attention on the music, not himself; he became the instrument of the music.

He played ballads, jump tunes, a concert arrangement of "Rhapsody in Blue;" he even sang. But the closing number brought everything in focus. Taken at a seemingly impossible up-tempo, "Anvil Chorus" literally exploded across the footlights. McKinley, revealing a capacity to uplift others that few possess, lit a fire under the band and built it to a high and provoking temperature. The drummer was not hampered by the weight and largeness of the Miller ensemble; he merely spread pulsation through the organization as if it were a far smaller unit. And all the while, he was quite imaginative. He used the drums and cymbals in a manner that was several steps beyond the merely functional. The attractive rhythmic ideas he executed so adeptly significantly enhanced the effect of the music. The most curious thing of all: McKinley didn't make a big deal out of anything. Even when he played a stirring solo during "Anvil Chorus," notable for press rolls with constantly varying accents, he stayed away from showmanly exaggeration. He illustrated what could be done without resorting to anything beyond drumming itself.

When we met briefly after the show and he found out that my friend and I were hopelessly involved with drums, Ray was as nice as could be. He offered words of encouragement, a friendly smile and, before going back to Yale University where the Miller band was based, he signed my autograph book.

It was quite a thrill for a fourteen-year-old.

Ray McKinley remains "young" and involved in a variety of things. Not the least of these is drumming. He reads voraciously; he listens to music, occasionally watches TV, plays golf, rests, and gets in shape whenever there are bookings coming up.

"I work out for a few days at the drums in order to get limber," he says, adding, "I just take a few jobs nowadays . . . and only for the best money." He plays places as widely separated as Disneyland in California and Australia, mostly with big bands; the tours Down Under have included several friends from the Glenn Miller band.

When McKinley isn't performing somewhere, he and his wife Gretchen spend the warm months in Canada; during cold weather months, the McKinleys live in Florida. McKinley mixes activity and work with quiet time in the ratio he most relishes—just enough of both. He's free in the best sense of the word.

How has life been for Ray McKinley? Not bad. Ray and I discussed the beginning, the middle, and later years and the present on the phone. He was born in Forth Worth, Texas and grew up and found his way into music there.

MCKINLEY: My initial connection with music was made when I was three, four, or five years old. I had a little tin drum that I really enjoyed playing. After a while, a gentleman across the street moved me up a notch. He owned an old Army drum, one of those deep parade drums. I liked fussing with that even more, and I did pretty well. I couldn't have been too old when my father stuck me in front of thousands of people at the old Northside Coliseum in Forth Worth, where the Elks were having what they called an Elks Circus. I played a little diddy-rum-dum, boom-boom-boom snare drum solo.

I guess I just fell into drums. The instrument felt right to me. Playing was great fun. The guy who really got me interested was Johnny Grimes—the pit drummer at the local Majestic Theater. I used to sit in the front row and just watch him. He had all the paraphernalia that pit drummers had in those days.

I got my first set of drums—if you could call it that—when I was nine years old. It included a snare drum, a bass drum with a pedal, a cymbal, and a little Chinese tom-tom. Up to that time, I had been beating on a variety of things, like pots and pans, pie plates, old pieces of wood—anything that sounded a bit like drums.

As soon as I had that set, my career began. I was asked if I wanted to become a member of a little five-piece outfit called the Jolly Jazz Band. The group had a girl piano player; I remember that. We played around town a good deal.

There were a lot of bands in the Fort Worth area in the early 1920s—Swayne Cummings' Southern Serenaders and Frensley Moore's Black and Gold Serenaders. . . . The others I can't remember at the moment. Anyway, at one time or another I played with them all.

It seemed each band I played with was larger than the last. I learned a little more with each experience. The last guy I worked for before leaving Fort Worth the first time was an Indian: Chief Gonzales. He had the band at the Texas Hotel. I had a good reputation in my hometown. I wasn't that terrific but everyone thought I was.

That's the first chapter. I got my start playing with all those local orchestras. Before I forget, there was one in Dallas as well: Cline's Collegians, the best of all the bands I played with before going out in the world.

McKinley is essentially self-taught. He's an instinctive, natural drummer. It's not that he doesn't believe in studying—as a matter of fact, he encourages most young people to do so. But obviously what he did *worked* for him.

MCKINLEY: I don't remember ever taking a *drum* lesson. I learned almost everything by just doing and observing. If I heard a guy play something I liked, for example, I'd try to learn it and then apply the technique or idea in the most musical way possible.

Hold on! There was a brief period of study, way back there. I was seventeen and working with Beasley Smith's band, out of Nashville. We were engaged for the summer at Lake Pawpaw, Michigan, which is sixty or seventy miles from Chicago. I decided to study timps with Art Layfield in the Windy City.

At the time [1927], Paul Ash, the conductor, was the big thing in Chicago with his elaborate stage presentations. Art was his percussionist. A fine tympani player and snare drummer, he later played snare drum with the New York Philharmonic. I guess I got the bug to play tymps because the more equipment a drummer had and could play, the better were his prospects—at least in those days. Vic Berton had just started doing his fancy stuff on the pedal tympani with Red Nichols on records. Art and a lot of other impressive players had chimes, kettle drums, every bloody thing. It seemed the thing to do.

Every Thursday for a period of time, I made the trip into town for a lesson. I bought a pair of tymps; the expense nearly broke me. But the studying stood me in good stead on a number of occasions with the Glenn Miller Army Air Force Band and, certainly later with my own band.

As a young player, McKinley wasn't too impressed with drummers in and around Fort Worth. But he warmly recalls George Marsh, who came through town with Paul Whiteman, and Dick Hamil, "a pretty good guy with the sticks in Jimmy Joy's orchestra— the best bunch of musicians in Texas."

Ray Rohel, who played in Dallas in 1925 with the Don Bestor band at the Baker Hotel, was the only drummer to have a major influence on McKinley during what was probably the most impressionable interval in his life.

MCKINLEY: Drummers were different in those days. They fiddled around on all the drums and equipment. They had woodblocks, temple blocks, gongs, snare, of course, bass drum, and tom-toms galore, all over the place.

They did a bit of everything, even played on the rim and the shell of the bass drum. Many drummers were fond of choking the cymbal in climactic spots—hitting it with one hand and then "choking" it with the other.

Supposedly time-keeping was the drummer's basic function. But too many of the guys were busy doing other things. Rather than providing a steady pulse and "interesting" background for the ensemble and soloists, the typical player of the period involved himself with "show" and using the whole set. Things got better later when the fad and fashion was to concentrate on snare drum, bass drum, top cymbal, and high-hat in a unified manner.

In 1926, McKinley left Fort Worth for the first time and toured with the Duncan-Marin Serenaders. Duncan led the ensemble; Marin was the booking agent. After a while, McKinley left the band in El Paso to join Beasley Smith, "a big name around Nashville in those days," says McKinley. He stayed on with Smith until 1928, by which time Smith had joined Adrian McDowell—"a hot fiddle player à la Joe Venuti"—to form the Smith–McDowell orchestra.

That same year (1928), McKinley moved on to Pittsburgh to still another hyphenated outfit, the Tracy-Brown Band. "Tracy was a bad fiddle player; Brown, an equally unlikely tuba player, was a good businessman," McKinley recalls. "There some fine players in the band, like clarinetist Matty Matlock and trumpeter Bruce Hudson."

MCKINLEY: I had two of the biggest thrills of my drumming career during the early years. The first one—getting to play with Jimmy Joy. I was about eleven or twelve. He had a marvelous jazz group out of the University of Texas—one trumpet, a trombone, a couple of reeds, and a rhythm section. Don't make a mistake about Joy because he later had a successful semi-society band at the Edgewater Beach Hotel in Chicago. The band I'm talking about was so good, some say Bix Beiderbecke once offered to come and play with it for nothing.

At any rate, the band had made a hit recording, "Mama Will Be Gone"/"Clarinet Marmalade Blues" [Okeh, 1924], and was in Fort Worth to play at a place called the Meadowmere. To come right to the point, the band performed at a local record store—to plug the recording—in the afternoon. And the drummer took sick; he had an appendicitis attack the previous night.

Jimmy Maloney—that was Joy's real name—was frantic to find another drummer for the job that evening. His trombone player, Jack Brown, got on the phone and couldn't get anyone. Then he turned around—I had just walked into the store with a friend of mine—and said rather boldly, "I hear there's a kid drummer in town who's pretty good." That scared me to death. I started to sneak away. But my friend, Russell Ward, a local clarinet player, grabbed me by the collar. "Yeah, and here he is!" he said.

The windup was terrific. I went out and played with the Jimmy Joy Orchestra at the Meadomere. I had to borrow a pair of long pants to do it; I didn't have any of my own.

That was a giant step forward for a kid drummer. Not only did these fantastic musicians *speak* to me, I *played* with them. It was absolutely thrilling. The biggest kick, however, came *after* the job. The guys in the band asked me if I could leave with them the next morning for Kansas City to make some records. Well, my daddy wouldn't let me out of school. And, of course, that broke my heart. But I had had the ultimate experience—being associated with the Jimmy Joy Orchestra.

The other thing that happened was memorable and, in some ways uplifting. But it had a disappointing ending.

In late 1927—somewhere in there—I spent some time with the members of the Ben Pollack band in Chicago. I had been on the road for a time. It was my hope I would get a chance to play with a really top band.

Pollack was appearing at the Blackhawk Restaurant. He had some fine players; Glenn [Miller] was in the band. They sounded terrific. Of course Ben was a great drummer and most influential. That night, I sat in and everyone seemed to like what they heard.

Six months down the line, I happened to be in Chicago again and Pollack contacted me. He said: "Look kid, I'm going to hire another drummer. I want you to join us. Just keep it under your hat; don't tell *anyone*—not a soul." I was very excited at the prospect of playing with this band.

Within a few months, I heard Jack Teagarden, the great trombonist, had come into the Pollack band and brought along Ray Bauduc to take Ben's spot at the drums. I can't tell you how badly I felt when I found out. But I did have the satisfaction of having been asked by one of the great drummers of that time to be his replacement in his own band. That partially made up for the great disappointment I felt.

In 1930, through some of my friends in the Pollack band, I got the chance to go to New York and join Milt Shaw's Detroiters. The group was sort of the house band at Roseland Ballroom.

BOB HAGGART: I was in high school then, a young guitarist in love with music. [He didn't switch to bass until two years later]. I used to hang out at Roseland on weekends. And I met McKinley and Will Bradley. I was just tickled with McKinley's playing. After a little while, we began to get together—Ray, Will on trombone, and maybe some other guys—to jam in McKinley's room at the Midtown Hotel on 61st Street and Broadway.

Ray would get out his washboard, don his thimbles, and off we'd go. He was so pulsating and tasty on the little outfit, which also included two small frying pans and two little cymbals. It was clear I was running with extremely fast company.

To this day, I remember all the details of one particular afternoon with McKinley, Bradley, trumpeter Stewie Pletcher (he later went with the Red Norvo band), and the great guitarist George Van Eps. It was *so* softly swinging.

Being associated with McKinley was very helpful. He taught me a number of things about music, not the least of which were some good jazz tunes: "Wolverine Blues," "Jelly Bean," and "Jazz Me Blues." He hooked me on Louis Armstrong Hot Five and Hot Seven recordings. And he introduced me to key people, like Artie Shaw, Glenn Miller, and Bunny Berigan.

I really got an education at Roseland, listening to McKinley play drums. He gave me a good idea of what music was all about. His approach to jazz performance was and is very individual and authentic. Because of this, his ideas generally filtered into the bands with which he played.

When the Dorseys started their band a few years later, McKinley's influence on the arrangements was unmistakable. The Dorsey charts mirrored the way he sang riffs and phrased. He actively participated in their creation, singing his ideas to the arrangers, describing just how he wanted the band to play. The Dorseys had a trumpeter named George Thow; he sounded just like McKinley. Ray's ideas also had an effect on Will Bradley—*then* and later when they had a band. And certainly McKinley's personality and concepts helped shape all of his own bands.

As time went by McKinley's drumming at Roseland kept getting better. The Chick Webb band shared the stand with the Detroiters for an extended period; that certainly had something to do with it. McKinley learned to play the high-hat from Chick. Like the little dynamo, he manipulated the "hat" with his hands and sticks in a very provocative and swinging way; he played a bunch of variations on the basic dotted eighth and sixteenth rhythm and really got the band moving. McKinley used the high-hat as an instrument in itself. Both Chick and Ray played the hell out of it! And the high-hat was a relatively new thing, back then.

The Depression had its effect. Even musicians as adept as McKinley felt the pinch. When Glenn Miller called in 1932, just as the economic downturn entered its deepest and most threatening phase, McKinley was quite open to Miller's invitation to join singer Smith Ballew's revamped band.

McKinley had been assured that Ballew, long a relatively undistinguished singing band leader, was determined this new venture would be top-flight. Indeed, Ballew followed through, hiring some of the best players: trumpeter Bunny Berigan, bassist Delmar Kaplan, and pianist Fulton "Fidgie" McGrath, and later, as replacements, trumpeter Jimmy McPartland and pianist Chummy MacGregor. Miller, the band's musical director, did whatever he could to make the ensemble distinctive and successful.

However, the Ballew crew traveled a bumpy road. It worked, then broke up, only to get together again when some other dates had been arranged. There were some long, well attended engagements, but not enough work to build momentum. The band continued until late 1933, when most of the men left to seek better situations.

McKINLEY: In 1934, after rattling around the country with Ballew and playing for peanuts, things began to look up a bit with FDR. A bunch of us out of the Ballew orchestra—Glenn Miller, myself, saxophonist Skeets Hurfurt, trombonist Don Matteson, guitarist Roc Hillman, and singer Kay Weber—joined the Dorsey Brothers Orchestra. It was March or April of that year.

The band had a different sound. That was Glenn's idea. Bing Crosby was the big thing then, and Glenn decided to pitch down to his [Crosby's] register. So instead of the usual couple of trumpets and just one trombone, we featured three trombones. Tommy and Glenn and Don, and just one trumpet. . . . The saxes had a different sound—two tenors and one alto instead of the usual two altos and one tenor.[4]

The Dorsey Brothers Orchestra was relatively short-lived. For a little over a year, it performed at some top spots, like Sands Point Casino on Long Island and the Glen Island Casino in Westchester, twenty-five miles outside of New York City. The orchestra was heard on radio, and recorded over 100 sides for Decca in 1934 and 1935.

But the Dorseys battled almost constantly about the music and how it should be played. The arguments culminated in a massive blowup at the Glen Island Casino in the summer of 1935. Tommy Dorsey walked away from the band; brother Jimmy took over, and most of the players, including McKinley, stayed on.

Despite the tense working conditions, the Dorsey Brothers Orchestra frequently managed to make fine music.

CLIFF LEEMAN: I caught the Dorseys on a one-nighter in Massachusetts. A buddy and I came down from Maine to hear the band. It was very much worth the trip. The band had an unusual sound and instrumentation. When it played softly, it really was a pleasure. Mac was just as good in person as he was on the radio. His drums had a marvelous sound; they were tuned to what seemed like different intervals. He used the set in a most musical way. I recall he played a lot of top cymbal and his rim shots were clean, sharp, and well placed. As in later years, he backed the band and soloists very well. He worked to make them sound good.

That concept was very much a part of him . . . and still is. Remember, Mac is a product of an era that preceded the emergence of the drummer bent on showing what *he* could do. Unlike many of the highly technical showman drummers, McKinley combined elements of showmanship and thoughtful, feeling performance. He never ignored his time-keeping duties.

Gene Krupa got the whole "showboat" trend started. I don't want to put Gene down; he was a great artist. But his effect on the field was not entirely positive. It was a healthy thing that there were a number of guys around, like Mac, whose work reminded other drummers what had to be done.

The McKinley recordings with the Dorsey Brothers—"St. Louis Blues," "Stop, Look And Listen," "Dese Dem and Dose," "Weary Blues"—confirm what was said about him by those who were there in the 1930s. On these records, his time flows; he never seems to press or rush. Warming to the player and listener alike, McKinley does not vary stylistically from most other drummers of the time. The difference—and it's a crucial one—is that he is consistently *interesting*.

He makes provocative use of the various elements of the drum set—snare, bass drum, woodblock, rims, high-hat, cowbell, tom-toms, cymbals—and creates a rhythmic climate that is simultaneously stimulating and comforting. Essentially a two-beat drummer, immersed in the instrument's tradition, McKinley was basic to the Dorsey Brothers' music and its traditional character.

Most of the Dorsey charts, McKinley says, were "heads," devised by members of the band. The more formal arrangements were written by Glenn Miller. *All* the music conveyed a jazz feeling and unity of conception, because the players had common roots. The Dorsey Brothers Orchestra made a point for art and craft, but never pretended to be anything more than it was—fun with a Dixieland accent. The players were young and hopeful and they often had a good time on and off the stand, despite the feuding between the Dorseys. This, too, shows in the music.

JACK EGAN: One night the band had a hell of a party at the Glen Island Casino. I don't know what the occasion was. We all got bombed. I remember going over the next morning to the apartment house in New Rochelle where all the guys lived. I can't tell you how hung over everyone was. We were slowly making our way out of the building; I believe some sort of breakfast was on our minds. And out of the elevator comes McKinley, bright as a penny, all dressed for a couple of sets of tennis. "Hi fellas," he said, seemingly unaffected by what happened the night before. Perhaps he hadn't had much to drink. Perhaps he absorbed it better than we did. One thing is certain: he looked like an advertisement for good living. It brought us all down.

The Jimmy Dorsey Band was McKinley's home until the summer of 1939. Lacking the potency of the best bands of the period, it was a versatile but not terribly distinctive outfit. Though the circumstances weren't ideal, McKinley continued to evolve. He remained very much a captive of music in general and his need to bring something to it.

McKINLEY: Evolution is a matter of elimination as well as acquisition. I've never sat down and said to myself, "I'm going to improve on this, discard that, polish this and lay off that." But somehow you do.

   Sometimes development is a subconscious matter. Sometimes it's quite a conscious thing. For example, when the press roll was taking hold in the late 1920s, I did my best to make adjustments in what I was doing and learn how to use it. It seemed such an important innovation. Ben Pollack and George Stafford—that marvelous black drummer who died too young— were responsible for turning many of us around, each with his own exciting version of the press roll.

   When the high-hat came in the early 1930s and Walter Johnson—with the Fletcher Henderson band—and Chick Webb played it so well, I worked hard to get the knack of performing on those cymbals. The same thing happened when bass drum technique was updated and changed—from playing on "two" and

"four" with double-ups to straight "four." I went with the flow.
I had to.

You can be *frightened* into modifying your style. I remember
Stafford did just that to a bunch of us with his press roll and
exciting rim shots on a record he made for Victor: "Stomp, Mr.
Henry Lee" [1929]. Eddie Condon was the leader on the session;
Jack Teagarden, Joe Sullivan, and one or two other fellows who
played with Stafford in the Charlie Johnson band at Smalls' Paradise in Harlem were on it. Those rim shots, in particular, put
the fear of God in drummers. I understand when Krupa heard the
record he thought Dave Tough had done it. Stafford scared Gene
a whole lot. He told me that.

One thing has to be said at this point. The drummer must
have a really good sense of rhythm—no matter what stylistic
alterations or advances are made. If you lack this you can have a
fine musical ear, original ideas by the ton, the fastest hands,
intelligence of a high degree, and the face of a handsome movie
actor, you won't be a great drummer or even a good one.[5]

You have to have that *feeling*. It starts by being intrigued by
"time" and trying to duplicate rhythmic patterns when you're
young. Then you have to translate what you hear and sense to the
drums. It's one thing to beat your fingers on the tabletop and
your feet on the floor, quite another integrating everything at the
drums. There are movements to be made, back and forth, up and
down and across the set. . . . It takes a little time to learn all that.
But once you have the techniques down and combine them with
an inherent sense of rhythm—I believe you have to be born with
it—you're well on your way to becoming a good drummer. If you
don't have that bone-deep, rhythmic sense or "feel," you should
be doing something else! That may sound autocratic. But that's
the way it is, as far as I'm concerned.

The highly rhythmic quality of McKinley's playing—"wild ideas
in syncopation," says George Simon—brings to his performances an
unusual sense of life and more than a few surprises. With a firm hold
on rhythm and how it operates, and enough technique to be expressive, a drummer is free to create as his instincts and intellect dictate.
He can take the listener far afield, if he so desires, and move with
relatively little inhibition.

One of the drawling Texan's most memorable efforts with Jimmy
Dorsey, "Parade of the Milk Bottle Caps" (Decca, 1936), a Dorsey-Pat
McCarthy collaboration, is an excellent example of rhythmic charm,
control, and ability to make ideas sound both spontaneous and tailored for the occasion. Set in a medium-swing tempo, this piece de-

rives its distinction from colorful time-keeping, facile high-hat work (heard in two-bar and longer bursts, with a little triplet wrinkle at the end of each comment), and quietly effective two- and four-bar breaks. There's nothing spectacular here, but the seamless, impromptu quality of performance makes it classic in its way.

A point of interest: like most leading drummers of the time, McKinley never went over the bar-line in the final bar when playing a break or solo. If he had four bars, he ended his comments on "four" of the fourth bar.

JIMMY MAXWELL: What I particularly remember about Ray during the Jimmy Dorsey days was the way he held the band together. He was authoritative *and* sensitive. And he really knew how to color and fill in the open spaces. Like Davey Tough and Sonny Greer, he seemed to come up with just the right figure and little touch. Sometimes he'd get into the cowbell kind of stuff that Dixieland drummers favored—"Way Down South" things that pushed the beat long. But it always felt good.

Another thing: Most drum soloists don't make a hell of a lot of sense to me. But McKinley is an exception; he seems to go someplace when he has the spotlight.

Ray also could be very helpful, if the feeling was upon him. He did a lot for trombonist Bobby Byrne, the youngest guy in the Dorsey band. Mac took him over and more or less taught him to play jazz.

Because the Jimmy Dorsey band was not a blazing example of the best around, I was curious why McKinley stayed on. Of course, there was the security of steady work, particularly the Kraft Music Hall radio show in L.A. with Bing Crosby. But there had to be more to it.

MCKINLEY: I had a lot of offers from other bands. I remember one week Paul Whiteman, Hal Kemp, Benny Goodman, and Tommy Dorsey all asked me if I would leave Jimmy. Someone wrote it up in *Down Beat*. Tommy wouldn't take no for an answer; he kept on my case. It got so bad that Jimmy finally called his parents and asked them to tell Tommy to lay off McKinley.

But I stayed with Jimmy. He was easygoing and liked several things in addition to music. He enjoyed golf, for instance; I went for that. And I was one of those guys, you know—loyal—and I enjoyed Jimmy's friendship.

I knew we didn't have absolutely the best groups of musicians in the country. But obviously that wasn't everything, as far

as I was concerned. After I left Jimmy, his band got better. Do
you think there's any connection? I certainly hope not. Anyway
that's the whole truth.

Willard Alexander, the well-known booking agent, was the
guy who approached me about forming a band with Will Bradley, then known as Wilbur Schwichtenburg. One of the really fine
trombone players, Will had been doing very well around New
York, performing in radio and on recordings. Of course I had
known him since the Milt Shaw days. Well, Alexander got us
together. And one of the first things Will had to do was change his
name.

WILL BRADLEY: Ray was playing with Jimmy in New Jersey at the
    Meadowbrook, so Willard and I met him in a cocktail lounge in
    Newark. All three of us were sitting there and everything was
    going along fine, when I'll be damned if Jimmy didn't just hap-
    pen to walk into the same place. Things were a little tense, be-
    cause I'm sure he knew what was going on, but Jimmy just smiled
    and said, "Go ahead. I don't mind. I know what you're talking
    about."[6]

However, it wasn't quite that simple. Jimmy Dorsey wanted very
much to retain his friend and ace percussionist in his employ. He kept
asking McKinley to stay on, long after he'd handed in his notice.
Dorsey claimed he was having difficulty replacing him. After a while,
McKinley, anxious to get going as a leader, also started looking for a
replacement for himself. He asked Dave Tough to take over for him;
certainly Jimmy would have no objection to Tough, whose creden-
tials were impeccable. The "little giant" came into the band, and
McKinley was free to leave.

The Bradley band was born in the summer of '39. The billing—
Will Bradley and his Orchestra featuring Ray McKinley—led to mild
confusion about who held the reins. "We were partners, co-leaders,"
says McKinley. Relatively undistinguished at first, the band began to
take hold early in 1940 after turning to boogie woogie during an
engagement at the Famous Door on New York's 52nd Street.

Tight, distinctive, almost slick, eight-to-the-bar arrangements
gave the band a means of connecting with a vast audience. In performance they combined precision and all the pleasures of infectious
pulsation. These boogie charts effectively gave the band an identity.

At least partially responsible for the Bradley band's impact were
Freddie Slack, a barrelhouse pianist of some distinction, and the
adaptive, creative Bradley on trombone. Certainly the jazz feeling

within the band and the quality and warmth of its soloists enhanced the impact.

But without a doubt, the jazz heart and soul of this blues-centered group was McKinley. All one has to do is to listen to "Beat Me Daddy, Eight to the Bar" (Columbia, 1940), one of Bradley's most important and successful recordings. McKinley's impact immediately becomes apparent. His hip yet assuming singing and his stirring drumming give the music character and a down-home quality. The record quickly sold 100,000 copies, a major accomplishment in those days.

The foundation of this and all the key Bradley jazz recordings is McKinley's sense of rhythm. It permeates his singing, and is undeniable in his drumming. McKinley is the source of natural movement and more than a little drive.

The bass drum—tuned low—is his key instrument. He blends it with the other drums, and sometimes the cymbals, of the kit. Only rarely is he too loud. The result has to be felt to be really understood.

Boogie woogie may have been introduced to jazz devotees by black pianists like Albert Ammons, Pete Johnson, and Meade Lux Lewis. But the public at large came to know and love this rhythmically relentless style via the Andrews Sisters—remember "Boogie Woogie Bugle Boy"—and the big bands, particularly the Bradley band. People then found the way back to the seminal, boogie figures.

McKinley and Bradley helped trigger a trend that extended through the war years. The country became increasingly aware of boogie after the Bradley band hit. The Bob Crosby and Tommy Dorsey bands—pioneering units in boogie woogie—and Bob Zurke's group of musicians, the Basie band, and Earl Hines, Harry James, and Woody Herman and their orchestras, and certainly the bands headed by Freddie Slack and Gene Krupa all performed in the tradition.

McKinley left boogie woogie behind in February 1942, when he and Bradley parted company. They had disagreed about the band's direction: Bradley wanted to play more ballads, which he felt suited him better, while McKinley insisted they had a good thing, musically and commercially, with boogie woogie.

Before the breakup, more than a few performances were etched in wax for Columbia in 1940 and 1941. There were a number in the boogie style, like "Rock-a-Bye Boogie" for big band and "Down the Road Apiece" for the trio; ballads by Carlotta Dale ("I Don't Stand a Ghost of a Chance") and Terry Allen ("Who Can I Turn To?"); novelties by McKinley like "Scrub Me Mama with a Boogie Beat;" 4/4 instrumentals like the best-selling "Celery Stalks at Midnight;" and "Strange Cargo," the unforgettable Bradley theme, which suggests boogie woogie with a lyric feeling.

MCKINLEY: While with the Bradley band, I introduced something unusual—the use of two bass drums. This was years before Louie Bellson had the Gretsch Drum Company build him a set with two bass drums—long before the concept became popular.

Bill Mather designed a little outfit for me, including two twelve-by-twenty-four-inch bass drums; I believe it was in 1940. I was with Slingerland in those days and the company manufactured the kit.

I used the set with a small boogie woogie combo we put together from within the big band. Playing the two bass drums—boom, boom, boom, eight-to-the-bar with two feet—might have been innovative. But as far as I was concerned, it didn't work out too well. I discarded the idea after a short while. Not entirely satisfactory on a musical level, the situation also made for added physical difficulty. I got tired of carrying around extra bass drums.

The first Ray McKinley band took form not long after the drummer left Bradley. McKinley rehearsed the best musicians available for several weeks in Patchogue, Long Island, away from all distractions. Then he introduced the band to the world.

MCKINLEY: The Japanese had done their little bit out in Pearl Harbor and that kind of messed things up. But we made a good start. Over the eight-month life of the band we played the Commodore Hotel in New York and Frank Dailey's Meadowbrook, recorded for Capitol, and made a picture called "Hit Parade of 1943." The film also featured the Basie band and the Freddie Martin orchestra.

We had some good charts and players. . . .

Clarinetist Mahlon Clark, valve trombonist Brad Gowans, and pianist Lou Stein were among McKinley's men. The band was somewhat unusual in having a tuba—played by Joe Parks—which was used in a variety of interesting ways, with the brass, reeds, and rhythm. The band caused excitement. *Down Beat*'s New York editor Mike Levin, in his 1942 review, was enthusiastic about the McKinley crew.

MIKE LEVIN: If a new band can buck the current transportation, radio, and disk troubles [there was a wartime ban on making records], this is the one to do it. Hope the Morris agency gets on the ball and does a job for Mac—this band deserves it.[7]

Ray McKinley and his Orchestra on the set of the Universal film *Hit Parade of 1943.* "This picture featured two other bands as well—Count Basie's and Freddy Martin's," says McKinley.   Courtesy of Ray McKinley.

But the band wasn't fated to be on the scene for long. McKinley tried his best to keep it going. When he realized he couldn't, because of the military's demand for men, and the growing shortages at home that made travel increasingly arduous, he put in a bid to enlist the band in the Marines as a unit. This last effort, made in the hope of keeping the band together, didn't work out. As a parting shot, before he too joined the service, McKinley called Tommy Dorsey to offer him his remaining men. Dorsey grabbed almost all of them.

McKINLEY: After I got my little billet-doux from the draft board, I joined Captain Glenn Miller in Atlantic City and became a member of his Army Air Force Band. About a month later—I believe it was April of 1943—we were transferred to Yale University in New Haven and really started getting the thing together. Glenn brought all his organizational talent and creative ability to the orchestra.

We performed all kinds of music, including jazz marches. The orchestra made appearances at bond rallies and during

WAAC and Army recruiting drives. Military functions, like re-
treats and parades, were primary; we devoted much of our time
to them. There also was a lot of local radio work. And each Saturday we traveled into New York to do a nationally broadcast
program called "I Sustain the Wings," for the Air Force.

Very possibly the AAF Band was the greatest dispenser of
popular music ever. Certainly it was one of the two best musical
organizations I had anything to do with as a player. My post-war
orchestra, which featured the adventurous arrangements and
compositions of Eddie Sauter, runs parallel to the Miller ensemble when it comes to general excellence.

We had an awful lot going that made Glenn's Army Air Force
Band distinctive and musical. The performance level was very
high. Our instrumentation made for a bit of difference. We had
over twenty strings, a French horn, rhythm complement, one
more trombone [four], one more trumpet [four], and one more
saxophone [six] than other bands used. Solo stars, like Mel Powell on piano, clarinetist Peanuts Hucko, trumpeter Bernie Privin,
and that fine bass man, Trigger Alpert, added to the band's quality. And the arrangers made a really major contribution. The
scores gave us an identity and the sort of warmth few bands
have.

The whole experience was very exciting. But there is one
thing I must make clear. Though a marvelous band, it was not
particularly innovative. Glenn brought popular music of the time
to those who needed it. The band helped the war effort. It did its
job!

Some of our best work was done overseas. We always wanted
to go and finally did in June 1944—a few weeks after D-Day. The
band was stationed in England until leaving for France on December 18. Glenn, of course, had gone ahead of us on that ill-
fated airplane, three days earlier. Unfortunately, that was the
last we saw of him. It certainly was a terribly sad experience for
all of us. We had no idea he was missing until the week after the
band arrived in Paris.

When it became clear Glenn was lost, they stuck me in front
of the group. And we carried on during the rest of the time over
there, with Jerry Gray handling the arranging and everyone doing his job, just as if Glenn was still around.

LOU STEIN: I was in the band in the States. Ray took care of business
both as a musician and soldier. He was meticulous about his
military duties. But unlike the captain, with his white gloves
during inspections, Sergeant McKinley never bothered anyone.

CARMEN MASTREN: I had heard things about McKinley. Some guys said he could be biting and a little bit difficult. But I had no problem whatever working with him. We had a good rhythm section. Mac realized that it's the section, not any one man, that's really important. He knew we had to function as a team. A lot of drummers don't care about the section. They play for themselves. McKinley seldom forgot why he was there and what he should do.

We had a lot of laughs in the band. McKinley knows how to communicate in various ways. He's a fine entertainer. He and Trigger used to do some things and break it up. What it comes down to is that McKinley is a good all-around musician and performer. I came to like him and his playing a great deal. I look back on my experience with the Miller Air Force Band as an entirely positive one.

BERNIE PRIVIN: Ray and I got along fine. His affability and easy, Texas-type feeling often were mirrored in his playing. Though he wasn't terribly aggressive, he did a very good job holding the band together. Over the time we were the Miller band, Ray continued to develop. He got better and better.

Clearly he had his own way of doing things. The only aspect of his playing that bothered me a little bit was his two-beat preference. Sometimes he brought that feeling to material where it didn't fit. I think he played best in a small band. We made some wonderful small group records with Peanuts, Mel Powell, bassist Joe Shulman, and the French gypsy guitarist Django Reinhardt.

The recordings by the Miller Army Air Force Band on RCA Victor tell us a great deal about the McKinley of the war years. More so than previously, he backs the sections of the orchestra and the whole ensemble, providing support through key phrases and figures. His time is firm and often inspiring. McKinley's high-hat work in the mid and up-tempo pieces has an unusual sense of freedom and style. His pulse on these cymbals guides the band. The predominant meter feeling is 4/4. McKinley's love for two-beat, however, sometimes affected the 4/4 flow. During this period, drummers (i.e., Jo Jones) who thought and played more naturally in 4/4, could be a bit more convincing in the 4/4 time signature than McKinley.

As a colorist, a swinger, and all-around percussionist, McKinley gets good marks. He is commendable as well for his leadership qualities and creativity—it was his idea to play jazz marches, like "St. Louis Blues March." He also deserves recognition for building morale in this wartime musical organization.

General Hap Arnold of the Army Air Force rewarded McKinley with the Bronze Star "for meritorious service in connection with military operations, as a band leader, Army Air Force Band." McKinley was further cited for "able and talented leadership (that) reflected high credit upon the U.S. Army."

MCKINLEY: We arrived back in the States late in August, 1945. Shortly thereafter, I got out of the Army on points. And I began rehearsing my own band. New ground was broken. Eddie Sauter, an arranger and composer who Glenn said was way ahead of his time, wrote most of the charts. Deane Kincaide did the rest. The players were young and enthusiastic—guys like Mundell Lowe (guitar), Vern Friley and Irv Dinkin (trombones), Nick Travis and Rusty Dedrick (trumpets), Ray Beller (alto saxophone) and Lou Stein (piano).

We got something real good going. If I hadn't been the leader, with all the headaches that go with the job, I would have enjoyed it even more than I did. But I had the sense to know I had an important band.

The recordings we made, however, don't do the band justice. The industry didn't have the capacity to capture the best of any large group of musicians in those days. Much of what was played in the studio was lost. Recording techniques were just too primitive.

Late-night remote broadcasts from various spots, including the Hotel Commodore in New York City, got the band's message across. As a youngster, I remember waiting anxiously, night after night, to hear McKinley and his men; though not completely aware of the implications of the music and the performances, I did realize it was quite hip and special.

Central to the McKinley band's impact were the Sauter charts which were well knit and often quite melodic. Unexpected harmonies, interesting rhythmic juxtapositions, a variety of colors moved quickly past as one listened. Sauter used the orchestra and its individual players to create provocative musical experiences.

In McKinley, Sauter had a very supportive leader who, despite his traditional background, played the music with extraordinary understanding and taste and sense of adventure. During many of the broadcasts (and later when I bought the Majestic recordings of the Sauter creations), I was agreeably surprised by McKinley's performances. Though his style hadn't radically changed over the years, he made the music work and swing. He had discarded the two-beat, inner coating of his playing. The music moved in "four," though as the scores unfolded, they sometimes suggested other meters.

Because the band was unconventional, McKinley had a struggle on his hands. Those who sought the comfortable and easy-to-understand—and this included bookers, musicians, fans, and critics—forced the McKinley crew to play more accessible music and to become progressively more "versatile," though the band continued to play the Sauter material. McKinley and his men recorded an increasing number of novelties such as "Hoodle Addle" (Majestic, 1946), "Red Silk Stockings and Green Perfume" (Majestic, 1947), "Pancho Maximillian Hernandez" (Majestic, 1947), and "Arizay" (Victor, 1947), generally featuring McKinley vocals. Some of these enjoyed great success. The focus was on McKinley the entertainer, in order to keep the band afloat and in the black.

MCKINLEY: We had a few good years. But in the late 1940s, the band business started to wobble and get sick. As a matter of fact, it began to die. To survive, I changed the format, let some of the fellows go, shaving down the band to a size that was "workable" as far as the bookers were concerned. We played a simpler library. But in the long run, it made no difference.

In 1951, after an attack of amoebic dysentery, I broke up the band, got off the road, and took it easy. It was over. It seemed the right time to work in and around New York. I did a variety of things on radio and TV—a DJ show, weather reports incorporating some drumming, and several TV variety shows as a leader of a studio band. Only occasionally did I take a big band job nearby. And then I just picked up some guys in town and played the easier charts in the library.

The great post-war McKinley band rapidly became a memory, as far as the public was concerned. But those who helped shape it and the critics who were around remember it with great affection.

LOU STEIN: I love Ray for many reasons. Not the least of these: he hired me to play with that great post-war band. The players were so *involved*. They really wanted to play well. There was such *enthusiasm*. You never forget that. That attitude is not too prevalent these days.

MUNDELL LOWE: After I joined the band, I knew it was going to be something great. And that's how it turned out. Of course the charts were fantastic. But even more important to me: I learned most of what I know about playing in big band settings from

McKinley. He had a very definite idea about the function of each instrument and how it fit into a jazz orchestra. I have to thank him for that.

And he's a hell of a drummer. A lot of guys I've worked with are wonderful soloists; they can play fast and read well. But what they bring to the band and the rhythm section doesn't make it. Mac's way with music and rhythm is outstanding. It always felt terrific in the McKinley rhythm section. And let's face it, if the rhythm section works, then the rest of the band can get on with playing the music.

In some ways, though, Mac was a paradox. He hired Eddie Sauter and really *played* his music. On the other hand, he didn't let himself become involved with modern jazz, even though he had the talent to play it.

Paradox or not, Mac had the courage to organize and keep going a wonderful, musically memorable band. For that and numerous other things he has done for music and musicians, he must be deeply respected. He's a dear man who I will always consider one of my best friends and, of course, my mentor.

MCKINLEY: I didn't get back into the band business again until the spring of 1956 when Willard Alexander talked the Miller Estate into rejuvenating the Glenn Miller Orchestra. There hadn't been a Miller orchestra since the Estate parted company with Tex Beneke in '51. I was asked if I would be interested in heading up the band. I said, sure, I'd give it a shot and see what happens.

Fortunately the band became very successful. We played Miller music and more contemporary material. I spent ten years traveling. You name it, we were there—Japan twice, all over Europe, North Africa, and boom, boom, boom. Some of the traveling was enjoyable and interesting; the hard part was the one-nighters on the bus here in the States. It finally got to a point where I didn't want to be on the road anymore. I couldn't sleep in a bed. When I couldn't take it anymore, I quit.

LENNY HAMBRO: It was Mac's personality and musicianship that made the Miller band a success. He knew what he wanted and got it. He was a very strict disciplinarian—in the tradition of Tommy Dorsey, a man he admired. Some of the guys in the band didn't like McKinley. They called him "Sarge" because he made demands on them.

Mac loves good musicians, can't stand bad ones. He doesn't bother with guys who can't play. Not an emotional guy, he can have very positive feelings about someone and show very little. He's a great friend. But there's no fuss. That pretty much de-

Ray McKinley and the "New" Glenn Miller Orchestra on a date in Chicago in 1963. McKinley headed the Miller Orchestra from 1956 to 1966. Courtesy of Ray McKinley.

scribes his drumming as well. It's natural, often melodic, always pulsating, never fussy. He can play with anyone. Mac doesn't throw the kitchen sink in; he just makes everyone feel good. And his solos tell a story.

MCKINLEY: Since 1966, I've done some TV, worked for Walt Disney, made a few records, taken jobs that I feel are suitable. As I look back on things, I'm pretty satisfied.

I still have strong feelings about music and drumming. Good "time"—the pulse—is what jazz is about—always has been.

I regret I've never taken drumming as seriously as I should. I've never practiced. Perhaps if I had, I would have become more technically accomplished. But I've always been able to execute what I felt was necessary.

Woodshedding [practicing] on a pad can be good and bad. It can focus attention on *rudiments* rather than *music*. And that kind of playing is about as interesting as a temporary filling.

I guess I never was a very ambitious guy—even though I've

had good bands and received praise from people. I'm not wired that way. I'm the kind of guy who likes to do a lot of things. For a long time it was tennis, then swimming, now golf. And I love to read.

McKinley's native ability has allowed him to do what he wanted. That he never felt motivated to move beyond an updated form of swing drumming is in some ways unfortunate. But on the other hand, he has never lost what attracted so many musicians to him over the years.

Listen to the many musical recordings he has made. The quality is consistent. The best of the bunch, McKinley and I agree, is an album he made for Grand Award in the 1950s, with Mickey Crane (piano), Peanuts Hucko (clarinet), Lee Castle (trumpet), Trigger Alpert (bass), and Deane Kincaide (baritone saxophone). McKinley's time is flawless; his playing with and for his colleagues makes the music both provocative and fun.

McKinley credits a number of drummers with having left a mark on him. He frequently mentions Ben Pollack as a major factor in his life; George Stafford and Chick Webb are two others who have been important. Walter Johnson offered a few insights into high-hat playing. Dave Tough's work with Woody Herman's First Herd made an impression. So did Krupa's work with Goodman.

Jo Jones is another drummer McKinley "loves." Ray Bauduc had an influence: "He was the first guy I ever heard syncopate the bass drum." Shelly Manne, Jack Sperling, Nick Fatool, and Louie Bellson are each interesting to McKinley.

The best of the youngsters, according to Mac, is Duffy Jackson, the former Count Basie and Lionel Hampton sideman. "He's got an ear, a fine sense of rhythm, technique—all the good qualities," McKinley says, adding: "These are the guys who mean a lot to me. Certainly, many others would make the list if I had heard them."

Rock drummers?

MCKINLEY: As for the rock drummers—some of the better ones I've heard do interesting things with the bass drum. They should be complimented for that. But they do have a problem when it comes to achieving the simple, straight-ahead, exciting pulsation in a big band. Unfortunately these fellows really don't know what to do. I think they're more lost in this context than veteran players would be in a rock band.

Again on the positive side of the ledger: rock drummers, by introducing new ideas and creating interest among fans and other musicians, bring a certain vitality to the scene. I must admit, though, that I'm just a bit skeptical about the sets many of these youngsters use. All those drums and cymbals. It reminds me of the drummers back in the 1920s who surrounded themselves with chimes, bells, temple blocks, kettle drums—just everything—and didn't play on them too much.

If the kids nowadays want to spend all the money on lots of drums and things and not use them—why, that's their business. Yet it strikes a funny note with me. I remember one guy in particular. I came across him at a Holiday Inn somewhere in Florida a couple of years ago. He had 13 drums set up around him, plus two bass drums, snare, two big floor tom-toms, and a bunch of cymbals. It looked as if he would need roller skates to be able to play them all. As it happened, he didn't use more than a few drums and cymbals. It wasn't anything but show. Nothing new about that.

The best drummer of them all?

MCKINLEY: Buddy Rich. I've listened to the guy and watched him since he was a kid. I first met him when he was working with his Dad in vaudeville. Then I heard him with Shaw and Tommy Dorsey. He always knocked me out. In more recent years, he just baffled me. I think he was far and away the greatest drummer who ever lived. His technique was unbelievable; he swung; he could execute anything he had in mind. He just had it all.

Jo Jones
(1911-1985)

"He is a totally alive performer and he communicates with everything he has and is."

—*NAT HENTOFF*

"I've played with everybody I wanted to play with. I've been everywhere I wanted to go. The people I didn't want to play with, I didn't play with. The places I didn't want to go, I didn't go. I'm like Elsa the lion, born free. Ain't nothin' ever controlled me, except the music."

—*JO JONES*

Jo Jones with the Count Basie band at the Trianon Ballroom in Southgate, California in 1942. The trumpeter on Jo's left is Buck Clayton. © 1942 Harry Tate.

Jo Jones was slick. A handsome man with a highly expressive face and communicative eyes, he had "the look of a matinee idol, particularly in the early years with Basie," according to John Hammond. Lean, lithe, an erect, commanding figure at the drums, Jones was marvelously visual. And not only was he an attractive man, he had wide-ranging experience in reaching audiences; he knew every trick in the book.

Beyond the surface characteristics and the "show business" of Jo Jones was his work. The man was serious and deeply dedicated. His great natural talent for the instrument, and his need to keep learning and to excel made for a powerful combination. Jones' impact, particularly during the peak years with Count Basie, essentially stemmed from a flair for the unexpected and unusual, a firm, individual sense of time, and the capacity to be convincing and inspiring.

You didn't have to *see* Jones perform—that merely added several dimensions to what he played. What you *heard* told his story quite well.

"Jo Jones was like Louis Armstrong. He did a lot of things first. Techniques and attitudes that today's musicians take for granted Jo developed."

—JOE NEWMAN

"Jo Jones took the clutter out of jazz drumming."[1]

—WHITNEY BALLIETT

"I don't know how much technique Jo Jones has. But he gives you that feeling. Like you're on cloud nine. In his day, Jo was an absolutely thrilling drummer."

—PEE WEE ERWIN

"Going to see Jonathan David Samuel Jones ... is like entering a time warp inhabited by sand dancers, musicians, slapstick comedians, chorus girls, blues singers, and nomadic musical gladiators."[2]

—CHIP STERN

"Jo Jones, an elegant, swinging dude, always had a style of his own. When he was with us, you could hear him, feel him—everything was right there. From then to now, he has done the job."[3]

—COUNT BASIE

"How many others in jazz history both epitomized their own era and made essential contributions to the next?"[4]

—BOB BLUMENTHAL

"I was never as completely overwhelmed by a drummer, before or since, as I was that first night in Kansas City's Reno Club in 1936. Jo was infinitely variable, mighty sophisticated."

—JOHN HAMMOND

"Talk about flash and fly . . . what he introduced was a revelation, an advance on everything that had been done."

—HELEN OAKLEY DANCE

"No one in the world played high-hats the way he did. The dotted eighth and sixteenth rhythm was so even; it just rolled along, smooth as you please."

—ALLEN PALEY

"His high-hat sound was like an ocean surf—moving in and out."

—IRV KLUGER

"Jo Jones discovered he could play the flow of the rhythm, not its demarcation."[5]

—MARTIN WILLIAMS

"I never felt better playing than when Jo was in the rhythm section."

—MILT HINTON

"Jo was a very, very sensitive person. He cared a lot about people he liked and respected."

—BUCK CLAYTON

"The man was independent *all his life, even toward the end when illness wore him down."*

—*WILSON DRIVER*

"Jo said what he believed. If he thought you were wrong, or that you had behaved badly, if he felt you were a terrible person, he'd say so right out in the open."

—*SHELTON GARY*

"There have been remarks made about Jo being 'outside' and 'unusual.' But that's not the truth. Jo was an original, as a musician and a person. That's the truth!"

—*CHICO HAMILTON*

MEMORIES

I first saw Jo Jones at the Roxy Theater in 1944, just before he went into the Army. His personality filled the great New York movie palace. Backing a line of thirty-six girls and a variety of acts, catching every nuance, he swung like mad, making it all seem easy as pie. "If you were there, you really heard me," Jones said. "I carried two bands—Paul Ash's and Basie's. After the Roxy ensemble's percussionist played the overture from the pit, conductor Ash pointed at me and said: 'You got it.' "

Onstage at the Strand Theater on Broadway in 1948: this was Jones' last engagement as a regular member of the Basie band. Rather suddenly, according to Basie, the drummer left one day between shows, taking all of his equipment with him. The band leader had to scuffle a bit to get a temporary replacement for the next series of shows but managed to fill the gap with a drummer from the Apollo Theater. Shadow Wilson, the sub for Jones during his service stint, ultimately returned to the band.

The Strand, on this occasion, offered quite an appealing show, both on stage and screen. Basie shared billing with Billie Holiday, Stump and Stumpy, and the Two Zephyrs. The picture was "Key Largo," which teamed Bogart and Bacall.

This stand was a learning experience for me. Instinctively I realized that there was much more to his playing than there seemed to be. Later it became clear that he drew upon his years in carnivals, medicine shows, and vaudeville and his experience with large and small bands of various kinds.

Toward the close of the show, he offered a composite of show business smarts and musicality. For a little over five minutes, during what he described as his "feature," he played with sticks, brushes, and mallets and with his hands, managing to please both the people who came to see the picture and the musical members of the audience.

Jones employed visual trickery, particularly when playing cross-over patterns on the floor tom-toms—one on each side of him. Essentially, however, Jones used the drum set to build a statement. Not technically gifted, he seldom resorted to speed for its own sake.

The solo kept developing. It was as if Jones were talking to the audience. The performance had an inner sense of design—ebb and flow, peaks and valleys, pace and movement. Through it all, he held the audience tightly, changing pace when you thought you knew just what he was going to do.

I couldn't take my eyes off him. His head and body moved gracefully; his face mirrored the emotions he was feeling. His hands and arms projected the elegance basic to a dancer, rare in a drummer. His rhythmic patterns were never boring. In each show, the solo was different.

PICTURES OF JO THROUGH THE YEARS

At the posh East Side Club in New York, the Embers, with Buck Clayton, Milt Hinton, and Joe Bushkin in the 1950s: Still a bundle of nervous energy that transformed itself into rhythm, he had lost nothing. Now his work, for the most part, was with small groups. I can still hear his brushes snapping and swishing over the calfskin of the snare at a very fast tempo. His execution was just about flaw-free.

In the open air of New York's Central Park early in the 1970s, in the company of Art Blakey, Elvin Jones, Tony Williams, Max Roach, Freddie Waits and Mel Lewis: the program, sponsored by the Gretsch Drum Company, took place during one of George Wein's early jazz festivals in New York. Jones contended with these drummers, using only his high-hat, and proceeded to wash all of them away.

At that concert, Jo also openly showed his love for an ailing Gene Krupa. He presented him with a special award, signed by most of the major American drummers. Frank Ippolito, the well-liked drum shop owner, and Jo made a special effort to get this done for Gene. They wanted to help cheer the "drummer man" when he most needed support from friends and colleagues.

Finally: at home on East 64th Street after his cancer operation in 1981: His hunger for playing had not abated. But his body did not respond as it once had. He ruefully admitted his "time had passed. Now it is the turn of others." He declared, "Drumming is a young man's work!"

Jones, Mel Lewis, and I discussed a variety of matters, from Jim Europe and early black popular music to the work of Tony Williams, a drummer Jo liked. The meeting had been planned as an interview, but it turned into a sometimes valuable, sometimes annoying stream-of-consciousness outpouring from Jones. He was oblique, occasionally, a bit salty but finally warm, open, and loving in his typically authoritarian manner.

Jo insisted we all play his high-hats. For me that evoked the sort of uneasiness a dancer would feel performing for Astaire. Then, quite suddenly, his mood changed. What had been diffuse became clear and more concentrated; obviously he felt more comfortable and trusting than he had when we arrived.

He accepted my invitation to play at the "Buddy Rich Retrospective," the concert I was going to produce for George Wein at Carnegie Hall the following June. "I may be in Spain by then," he said gently, with a smile. "But I'll do my best to be there."

His son David came for a visit as late afternoon was turning into evening. Mel and I had been there almost four hours. It was time to make the break. When I put on my coat and walked toward the door, Jo followed me, grasped my hand and said: "Come back. But make it soon!"

Jones lived for four more years. I remained in contact with him, but I saw him only once more—at the Rich concert. Frail and older-looking, he was warmly announced and greeted by Buddy and encouraged to play. Jo smiled, bowed, then sat at the drums. It soon became clear that his illness had ravaged his beautiful talent. But he had enough to carry him through. And the audience responded strongly to the man who once was the very essence of what a drummer should be.

He died in 1985 after more than a little pain and difficulty, and the inevitable sense of humiliation that comes with an illness that transcends all else. The jazz community grieved. A bit of my youth went with him.

The best introduction to Jo Jones is provided by the recordings he made with Count Basie. Certainly pianist Basie gives the music undeniable character. Tenor saxophonist Lester Young's solos bring a floating sense of flight and undeniable swing to the best performances. Comments by trumpeters Buck Clayton and Harry "Sweets" Edison and trombonists Dicky Wells and Benny Morton add to the dancing pulse. And the band, as a whole, exemplifies a togetherness and a unity of conception that almost defy description.

But mostly it's Jo's breathing, sizzling, high-hat that makes everything just right. His playing charms the ear and brings to the body the urge to move. He smooths out and opens up the rhythmic flow, never becoming overly assertive, remaining ever consonant with the feeling of each arrangement. Grace and subtlety predominate. Jones is cool, yet the underlying heat that heightens excitement at any tempo permeates what he does.

Jones, Young, Clayton, Edison, Wells, Walter Page, Freddie Green, Basie, and the rest altered the conception of how jazz could and should be played. By exploring natural, flowing pulsation and marrying it to relaxation, the band offered a fresh approach to soloing and sectional and ensemble performance. The use of space, understatement, surprise, and constant swing made the ensemble very effective.

The Basie band could get to you while playing a suggestive, slow blues or a medium-tempo swinger, or while shouting and exploding over charging rhythm. The band's hallmark was simplicity. But the band could fool a listener who wasn't paying close attention. A lot was going on—among the soloists, in the sectional and ensemble playing, and particularly in the rhythm section. The major Basie players helped move jazz toward what many describe as the jazz revolution of the 1940s.

The Basie recordings remain quite hip, specifically those made while Lester Young was in the band (1936–1940, 1943–1944). And at the very center is Jones—a quiet delight, ever musical, ever pushing the beat, always encouraging the band to sing its song. With a touch here, a bomb there, a well placed accent, or a highly relevant break, in addition to his beautiful high-hat and cymbal playing, he brings to the Basie repertory rhythmic individuality, substance, and weight that it would not have without him.

Somehow, however, the sweep and value of his work eluded some critics. George Simon, a longtime observer, recently commented that he always felt the drummer had time problems, stemming from disinterest, when playing ballads. It's possible. One or two others suggested Jones was overrated. I couldn't disagree more. Jo had his faults—most of them the result of temperament. But in circumstances that pleased him, with players equal to the task, he seldom disappointed musician colleagues or anyone who came to listen.

BUDDY RICH: I've never forgotten those nights at the Famous Door on 52nd Street when I first heard Basie and Jo Jones. It was 1938. The Basie band had begun to catch on in New York. All the cats talked about it. I loved what Jo did and how he *felt*. His playing was innovative. I was a kid. I'd just gotten my start in jazz with Joe Marsala down the street at the Hickory House. I was open to all kinds of experiences when it came to music. Jo, Pres, Sweets, Buck, and my man Basie—the whole band—gave me some of the most exciting nights of my life.

There's no doubt about it. When Jo was a key member of what became known as the "All American Rhythm Section," with Basie on piano, Walter Page, bass, and Freddie Green, guitar, he was the greatest time-keeper of all. He might have been a limited soloist. But his solos were devastating because they worked and were so right. If Jo had four bars to play, he did exactly what was necessary, with a great sense of creativity. He wasn't into speed or technique for their own sake. The man played exactly what was called for in the chart. You have to have special ability, ears and a true understanding of what music really is in order to do that.

One thing is for sure. Anyone who plays drums or supposedly appreciates drumming should experience Jo Jones.

ALLEN PALEY: Jo and I got to know one another during the Basie band's first engagement at the Famous Door in 1938. I became deeply involved with him and his playing. We talked almost every night between sets. I'd hang around until he was through and we'd talk some more. It wasn't unusual for us to still be talking on Broadway as the sun came up. Some days we'd get together and play. I was studying—first with Sanford Moeller, then with Billy Gladstone—and constantly practicing and playing around town and on the road. At that time, for me and certainly for Jo, drums were what life was all about.

I learned a lot from him. He was very giving, very helpful. On a couple of occasions, he asked me to sit in with the Basie band. "Go ahead, play!" he insisted." I was scared but it felt marvelous each time. Let's face it, if you couldn't play with *that* band. . . .

Many nights after Jo finished work at the Door, we would go uptown for a session at Monroe's or some other place. Other guys in the band, usually Lester Young and Harry "Sweets" Edison, also made these sessions, that sometimes lasted until late morning.

The whole thing is almost unreal to me today, after not having been part of the life for so long. But it was something for the books, being involved like that with someone like Jo. Night blended into day. What started early in the evening generally would end with ribs and more talk at Eddie Green's in Harlem.

STANLEY KAY: I was fourteen in 1938 when I *saw* and *heard* Jo Jones for the first time at New York's Loew's State Theater. He was quick, precise yet loose. He didn't play like most of the white guys who just jumped up and down and accomplished very little. Jo knew exactly what he was doing. There wasn't a wasted gesture. He sat up straight and used his hands and arms in a way I can only describe as very graceful. Every accent he made with the Basie band was a picture.

As I talk, it comes back. . . . The guys wore yellow jackets and black tuxedo pants. Most of the reed section had dark glasses on because they didn't like the spotlight. Everyone was relaxed, not methodical and military like the musicians in some other bands. The ease, lack of strain, and the time feeling were the key elements with Basie. The band never pressed. Jo helped make the music a light delight.

Somehow I managed to get backstage that day and saw Jo's drums up close. They were far from anything special—a twenty-eight-inch Leedy bass drum, a snare drum made by Ludwig, Gretsch-Gladstone tom-toms, large high-hats, a few cymbals. It was *what* he did on the rag-tag set . . . the sounds he created.

Later when we got to know one another, while I was in Buddy Rich's band, I noticed a few things. He used special soft shoes when he played, almost like ballet slippers. And he generally rolled up his pants on his right leg. This was to avoid getting the pants caught in the beater ball of the bass drum pedal.

He gave me some hints about what I should wear when I played—a T-shirt under my dress shirt to absorb perspiration and *always* clean, white socks. Jo was full of ideas; he talked a lot and I listened. All the while he continued to play in a way that none of the drummers could quite duplicate.

That day at Loew's State was the beginning of something important for me. I didn't know exactly what Jo, Pres, and the band were doing. But it was better than anything I'd ever heard.

LOUIE BELLSON: I remember one of the last jazz festivals in Newport, George Wein decided to get all the drummers he thought were the top echelon at the time. Buddy was there. Mel Lewis, Elvin Jones, Roy Haynes, maybe two or three other players. Buddy did his thing, pulling out all the stops. I did everything I could with the two bass drums. Elvin played real well. Everybody just—boom!—played hard and creatively.

Came time for Jo Jones: He went out with a high-hat and a pair of sticks and tore everybody apart. We all threw up our hands and said, "Okay, you got it, man. That's all." No drum set. Just the high-hat. And he broke it up.

Jo Jones did what was right for him. He became a part of what he loved. From childhood, he had been strongly drawn to music and entertainment. They made him feel good, igniting a spark within that added buoyancy to his days. His talent as a musician and entertainer brought him even more—that special joy reserved for those whose work is also their play.

Jo always wanted to learn, to be able to give more and more of himself. Because he was by nature a curious and highly sensitive person, with a capacity for absorbing what he saw and heard, Jones assimilated and integrated what he experienced musically. The process was never-ending; that's why Jones never got "old" as a player. He also used what he learned in his own way. He wasn't a copy.

Growing up during the 1920s, Jo Jones was on intimate terms with the growth and development of multiple types of popular music and entertainment. He was *there*, taking it all in, participating: he traveled around the country in carnivals and vaudeville, medicine shows and circuses; later, with bands and groups, he added to the sum of his knowledge. Responsive to and respectful of those who really knew the field, he became an informed, increasingly colorful figure—sure of his ground, seemingly always putting others to the test.

An artist who knew how to manipulate audiences, Jo Jones was a *performer*. How he dressed, how he carried himself—*everything* was part of the impression made, he said.

He and his contemporaries were "show business" because that's the way it was when they were coming along. Though many things about Jones changed with the years, the way he "performed" in front of an audience remained unchanged.

Like Count Basie, his great friend and longtime employer, Jones was completely and thoroughly stagestruck. He enjoyed being around musicians and performers, theaters, clubs, and concert halls, and loved anything that had to do with music and entertainment. He relished talking shop. More than most, he cared for and nurtured young players. Jones was deeply proud of being a musician and realized his responsibility to up and coming musicians.

Despite protestations to the contrary, he never really thought seriously about being anything but a performer. His fascination with the business was permanent. His need to play and be a part of music never left him—even as life came to a close.

He once said: "I want to play twenty-six hours a day, even though I know I need sleep. I don't want to go near music when I can't play. I sit there and the palms of my hands are perspiring. It's a real feeling of frustration."[6]

Jonathan David Samuel Jones was born October 7, 1911, in Chicago, the son of Samuel and Elizabeth Jones. His most vivid childhood memories centered around his father, a man of uncommon abilities, who worked as an electrician and boat builder, among other things.

The Jones family moved from city to city, wherever Samuel Jones' work took him.

Jo's early years were filled with drama and some of the terrible realities of life. His father was killed before he reached his eleventh birthday. Before that—"I was four, five, or six, I don't quite remember"—Jones seriously burned himself playing with fire. The accident shut him away from the outside world for a period of time. Living in a world of adults, he put aside childish interests. He read a great deal and became unusually thoughtful and philosophical for a youngster. And he became infatuated with musical instruments, particularly the drum, and the world of dancers, singers, comedians, and musicians.

Jo's fascination can be traced back to his father, who suggested that entertainment was a more than feasible career for the black man of Jo's generation.

PHIL SCHAAP: Papa Jo was responding to his father. His Dad had indicated to him that sports and certainly entertainment were two areas in which the black man could excel and get respect. They were ways out of a bad situation. It soon became clear to Jo that his Dad was right, that he had been given good advice.

JO JONES: My father was connected with the Government; he was known as an artificer. Aside from being an electrician, building boats and things, he was called on to do other jobs as well. He was in a unique position. You must remember how the situation was for the black man then. My father had to be four times better than anybody else to accomplish what he did.

Then suddenly it was over. He died trying to help others. The date remains fixed in my mind: July 17, 1922. Some college students in Tuscaloosa didn't know how to fix a large piece of machinery. They were earning money so they could continue their education. My father got up on this barge and the machine—it was like a plow—failed, came apart, and a piece of steel struck him in the back, cutting him from the neck down to the base of the spine. I had gone to visit him with my sister Lillian the day before it happened. He passed on a Monday.

As for my accident—I remember being an invalid for a year and a half. It took me until I was sixteen or seventeen to put the experience behind me. Even now, I find it hard to think about it. I was burned from head to foot in a fire. I wanted to copy one of my uncles who lit his cigar with a piece of newspaper. All of a sudden I was on fire. Doctors didn't know too much about treating burns. I used to sleep in a tub filled with ice and cold water.

I'll never forget one thing. My father brought me silver dollars and a ukulele.

I wasn't allowed to do what the other kids did. I missed growing up the way they did. So here I am, having lived a lot of life, and there are certain things I know nothing about. But the whole thing taught me *understanding*. It convinced me you have to help people, every day, if that's possible. I guess that's why I got involved with Father Flanagan and Boys Town, Lighthouse for the Blind, and the Children's and Domestic Relations Court in New York. Having had a real bad experience, young, made me the way I am.

I was forced to learn certain things that others didn't have to deal with until much later—if at all. You could say I wasn't born no child. I was born a man. Not a baby. Not a boy. A man, in capital letters. No questions, no semicolons, no parentheses, no commas. Period. A man!

Music began to filter into Jo Jones' life during his convalescence. Sister Mattie, an aunt on his mother's side, took him to the Ringling Brothers Circus, where he had a "fantastic" experience.

JONES:　I saw, heard and felt Mr. Emil Helmicke, the greatest bass drum player that ever lived. The impact of the bass drum got me right in my stomach and I never relinquished that feeling. That was my real introduction to music. I couldn't keep still; my Aunt Mattie held me in her arms. Right after that, she bought me a snare drum.

During childhood and early adolescence, Jones spent a number of years in Alabama, particularly in the Birmingham area. He had family there, and attended black schools: the Tuggle Institute, Lincoln Junior High School, the A & M Institute in Huntsville. In addition to the drum, he played trumpet, saxophone, piano, chimes, vibes, and tympani, sang and danced, and "did the dramatics," sometimes leaving town with carnivals and shows, living many a young kid's fantasy.

JONES:　I didn't think I was going to end up a drummer. I was trying all these instruments. But somehow I played drums on all of them. After a while my feelings for the instrument became quite strong.

I don't know why all these guys jump on drums and think it's the easiest way out. . . . When I first met Mr. Wilson Driver [one of the first drummers to come out of Birmingham], he had a set of drums, a xylophone and cornet, and he could teach the whole thing.[7]

WILSON DRIVER: When Jo was twelve or thirteen, he used to come by the Famous Theater in Birmingham, where I was playing accompaniment, with a pianist, for silent pictures. He'd be there every day in the second row, staring at me the same way a rattlesnake does at his victim. For a time, he just checked me out and never said anything. He was aloof; he wouldn't let me show him anything at first. He said, "Wait until I ask!"

After a while I put a question to him, "Are you playing hooky from school?" He quickly answered, "No. My people know I'm here!" When he finally let me show him some things, he would often question my methods. Occasionally he suggested how I might do better. When we discussed the best way to hold sticks, he had me show him what I had been doing. Then he came back with "That's very good. But I want to hold mine in my own way."

On a couple of occasions, when we added a few more instruments for a special picture, I asked him if he wanted to know what notes meant, because we were reading. His answer: "I don't want to read no notes because anything anybody plays I can play. So I haven't time to be bothered reading notes."

Sometimes his tremendous confidence and independence could be a little trying. But I couldn't help feeling good about his possibilities. He wanted to play so badly. One time though, he made me quite angry. I said, "Don't come back any more!" He kind of smiled and said, "I'll be back when I need something else." Jo was very singleminded about drums.

In all, Jo was with me for about six months, several hours a day, almost every day. When he left town, after I had sent him over to the Frolic Theater to play with Butterbeans and Susie, the music and comedy team, he was gone for quite a while. He made a prediction before leaving, "When I get back, I'll be better than you." I said, "We'll see."

Jo was in and out of town over the years. There was a lot of talk about what he did in Omaha and Kansas City. How well he played became quite clear to me when I heard him on the radio—after a number of years—from Cincinnati, shortly after Basie left Kansas City.

Our relationship lasted through his life. I loved and respected him. And his prediction came true. He outdistanced me in almost every way. The roles reversed. He became the teacher. Funny thing, though; he never really wanted to show me anything. He'd say: "The student doesn't tell the teacher. Come watch me to-night. Listen to what I'm doing!"

HAYWOOD HENRY: Jo and I went to Lincoln Junior High School in Birmingham in 1926, or thereabouts. He lived in Ensley, a suburb of the city, five miles from Birmingham proper. Because there were no schools for blacks in the area, Jo had to ride the streetcar into the city every day.

When he was at Lincoln, Jo was a fine athlete. Most people don't know that side of him. He was an excellent boxer. I also remember few could beat him at the game of checkers. He'd take his front line off the board and still beat us.

Even back then he was a wonderful drummer. There were a bunch of good drummers in Birmingham. But I preferred Jo because he was smoother than the others. And he was just fifteen years old.

He was impressive from the beginning, a natural. He didn't have to go in for formal training. He was just good . . . at everything he did. This is 1926 I'm talking about, not after he had a whole lot of experience.

Jo also was very wise for his age. He was way ahead. He had his life planned. Often he discussed what he was going to do, how he would become a famous drummer. And not only was he a drummer, he danced and played the piano.

After I went to high school, I didn't see Jo for some time. I began playing saxophone in the band that Erskine Hawkins led, the Bama State Collegians. In 1935, we went to New York to play the Uproar House at 51st Street and Broadway. Jo came into town a year later. The Basie band opened at the Roseland Ballroom. One night, he came down to the club to check us out. I had been hearing so much about him, so the reunion was exciting. Jo was surprised to see me with the Collegians. I hadn't started on my horns until after he left Birmingham. We reminisced about Birmingham and talked music. Then he sat in with us and really was swinging.

After that, we got together at band battles at the Savoy Ballroom—Basie against the Erskine Hawkins band. On these occasions we talked a great deal. There's nothing like spending time with someone you care about from home.

You know one thing? In those days, musicians didn't admit they came from places like Alabama. They always claimed they were from New Orleans, Chicago, or Kansas City, where all the action was. It made them seem more impressive to people in music. But when you get right down to it, a lot of great players came from out-of-the-way places, like Alabama. Cootie Williams, for one; Jo Jones, for another.

As far as much of the music community is concerned, Jo Jones was born when he joined Count Basie. But going with the band, first on Valentine's Day of 1934 for a brief stay, then a little over a year later during the band's engagement at the Reno Club in Kansas City, was merely the culmination of many experiences for the drummer.

JONES: A lot happened to me before I settled in with Basie for a fourteen-year stay. I was involved with a bunch of things and met many people who taught me what I had to do as a man and a musician.

I always hung out with older experienced people—I never hung out with no one my age. In my formative years, having dabbled in Chautauqua shows, medicine shows, carnivals and circuses and little girlie shows.

You had a whole lot of fathers and uncles and mothers out here, you see, and that's what's so remarkable about it. I remember that I was connected with people that had "foreign intrigue."

These people—Hungarians, Lithuanians, trapeze artists, and what have you—they taught me how to eat, how to think; they taught personal hygiene, moral and civil discipline. We weren't allowed the luxury of playing around like teenagers, because we were around old people with experience. They didn't lecture us, but they showed youngsters the way. The people I'm talking of were passing on the benefit of their know-how to us. When we got so smart that we knew everything, they let us go and jump off a cliff. But they'd have a net there to break our fall, and then they'd let us know we weren't so all-fired smart.[8]

No drummer influenced me. Any time I saw a drummer, I knew what he was going to do after he had played two bars.

But there were several drummers Jones admired during his early years in music, including Kid Lips Hackette, Manzie Campbell, Crack Johnson, Holland "Tubby" Harold, Jimmy King, Sylvester Rice, and Jimmy Bertrand.

JONES: Kid Lips Hackette was a sensational drummer. He could flip sticks, run around the room, juggle sticks, and do all that [show] business. But at the same time, he could play the "Poet and Peasant" overture, a symphony. You must remember, the black musician, like the black player in the early days of semipro baseball, had to clown. He had to have that simple thing called showmanship—a certain flair. Kid Lips, he not only could write music and drum parts, he could play the whole bit. He had the ability to sit in with a straight orchestra and still do his act. You see, he had an *act*.

He also was a terrific prize fighter. When the people in the show were stranded, he'd book himself a fight down at the YMCA or some club somewhere and pick up $20 or $25 and come back and feed the company. Then he'd do the show. . . . At one time Sid Catlett, Kid Lips, and I were going to have an act.

The greatest drummer who ever lived in the whole world, the guy who made me what I am today was a fellow by the name of Manzie Campbell. He was the only man I have ever seen that could take his left hand and play a perfect drum roll. I met Mr. Campbell with the Collier Show, which toured just the South. Crack Johnson played in the big tent with John Philip Sousa. He looked like Jack Johnson, the boxer. And he taught me a great lesson. After I had known him for several years, he sat down at my drums one night and said: "Son, you might go far. But don't make that mistake anymore." He told me how to learn to play drums. I had been trying to emulate the popular drummers in the territory where I was working. I wasn't going anywhere. He taught me *not to imitate*. . . .

"Tubby" Harold was the second greatest drummer on my list. He played the whole bit and taught. He helped me with my musical education and opened my eyes to many things.

When you speak about musical drummers, the most musical drummer I know was a fellow by the name of Jimmy King. His career was short-lived. He died in the 20's. He was with Rex Stewart. He played with Rex and Horace Henderson in the Wilberforce Collegians.

The greatest all-around drummer that I remember who also was a conductor was Sylvester Rice. I have never seen a percussionist, with the exception of Mr. Billy Gladstone, who played in Radio City, that could conduct a symphony. Sylvester Rice could conduct anything.

He played with the Eli Rice band, his father's organization. It was a Midwestern band . . . He came to New York for a moment. But he went back to the Midwest because New York musicians didn't have his knowledge. He was disgusted because they were too slow in their thinking.

As for Jimmy Bertrand: I didn't know anything about tuning drums until I rubbed elbows with him.

What I learned from these fellows, and later from men like

Billy Gladstone and Lou Singer, is that most people don't know how to *play* drums. They *beat* them.

If I were a lady of the evening, I wouldn't go with a drummer. Most of them aren't tender enough. Bang, bang, bang— that's no good. I told Duke [Ellington] forty years ago: a drum is like a woman. You *play* it.

I just went through something here with you and Mel [Lewis]—playing my high-hat. I tried to show you fellows that it's *touch* on cymbals and drums. Can we learn to be gentle? I don't know whether we all can learn. Tell you one thing: I've been out here on the street since I was eleven years old. You *do* acquire something. But it really depends who and what you've heard, the people you're close to, musically. And you can only play what's inside you. It comes out. The instrument will bring it out of you. But you must hit the drum gently. It's just that simple!

There were other people and circumstances that shaped Jo Jones during his formative years. During our conversations, he mentioned his trumpet teacher in Alabama, George Hudson, who later led a band out of St. Louis, and cornetist James H. Wilson, another Alabama mentor, who introduced him to the work of Louis Armstrong. And, of course, Jones learned a great deal while traveling.

JONES: I had an unusual background from being in shows and carnivals, starting out when I was eleven years old. No one can tell me about drums—no one has my reflexes, my *musical background.*

Jones was challenged by the variety of situations which he faced in carnivals and shows. His ability to improvise, most often on inferior equipment, was constantly called into play and tested. These traveling shows, though structured, had more than a share of freedom and unexpected events. Jones not only had to be an inventive drummer but an all-around entertainer as well. He exercised his talent as a singer and dancer and even played "the cute black tyke" in black vaudeville.

What did he remember or want to talk about regarding those years? Mostly his involvement with all kinds of performers, ranging from those previously noted—"with foreign intrigue"—to top black comics like Pigmeat Markham, and leading blues interpreters. "I once took over for Stepin Fetchit on a medicine show," he recalled, smiling.

It was Jones' feeling that other musicians missed a lot by not having the benefit of widespread experience. At the close of his life, he often said that Roy Eldridge was one of the few remaining players who had "gone to the same school." Only Eldridge had shared with Jones the wonder of travel and the diversity of show business. The others "never saw the people . . . they didn't hit the forty-eight states—villages and hamlets," he declared. "After World War II, it got so they could get an airplane and they never saw nothing!"

As vaudeville, carnivals, circuses, and other traveling shows felt the effect of talking pictures, radio, and recordings, it became apparent to Jones that the future was elsewhere. Because of the change in the entertainment business and the response of people to it, Jones became increasingly involved with drums and the performance of music with bands.

From the late 1920s until linking up with Count Basie in Kansas City in 1934, Jones played his way through a number of bands. He traveled a good deal of the time, using Omaha as his center of operations, all the while becoming immersed in what was happening in music through the Midwest and Southwest.

Jones set a pattern that he followed to the end of his life. Wherever there was a prospect of great music being made, he turned up. He found out, or instinctively knew, where the great sessions would be held in any city or town. He played piano, vibraphone and drums, depending on what was necessary and how he felt. He soon realized that he could be most expressive on the drum set. By the time he joined Basie, Jones had forsaken the other instruments for the most part. Besides, "being a drummer paid better."

Jones didn't talk much about playing with the pre-Basie bands. But he indicated that performing with the Ted Adams Band, Harold Jones' Brown Skin Syncopaters, the Grant Moore Band, the Jap Allen Band, the famed Bennie Moten Ensemble, and Lloyd Hunter's Serenaders—with whom he made his first record in 1931—helped him develop his distinctive manner of playing.

The style he brought to the Basie band was a product of "the people he rubbed elbows with" and the parts of the country in which he did his performing and listening. The Midwest and Southwest, where his activity was centered during the pre-Basie years, were geographically open areas. It is not incidental that the way bands and individual players from these two sections of America expressed themselves often reflected the spaciousness of the areas. The rhythm was generally looser and lighter than in other places. Drummers allowed the beat to flow, so the rhythmic line straightened out, and ultimately became a rolling 4/4 in the Basie band.

The performers of the Midwest and Southwest were noted for

rhythmic invention and change. During the 1920s and the first years of the 1930s, there was a progressive modification of the pulse of Midwestern and Southwestern bands. One has only to listen to the early Bennie Moten recordings on Victor—cut in the 1920s—and the 1932 session for the same label by this premier Kansas City band. The time feeling moves from two beats to the measure to straight four. Other influential bands within this general territory, such as the much-admired ensemble led by Alfonso Trent, and certainly Walter Page's Blue Devils, were going in the same direction as Moten. They were starting to relax and *swing*.

Jo Jones was in the midst of the turbulence and creativity in these areas, moving as he did from band to band. What was being experimented with in the Midwest and Southwest would, within a few years, affect the entire musical community from coast-to-coast. On a recording by the Grant Moore band, "Mama Don't Allow No Music Playing Here" (Vocalion, 1938) are bass drum "bomb" patterns (by Harold Flood) that became common in the mid-1940s. Willie McWashington, the drummer who preceded Jo Jones in the Bennie Moten band, was also experimenting. "He played 'stumbles'— they now call them bombs. He made that connection between the interlude and the out chorus. Nobody could drop it in the bucket like him," Jones said. Though Roy Eldridge said that Chick Webb was among the first to "shoot bombs," and others claim Kenny Clarke was a primary pioneer when it came to bombs and snare and bass drum coordination, it was in the bands of the Midwest and Southwest that this rhythmic idea initially took form.

Jones was never too open about the influence of others on his playing, but he did acknowledge the strong effect on him of Walter Johnson, the great Fletcher Henderson drummer. An artful and subtle high-hat stylist before Jones became famous in the Basie band, Johnson provided the foundation for what was later played by Jones, Alvin Burroughs, and other drummers who leaned on the high-hat.

LAWRENCE LUCIE: Jo Jones was working with the Jeter-Pillars band in St. Louis when I came through with the Fletcher Henderson band. No one knew him back then. It must have been early 1934, for I was with Fletcher until moving over to Lucky Millinder later that year. Anyway, Jo would come in every night during our engagement. He was a great admirer of our drummer Walter Johnson. Jo got a lot from Walter, particularly the smooth way of playing the high-hat and other cymbals.

Jo always comes to mind when I think about Walter. They both knew how to play softly; you could hear every instrument in the band. Jo developed a lot of other things, like unusual coordination, that Walter didn't emphasize. But in so many ways they were alike.

DANNY BARKER: One of the greatest drummers I ever worked with was Walter Johnson. He'd sell it soft, you know. Walter would sit up there, saying nothing, just laying it down. He was a machine, but smooth. He never hit cymbals too hard. His drums were well tuned. Drummers could learn from Walter Johnson.

I'd sit in front of him with my head in about the center of his bass drum. He didn't get in nobody's way. He never was annoyed by anything. He just kept looking straight ahead. And he was the handsomest man I ever saw. There'd be fifteen, twenty women standing by the bandstand, looking over my head at Walter Johnson. If you were looking for a woman, you just hung around Walter.

I can't forget his drumming. Everything he did, man—it was in the right place. He knew how and when to play the cymbal, when to hit the bass drum, the snare drum, how to run that high-hat. It was a pleasure. He looked at you with a nice expression. And he never got wringing wet, like other drummers. He was cool; his tie and suit remained fresh and in place.

Walter helped a band. When the excitement began to build, he was right there, supporting the feeling. The man was precise, quick. All the younger drummers came around. All of them, including Jo Jones. Walter made his reputation with Fletcher's band in the early 1930s. And everybody wanted to hear *that* band.

JONES: I learned from everyone, and I always tried to hang out and pick up as much information as I could. You had to play every kind of music with these territory bands, so I would find the guys that knew.[9]

The one I learned *more music* from than anyone else was Henri Woode. I roomed with him when I was with Lloyd Hunter's band. He played piano and accordion, and sometimes I wanted to get my pistol on him because he would have music paper spread all over and he'd be using the bed as a piano, writing and singing. "This guy's going crazy," I thought . . . When we were on one-nighters in Iowa, I used to watch him. He'd come back in with another idea and start writing—with no piano. I picked up so many things with that ten-piece band, and he really gave me an insight into ear training.[10]

FRANK DRIGGS: The Hunter band was the leading band in Omaha. Jo started with the Ted Adams band; it was a semi-society group like the one Noble Sissle led, and probably played stock arrangements. Then he moved into the Hunter band. He played with other local organizations in and around Omaha, like Hal Jones and the Brown Skin Syncopaters. But he was probably with Hunter most of the time in the early 1930s, moving back and forth between Hunter and Grant Moore, who worked out of Milwaukee. Herschel Evans, the great tenor man who was in the Basie band and meant so much to Jo, also worked with Moore at one time.

As far as Jo and Basie are concerned, their getting together was an accident of history. Jo was in the right place, at the right time, with the right kind of talent. Jesse Price or Baby Lovett, or one of the other guys around Kansas City, might have gotten the job.

A series of events led Jo to Basie. He was in the Bennie Moten band when Moten died. Several of the Moten men joined Basie. It was almost inevitable that Jo would wind up in the band. Moten's band, according to Billy Hadnott, who replaced Walter Page with Moten, was a great organization that did everything Basie would do two or three years later. It had the same guys—Pres [Lester Young], Herschel Evans, Jo. That was 1934. Jo was right there, helping establish that laid back, Midwestern/Southwestern kind of swing.

HARRY EDISON: The Jeter-Pillars band stayed in Cleveland about a year and then went to St. Louis for about two or three years. . . . After A.G. Godley left, we got Sidney Catlett on drums . . . Then Sidney Catlett got the call to join Fletcher Henderson in Chicago, so that was when Jo Jones . . . joined us.[11] When Basie finally reassembled Bennie Moten's band to go into a place called the Reno, this place in Kansas City, Basie sent for Jo Jones.[12]

COUNT BASIE: I don't remember how many different drummers I had in the rhythm section with me and Walter Page before Jo Jones came in. But it seems to me that Jesse Price was there at one time, and I also got Willie McWashington to sit in with us for a while. Now, Willie Mac had been Bennie Moten's drummer for most of the time I was with the band, but he wasn't in the band when Bennie died. Jo Jones was. So he wasn't in the band when it broke up. Actually I don't think Willie Mac was very well at the time. That may have been the reason why we got in touch with Jo when we did. He was in St. Louis playing in the Jeter-Pillars band at the Plantation Club by that time, and he came right away.

But for a while we thought we had gotten in trouble with the people in St. Louis about that because Jo had left without giving them notice. We were very concerned because there were some pretty tough people with interests in that club, and they could get pretty mean if somebody was trying to steal their musicians and entertainers. I don't know what all Jo Jones was into, and I don't know what happened. I don't know whether some of Sol Streibold's friends fixed it up or something. They just let it go, and Jo was free to stay at the Reno with us. So he took over from Willie McWashington, and that's when the band really started swinging.[13]

Bubbling with activity and good feeling in the 1930s, Kansas City endeared itself to musicians and entertainers and any and all who liked to swing and *live* through the day and night. Free and easy, the city encouraged you to get involved with music and good times and stay with them as long as you liked. No matter what the clock said, it was always the right time. Here the Basie band developed into a musical explosion and began making a reputation, via its broadcasts. Here Jo Jones made a name and gained great respect.

BOB BROOKMEYER: Kansas City, eh? Well, I guess everyone got some kind of bell that gets a tap from that town.

When I was old enough to sneak into the night clubs and dives where the good bands played, it was always the same feeling, to my heart anyway. Smooth, deep, rich, mellow, like a fine cigarette. But with the "clean-up" local government, the end of the war, and the advent of the ofay bopper [white modern jazz musician], that pretty much washed up swing music in KC. Long before the ghost went elsewhere, the gospel had been heard, luckily enough. Almost every musician who could play spent at least a week or two there, playing, soaking, loafing, waiting.

I do know that some lovely and lasting talk came out of there—some gentleness (genteelness, if you will) that could only be found around men who so fully knew what they did and wherein they spoke that relaxation was the only way to express it. When you're not sure, it gets very nervous, but that utter confidence in swing is hard to beat.[14]

JAY MCSHANN: You take a town as wide open as KC and you know we're all going to be there. The vice line of the town—everything depends on it being wide open. The pimps, the babes, you know what I mean? The night life, the musicians, the entertainers. All that is what kept it going.

I remember how good it felt and all the stuff that went on after hours. There always was a spot where everybody went after they got off work in the clubs and theaters. One spot on Monday; another on Tuesday. Maybe another the next early morning. Musicians, all kinds of entertainers, bartenders, waitresses—night people got together.

They had shows in the clubs. That meant great dancing and comedy. The dancers were *dancing* in those days. The drummers—the reason they played so good in Kansas City was because they learned by cutting those shows. . . . Some top drummers came to town and couldn't do those shows. They wanted to stick to just what they saw. But that wasn't good enough; the drummer had to be flexible, *loose;* he couldn't stick to the straight script. And he had to swing.

Going back to that school, learning to catch the little things that dancers and comics did, made the drummers free and creative. A lot of the cats who got that experience did real good when they went somewhere else, like Chicago or New York or Los Angeles.

Tap dancers had a big influence on drummers, no doubt about it. They taught drummers when to play and when to stay out of the way. Reading music had little to do with it; it was a matter of developing your instincts. Drummers and dancers get to understand one another, particularly if they work together for a while.

Jo Jones had that thing, that swing that everybody dug so much. All the drummers 'round town learned from him. Jo could play with sticks and then brush you into bad health. Like the other drummers out there who could *really* play, Jo was relaxed and not too technical.

His rhythm was light and natural. It was *there*, easy to feel. It got you going. See, it wasn't 'right to it, right to it, right to it,' you understand? It was somewhere between tight and loose. KC rhythm might seem straightforward. But it's really sophisticated and subtle.

Jo and Baby Lovett and Jesse Price were the boss drummers in Kansas City during the 1930s. Jesse played with Basie and with my band. Baby and I worked together but not regularly.

Jo had the greatest respect for Baby Lovett. Baby does a lot of technical things. Jo loved Lovett because of his technique and Lovett dug Jo because he could really swing.

JONES: I moved to Kansas City because I had to leave Omaha. It was some time in 1933. I had been working with a ten-piece band with revolving leaders. A gangster who ran things told us what to do; he named the leader for each job.

I left Omaha and joined the Tommy Douglas band in Joplin, Missouri. The job didn't last long. Then I went on to Kansas City. I played piano there and had my vibraphone. I wasn't going to play any drums. But then a special dance job with Douglas came up and I played drums. Walter Page, "Big 'Un," the great bass player who had led the Blue Devils, sat in with the band. He asked me if I would like to join Count Basie's band. I said, "Sure." I played one night and quit.

Phobic about KC and the excellence of its players, Jones didn't feel he had enough experience to deal with what was happening in the Basie band. "I'd been isolated in Omaha for over three years and I felt I couldn't handle the situation," he said. That first night with Basie in Topeka made him want to run and hide.

JONES: The first night, the band played "After You've Gone" and Lester [Young] took his chorus, then he took a break and it put my heart in my mouth. I went over to Basie after, planted a pint of whiskey on the table in front of him, and said: "You've got a great band. Good luck. I'm going to Omaha."

Ben Webster got real angry; he wanted to slap me. "Why? Are you crazy?" he said. Herschel Evans, who I admired so much, told me, "You can play in the band." So I finally came around. I said to Basie, "All right, I'll play with you for two weeks until you find a drummer." That lasted fourteen years. And I'm still with the bum!

There were three editions of the Basie band preceding the band that went out in the world after making a momentous impression on the influential jazz critic and recording man John Hammond in 1936. Jo Jones said these earlier bands were quite good, but there is no documentation of their excellence other than the memories of those who were on the scene.

Drummer Cliff Leeman was there. Stranded in Kansas City for a period of time with Dan Murphy and his Musical Skippers, he vividly recalls the Basie band being organized, shaping up, and ultimately taking flight when Jo Jones rejoined the rhythm section. Jones had played with Basie at the beginning in 1934, and then left to work with Rook Ganz in Minneapolis and the Jeter-Pillars band in and around St. Louis. As noted, Jo returned at Basie's bidding.

CLIFF LEEMAN: How did I find out about Basie? I was walking across the street in KC one night. I met a girl who asked me what I was looking for. Music, I said, smiling. She guided me to the Reno

Club on 12th Street. She said things started after twelve o'clock. Little did I know that the club was going to have what was called a breakfast dance.

The Reno was a *white* place where ranchers came. It wasn't anything fancy. The show was black. For a fifteen-cent beer, I heard this band and almost fell through the floor. It was one of the first bands Basie put together, with Joe Keyes and Oran "Hot Lips" Page, trumpets; a trombonist called Rabbitt who had been with Fletcher Henderson. The guy on bass also played sousaphone; he wore a cap. I can't remember his name. One thing I recall quite clearly was this big round shell down front with a sign that said: FEED THE KITTY!

The drummer—he wasn't right for the style of the band. Often I got a chance to sit in on brushes. Basie seemed to enjoy my playing and encouraged me. Jo came in five or six months later. I walked in one night. I'll never forget it. Jo was sitting up there above the band, smiling and cooking. The band was on fire. Basie had found the recipe and Jo was a key part of it.

Let me tell you, the band became unbelievable. You never *felt* anything like that! Jo scared the life out of me. I had never heard anyone play that way in my entire life.

Jo Jones had a great influence on every drummer who heard him, particularly in those early years. He played the high-hat with so much finesse. He did so much on it that he turned it into an independent instrument. So many techniques and touches for the hat are his creations. Jo was the first person I ever heard keep time on a closed high-hat while developing counterpoint-in-rhythm with his left hand on the high-hat stand. So many things: the feeling of variation he brought to high-hat playing—how he changed the accents and the feel of the dotted eighth and sixteenth rhythm without interrupting the flow. His little kick beats on the bass drum behind Basie's piano—so unusual for the time. The way he tuned his drums, to intervals, also was a plus. His drums had an open, unmuffled sound. This sort of tuning is difficult for many drummers because it demands great control of the hands and the right foot. The tuning worked well for him; he found he could get out what he wanted to say *because* the situation was so challenging.

One of Jo's most charming bits of business was a thing he did with his right heel. He kept time with it on the floor, combining this sound with what he did on the high-hat. Frequently he would take his foot off the bass drum pedal and use the clicking of the right heel on the floor, alone, as an extra bit of color.

While playing brushes, he'd sweep with the left hand and

play a shuffle beat with the right. It was a particularly powerful technique when the tempo was up there—real fast. The beat became so *strong*. It wasn't the kind of shuffle beat you associate with bands like Jan Savitt; it had the feeling of a triplet while retaining something of the shuffle. It made you think of a tap dancer. So many great drummers have been tap dancers and come from that tradition: Jo, Big Sidney [Catlett], Buddy [Rich], Louie Bellson.

It's hard to believe that Jo did all that great stuff on drums [that were] held together with ropes and on cymbals that were just awful. Until Jo became more widely known, and replaced them, he had a rag-tag bunch of drums and cymbals. Still he made them *sound*.

His ideas and some of the things he played had a base in the past. But a large number of his techniques, patterns, concepts did not come from any place or anyone. They were original with Jo Jones. I can only say about Jo what you have often written about Buddy Rich, "There will never be another like him."

To remain sharp in the highly competitive Kansas City atmosphere, Jo Jones played in every circumstance possible around town.

EDDIE DURHAM: After the job, the musicians would meet on 18th and Vine . . . right in the middle of the street. I'd get off around 3:00 or 4:00 A.M. at the Cherry Blossom or any of those places and go to Piney Brown's or to where Joe Turner was bartending. When I walked in, I'd have my guitar throwed across my neck.

I'd jump on the stage and sit up on the bar and get the guitar. Joe Turner would wipe his hands . . . and he'd sing. Jo Jones would have his sock cymbal. And it'd be the three of us . . . we used to work there until about seven in the morning.[15]

Jo was playing that modern stuff and it sounded good. He was sharp on it and he was really creating a style. I don't know where he got it from. He hadn't been East—he hadn't been any place. But he was something else. It was *natural* with him, and maybe he doesn't get enough credit for it now.[16]

At the same club, the Lone Star, where Pete Johnson, the boogie woogie master, was playing, drummer Gus Johnson had his first experience with Jones.

GUS JOHNSON: He came over and said, "You play a nice drum. I'll take over now." I think we were playing "I Got Rhythm," and the way he played . . . I never saw anything like it, the way he was with those brushes. It was smooth as you'd want to hear anybody play, and it was just right easy. He was smiling, doing little bitty things, and he wasn't *working*. The personality and everything knocked me *out*![17]

Jo knocked out a lot of people. One of the most important was music man John Hammond. He was so impressed that he used his influence to thrust Jo, Basie, and the rest onto a larger stage, bringing them to a nationwide audience.

JOHN HAMMOND: In January 1936 I heard Jo Jones for the first time. I was sitting in my car listening to the radio outside the Congress Hotel in Chicago, biding time between Benny Goodman sets in the Urban Room. All of a sudden I came across this exciting little band from Kansas City on Station W9XBY. It was that grand Basie nine-piecer from the Reno Club. Basie had the most wonderful rhythm section I'd ever heard.

In March of that year, I went down to Kansas City to hear the band live. What was the Reno Club like? Well, it was on street level. I believe the second floor was a whore house. Food and drink were relatively inexpensive in the club, even for those times. The building was run down.

That first night I got to the club at 8:20 P.M. and left at four in the morning. It was a great night for me. Not only did I hear Basie, I went out, after hours, to hear Pete Johnson and Joe Turner at the Sunset and finally ended up on 18th and Vine Street where I listened to Clarence Johnson, a great boogie woogie player who never made records.

As for Jo: I never was so completely overwhelmed by a drummer before or since as I was that first night in the Reno. He was . . . the best show drummer I ever saw.

Jo had a delightfully light foot; that was rare to find in those days. His concept of drumming was completely different—so natural and flowing. The way he played those high-hats and his other cymbals.

I kept an eye on him each time I was in the club. He spent a lot of time tuning his drum heads. That just wasn't done in those days [ed. note: it was more prevalent than commonly thought]. I generally positioned myself at Basie's left hand and looked up at Jo—he was on a riser—and just watched his foot. It was utterly fascinating.

In those days, Jo was an extraordinary ensemble performer. He played for the other men in the band, supported and helped them. He had *ears* and a sense of the dramatic. That certainly enhanced the effect of his work.

Those nights at the Reno are lodged in my mind. When I go back over them, I am reminded how hard the guys worked for little money. But they loved what they were doing. Believe me! Jo was always smiling. What he did *worked*. He lifted the band and he knew it! It was a wondrous time for Jo, Basie, and the others. And certainly for me. I wanted to do all I could for them. One of the first little things I did was to shorten Mr. Jones' name from Jonathan to "Jo." I felt it had a better and more direct quality.

When the Basie band moved from Kansas City to Chicago to play the Grand Terrace, it entered a new, more complicated world. The demands made on this group of "instinctive" players at the South Side night club were vastly different from those the band had faced at the Reno. The Grand Terrace was big-time, black show business. In a way, Jo Jones saved the day for Basie.

JOHN HAMMOND: After playing a final Kansas City date, the Basie band boarded a bus for Chicago and the future. It opened ... at the Grand Terrace, the home of Earl Hines and Fletcher Henderson, a night club with an elaborate floor show that was a challenge to any band. Although Basie had by then enlarged to the usual dance band complement—four saxophones, five brass, and four rhythm—he had few arrangements. Worse, only about half the band could read music well. Remembering those first nights at the Grand Terrace, I am astonished they were not fired. They struggled through Ed Fox's show arrangements but the chorus girls loved the band because it was so easy to dance to. Jo Jones, a dancer himself, knew how to play for dancers.[18]

The band hit the road after closing in Chicago. It played a series of dates and then came New York, the ultimate challenge. The site of Basie's Gotham debut: Roseland Ballroom.

COUNT BASIE: We didn't raise any hell in there either. It was not as bad as the Grand Terrace, which was the worst. But we definitely were not a hit at Roseland either.[19]

JONES: We opened at Roseland on Christmas Eve of 1936. The bill: Count Basie, Woody Herman, and the Zinn Arthur Orchestra. Zinn later became a photographer.

It wasn't an easy engagement in any way. I remember going around the corner opening night to get a hot dog from a vendor on the street. And the man said, "I can't serve you." I pulled out my pistol and said, "If you don't serve me I'm going to get you in both your arms and your kneecap." And I'm a crack shot because Frank Newhart taught me how to shoot. A New York City detective walked up to me and said, "Son, you're not supposed to have a gun in New York." He settled things and I got my hot dog. But I was torn up by the incident. I knew about this sort of thing. But yet I didn't. After all, I was just a farm boy from Nebraska.

I went back to Roseland and spoke to Brecker (the owner), John Hammond, and Basie. I said, "Look, I'm leaving. And the sooner the better." All kinds of people gathered around and encouraged me to stay: Duke (he was at the Paramount Theater down the street), Gene Krupa, and Vido Musso. But it was Chick Webb who convinced me. He came down the next night with Bardu Ali, who often led his band. I said, "Chick, I don't like the hot dogs here." He smiled and then answered, "Why don't you try it?" Mr. Chick Webb made me stay in New York with Basie.

There is so much ignorance out here [in the world]. So many people don't know us [blacks]. They see us but they don't have any idea who and what we are. I play tennis. In the 1930s, when we came to New York they didn't know colored people did that. All they ever saw were cooks, maids, butlers, chauffeurs, and bellboys. These people had no idea there were doctors and lawyers and teachers among us.

When John Hammond took Jimmy Rushing and the rhythm section in a *limousine* to play a special gig, *we* became something different. Jazz musicians moved up in the thinking of many of the uninformed.

One thing is for sure. Without John Hammond, there would be far less understanding. Without him, many of the historical events in jazz wouldn't have taken place.

Race? I always told my children: there's a boy, there's a girl, there's a man, there's a woman. I never allowed them to use no names, ethnically speaking. You see, this is a luxury you can't afford, particularly if you're going to play music.

What do I believe? I'm into 400 religions and 500 cults. There's my Bible; I live by it. I sleep with the door unlocked. I've never locked my door in my life. I don't fear anyone or anything.

JOHN HAMMOND: When Jo came to New York, the first couple of years he was around he got a lot of attention. What he was doing was new and drew a lot of musicians to him. Gene Krupa would visit

Jo every day and practice with him on a pad. You have to remember how influential and busy Gene was in those days. That he took the time indicated how much he thought of Jo. All kinds of drummers came to hear Jo at Roseland in 1936 and later, in 1938 and 1939 at the Famous Door on 52nd Street. And he was as much of a sex symbol as Gene. Handsome, a shade arrogant, a man with a great smile, Jo had the chicks just falling all over him.

His drums, however, always were his primary means of communication.

IRV KLUGER: I heard Jo on a couple of early Decca records with Basie. When I found out the band was returning to Roseland, I got there early, opening night. That rhythm section—the four guys breathed together like a family. And each one of the players knew what his role was.

Basie played simple, syncopated "comps" in his right hand and didn't overwhelm the rhythm section at any time. Guitarist Freddie Green held the four guys together. Walter Page, the veteran, brought a special quality to the time. Jo created colors, laid down the down beats and up beats, and brought the band in. A revolutionary change had taken place. The Basie feeling was so different from the 4/4 thumping of other sections. Jo's cymbals, the guitar and the bass walking together, the plinking of Basie and the way he edged in his left hand once in a while—it just lightened everything up and made the jazz rhythm *section* come to the fore. What these guys did was very difficult to imitate. You had to be so fine. You had to know why you were there.

"The All-American Rhythm Section" of Basie, Page, Green, and Jones had its own recipe. Relaxing, being natural, responding consonantly and with feeling to the music—all of this gave the section distinction. The section blended flow and interaction, flexibility and freedom, bringing to the Basie music a lightness and a provoking sense of pulsation that carried one along.

Very simply, the section swung as none had before, providing a potent example of what could be done if rhythm players moved in the same direction. The beautiful part, though, was that each person in the section never forgot who and what he was, or what a variegated role his instrument could play.

JONES: It took a lot to do what we did. What was happening to us on and off the bandstand—it all came out in our playing. That's what made the Basie rhythm section what it was.

Jo Jones in the 1940s.   Courtesy of the Institute of Jazz Studies at Rutgers University.

HARRY EDISON: It used to send chills up me every night when I'd hear the rhythm section. The whole band would be shouting, you know. And we'd go to . . . the middle part, the bridge, and all of a sudden . . . everybody would drop out but the rhythm section. Oh, my goodness. I've never heard a band swing like that.[20]

At the center of the rhythm section was bassist Walter Page, a man of wisdom and great musical expertise and experience.

JONES: I learned how to play the drums from Mr. Walter Page. He was a musical father to me because without him I wouldn't know how to play drums. For two years Page told me how to phrase, he taught me how to turn on what the kids now called "dropping bombs."

Now bombs are just pure accents. The accents in drum playing are going to be here for years to come just as they've been for millions of years before now.[21]

Jones took Walter Page's lessons to heart and added to his performances what he had inside. The result was a highly stylized individual approach to drumming in a jazz ensemble. Jones helped open up a number of possibilities for the drummer, not the least of which was the option of being a colorist, a contributor to the feel of the band. He made the drummer less of a mechanical presence, more of a musician.

ROY ELDRIDGE: Nowadays, most everybody out here is playing the same type of things. Back then, all the good players had their own thing that they played.

Jo was a pusher; he kept the beat moving. He had that high-hat and them cymbals down. When he came to Chicago with Basie to play the Grand Terrace, me and him and Pres used to hang out. I used to pick them up every night. And we'd go out and look for a place to jam.

You know one thing that people overlooked about Jo's playing in the Basie band? His bass drum. He didn't stop playing it, as some say. He kept a *light* four going, giving a bottom to the rhythm. Drummers in those days used to tune their drums to a G of the bass fiddle. And the way they used their bass drum didn't come out boom, boom, boom, but just blended with the bass. The guitar was also playing four, right? So everything was going along the same course, *together!*

Swing identified the Basie band. But there were a number of other elements like tempo, that made this group of musicians so persuasive. Jo Jones had a lot to do with setting tempo.

EDDIE DURHAM: Jo was responsible for a lot of that. (He) was a master of setting tempos. I think Basie learned from Jo Jones.[22]

Jones' chief means of defining his time feel and establishing the right tempos was the high-hat. Over the years, his name became synonymous with this contrivance, usually placed to the left of the snare if one was right-handed, to the right of the snare if one was left-handed. Fletcher Henderson's Walter Johnson and Chick Webb and Alvin Burroughs from the 1930s edition of the Earl Hines band helped bring the high-hat to the attention of the music community. But it was Jo Jones who made the hat an integral part of every jazz and pop drummer's life. The high-hat, he often insisted was "my thing." Jo Jones "swung a whole generation with the high-hat," Jake Hanna, the former Woody Herman drum star, insists.

Early in the 1930s, the high-hat, also known as the "high boy," was developed. The instrument, at the beginning, was about waist-high. At first, drummers used relatively small cymbals, ten, eleven, or twelve inches in diameter. Only Jones used "large" cymbals—

thirteen-inch. The high-hat could produce a variety of sounds and effects with the use of the pedal, ranging from the hard-hitting sock sound, when using heavy cymbals, to the less intense "chick" or "swish" sounds when lighter cymbals were employed.

When drummers discovered the possibilities for sticks on the high-hat the general nature of time-keeping radically changed, and the high-hat became a central element of the drum set. The drummer increasingly became a cymbal player and not a performer who used only the drums. Jones was primarily responsible for moving the time to the high-hat and suggesting what could be done on cymbals. The bass drum, the key time center, began to assume a lesser role.

JONES: It was because of *necessity* that I went out and got a pipe. I couldn't play that sock cymbal on the floor. (In one of its original forms, the high-hat or sock cymbal, then called a "low boy" or "low hat," was 15 inches off the floor.)

JONES: As recently as 1934, nobody had a sock cymbal but Alvin Burroughs. George Wettling, Gene Krupa—they didn't know nothing about a sock cymbal. They had a sock cymbal but they put it in the closet or left it home. Tubby [Harold], Zutty [Singleton], those guys, they never played the sock cymbal. But mine was through necessity because that's all I had.

The years with Count Basie formed the core of his musical life. Subconsciously, he compared everything before and after with the Basie experience.

In many ways, Jones never left the band. Until the end of his life, there was that link with Basie. In the mind of the public and many of his colleagues, Jones remained Basie's drummer, despite the fact he played so well with others and on his own.

In spirit, Jo and Basie were together until the pianist's death in 1984. The love and respect Jones had for his old friend and former employer often were quite touching. As Basie wound down his life, encumbered by illness, Jo kept at him to slow down, in his typically gruff manner: "All the man has to do is maybe ten concerts a year. He could get Pep [Freddie Green], a bass player, and me and not work so hard," the drummer insisted. "But he has to have that band and travel all the time. No need for that at this point!" Every time he discussed Basie's schedule, Jo revealed his concern for what might happen to his buddy, his deep voice sharpening into an exclamation point.

Jo found it difficult to view Basie in a mechanical wheel chair. He only wanted to remember the glory years when everything was in a good groove.

JONES: I laughed for fourteen years. I sat up there behind the drums and laughed. . . . I stayed because it was a challenge. And also because the band operated on a strange spiritual and mental plane. In my fourteen years, there were no arguments. We'd meet guys from other bands who always asked us, "How come you guys don't fight like the rest of the fellows?"[23]

Admittedly, rapport within the Basie band was unusual. But, like any group of individuals in a close family situation, there were times. . . .

EARLE WARREN: Jo could be quite aloof and difficult. It took several months after I joined the Basie band in 1937 for us to get it together, personally. How did we do it? I challenged him. He wanted to chastise me for something. And I said to myself, "Hey, wait a minute; I'm pretty good at boxing." So I put it to him this way, "I don't think you want to be bothered with me. I don't have time to fool with you!" That was the end of that. We just forgot the argument.

As I recall, one incident solidified our relationship. It really broke the ice and got us both laughing. We were playing the Paramount Theater, downtown, on Broadway. One day during an early show, I tried to do my feature, "I Struck a Match in the Dark," a record I had out with the band. We had a regular routine on the tune. The trombones played a sort of ad lib pattern. I stepped out to the microphone on a dark stage and lit a match for my cigarette and started singing.

This time, I stood out there for what seemed like forever, trying to get my matches to light. Jo had really done it to me; he wet every last one. Was I embarrassed! After a short while, Jo hollered, "Come on Smiley, light it up." And the whole band broke up—me included. Even though Jo had ruined my piece of business, which was quite effective, incidentally, I couldn't stop laughing.

Pres got to me around the same time. And it was on the same number. All the guys in the band were supposed to light a match at the same time as I lit my cigarette. They did it on cue, except for Pres. He held up his music and just set it on fire. . . .

Humor took the pressure off the band. It chased boredom during the increasingly oppressive schedule of theater engagements; seven days a week, five to ten shows a day. The rush of the road, where there never seemed time enough to eat, clean your clothes, or sleep, was slowed by a joke or some well-planned funny business. Jo and Pres, more times than not, were at the root of the merriment.

DICKY WELLS: It was at the Lincoln [Hotel] in New York in 1942 that Pres got his little bell. If somebody missed a note, or you were a new guy and goofed, you'd hear the bell going "ding-dong!" If Pres was blowing and goofed, somebody would reach over and ring his bell on him.

Jo Jones had another way of saying the same thing. "Bing-bing-bing" he'd go on his cymbal rod. When you first joined, you would take it kind of rough, but later you'd be in stitches with the rest and take it as a joke. They'd ring the bell on Basie too. . . .[24]

Whatever the difficulties, day to day, the musicians in the Basie band thrived. Uncomfortable and unlikely situations, bad food, irritating, and sometimes racist people on the seemingly never-ending "road," were transcended by the music itself.

HARRY EDISON: One of my most glorious moments . . . was when I joined Count Basie at nineteen. [The night] I joined him, we played a dance in Owensboro, Kentucky, which is about thirty miles from where I was raised. My uncle and aunt came to the dance. [My uncle] came up on the bandstand and told everybody, "I taught him what he's doing today. I taught him . . ." Oh he was so proud.[25]

JOE NEWMAN: I left Lionel Hampton in December 1943 after Jo asked me to join Basie. I took the job so I could play with Lester; he was my friend. Pres, Rodney Richardson, (the bass player), and I used to hang out. Being with the Basie band—with Pres, Rodney, Jo, Basie, and all those cats—was a dream come true.

I sat next to Jo in the band. Because of this, I got to know a lot about him and his playing. He was a very interesting person, particularly in those days. He always had a little quip. Jo and Pres coined phrases that most people picked up. Some of the phrases are now widely accepted and used; they're in the dictionary.

As a player, Jo had extraordinary style—so much personality. That million-dollar smile of his would light up a stage. He knew how to get attention. But what he did went far beyond showmanship. He knew how to fire up the band. And he did it in his own way.

Jo came up with a whole different approach to playing drums. He developed new ways to play cymbals, getting the best out of them—whether he was just playing time or making colors. The cat was always experimenting with his sticks, trying new holds, using half of the stick, three-quarters or all of it so he could get different sounds. One thing is for sure; Jo Jones could take any part of the drum set and make music out of it.

The man was most alive during the Basie years. He was happy and felt people were listening to him. His style, as far as I'm concerned, was an update of New Orleans rhythm. You could march on it, dance on it . . . because it was so swinging.

EARLE WARREN: During the heyday of the Basie band, it was essential—certainly when you played theaters—for the drummer to play an extended, interesting solo—not a lot of noise. Jo came up with some of the sharpest drum solos I ever heard. His vehicle was "Prelude in C Sharp Minor," a Rachmaninov thing. Jimmy Mundy made an arrangement on it for him.

Jo put together a composition each time he played that feature. What he did was tasteful and very rarely did he go over the same ground twice. His solos could begin on any part of the set. He moved all around; I particularly liked what he did on the tom-toms.

When he got to the high-hat and the cymbals—that was the climax. He worked the high-hat, made it talk, then went up on the cymbals, mixing colors and patterns.

You could forgive his being temperamental every once in a while when you listened to him play.

There was a very special musical relationship between Basie and Jones. It grew out of love, respect, and musical intimacy on the stand. A matter of give-and-take and mutual momentum, their connection was often uncanny. One anticipated and motivated the other. Often they united and glided along in a graceful, seemingly effortless manner.

The kinship that existed between Jones and Lester Young, however, went beyond what the drummer had with Basie. It was the essence of musical compatibility. The Basie recorded repertory featuring Pres—"Song of the Islands," "Doggin' Around," "Pound Cake," "Shorty George," "Miss Thing," "Taxi War Dance," "Clap Hands, Here Comes Charlie," and the small-band sides like "Lester Leaps In" and "Shoe Shine Boy"—makes clear how strong their feeling was for one another.

Jo was a positive presence behind Pres. One always felt an undercurrent of excitement when Jo fed Pres the time and his ideas. As the saxophonist's solo unfolded, the intensity built. But the heat and strength of the experience did not overcome either Jo or Pres. There was control; the music retained a sense of cool flow. There was almost an objectivity about it.

Yet these recordings are hardly examples of detached performances. The drummer is *there*, very involved; he supports his friend and the band but never forces either to play any particular way.

JOHN LEWIS: You heard the time but it wasn't a ponderous thing that dictated where the phrases would go. The band played the arrangements and the soloists were free because the time didn't force them into any place they didn't want to go.

MEL LEWIS: Of course Jo played the high-hat for Pres. But he did something else for him . . . and only for him. He did what he called his "ding, ding-a-ding" on a small, heavy cymbal sitting on a spring holder. Mounted on the right side of the bass drum, real low, it had a sound that carried and surrounded Pres with a strong rhythmic foundation.

Jo said that it was really the beginning of ride-cymbal playing for him. There might have been others, maybe Dave Tough, who played time on a cymbal in that way. But I think Jo was one of the first to loosen things up. He was a pioneer when it came to playing what is now called a "ping" cymbal. The dotted eighth and sixteenth rhythm was clearly stated and felt, yet floated, the shimmer of the cymbal providing a cushion for the player or the band. I had never heard anyone do that before Jo. It knocked me out.

As Jo Jones' sound and ideas became widely known, more and more drummers endeavored to imitate his style. Few if any could do it. What Jones did was too elusive.

BUCK CLAYTON: Jo came into the Basie band, pretty much full grown; his style was already almost as you know it. He was a perfect drummer. For our kind of music, you have to have a good sense of rhythm in your hands. Jo had that; really, it was his main thing. Not only that, he could execute anything he heard or had on his mind.

Most of the drummers in the Mid- and Southwest—in those territory bands—were stylistically like Jo. But Jo did it better.

J.C. Heard was the only one who truly played like Jo. Most of the others just didn't think they could ever play like Jo Jones, so they didn't even try. J.C. had certain feelings for Jo; they were tight. J.C. even played with us briefly. I must say he really got close to what his mentor was laying down. Gus Johnson was sometimes compared to Jo because he did things in the same general way as the guys in Kansas City. But he later found his own style.

Jo had an *attitude* that got us all going in the Basie band. Every time he and Pres sat down they wanted to swing. That made the rest of us want to swing too. It was a feeling we all wanted to continue indefinitely.

Life in Kansas City set the pattern for a number of guys in the band. They'd play the gig with us and, after work, go somewhere and start playing again about 5 A.M. It'd be noon before they went home to sleep for awhile. When they got up, they would do the same thing all over again.

Jo didn't like to read music. He thought he could play better than anything written on paper. Fortunately, with the Basie band, there was no need for reading. Most of our things were "heads;" we couldn't afford arrangements. The only written charts we had were the ones others gave us. There were a few Benny Moten and Fletcher Henderson arrangements in the book.

Our charts just happened. We'd get together in a club or rehearsal room. Lester would say, "Let's do this." Maybe Jack Washington or Herschel Evans would make a suggestion. I might have an idea. We'd figure out what to do. Each person had his "notes." Then we'd put it all together. Jo would learn just from rehearsals. That's how he figured out where to put the accents and things. Sometimes he would play with the brass, sometimes with the reeds; all the while he and the other rhythm players would give us a good feeling to play against.

Jo stayed by himself a lot. I barely knew his family. I'd see him on the bandstand and on the bus. We both did have special doctors we'd visit to check our health—in Washington, Chicago, New York, all over. Every time we hit a city, we'd go in for a checkup. But other than that, we didn't do too many things together.

All I know is that we'd play with Basie. Then Jo would play again in some after-hour joint, no matter what city it was. He and Lester usually would find some place. Jo built his whole life around playing. I couldn't imagine him going to bed. I knew he went to bed. But somehow I couldn't picture it with the hours he kept.

Jo Jones and Lester Young had a lot in common. They were together a good deal and trusted one another. They inhabited a special world where music and playing were the focus of every waking hour. Both helped younger players, freely gave advice, even watched over them. Music was an obsession.

Jo and Pres went into the Army at almost the same time.

JONES: Les was too tender. He didn't like to see nobody, not one human being, mistreat another human being. You could tell it in his playing. I always took care of a lot of things for Les because you must remember, [he] would not go to a doctor or nothing unless he consulted me. Remember I buried Lester. His mother, his wife, his sister, and everybody said, "Jo, you got it."

Time passed rapidly for Jo Jones. Theater engagements, locations, one-nighters, and recordings melded into a long, single line of events that make up a life.

The recordings remain. They speak volumes about Jo Jones during the Basie years and, in many ways, indicate how he would proceed, stylistically, for the rest of his life.

The first thing one notices is Jones' attention to detail. Never a fussy drummer, he was precise and organized. He knew the value of space, intuition, and surprise. His firm, delicious time under the band was a natural phenomenon; he just allowed it to flow, adding what seemed right to him.

His commentary behind soloists, and highly selective accenting during sectional and ensemble performances, reveal inner direction and a facility for self-editing that cuts away the extraneous before it surfaces. Jones' playing never cluttered the rhythmic and melodic lines.

His solos grew from the fabric of the music itself. His technical limitations were frequently an asset. He said what had to be said, in an original manner.

There are so many examples of excellence: his high-hat solo on "The World Is Mad" with the Basie band (*Evening of a Basie-ite, Lester Young, Volume V*, Columbia); the short burst of high-hat work on "Beau Brummel" (*The Complete Count Basie, 1–10, 1936–1941*, French CBS), during which he varies the sound of the hat and the accents; and his solo on "Basie Strides Again" (*Count Basie–V Discs 1944–1945*, Jazz Society), eight bars of simply rendered rhythm that could easily have been a tap dance.

"The Jitters" (*The Complete Count Basie, 1–10, 1934–1941*, French CBS), a Tab Smith original recorded in January 1941, provides the whole picture. The breathing, living high-hat, the intuitive fills, a marvelous time feeling, and a four-bar entry into the out-chorus that lifts the band up high—you can actually hear the change in emotional

quality. What Jo plays in that four bars is a revelation of simplicity—
and so fitting.

The dancer in Jo Jones is everywhere in his playing. Strongly
influenced by a wide range of dancers, from Bill "Bojangles" Robinson to Baby Laurence, Jones remembered in detail their routines and
the way they carried themselves. When one least expected it, he
would offer his version, in a solo or fill, of a dancer from long ago, or
one he had heard the night before.

DAN MORGENSTERN: The effortless grace of his movements, on or off
the stand, bespeak his early days as a dancer, just as his solo
work may sometimes remind of the fascinating patterns created
by the masters of the vanishing art of jazz tap dance.[26]

LOUIE BELLSON: As Buddy Rich said—and I agree—if you have to
choose one guy it would be Jo Jones. When he came out with the
Basie band, it was as if we had been waiting for him. Drummers
listened and said, "Yeah, that's where it is. That's the way drummers should sound." Jo brought fluidity—a musical, legato
feeling—to drumming. He also showed us how to set up a band
for the finale—the shout chorus. When he played that four bars,
it was like saying, "Here it is!"

Jo answered all the questions as to what the big band drummer should sound like. Later, when he got more deeply into small
groups, he established precedents for trios, quartets, quintets,
sextets.

The Army temporarily separated Basie and Jo Jones. In September of 1944, Jones got Shadow Wilson, "the greatest natural drummer that ever lived"—that's Jones' appraisal—to replace him, and
entered the service three days after Lester Young.

JONES: I was supposed to go to Washington and join the Navy band.
They were going to make it very racial. I was going to be the first
black in the band. All they wanted me to do was to stay in Washington. I said no and got Shadow.
I didn't have to go into the Army; I had a choice. I said, "I'll
take the infantry." I refused to play drums. I soldiered in the
Army.[27]

BUCK CLAYTON: I remember one time at Camp Kilmer, where I was
stationed with an Army band, Jo came over from New York for
something. He was on furlough from Alabama, or wherever he
was. We had a retreat to play. The whole ceremony took about an

hour. Jo stood at attention the whole time. He said he was trying to show all them other kiddies how a real soldier should act. He wasn't in any band. He went through combat basic training. So did Lester.

It was a bad period in Jo Jones' life. He saw Lester Young suffer multiple miseries. He never fully adjusted to the military, with all its rigidity and prejudices.

WILSON DRIVER: Jo came to my house in Birmingham every Sunday that he was in the service. Fort McClellan was only sixty-five miles from Birmingham. Each time he sat on the floor with my two young daughters—they must have been five and six at the time—and made puzzles. You know, those block puzzles that end up being a picture. That's all he did. Occasionally we'd go downtown and get a beer or two or more at a place I was running. He'd just sit there, looking around and out into space, listening to music. He didn't have a terribly good time in the Army. And he fretted about Pres. I asked him to bring Pres with him. He said, "I can't get him out of camp."

Life began again in February of 1946. Jones allowed himself what he deemed a "debriefing" period of several weeks before joining Basie on the road. During this time, he also stopped in at a Basie recording session, stepping in for Shadow Wilson on "The King" (Columbia). Jones established two things: he could play as well as before, and he had been listening to younger, adventurous drummers like Max Roach. Though not as far along polyrhythmically as Roach and Kenny Clarke, Jones had assimilated some of their notions, which were, in essence, extensions of his own. On "Muttonleg," a Basie recording (Columbia, 1946) with Illinois Jacquet, it is clear that Jones was quite aware of what had happened musically while he was in the service.

Jones was depressed by the new drummers, as he confided to close friends like Buddy Rich. He felt he was being displaced. He sensed that younger drummers were moving away from him, looking to others for direction. It wasn't entirely true. But this impression, in combination with the death of his wife Vivian in 1946, brought him way down.

BUDDY RICH: This thing began in the mid-1940s. He didn't think he could play anymore. So many people said that Max Roach was the greatest. I remember he came up to see me when my band was playing at the Apollo and asked me what he should do. I said punch out anyone who says you can't play. How dare they! I said, "You *can* play and there are hundreds of records to prove how great you are."

When you reach Jo Jones' stature—when you reach that level—how can you ever play badly? You can't. Jo was great until illness took hold of him. He was *Jo Jones.* The man was no mystery. Because of the way he came up, Jo was the history of our music.

Jones left Basie in 1948 under veiled circumstances. Basie insisted he just cut out during a New York theater engagement. Jones said he was ill—a delayed reaction from the loss of his wife. "It didn't dawn on me until that particular time in 1948," he explained. "I stayed on with the band for three weeks. I said, 'Mr. Basie, I'll get somebody.'" He got Shadow Wilson. And when Wilson left after a brief stay, he persuaded Gus Johnson to come into the band.

Jones then busied himself freelancing with New York as his base. He recorded a great deal and traveled the world, often with Jazz At the Philharmonic, and later with his pal, pianist Milt Buckner. He appeared often with Lester Young; he worked in Illinois Jacquet's memorable little band soon after Jacquet left Basie; and he led his own trio, which made some excellent records, illustrating Jones' ability to make use of his hands and feet in a way that brought color, meaning, and interest to the music. His affair with the high-hat continued, no matter who he had with him on the stand or the recording studio. He listened to the younger players and encouraged them, or laid out what they had to do in no uncertain terms. He kept working and talking. The names on his resume could fill pages: Teddy Wilson, Claude Hopkins, Vic Dickenson, Benny Carter, Benny Goodman, Joe Bushkin. . . .

MILT HINTON: Joe Bushkin is a smart little cat. He knew about Jo's little things. He never told him what to do. When we had twenty minutes off at the Embers or somewhere, he never expected Papa to show on the minute. He would come up on the stand, play around the piano, indicating it was time to go to work. I'd play with Joe; Buck (Clayton) would amble over, pick up his horn and join us. He'd play a ballad. By that time, Papa had finished his conversation and gotten behind his drums.

There was little letup in the demand for Papa Jo's services until the 1960s. He played most of the festivals and remained an influence across the world. But somehow the situation began to change; other drummers, sometimes younger, were preferred. His temperament also played a role in the change. There were more outbursts as he sensed what was happening to his career. His friends did all they could for him.

EARLE WARREN: For a while Jo didn't get much work because of his attitude. I guess it was in the late 1960s. I offered him a job to work with me in a Brooklyn theater with some R & B and rock acts. I gave him a fifth of Martell as a little gift. He worked well with blues singer Big Maybelle, who was on the bill; she liked his playing. But the other acts wanted something different. I defended Jo. But he wouldn't lean; he had to play his own way. He wouldn't do what the rock cats wanted.

The man who played like the wind in 1959.   Charles Stewart.

Around that time, Jo got depressed. He was beginning to drink too much—Hennessy Five Star. Yeah, cognac. He'd sit at the end of the bar at Jim and Andy's on 48th Street—you know the place a lot of the musicians used to go. When I came in, I'd sit with him for a long time.

One of Jo's other friends recalls more than one record date during which the drummer refused to play arrangements he thought didn't swing. He made a big to-do about the situation, slamming his drums on the floor each time. On one occasion, the arranger brought in a waltz. Jo shouted, "I ain't gonna play no goddamn waltz." And he packed up and went home.

Jones had occasionally been rambunctious with the Basie band. He finally got to Basie. The band leader pointed out to his friend, "Look, man. I'm the star of this band. You're just the drummer."

BUCK CLAYTON: Pres really got on Jo one time. They were playing in a group that included tenor man Bud Freeman. When Pres played, it was fine. But Jo didn't like Bud. So when it came time for Bud to play, he would try to drown him out. Lester gave Jo hell. "Lady Jo," he said, "you're not a trouper. Troupers don't do that."

JOE NEWMAN: The thing that made it hard for him at certain times in his career was the lack of recognition.

In the later years, a lot of people didn't even know who he was, especially in America. Fortunately, in other parts of the world, jazz fans and musicians were very conscious of what he had done. They gave him work and respect. Sure, there were drummers and musicians in this country who admired him and let him know it. But it was nothing like the old days.

Because he didn't read music—or want to read—his money-making capacity was not up to what it should have been. His way of thinking cut him off from what could have been an easier life in those last years. But you have to understand. He came up in another time, when everything wasn't so mechanized. When you think about Jo Jones, you have to go back and reflect on what was happening in *his* time.

Change, attitude be damned. He revolutionized jazz drums. A man who did that deserves respect for his entire life.

GEORGE WEIN: Jo Jones may have been the most important drummer in the history of jazz. But he was never the same after he left Basie. He had been on the mountain, as they say. When he came off the mountain, he was always looking to go back up on that mountain—to stay on the level he was used to in the Basie band. Unfortunately, most musicians couldn't maintain the standards, the excellence that satisfied him.

Jo had his own language. There was an essential wisdom within what he said. And he had enormous respect for what he did and for other musicians. I heard this story about him, recently, and it touched me.

Every time Jo went to Europe, he would stop in Lourdes, France. He'd buy these very expensive candles and have them lit. One time, a priest asked, "For whom are you buying these candles? They're very big." Jo answered, "They're for *very* big people: Sid Catlett, Louis Armstrong, and Duke Ellington." This went on for years.

The character of Jo Jones' life never really changed. He lived to play well, to bring more dignity to his calling. When he no longer had the facility because of illness, he fought, trying to make the impossible possible. A cancer operation in the late 1970s, later a stroke, and assorted physical difficulties bedeviled him. Many of his friends were gone. He spoke frequently of Roy Eldridge—the only one left with whom he had much in common.

The last years blended a bit of good with a lot of bad. At a "We Remember Billie" program in 1979, according to *New York Times* writer Ken Emerson, Papa Jo still had the goods: "Jo Jones grinned like a gambler with four aces in his hand and a fifth up his sleeve as he traded tricks with genial Milt Hinton on bass."[28]

The destructive effects of illness and age began to bring him down as an artist. Yet:

LEE JESKE: He was a constant presence at jazz clubs and concerts, always carrying a rolled-up tabloid with which to jab the air and beat time against the chair. Even after having been sick for a number of years, Jo was still hanging out, still dazzling younger players with his wit and wisdom, still accepting offers to sit behind the traps.[29]

But as his time came closer, he grew increasingly vitriolic. All but the closest fell away. As Chip Stern, a devoted friend, notes, "He was tired, broke, and alone." The fight went on until September 3, 1985. "I've been lucky three times," he said a few months before he passed on. "The man ain't ready for me yet. . . . When he gets ready for me, he knows where to come."

The funeral at St. Peter's Church in New York was something of a jubilee. Music, films, and speeches by those who cared brought him sharply into focus. The films showed Jo at his height, totally alive, very much in his element. A description by Nat Hentoff gives you the picture: "There is a nonstop choreography of what could be called accents in his eyes, in the motions of his face and body, in the vocabulary of grins and grimaces with which he accompanies his drumming. He is a totally alive performer, and he communicates with everything he has and is." That's how I'll remember him.

Sid Catlett
(1910-1951)

"He reined in the obstreperous, pushed the laggardly, and celebrated the inspired."

—WHITNEY BALLIETT[1]

Sid Catlett at the Paramount Theater in Los Angeles where he was appearing with the Louis Armstrong Big Band. The year: 1942. © 1942 Harry Tate.

The significance of an artist is measured in many ways. One of the most important is the test of time.

Few drummers survive as key figures beyond their primary period of activity. Continuing relevance, that ageless quality that makes a drummer's work consistently fresh, is elusive indeed.

Sid Catlett is one of the drummers who erased the line between the then and now. From the 1920s until his passing in 1951, he had the capacity to be consistently interesting and creative in small groups, big bands—whatever the context. Almost 40 years after his death, his work continues to speak well for him.

Much of his continuing impact had to do with his talent. A good deal of his longevity, however, is related to his attitude. An artist who faced the future squarely and without fear, Catlett moved forward unintimidated, welcoming whatever challenges the music offered. He was open and adventurous. He put his mark on many styles of music, including some of the most advanced performances of his time. Even a partial review of his recordings and radio broadcasts reveals his unusual ability, liveliness, and sense of invention.

"Sidney Catlett . . . a prince among fellows . . . a king on the drummer's throne."

—CLIFF LEEMAN[2]

"Sid was totally wrapped up in music and his own concept of what it was to be a fine drummer. Lovable, pleasant, well liked, he was not the sort of drummer who threw his weight around or had a big ego thing."

—HELEN OAKLEY DANCE

"He was what I call spiritual. The guy had a lot of feelings in his playing."

—LAWRENCE LUCIE

"Big Sid felt that drums were to lift and drive the others, not to go it alone."

—BILL ESPOSITO[3]

"It was impossible to play with him and not to feel the essence of jazz."

—*BILLY TAYLOR*

"What he did seemed right, the way it was supposed to be done. I think he was far ahead of a lot of drummers. When he performed there always were a lot of drummers around."

—*RAM RAMIREZ*

"He could play with anyone. That's the main thing about Sid. And his solos were beautiful. Like a dancer, you know. Like Baby Laurence tapping."

—*HARRY LIM*

"It isn't that he played any style; it's that he played so good that it fit anything."

—*RUBY BRAFF*

"He didn't have a lot of technique. But he created that groove. He could cook you out."

—*STANLEY KAY*

"Catlett brought a more melodic concept to jazz drumming. There was melodiousness in jazz drumming before him, but it was covered with the military."

—*DON DEMICHAEL*[4]

"Sid was one of the real giants of drumming. 'Big' was not irony. He really was 'Big' Sid. He had the most sensitive touch of any drummer. A great sense of pitch. He could be restrained and convey fervent excitement."

—*MEL POWELL*[5]

"He was like a big baby, real gentle, real fine. There's nothing bad anyone could say about Sid."

—*BARNEY BIGARD*[6]

"If he were still around, he could show some of these modern drummers a thing or two about communication, both with his fellow musicians and the audience."

—REX STEWART[7]

MEMORIES

Sidney Catlett was a mystery to me when I was a kid. Musicians spoke reverently of the man. And I just couldn't understand what motivated such intense devotion. I had been fascinated by Gene Krupa, Buddy Rich, and Jo Jones—all wonderful players—for many of the wrong reasons. Fed on flash, immersed in technique, I felt "chops" were everything, looking good the key, and speed the ultimate. Though Catlett was a technician and a showman, a great drummer in every way, he didn't have the kind of image that made my pulse race. I didn't fully realize the value of musicality; at least I failed to give it primary emphasis. My obsession was execution. *For the most part, the charm, power, the artistry of "Big Sid" eluded me.*

I sensed how well he played on recordings and was particularly impressed with his work with Coleman Hawkins on Keynote—the All-American four sides—and with Charlie Parker and Dizzy Gillespie on Musicraft. But the few Catlett performances I attended—with the Louis Armstrong big band in New York theaters, and with a variety of small groups on 52nd Street—failed to light a fire in me. It's hard to believe. Catlett played well and with individuality; his time was rock firm; he swung and had stage presence. Yet I failed to get the message. I didn't really understand what made him so special until later.

Only after his death did Big Sid emerge as a hero to me. Finally it became clear what all the comment was about—how deftly he communicated with and supported other musicians, how well he soloed, how instinctively he understood audiences. Listening to his recordings, I am repeatedly impressed with the range of his work and the depth of his capacities. There is art and a foundation of feeling in his work. It is bright and distinct and reaches out, even without the visual dimension that was so crucial to his performances.

Unfortunately, because the dawn was so late in coming in my case, I am without significant personal memories of Big Sid. But luckily, there are Catlett's friends and musical colleagues, his fans and observant writers all with keen recall of this visionary drummer. They tell his story from a number of vantage points, thus affording us a wide-ranging and revealing view of Catlett.

REX STEWART: I fell into Smalls' Paradise [in Harlem] one morning [in 1930] and found a drummer's session in full swing.

I don't remember everyone who was there, but I recall seeing Walter Johnson, Manzie Johnson, Nightsie Johnson, George Stafford [drummer with Charlie Johnson, who had the house band], Chick Webb, Kaiser Marshall from Fletcher Henderson's band, and Kid Lips Hackette. It seems every drummer in Harlem was there, standing around eyeing the stranger, Sid Catlett.

As daylight broke, Catlett not only proved to have as fast and skilled hands as anyone around town, but he also took one of his rare solos. I suppose he sensed that this was his debut in the Big City [Catlett was working in town with the Sammy Stewart band from Chicago], so he performed like a champ—not the usual drum gymnastics coming on like thunder, either. On the contrary, Sid gassed the house by taking a medium, relaxed tempo and working his snare and bass drum in conjunction, as if they were kissing cousins. Then he topped off the sequence by doing a stick-bouncing and stick-twirling spectacle that caused the entire house to burst into applause. . . . Catlett's performance was the epitome of grace and beauty.[8]

PEE WEE ERWIN: I principally remember Sid with Rex Stewart's band at the Empire Ballroom here on Broadway. The year: 1933. I never worked opposite a more thrilling band. I was with the Joe Haymes orchestra. Of course the band swung an awful lot. Sid sat there on his perch; he was the king of the band. I couldn't wait to stumble to the bandstand so I could listen to Rex and Sid.

JOHN SIMMONS: We get to Toronto [in 1941]. They're supposed to have reservations for the [Goodman] band. What's the name of the hotel in Toronto? King George? King Edward? James? Something.

Anyway they didn't have accommodations for Big Sid, Cootie [Williams], and myself. So Pee Wee Monte [who worked for Goodman] pulled Cootie over to the side and said, "Don't worry, we'll get you a room. Stay here." So Sid and I—we got out and got a cab and went to the train station. He saw a red cap and called him over. "Hey brother," he said. "Where can I find a house of ill repute?" I told him, "Sid, I don't want to see any woman. All I want is a bed." "Well," he smiled, "where you find a woman, you find a bed."[9]

JO JONES: Big Sid was like my brother. I never go anyplace without a picture of Big Sid. I've got a little picture of him that I carry with me. That's why I'm never afraid. I know I've got Sid with me. I was very privileged to play with Count Basie, to be around so many creative people. I remember one time Sidney sat in and said, "Man I ought to knock you down—now I got to go back to the coal mines." Did you see *Jammin' The Blues*? Remember when Sid threw that one stick at me? We used to do a thing every Thursday night at the Apollo when we closed. The theater's packed, but there are two seats set aside for Sid Catlett and his wife. I used to throw the sticks to Sidney and a man would put a light on him and BOOM—he'd catch it. Then, BOOM, he'd throw the stick back to me and we'd go into "One O'Clock Jump." Don't ask me. Ask the people that were there. They done saw it. They saw show business. Yeah, we did some strange things out there.[10]

ED SHAUGHNESSY: Sidney Catlett was kind of a mentor of mine. I met him in about 1946 when he was working on 52nd Street with a variety of groups. He was very kind to me. I'd only been playing drums about three years. And he used to let me sit in, usually in the last set. I couldn't have been more than seventeen.

He was the one who approached me because I was certainly too shy to approach him. He asked if I was a drummer. I told him I was trying to be and Sidney said, "Well, I'll tell you what— you're going to play part of the next set." I almost flipped because the group included Ben Webster and John Simmons, one of Sid's favorite bassists.

I was too scared to say no and too scared to play! When it was time for the next set, Sidney came over and said, "Let's go." And I said, "I couldn't do that—I'm not good enough." And he replied, "You'll never get good unless you play with better players." And with that he just picked me up and scooted me along to the stand. All the sidemen were friendly and I played two or three tunes. I'm sure I was anything but good but they were gracious.[11]

CONNIE KAY: When I was about seventeen, I met him when he played on 52nd Street. He couldn't get a taxi home from the gig. I had a car so I said, "I'll give you a ride." On the way home, we started talking, and he found out I was trying to play drums. When I got him to his door, he said: "Hey, Bub. See this building here? I live on the ground floor on the right. Anytime you want to, come by." I was there the next day. I could hardly sleep that night after I dropped him off.

In all the years that he and I were friends, I never once asked him anything about how he did certain things on drums. It was just osmosis, man. I learned from him from having conversations on anything: baseball, women, life in general. Just being around this guy, man, you could see why he played the way he played. I didn't want to impose on the cat to make him think I was trying to pick his brain. I figured that, if I was going to get lessons, I should pay him. If he had asked me if there was anything I wanted to know, then I probably would have asked him how he did certain things. But he never asked me. Basically I wanted to be his friend.

At one time, he asked me what I had been doing lately, and I told him I had a gig. I said that, if he wasn't doing anything, he should come by and tell me what he thought of my playing. Sure enough, he showed up. I was shocked, man. He heard a set, and after I got off, I sat down with him. "You play good," he said. "There's only one thing I think you should do. You should do more with your left hand." That was the only advice he ever gave me. Other than that, it was all osmosis and knowing the man.[12]

Big Sid Catlett loved playing drums and being part of the music and entertainment and gaming scene. He blended night into day, while pursuing music, fun, a wager, a gambling venture. He seldom slept. When he did go to bed, it was a brief sojourn; his need to be out and around predominated.

No matter what the city or town, this imposing figure of a man gravitated to wherever musicians, show people, and those involved with games of chance gathered. Catlett was the constant participant; he feared he might miss something if he turned out the lights and said good night. He was constantly on the move, seeking good talk and music, a hilarious story or joke, the best game around, a unique horse race. Sometimes he paused for a drink or two, often using his charm on an attractive woman.

Big Sid carried on as long as he could—until all others had gone to bed or to day jobs, until fatigue made it impossible for him to play or party any longer. Then he took a short break—a bit of sleep, a shave and shower—and went out again, to a theater, club, concert, or just in "the street," telling stories to musicians and friends.

Catlett rebelled against rest, but the body can be tampered with only so much. Louis Armstrong and all of Catlett's friends warned him that he could not follow this regimen forever. Catlett wore out as the 1940s were coming to a close. He had trouble with his kidneys and his heart, and was forced to leave the Louis Armstrong All-Stars in the spring of 1949. Two years later, while hanging out backstage before an Easter Sunday concert at the Civic Opera House in Chicago, the great drummer left us. He was only forty-one.

That night, as usual, he was on the scene, among his friends.

HELEN HUMES: There was a whole bunch of us standing around backstage at the Opera House, where a concert was going on. Sid had come over to say hello from Jazz Ltd [a club where he was appearing]. He was standing behind me and had his arms clasped around my waist, and he was telling me one of his stories. It came near time for me to be onstage, so I said, "Sid, let me go put some powder on. I'll see you after." I walked away, and right off I heard this funny sound: a kind of *whummpp*. I turned around there was Sid lying on the floor, and that was all there was to it. He died right away.[13]

SID CATLETT, JR.:   I was too young to remember my Dad, first-hand. He died when I was a year old. But I am quite uplifted by what everyone has told me about him. He was a worthy man and a great player. Louis Armstrong and Buddy Rich and Art Blakey and Max Roach told me how much they admired him. So many people, even those not at all concerned with music, respected him.

EARL HINES: All the harm he did was to himself, never to anyone else. Trying to be nice to people who took advantage of him, and a few other worries he had, were the cause, I think, of his drinking as much as he did.[14]

EDDIE BAREFIELD: For some reason, Sid hated to go to bed before daybreak. Even if everybody had gone home and nothing was happening, he'd be standing out somewhere in a restaurant, telling jokes and things until daybreak. Sid never went to bed. And neither did Art Tatum.

NELLIE LUTCHER: All the musicians were crazy about Sid. When he'd walk into a room, you'd hear all the players whispering, "There's Big Sid!" He returned the feeling, the warmth. Above all things, he loved music. He was crazy about those drums. When he worked with Duke for a while in the mid-1940s, he was so thrilled. He was just in heaven. He told me, "Just think, I got a chance to work with Duke"—you know, as if he was nobody. But he loved Duke; he had great admiration and respect for him.

JOHN WILLIAMS: Sidney would go around and listen to everyone. If a band he wanted to hear was playing a theater and we were working until late at a club with Louis Armstrong or Teddy Wilson, he'd finish work, go home, shower, change his clothes, and go out again. He'd hang around the theater all day, just to be with the cats and dig the music.

I don't remember his getting drunk or drinking a whole lot of whiskey. It was hanging around with the musicians that was important to him. If there was a jam session, Sid would usually be there. We had so many of them on 52nd Street. After the blowing was done, we'd go to this after-hours club on Sugar Hill in Harlem where they served whiskey in coffee cups.

Life began for Sidney Catlett in Evansville, Indiana, January 17, 1910.

REX STEWART: He told me years later, jokingly, that his parents were concerned about his tiny size at birth but that the doctor reassured the anxious parents that the seven-pound child would become a big fellow. These words were prophetic as little Sidney Catlett grew until he outgrew the town of Evansville and went on to Chicago.[15]

GLADYS CATLETT: His parents were very unselfish, loving people. He was an only child and they thought there was no one good enough for him. He father chauffeured and his mother was a good cook who worked for wealthy people. I believe his Aunt Minnie worked for those same people. It was through them that he took some drum lessons from an old German teacher. Sidney was the only colored student he had. His mother wanted him to be a lawyer, but the teacher had told her, "You let this boy play the drums and he'll be the greatest drummer in the world."[16]

Catlett's great feeling for the drums was apparent very early on. Shortly after his family moved to Chicago, he got a good drum outfit for around $150. He studied the instrument, learning to read, becoming familiar with rudiments, the building blocks for any "schooled" player. While still a teenager, Catlett moved around from club to club, hoping the topliners like Zutty Singleton would let him sit in.

LOUIS ARMSTRONG: I remember when I was playing with Carroll Dickerson at the Savoy [Chicago, 1928]. Big Sid showed up in knickers and pestered Zutty to let him take over the tubs.[17]

REX STEWART: He would slip away from home to venture into some joint on Chicago's South Side, where perhaps Jasper Taylor or Baby Dodds was playing. . . . He was always careful to be home before daybreak. As he later explained to me, he didn't want to worry his mother.[18]

Milt Hinton, who lived and worked in Chicago, knew the young Catlett. The drummer went to Tilden High School, but spent a lot of time at Wendell Phillips High School, where Hinton and some other budding musicians were students. Hinton remembers that Catlett was a particular fan of Zutty Singleton. He hung around the New

Orleans pioneer, paying close attention to everything he did. There were several others who influenced Catlett, Hinton told critic Whitney Balliett: "There was a drummer around Chicago named Jimmy McHendricks. He was dark and short and had a lisp, but he had flash, throwing his sticks in the air and carrying on like that. [Lionel] Hampton and Sid would watch him all the time."[19]

SID CATLETT: There were a lot of terrific drummers around Chicago in those days. Johnny Wells, Zutty Singleton, Baby Dodds, and Jimmy Bertrand come to mind offhand. Bertrand was the most finished of all. He was really the sepia Vic Berton, a master of technique and an excellent tympanist. Another powerful drummer I admired in those days was Orm Downes [who became widely known with the Ted Weems band].[20]

TOMMY BENFORD: I believe he picked up a lot around New York when he first came from Chicago. He listened to Kaiser Marshall, and George Stafford and Walter Johnson and old man Brooks, who played at the Lincoln Theatre. And he learned a little from me, too.[21]

LAWRENCE LUCIE: When we were together in Louis Armstrong's band a little later, I used to hear him talk about Cuba [Austin, the drummer with McKinney's Cotton Pickers] and I know he admired Chick Webb. But he was a drummer who could play everyone's style. Zutty was his man, though; he used to mimic Zutty on the stand and Pops [Louis Armstrong] looked back and just laughed because he loved Zutty, too. Sid and Pops had a special relationship. Sid would play certain things behind Pops and he would just smile at the big man on drums and look so pleased.

You know, Sid was all music. Back then, most of the guys were all music. We played for the pleasure of it and were happy we had the talent and luck to work with a top band. The thing we strived for was to work with a band like Duke's or Smack's [Fletcher Henderson's] or Pops'. Sid had enough ego to feel he was doing the job. And he was happy to be with Pops.

EARL HINES: Sidney and Louis Armstrong and I ran together in Chicago in the late Twenties. We were full of jokes and were always kidding each other, and we were all batty. We drove around in this broken-down automobile we had, and when we got home from work we'd leave it parked in the middle of the street or in front of someone else's house. Sid left Chicago for New York in 1930, in Sammy Stewart's band. It was a hotel-type orchestra, a hicky-dicky group. Stewart only hired light-complected guys, so when the three of us went to see him for jobs he took Sid but he wouldn't have anything to do with Louis and myself.[22]

Catlett's ability to play shows, read music, and handle intricate arrangements got him the job with Stewart. He replaced David Smallwood, who left to join Dave Payton's band at the new Regal Theater in Chicago.

GEORGE HOEFER: Catlett's career really began to change in 1930 when he left Chicago with the Stewart band. The outfit—with pianist Alexander Hill, trumpeters Walter Fuller and George Dixon, Banjo Ikey Robinson, alto saxophonist Ken Anderson, and several Stewart Brothers—played one-nighters on its way east to open at Harlem's Savoy Ballroom. In Bluefield, West Virginia, they discovered and hired a young, heavy-set tenor saxophonist Leon (Chu) Berry who had recently left his hometown, Wheeling. In New York City, the Stewart band played both the Savoy and the Arcadia on Broadway before disbanding in 1931.[23]

Because he played so well and was an affable presence wherever people gathered, leading musicians sought out Catlett. He brought to music a dimension, a completeness that became only truly apparent after he had moved on to another band or project. Big Sid shaped performances and developed them in a manner that was uncommon in the 1920s, 1930s, and 1940s. He had a great sense of form; he seemed to know how things should be structured. Regardless of the style in which he was involved, he allowed the music to speak to him and reacted in a way that was consonant, affirmative, creative, and right.

From his recording debut with the Sammy Stewart band on "Cause I Feel Lowdown" (Vocalion, 1928) until the close of his recording career in 1950, Catlett brought character and *his* feelings to music. Big Sid transcended style and anticipated what was to come. Listen to him on the May, 1933, Spike Hughes version (with Benny Carter, Coleman Hawkins, Red Allen, Chu Berry, and Dicky Wells) of "Sweet Sue" (originally English Decca). While many drummers of the period were stiff and unresponsive, Catlett gives every indication of being on intimate terms with the demands of his job. His drumming is never loud and always serves as a provocative undercurrent. It's the very essence of swing at the very beginning of the Swing years. His four-bar solo flows and has color rather than being merely a combination of rudiments (ruffs and triplets in this case). Big Sid adds valid musical *comment*, rather than just filling space.

Catlett could play in all styles and work with ease in a variety of contexts, without ever sticking out like a sore thumb. These capacities, combined with rare instincts and reflexes, made him a far more complete player than other major Swing-era names. But because he was not as technically startling and sensational as Webb, Krupa, or Rich, Catlett did not get the public attention he deserved. Musicians, however, knew the value of his work—its depth of humanity, its musicality, its fire, its humor, its sense of surprise.

RAM RAMIREZ: I admired Sid from a distance at first. I heard him when I was young—very young. I went to the Lafayette Theater in Harlem and he really attracted my attention. He was working with Sammy Stewart. The band played the show from the pit and then went up onstage. Sid seemed so nonchalant, you know, with a toothpick in his mouth. His solo was the highlight of the stage presentation. He played on the set, then got up and drummed all over the lower floor of the theater—up and down the aisles, banging on the chairs, the walls, the floor.

A bit later, in 1933, I got to play with Sid in the great Rex Stewart band at the Empire Ballroom in midtown Manhattan. Aside from Sid, there were some real good players with Rex: Nelson Heard on trombone, trumpeter Ward Pinkett, Edgar Sampson played alto sax and wrote for us. Our theme song was called "Misty Morning;" later it became known as "Stompin' At the Savoy." Sid really made the band swing.

Down the line, I worked with Sid's six-piece group at 52nd Street's Famous Door. Billie Holiday was on the bill with us. We had Freddie Webster on trumpet, then Jesse Drakes. After Jesse left, a little fellow by the name of Miles Davis came into the band. Eddie "Lockjaw" Davis and, following him, Hal Singer played tenor sax in the group.

Sid was so light on the cymbals—so flashy, full of humor, and playful. To relieve the monotony on a slow night, he would entertain the guys in the band by imitating all the great drummers. He'd say, "Here's Gene Krupa" and do his things, then follow up with Sonny Greer, or Cozy or Buddy. He really gave the band a lift that way. We had some good times together. But Sid's performances with the Rex Stewart band really remain in my mind.

In the early 1930s, following his stint with Sammy Stewart, Catlett played the with the Elmer Snowden band, an all-star ensemble that worked at Smalls' Paradise in Harlem. The band featured many musicians who would become major stars: trumpeter Roy Eldridge, tenor saxophonist Chu Berry, Wayman Carver (one of the first jazz flutists), and trombonist Dicky Wells. The drummer also spent time with the Jeter-Pillars band at the Club Plantation in St. Louis, Sam Wooding, McKinney's Cotton Pickers, and with his own group at the Stables in Chicago.

DICKY WELLS: Sidney Catlett was very instrumental in the success of Snowden's band. He was always pushing the guys. He was a musician's drummer. He would ask you, "What kind of rhythm should I play for you? What do you want?" That was as soon as you came in the band, and after you told him, you would get the same thing every night, unless you told him to change it. He was a loveable guy. All he had to say was "Let's go jam," and he had a mob following him. Everyone loved the way he would push you.[24]

Unlike many modern drummers, who specialize in a particular style of drumming, Catlett was a generalist. Remember, jazz and entertainment were synonymous when the drummer the late Tiny Kahn called "Big Veal Catlett," was coming along. There was work in carnivals and theaters, on the vaudeville circuit, and in burlesque, shows, ballrooms, hotels, and clubs. A drummer had to have many arrows for his bow. Sid did. Older show people and musicians often comment on how adept he was at playing shows. Catlett could read music well and was alert to the subtleties of performances—by dancers, comedians, jugglers, whatever.

CLIFF LEEMAN: Big Sidney played the shucks out of a show. He used to love to work with dancers; all the fine drummers I knew liked the give-and-take with dancers. Sid always came around to check out how other drummers played shows. He was there every time he was in town when we rehearsed a new Apollo Theater show with the Charlie Barnet band in the 1940s.
       You know what I noticed every time Big Sidney played a show? His timing was nothing short of fantastic. And he had great taste. He could execute anything that was necessary. The guy had to have studied more than a little. But we never talked much about that. Getting back to it—dancers were his thing, tap dancers, lines of girls. He really enjoyed playing for them.

DIZZY GILLESPIE: [The drummer] must have the tools to work with. He must have the most astounding reflexes 'cause a guy might do anything, and he's supposed to catch him. Like Sidney Catlett used to play shows, if somebody blinked an eye he got it.[25]

JOHN HAMMOND: There was no such thing as a bad chorus girl when Big Sid was around because he made everybody in a show *perform*.

Catlett told a very young Ed Shaughnessy, "Learn how to read and play a good show, because that'll bail you out when you don't have other gigs."

ED SHAUGHNESSY: Sidney believed in that because he himself played a magnificent show. There were dancers on the circuit who used to make special inquiries as to Sid's availability. They wanted him to be the guest drummer because he grooved them so much when he played.[26]

At the time he began playing with good musicians and bands in Chicago, Catlett realized the need to play shows with flair and to be noticed. The drummer of the 1920s and 1930s, before Krupa, was a victim of a number of misconceptions: he was not a musician; he was merely a subordinate novelty player. Many times his living depended on how much of a showman he was. He was tolerated because he kept the band together. If he was gifted and swinging, he had the support and recognition of discerning musicians, but everyone else thought him a noisemaker. Drummers did their best to live with this attitude; many adjusted, learning to call attention to themselves by twirling sticks, throwing them in the air and catching them, and so on. It was particularly hard on those who were very serious about music and the instrument. Catlett, however, apparently was not bothered by the emphasis on showmanship, accepting it as fact.

GEORGE HOEFER: For the rest of his life, Catlett was to have the utmost respect for showmanship, something instilled in him from the beginning of his career. During a 1941 interview, Catlett, asked whether he deemed showmanship or musicianship more important, replied, "I'd say showmanship. Think of all the first-rate musicians you've met who are playing for cakes because they haven't got showmanship. In other words, it's not what you do, it's how you do it that counts.[27]

Despite the emphasis on showmanly qualities, Catlett looked to the music for his essential motivation. Like all the great ones, he listened intently to what musicians were trying to say in their music; he acted in response to arrangements, which gave him direction.

BILLY TAYLOR: Sid *listened* when he played. He worked very closely with the bass player. He locked in with the guy playing bass; they functioned as a team. The piano player in a trio could get up and take a walk; I mean the rhythm was *right there.* Rhythm sections with Sid at the drums were among the best I ever heard. His playing not only had form, it mirrored his consciousness of dynamics. Above all else, he swung. His vitality permeated everything. When we worked together, every night was Christmas Eve. He did what was appropriate in any situation. If he was with a traditional band, such as those often led by Louis Armstrong, Sid knew all the repertory and all the moves the drummer should make. And he made them lovingly. It wasn't a caricature. He wasn't saying, "Hey, I'm more modern than this; I can play swing and bebop and all those things." Sid went right into what the music was about and *played it.*

Chick Webb and Sid had things in common. They could be thrilling and both were great showmen. Sid didn't do what Chick did because he was a big man who was very comfortable with his size. It wasn't necessary for him to keep proving that he was a great drummer. He just played softly; he didn't have to be the bombastic, takeover drummer. He always was *the musician.*

I remember once on the Coast [around 1945] when Buddy Rich, Dodo Marmarosa, and Buddy DeFranco were all with Tommy Dorsey, they used to come into the clubs and cut everybody. Buddy was cutting all the drummers, but not Sid. It used to annoy Buddy so much. He'd play all over his head—play fantastically—and then Sid would gently get back on the stand, and play his simple melodic lines—on drums—and he'd make his point.[28]

CLIFF LEEMAN: Sid was an impressive figure. Well over six feet, with long arms and extraordinary large hands, he'd pick up a pair of normal size sticks and they looked like toothpicks in his grasp. And you'd say to yourself, "Jesus, this guy is going to raise some hell." And unexpectedly, you'd get something else entirely. There he'd be on the stand with Don Byas or Ben Webster and a piano player and a bassist and playing so softly it was ridiculous. I didn't think you could play that softly with sticks or brushes and make it work. He had facility. Playing fast and soft is quite a difficult feat. You gotta have chops. You gotta have a lot of chops. Sid had the sort of technique that made this possible.

One or two other things: Sid moved easily around the set. He could make changes, from brushes to sticks to mallets without it being apparent. And when he soloed, he played ideas. But it all was structured. Yes, it was a song he'd be playing . . .

How did Catlett look when he played?

Critic Whitney Balliett, who admires Big Sid above all other drummers, and has written with unusual insight about him, remembers, "Majestic expressions flowed across his face when he played. He would stare into middle distance and look huge and mournful, or he would send out heavy, admiring glances to the pretty women in the room."[29] On another occasion, Balliett was even more specific:

> Catlett sat at his drums with Prussian erectness, his trunk motionless and his arms . . . moving so fast that they seemed to be lazily spinning in slow motion. It was an unforgettable ballet. Once in a while he would twirl his sticks over his head or throw them in the air, allowing their motions to silently measure off several beats. The effect was louder than any shout.[30]

EDDIE BAREFIELD: I think Sid's [physical] attitude was taken from Walter Johnson because the way they looked when they played was similar. Both sat very erect. Sid and Walter weren't the kind of drummers who made all kinds of motions and things. They made it all seem easy. Walter, in particular, always looked immaculate sitting up there in his collar and tie.

JOHN WILLIAMS: A lot of drummers move a lot—say if they make a roll or something. The whole body shakes. Baby Dodds used to do that when he played his shimmy beat. But Sidney and Walter, they looked like statues up there. They'd get into paradiddles and rolls and everything without making too much of it.

ARVELL SHAW: I guess Sid was the original "Mr. Cool." When he played there weren't any of those gyrations. He just sat up straight and played. He sometimes cocked his head to the side, rocked it on "2" or "4" of each bar. You know, he was spectacular without being a showboat.

RUBY BRAFF: When I first came to New York so many years ago, Sid and I shared an apartment for a while. We went out at night to hear people play and stuff like that. It was wonderful to be with him. But he never talked about himself very much. I never really got to know what he really thought about things on the inside. You know what I mean?

When we worked together in Boston, I realized he was a marvelous player. Not only that, he was a tremendous master of ceremonies. A terrific storyteller. He could fascinate you all night at the microphone, just talking and saying things. And the drumming—it was just wonderful to watch him. He was so graceful. When he soloed, you'd never get bored or tired. And when he played behind you, it was impeccable.

ERNIE ANDERSON: Sid was a man of strong temperament; modest, he was nonetheless completely aware of his talent.[31]

GEORGE HOEFER: Catlett's moods varied. He could be soft-spoken and relaxed, very friendly; or he might be tense, sullen, and agitated; or unusually gay, full of jokes, and ready with a put on.[32]

GEORGE WEIN: The thing I remember about him was his warmth as a man. He actually conveyed that warmth as a drummer. That's the word to describe Sid—*warmth*. He had it in his singing as well; it was so much a part of his personality, particularly when he was communicating with you on a one-to-one basis. He could be just one of the warmest human beings around. And how well he could sing. Not too many people know he sang and wrote songs.

One of the great stories about Sid Catlett has to do with his 1950 Boston "rent party," except we didn't know it was a rent party until we got there. It was around the time I first opened Storyville, my club in Boston. We got this invitation at the club: "Party at Big Sid's Place" was what it said, with the date and the address. Sid had a little apartment in Roxbury with Vic Dickenson at the time. Everybody came—you know, the Boston jazz people. I remember going over to the bar to get a drink and Sid said, "That'll be two dollars, please." I'll never forget Vic Dickenson's expression when Sid said to people who came by the bar, "A dollar for your drink; two dollars for your drink." Vic looked at me and said, "Well, kiss my waist!" Sid had this wonderful way of pulling surprises like that. But nobody got angry at him.

Sid knew the value of friendship when it came to his career. I'm not saying he wasn't sincere. He was very sincere. But Sid had a little *con* to him. But, it was a beautiful con.

MAX KAMINSKY: It was in 1934 that I made "The Eel" (recently released on *Swing Street*, Epic SN 6042) with Joe Sullivan, Bud Freeman, Pee Wee Russell, Floyd O'Brien, Eddie Condon, and Big Sid Catlett. . . . I had never met Big Sid until he showed up in front of the Brunswick studio at 1776 Broadway, where I was waiting for the rest of the guys. Big Sid was so big that instead of shaking hands he simply picked me up bodily, as if I were a toy, and when I was on eye level with him he said, most politely, "Man, I'm glad to know you." It was so spontaneous, and he was such a nice, plain guy in such nice, plain clothes that he was tops with me from then on. Every time I looked over at Sid during the recording session and saw that grin of his, it gave me confidence.[33]

This recording, an exceptional example of the rhythmic vitality and inventiveness of tenor saxophonist Bud Freeman, is evolutionary in character. With Catlett's unstinting aid, Freeman builds a stirring, burning performance. Using only snare drum and a cymbal, Catlett increases the heat and intensity as the record unfolds, his quiet momentum provoking Freeman and pushing the other soloists right along. Emotion and pulsation mingle; one is not entirely conscious of how well Big Sid is playing until the group has attained a high level of animation and things are really swinging. Then, suddenly Freeman goes into the coda and it's over. It is clear why Catlett gave Kaminsky confidence and why Lester Young listened closely to Freeman in the first half of the 1930s.

Kaminsky was only one of many musicians whom Catlett affected in such a positive manner. Louis Armstrong, who taught several generations of jazzmen—and continues to do so on record—had great affection and respect for Catlett's playing. The drummer was in and out of the legendary trumpeter's big band from late 1938 until 1942, rejoined him to play with a small all-star group from 1947 until 1949, and enjoyed a rare rapport with Satchmo. Big Sid had learned a lot in Chicago from Zutty Singleton. Armstrong had a long-term relationship with Singleton, a fellow New Orleanian; he cared about him and admired his playing. By aptly applying what he picked up from Singleton and combining this knowledge with his trigger-sharp manner of performance, Catlett managed to do all the right things for Armstrong.

LAWRENCE LUCIE: Whatever the tempo, whatever the song said, Sid was *in there* behind Pops, playing so good, gathering ideas from whatever was happening around him.

NESUHI ERTEGUN: Sidney, Zutty, and Davey Tough had something important in common: the ability to swing. It may sound trite but it's so very important. Sid would play a little rim shot or something and everything changed. It was electrical; the music came alive. Davey could do that. So could Zutty. Zutty and Sid were alike in many ways. Both were *big* guys who played softly—softly in the sense they never banged. Maybe on the last chorus of a Dixieland thing, or the last sixteen bars, they might bring up the volume. But they basically were drummers who played softly, reasonably, persuasively.

HARRY LIM: Louis dug Sid so much. When Louis soloed, Sid used to play on that big Chinese cymbal of his and knock Pops out. The lightness of his playing, the *sense* of what he did. His *taste*. That sums it up: Sid had extraordinary taste.

ERNIE ANDERSON: Louie Armstrong often pronounced him the greatest
jazz drummer and hired him on every possible occasion . . . [Sid]
made more records with Armstrong than any other drummer. . . .
Satchmo tells of performances in Southern dance halls where
Big Sid's twenty-minute impromptu spot reduced whole audiences to a state of hysterical frenzy. In theaters and at concerts,
when the mood was upon him, he would sometimes dance around
his drums while playing, generating a tumult of excitement.[34]

JOHN WILLIAMS: Sid always was playing. When we were on the road
with Louis, he'd generally have his rubber pad with him. As soon
as we got the hotel, he'd turn on the radio and play along with
the music. If we had a day off and didn't have to play until the
evening, we'd have a jam session in the hotel room. That's the
way Sid kept up.

There were some good guys in Louis' band: Red Allen, George
Washington, Scad Hemphill, Luther Coles, Charlie Holmes,
Prince Robinson, Lawrence Lucie, Joe Garland. Joe Garland was
the musical director.

In those days, we traveled Pullman. I remember Sid and I
would go to the back of the train and sit outside on that little bit
of a terrace. We'd get all smoky and dirty out there talking about
music. Sid would start beating out a rhythm with his hands on
that fence that surrounded us, inspired by the rhythm of the train
running over the tracks. It was great, man. We'd sit there and
hum songs and arrangements and Sid would get the rhythm
going. When he came up with a good idea, he'd say: "Look, I'm
going to play this rhythm behind so-and-so;" he knew what
would get to each one of the guys in the band. Like Duke [Elling-
ton], Sid was fascinated with the sounds and rhythms of trains.

You know, we had a wonderful setup on Louis' band. We
were close. You could say, "I don't have any money." Very
quickly one of the players would come over and ask you how
much you needed. There were no cliques that shut you out or
caused you any pain in that band. The chemistry was there. You
hated to stop playing because everything felt so good.

But racial problems were around every corner for black bands in
the late 1930s and early 1940s.

JOHN SIMMONS: We [the Armstrong band] got to Atlanta, Georgia, and
they had chicken wire down through the middle of the auditorium. It was a dance. Whites on one side, blacks on the other. If
the dance (and the music) got too good . . . and some more whites
wanted to get in there, the blacks had to go . . .[35]

One of the ways that Catlett and Armstrong put difficulties of this sort temporarily out of their minds was to exchange funny stories. John Simmons recalls, "They would tell jokes from one town to another. Every time I would hear them repeat one, it'd be as funny as the first time."

And there was the primary mitigating factor: the music. What the musicians went through found its way into the music. Particularly in the blues, feelings would roll out almost unedited. Generally, the musicians kept any negative vocal comment oblique, but it was fully understood by those on the inside. The music was many things: a forum, a shield, a world within the real world that was freer, more comfortable, and less threatening than the stark and often taxing day-to-day, night-to-night life.

The Armstrong band derived its distinction essentially from its leader. The band was not on the same level as the Ellington, Basie, Goodman, or Lunceford organizations. But it did have jazz's most influential soloist and singer up front. The sidemen responded strongly to Armstrong. Catlett was no exception, as some of the band's better records demonstrate: "Bye and Bye" (1939), "You're A Lucky Guy" (1939), "Savoy Blues" (1939), and "Wolverine Blues" (1940), all on Decca.

"Wolverine Blues" was Catlett's favorite of all the recordings he cut with Satchmo's big band. The record certainly has a number of things to recommend it. The band handles a fast tempo with elan; the performance has a feeling of precision, balance, and subtlety lacking in most other performances by the band. Armstrong plays well and Catlett is a delightful rhythm presence.

But "Bye and Bye," with its spicy New Orleans flavor, is particularly captivating. It follows the Crescent City formula, strongly suggesting small-band counterpoint. Pops sings and the band responds vocally and instrumentally. From Catlett's marchlike four-bar kickoff to the close, there is a buoyancy and freedom that make the performance distinctive.

Catlett's pulsating solo (six bars plus a two-bar pickup) shows how effectively he could mingle press rolls and single strokes. The record aptly combines entertainment and good jazz feeling, as Catlett fills the band with a controlled vitality.

These Armstrong sides, like a number of other Catlett recordings from the 1930s, indicate that only a natural response to music—without undue pressure from the drummer—can create a swinging environment. The drummer balanced strength and suggestion in his work, allowing the rhythm to make its own way. This attitude toward time was typical of Southwestern and Midwestern bands of the period. Quite likely Catlett's stay with the Jeter-Pillars band in St.

Sid Catlett throwing those sticks, a Big Sid specialty, with the Armstrong band in 1942 at the Paramount Theater in Los Angeles. © 1942 Harry Tate.

Louis, further ingrained in him this manner of playing. Drummers active in the Midwest and Southwest, notably Jo Jones, Baby Lovett, A.G. Godley, Jesse Price, and others, set telling examples of this rhythmic approach to music.

However, the Catlett recordings with Benny Carter, Spike Hughes, and Fletcher Henderson tell us he already knew the value of being natural. Certainly, his stay (1936–1938) with a band headed by

Don Redman, another important architect of big-band swing, must have been educational. In essence, Catlett learned that you can't lay back and expect things to happen. You have to push a band or group, give it direction. But the music moves only when the drummer doesn't put too much stress on his colleagues, only when he permits a chemical reaction among the players to take place.

BOB HAGGART: What Sidney Catlett did with Louis Armstrong's big band wasn't complicated. It never was complicated. It was just right. And very subtle. I heard Catlett quite a bit with Louis at the Cotton Club in L.A. when the Bob Crosby band was out on the Coast in '42. How well he did things! He laid the beat right in there, backing Louis with marvelously placed rim shots and bass drum explosions. He was so good that I tried to catch the band on the radio as much as possible, so I could record some air checks.

Between stints with the Louis Armstrong big band, Catlett worked with Benny Goodman. He signed a one-year contract with Goodman, leaving Armstrong in June 1941. The stay with the Goodman band, which brought him widespread public recognition—a natural result of working with one of the nation's top bands—was not a pleasant one. The relationship with the band leader started off well but deteriorated. Being a strong player and an outstanding showman, Catlett often took the spotlight away from Goodman, which annoyed the band leader. Goodman had to be in complete control, and generally didn't get along with his drummers. When he was disturbed with a drummer's behavior, Goodman gave him "the ray," staring the player down and making him uncomfortable.

ROY ELDRIDGE: I knew Sidney for a long time. We played a lot together. When we both were with Fletcher's band in 1936, Benny didn't like Sidney. He came over to hear us at the Grand Terrace in Chicago and asked me, "How do you like that drummer?" I said, "He's great!" He answered, "Man, in about three or four weeks, you ain't gonna be playing nothing with that drummer." I just told him, "Look! You, Fletcher, Paul Whiteman—nobody can tell me about Sidney because I've worked with him before. I'll probably be playing better and better the longer he stays around."

The next thing I know he had Sidney in the band—Sidney and John Simmons. I guess that was five years later. I used to meet them going to work in New York. But Benny badgered them so much. . . .

John Hammond, who was very close to the situation, contends that the rhythm section—Charlie Christian (guitar), John Simmons (bass), Mel Powell (piano), and Big Sid (drums)—was beyond Goodman's regulation. Highly creative people, they communicated with one another and all but ignored Goodman, who tried to tell them how to play.

JIMMY MAXWELL: Sidney and I came into the band at the same time. I returned; he joined for the first time. Yes, it was a deteriorating situation for him right from the start. We joined in June. Very soon thereafter, we went out to Chicago with the band. We did a weekly broadcast on NBC for the Holland Furnace Company and played at the Panther Room of the Hotel Sherman.

Benny took off a month at about that time because of his back. During this period the band sounded better than it ever had. With Benny away, all the guys felt free; it was like getting out of jail. Cootie [Williams, the solo trumpeter who came from the Ellington band] was playing great. Vido [Musso, tenor sax soloist] sounded fine. Everybody was playing good. Benny came back to a different band than the one he left. That's when things really started going downhill for Sid.

With Sid in the band, it was as if the sun had come out for me. It was so much easier to play. Lionel Hampton had been playing drums, splitting the job with Nick Fatool. Lionel used too much bass drum for my taste; it was distracting. Sid took the beat where I thought it should be. When I played the lead part or a solo, I didn't have to beat my foot or anything. The time was right there. Sid was strong but didn't *pull* the band. The pulsation had a very basic feeling to it, wasn't too loud and allowed you to concentrate. During my solos, it was as if Sid knew what I was going to play next. He'd set me up; he would motivate me to do things I wouldn't have thought of if he hadn't led me into them. He knew what I was going to do before I did.

Everybody in the band dug Sid. When any of us would solo, we'd turn around and smile at Sid and, you know, say *"yeah!"* He had a way of doing what had to be done for every player. On last choruses he could really lift the band up. I think that bothered Benny. He didn't want anybody to lift the band up except him. Once he told me when I went to hire Roy Eldridge—Cootie was leaving—that he didn't want any fast, high-note trumpet players. He said, "I do all the fast, high playing in this band!"

He liked to be in complete command! He'd often try to tell the soloists what to do. Just for fun, I stuck in the Bunny Berigan solos on "King Porter Stomp" and "Sometimes I'm Happy." I knew the records so well; I just couldn't think of anything else. Then when I didn't do it, he asked me, "Why don't you play Bunny's solos?" He liked the same solo every time. Sid played something different and fresh each time; he always would surprise you.

Sid and I got along very well. On the road, we slept across the aisle from each other in the trains. We talked a lot and liked to eat together. Generally, we'd talk about Louis [Armstrong].

As for Benny, he wasn't *all* bad. When we were at the New Yorker Hotel here in town, the management didn't want Catlett to come into the lobby. They wanted Sid and John Simmons to use the back door; I don't think Cootie was at the New Yorker. Benny was dynamite on stuff like that. He told the manager of the Terrace Room: "You knew we had Negroes in the band when you hired me. You shouldn't have hired me. These men don't walk through the kitchen." Then Benny said: "Why don't you get somebody else?"

I was at the table opening night. That's the way it was. He told the man where to go. The guy said: "I want all the musicians to walk in through the kitchen." Benny said: "All the musicians walk in any way they goddamn please." The manager added: "Well, they can't walk through the room in their uniforms." Benny raised his voice: "Just get somebody else!"

But Benny had so many idiosyncrasies, particularly about tempos. Sid didn't always go along with Benny's ideas about tempos; the band didn't either. For some reason Benny used to fool around with Sid. He'd slow down the count before the band came in; then he'd pull it up.

JOHN SIMMONS: One night they came off the stand and Sid collared [Benny]. He said, "Looky here, Pops, you gave the downbeat. I'm supposed to keep *that* tempo." Then he told him, "As long as you've been playing, you know it's unprofessional to change the tempo once the dancers are on the floor."[36]

JIMMY MAXWELL: Benny always gave "the ray" to drummers. He told me, "You've got to look someplace and the drummer is always at eye level. So I look at him." Benny was very surprised when I told him about "the ray."

Luckily Sid's reaction to Benny was nonviolent. Benny would make him so crazy he'd be in tears. Lucky for Benny, as I said, because Sid was a powerful son of a bitch. After a while, Sid finally quit, or was put on notice, depending on who tells the story.

SID CATLETT: It was one long nightmare with Goodman.[37]

Those who know Catlett's work very well say the stress of the relationship with Goodman did not adversely affect his performances in any discernible manner. Goodman and some writers and critics felt that while Catlett brought much of himself to the sound of the ensemble, he played too boldly. But the records and radio broadcasts of Catlett with the band tell a different story.

Unlike most of Goodman's earlier drummers—with the notable exceptions of Gene Krupa and Dave Tough—and a good number of the drummers who played with Goodman after Catlett was long gone, Catlett made a declaration of self in his interpretation of Goodman's music. He was, like all good band drummers, supportive, firm, strong, and responsive. More than that, he freed the rhythmic movement of the band considerably and pushed Goodman with feints and jabs and explosions, making him play in a manner that was not at all typical.

Though often an emotional player, Goodman seemed to hold back on occasion; he was reserved, perhaps too tidy, in certain circumstances, particularly on ballads. With Catlett at the drums, the clarinetist could not lay back; there was no place to hide. Even on ballads, the drummer was mildly provocative. On the dance tunes, he played a subsidiary role as Goodman improvised in a well-edited yet romantic manner, but his ideas shaped the leader's comments.

"Caprice XXIV Paganini," recorded for Columbia in October 1941, provides a good example of the drummer's rhythmic strength and prodding ways. Driving hard, he seems about to burst out of the arrangement by Skip Martin. "I'm Here," a Mel Powell composition and arrangement, finds Catlett under everything, exploding, firming up the accents, laying down a powerful time pattern. Catlett's melodic leanings are well illustrated on Eddie Sauter's "Clarinet A La King," from the same session as "Caprice" and "I'm Here." Catlett moves from drum to drum on fills, offering bits of color that add to the continuity and depth of the piece. He plays loudly when necessary and with controlled muscle most of the way, keeping the band expectant and excited, often electrifying the players, and listeners as well. (All three items—"Paganini," "I'm Here," and "Clarinet A La King"—can be found on Epic's *Clarinet A La King).*

The broadcasts, by nature freer, longer, and more relaxed in character, give the truest picture of the band and Catlett's effect on it. On a number of nights, caught for posterity on wire and wax acetate recordings, we hear Goodman and his men from the Panther Room of the Hotel Sherman in Chicago, the Steel Pier in Atlantic City, and Frank Dailey's Meadowbrook in Cedar Grove, New Jersey. The results are generally stirring.

The band reacts strongly to Catlett, who fashions each number in ways that elude, tax, or simply fail to occur to most drummers. He plays differently for each soloist, following and sometimes anticipating each player's thoughts. Now heavy, now soft, moving from sizzling, half-open high-hats to crisp rolls, to melodic tom-toming, to pinging, ringing cymbal playing, to damping routines on one cymbal or another, he plays ever-firm, gritty, grabbing time.

Mel Powell's "The Count" provides a classic example of Catlett's playing. The drummer mixes a provocative potpourri of color and rhythm; he moves from an opening damping cymbal pattern behind trombonist Lou McGarity to searing pulsation through Goodman's solo, trumpeter Cootie Williams' comments, tenor saxophonist Vido Musso's impassioned bit, and well-integrated ensemble and sectional segments, concluding with a repeat of the damping cymbal routine behind McGarity.

The 1941 Goodman band rates with the clarinetist's best. Certainly the arrangements and performances stand up after more than 40 years. But Goodman didn't agree. When we briefly got together about two years before his death, I indicated how much I admired the band featuring Catlett and the Eddie Sauter and Mel Powell charts. Goodman seemed surprised. He spoke warmly about the 1935–38 band, with Gene Krupa, Teddy Wilson, Lionel Hampton, Jess Stacy, and Harry James, which played Carnegie Hall. But he seemed uncomfortable with the 1941 band. Certain kinds of experimentation bothered him. He was equally out of his element during his abortive bebop experiment several years later. Goodman could not change or adapt to what challenged his view of how things should be. Catlett, in particular, was a burr on the bottom of his foot, and he couldn't put up with him for long.

RUSSELL CONNOR and WARREN HICKS: A large man, addicted to green chalk-striped suits and flowered ties, he [Catlett] enjoyed life and he played drums enthusiastically—at times overenthusiastically. He had a bubbling sense of humor and he played with what Chicago musicians call "a lot of side"—a kind of stagey exhibitionism. His droll "Watch the drummer, boy," his use of an oversized powder puff with which he patted his armpits, his trick of tossing a drumstick high overhead and catching it seemingly without looking—marking the catch with a heavy foot on the bass drum—were mannerisms knowing audiences came to look for.[38]

It was Catlett's hold on audiences—his showmanship—that did him in as far as Goodman was concerned. A concert at Soldier Field in Chicago was Big Sid's finale. The drummer captivated the audience during his solo on "Don't Be That Way" with his show-business shtick, walking around the drums and throwing sticks in the air. Then he played a great solo and, as bassist John Simmons remembers, "nearly blew the place up."

Goodman was not at all happy with this display. John Hammond, Goodman's brother-in-law and intimate back then, said when he heard about the extraordinary response to Catlett at the Soldier Field concert, he thought, "Oh, Jesus, Sidney's cooked."

Indeed he was. Upon its return to New York, the band took a few days off before going into the New Yorker Hotel for an engagement. The first night Catlett came to work in the Terrace Room, another drummer was sitting in his place on the bandstand. He got his two-week notice and was asked to show up every night in case he was needed.

Peggy Lee, the band's vocalist at the time, told Whitney Balliett, "He cried when he learned Benny was letting him go."[39]

JOHN MCDONOUGH: Catlett made a massive mark on this Goodman band. He was never shy about drawing attention his way. Yet he was one of the purest ensemble drummers of them all. He could weave into a musical phrase with a rimshot, bass [drum] accent, cymbal splash, or a combination of all three, and suddenly the lucky musician's solo would snap into bold italics. But he wasn't polite. He could ride hard on a soloist and band. His playing could be insolent and insubordinate. It challenged and dared as it supported and nourished. Any band with Catlett on its back was in harm's way if it didn't watch out. He had an imaginative sense of rhythmic motion that was coupled with an appreciation of a drum's melodic potential.[40]

When the ax was about to fall, Catlett told John Simmons, "Come on, brother, let's go back to Louis Armstrong. Let's go with Louis."[41] And that's ultimately what they both did.

Catlett spent a year with Armstrong, followed by a two-year stint (1942–1944) with pianist Teddy Wilson's small group. The Wilson band included excellent mainstream jazz players: Emmett Berry or Joe Thomas (trumpet), Benny Morton (trombone), Edmund Hall (clarinet), and John Williams (bass). It was a most compatible assemblage of musicians, which performed much of the time at New York's Cafe Society Uptown. According to Whitney Balliett, who heard the unit at the Cafe, Catlett seemed very much at home with this set of colleagues.

JOHN WILLIAMS: Sidney was a pleasure to work with, no matter what sort of band it was. He played with great imagination and swing in both small and big bands. The man did the job wherever you put him.

GEORGE HOEFER: He was welcomed on 52nd Street where small groups made up of musical rebels were beginning to get a hearing. . . . Catlett was a very important influence in the transition from old-fashioned time-keeping to the making of the instrument plus the traps into "a melodic voice." Using pitch variation, he embellished riffs he would set in his opening statements with the result he would create original tunes of his own. Among the avid students of Catlett's work was a creative group of young drummers that included Max Roach, Shelly Manne, Art Blakey, among many others.[42]

Catlett was everywhere as World War II was coming to a close. On 52nd Street he played with Ben Webster, Don Byas, and so many fine musicians, and also headed his own groups. He was the drummer on countless jazz record dates for a variety of small labels. Because of his extraordinary ability to adapt to any musical circumstances, he sounded equally relevant playing with Dizzy and Bird or with Webster; with Edmund Hall and James P. Johnson and Sidney DeParis on the famed Blue Note sessions; or with Coleman Hawkins, Teddy Wilson, and John Kirby on Keynote. He worked in a manner that was simultaneously potent and unobtrusive. The musicians would blow and Catlett would flow.

The Hawkins Keynote session of May 29, 1944, yielded two gems: the standards "Just One Of Those Things" (Porter) and "Hallelujah" (Robin-Grey-Youmans). The tempo is up—"Hallelujah" is the faster of the two. Balance and high-level creativity identify both efforts. In these homogeneous performances, everyone moves in the same direction, bringing something of his own to the music while adding to the overall meld.

Hawkins is bold and inventive: his big sound and confident, precise, and enviable execution of ideas consistently adds strength to what is played. Teddy remains light; his articulation is crystal clear as he moves through always logical, sometimes surprising sequences. Bassist Kirby provides a strong, dependable foundation. Catlett plays extraordinary brushes, making each stroke a matter of strength and clarity. He propels his colleagues with rhythm that is gay and carefree. The Porter opus benefits from Catlett's almost perfect blend of tension and swing. On "Hallelujah," he is highly affirmative and aggressive, thrusting everyone forward, changing pace by playing high-hats behind the bass. His solo is among his best on records. Two choruses of crisp, inspiring, diversified commentary add up to a major, highly integrated declaration.

The records Catlett made with Lester Young for Keynote—a December 1943 session—also have a marvelous flavor. Catlett is receptive and relaxed regardless of the tempo. He never overplays, and gives and takes with the members of the quartet as though he had been working with them for a long while.

Catlett never gets in the way and serves the unit—Young (tenor sax), Johnny Guarnieri (piano), and Slam Stewart (bass)—in an exemplary manner, responding to nuances, being supportive while adding his own impetus. All the elements fit so well on "Sometimes I'm Happy," a medium-tempo offering, that it seems it could be no other way. Stewart's rapport with Catlett is memorable. Big Sid's snare drum/bass drum responses during openings in the bassist's sung/bowed solo are endearing. In short, all the elements compounded—Young's deeply melodic playing, Guarnieri's performance within the group and his telling, spare solo, Stewart's firmness and humor, and Catlett's inventions in rhythm—make this a landmark performance. More than anything, it provides a revealing, highly edifying view of Catlett in a small band.

HARRY LIM: Lester didn't like heavy drummers—the guys who play for themselves. He couldn't stand drumming that got in the way of his thoughts. Pres liked to *feel* the time. Sid gave him exactly what he wanted on the session we did for Keynote. He was light, provided Pres the time to work against and stayed in the background. Sid astonished everybody every time he played. Musicians loved him because he was supportive of the band and the soloist, and made everything feel good.

TONY SCOTT: During the 52nd Street days, Sid was a big star. He was "the man" on drums. His playing was solid. It had weight to it. And that back-beat he played! That's the thing I really remember . . . plus how he tuned his drums. Such beautiful sounds!

Did you know that Sid was a very humorous cat? When the club wasn't crowded, he would take a solo. The kitchen was right behind the bandstand at the Down Beat. The shell at the back of the stand curved into it. Sid would get going on a drum solo, play on the outside of the bass drum, then go onto the wall, then the floor and into the kitchen, where he would play on the pots and pans before coming back out and sitting at the set again.

When I was working with him, he would play the off-beat in a flexible way. Sid did a marvelous thing with the sock cymbal.

He would use the front part of his left foot and close it on 2 and 4 and then bring down his heel on the other beats. Sometimes he used his heel on the bandstand and you got a hell of an effect. There were a whole bunch of different sounds going down.

We worked a lot at the Down Beat, often opposite Billie Holiday. I recorded with Sid and my friend and mentor Ben Webster. Sid was superb. He played all these interesting ideas! And he certainly was a master with the brushes.

Sid was very beautiful to me. I was a young kid when I first started coming around. Every time I went into a 52nd Street spot where he was playing, he asked me to sit in. During the war years, I was with the Army Band at Governor's Island in New York harbor and got to "The Street" every night. After a while, I went straight to the bandstand. Sid always made me feel welcome.

I was so happy when he hired me. The group had Thelonious Monk on piano—later, Argonne Thornton [Sadik Hakim] took his place—and Idrees Sulieman [trumpet] and Gene Ramey [bass]. "What!" Sid always said, nostrils flaring, if somebody made a mistake. It was the funniest thing. He'd just glare at you with his eyes popping out. The man was so comical and beautiful; he never gave cats a bad time.

Big Sid covered all the bases as a player. I don't know exactly who he came from. But it seems to me he might have listened to Baby Dodds or Zutty Singleton or someone like that. He knew all the drummers; he had them down. But Sid used all he knew—his background—in his own way. He made some bridges—from Dixieland to swing to bebop.

AL CASEY: I was with him on 52nd Street. I had a trio at the Down Beat. The club would bring in different groups—Diz and Bird, Ben. Sid generally would work with his own little band.

Drummers idolized him. Max Roach used to come in all the time. It was because Sid knew exactly what he was doing. And he did it in his own way. His beat and what he felt about it, his way of putting in the right things when they were needed, made him special. Sid had a great soul.

How did Catlett view himself as a drummer? One of the only interviews available, with Robert Fletcher in the April, 1941 issue of *Music and Rhythm*, provides some valuable information.

SID CATLETT: Man, I'm no technician. I play what I feel and it usually comes out the way I want it. . . . I'm a drummer and that means

I spend a lot of time on my snare drum. You can get some mighty powerful effects with press rolls behind a band.

When asked about favorite drummers, he responded: Jo Jones and Buddy Rich. Both are technicians with powerful beats and a great deal of good taste. Gene [Krupa] has more stuff than any other drummer, but it's running away with him.

Advice to young drummers: work on your sense of time and your feeling for the beat. That's the important thing in drumming and without it all the technique in the world doesn't mean a thing.[43]

Whether he realized it or not, Catlett was an authority figure, particularly to young musicians.

ILLINOIS JACQUET: I was twenty-two in 1944 and involved with a film that has turned into an historical jazz picture. Big Sid, Lester Young, Jo Jones, Marlowe Morris, Barney Kessel, John Simmons, and I were on the Warner Brothers lot in Hollywood making *Jammin' the Blues*. Humphrey Bogart and Errol Flynn came by the set one day. Then director Billy Wilder visited us and asked, "Are you guys getting paid pretty good?" He wanted to know who was in charge and I said Sid Catlett. He was the oldest and certainly one of the most respected guys on the picture. Bogart spoke to him; he asked what was going on with the film. "Are you guys being treated right? he asked. He wanted to get an idea of what we were getting paid. I said we were getting $50 an hour. And he thought that was a disgrace. We didn't have no one to speak for us at Warner Brothers, just Sid Catlett. Bogart insisted we should be getting more money for this film. Sid spoke with him and Bogart suggested a strike. So Sid called a meeting on the sound stage and said we were going on strike. I followed his lead and so did the others, because we respected him so. And he took care of business. We got more money, with the help of Bogart.

The young drummers, in particular, hung around where Big Sid was playing because he set a great example.

MAX ROACH: What I learned from being around Sid, Hawk, people like Charlie Parker was. . . . "You don't join the throng until you write your own song." Like, stylistically, you don't deal with a person's style who has such a strong personality, like Sid or Baby Dodds or Chick Webb. What you should get from them is at least a measure of your own individuality, of who you are. You want to be as creative as they are—not to stylistically recreate. That's what I got from Lester—the fact that what he did was different from Hawk. You don't try to copy Sid Catlett's licks—that's not what you're after. . . . I didn't hear that much of Big Sid, except on records, apart from the little I heard on 52nd Street, but I was influenced by his kindness, his generosity.[44]

STAN LEVEY: I got to know Sid in 1945. I was with Dizzy; we were going to California for the first time. We took the train out of New York. In the little group were Dizzy, Charlie Parker, Ray Brown, Milt Jackson, Al Haig, and myself. In those days, you took the Twentieth Century Limited from New York to Chicago. Then you had a six-or eight-hour layover in the Windy City.

When we got off the train, Parker and I went to one of the hotels where the musicians hung out. We saw some people we knew and ran into Sid Catlett, who was working with Louis Armstrong at the Chicago Theater. Sid asked me to come over and catch a show. And I did.

I was really impressed with this big guy. He had a great touch and all the nuances that are possible on drums. He could play loud and very, very soft and everything in between. We hung out for quite a while in his dressing room between shows.

Sid was a pussycat. He knew I was quite young—only eighteen at the time. I told him what I was doing; we discussed the interest I had in music. That I was with Dizzy and happy to be there. He had a practice pad in the room and we began talking about how he did things. He showed me whatever I wanted to see.

The guy had a beautiful stick control. Without a lot of arm motion, he could go from high volume to nothing. He did this on the practice pad and during the show as well. All through the stage presentation, he gave every indication he knew exactly how to use the set and the cymbals. I was in awe of what he could do.

While we were together, Sid had a few drinks; he liked to nip at his scotch. At one point, he showed me some tricks involving the fingers. He said I would control the sticks better by snapping them up after each down stroke. "Use the bounce, the momentum of the down stroke," he insisted, "and flick the stick up after each down stroke." In other words, utilize the impetus of the down stroke to keep the sticks moving. The lesson was a big help to me.

You know he took my place on those Musicraft sides with Diz: "Shaw 'Nuff," "Lover Man," "Salt Peanuts," and "Hot

House." That May 1945 session showed what he was capable of doing. Remember, what Diz was playing back then was right up to the minute. And Sid dealt with it all. Listen to the records again. He was perfect.

CHARLI PERSIP: How about the melodic snare drum playing on those records with Diz? And then, of course, Big Sid was one of the first drummers to start with the bass drum accents, which Mr. Roach and Mr. Blakey took on to a great degree.

ED SHAUGHNESSY: I never got over his flexibility and ability to blend, most of all, to really play the music well. As I've said, I learned a great deal from Sidney, by watching and listening. I think he had the smoothest style of any drummer of that era and possibly since. Everything flowed. And that's aside from his great originality, inventiveness, and melodic quality. But he was unrelenting, remarkably steady, and always had great sympathy for the music, regardless of style.

When you hear a record he's on, you know it's Sid Catlett. He had a way of playing simple things that gave him a trademark. Even simple rim shot and bass drum combinations, maybe just two beats in a certain spot . . . . the way he did it was sort of his thing. He could take a press roll and do so many things with it . . . volume, colors. Very similar to the way Jo Jones also established a rather simple, spare style as a trademark.[45]

The war years were extremely fruitful for Sid Catlett. He became highly visible working with key big bands and small groups and appearing on many records. Winner of *Esquire*'s Gold Award in the drum category for 1944 and 1945, Catlett rose to preeminence among musicians and critics, though mass acceptance on a level with Krupa, Rich, and Jones still eluded him. Catlett played in a variety of settings, and, challenged by the diversity—the new music in particular—played better than ever before. It was clear that Big Sid could do just about anything that had to be done on drums.

Listen to him on the May 11, 1945, Musicraft sides with Dizzy Gillespie and Charlie Parker: "Shaw Nuff," "Salt Peanuts," "Lover Man," and "Hot House." His drumming anticipates the modern jazz drumming style generated by Kenny Clarke and Max Roach. He loosens up the feeling of the rhythm, while simultaneously bringing to it the discipline that makes the performance work. Though essentially a four-beat drummer who uses the bass drum as his primary time reference, he places accents—with his left hand and right foot and with his foot alone—in appropriate and unexpected places. He changes the feel and texture of his performances, depending on the music's demand. His ability to deal with lightning tempi particularly impressed young drummers.

VERNEL FOURNIER: "Salt Peanuts" was something! Big Sid played that sock cymbal solo. I mean that shook everybody up. We had been dealing with the sock cymbal. But we never played it at a tempo like that. And what he played was so clear.

The intricacy and linear quality of bebop, and the ultra-fast tempi called for, placed additional responsibility on the drummer. Unlike Dave Tough, Catlett was not intimidated by the challenge. He adapted early to bop, laying down time in his own way and filling the openings in the music with inspiring ideas. His talent and receptiveness to what was current made it possible for him to sound quite *contemporary*. Yet his identity remained intact; he was always Sid Catlett. Big Sid's freedom as an artist, and the confidence that permeates his work, steadied Bird, Dizzy, Al Haig, and Curly Russell. Yet even while reacting creatively to a 1940s avant-garde environment, he revealed in his solo on "Salt Peanuts" that, for all his visionary tendencies, he was a product of earlier forms of jazz, as well as military roots of drumming.

On the face of it, Catlett seemed to have most everything he wanted. He was a group leader, the drummer generally called on to make all kinds of jazz dates; he was appreciated by his peers. As Nellie Lutcher noted, he even got the opportunity to work and record with Duke Ellington in 1945, subbing for Sonny Greer, achieving a dream that had taken form in the 1930s. With Ellington, he recorded "Come To Baby Do" and "Tell You What I'm Gonna Do" on October 8, 1944, for Victor.

But by the end of the war, it was clear that popular music was going in new directions. Though Catlett had helped to alter jazz, making it more modern, he was of an older generation. Like other pioneers who paved the way for the new jazz, notably Roy Eldridge and Coleman Hawkins, he gave way to the children he had helped develop: younger drummers like Max Roach, Kenny Clarke, Shelly Manne, Stan Levey, Art Blakey, Ed Shaughnessy, and Irv Kluger. Indeed, bop took the attention of many jazz fans, although the press exaggerated the conflict between the modernists and those who favored earlier jazz.

Catlett, Hawkins, Eldridge, and others were losing ground. The situation did not become terribly apparent until the late 1940s, but already certain musicians were realizing the times had changed. Eldridge, in fact, went to Europe to clear his mind and to determine where he would ultimately fit in. He realized being himself was the only answer. The others eventually came to the same conclusion.

Meanwhile instrumental music, though still prominent, was no longer at its height. Singers had begun to replace it for several reasons.

JOAN SWALLOW REITER: We were crossing several watersheds in the entertainment world. Television was about to take over the American living room. . . . The big bands were breaking up: as early as 1946, eight bands called it quits within a few weeks of each other. On records, singers were taking the place of bands, and the industry as a whole was adjusting to the introduction, in 1948, of the long-playing record.[46]

James Caesar Petrillo, president of the American Federation of Musicians, had more than a little to do with changing the situation in favor of the singers. He called a strike against the record industry in 1942. He may have wanted to benefit the musicians. But that is not how it turned out.

GEORGE SIMON: His argument was simple but specious. If the record companies couldn't devise some system whereby musicians were paid for the use of their recordings on radio programs and in juke boxes, then he wouldn't let them record at all.

For more than a year no major company made any records at all with instrumentalists. They did record singers, usually with choral backgrounds.[47]

Petrillo got what he wanted after two years: a royalty to the union for all records released. But by that time things had changed, despite the release by independent, small record companies of small band jazz sides during the strike of the majors. America wanted to hear the words.

With the advent of modern jazz, the rise of the singers, and, in New York, at least, the demise of 52nd Street as a center for jazz, musicians like Catlett began to lose out. Work became less plentiful; more and more, the older players had to work with contemporaries or even musicians older than they.

Catlett did not really feel the change until 1949, when health problems forced him out of the Louis Armstrong All-Stars, a band of the drummer's contemporaries. From 1945 until 1947, when he joined the All-Stars, he worked steadily, taking some club dates, playing with his small band and briefly leading his own band. During this period, Catlett may not have been "in," but his playing remained excellent.

BILLY BAUER: Dave Tough kept saying, "You gotta listen to this Big Sid guy!" Tell you about Sid: he had a terrific act. The whole band used to leave the stand and he'd solo. We were on tour, playing these summer ballrooms. I guess it was sometime in the mid-1940s. Charlie Ventura, the tenor man who had just come off the Gene Krupa band, was another of the musicians who was on this thing with us.

Well, one night, we had a couple of thousand people out there. And Sid kept them spellbound, going from soft to loud, building, building, building this solo. It was something! He didn't get his thing together like that every night. But he always pleased his audience.

When Catlett joined Louis Armstrong's small band in 1947, he felt very much at home with his old friend and employer. It was a traditional band, showcasing older, mainstream star players, with the exception of a 24-year-old bassist Arvell Shaw. The rapport and chemistry among the players was exceptional. With Satchmo up front, Dick Cary then Earl Hines at the piano, Barney Bigard playing clarinet, and Jack Teagarden on trombone, how bad could it be?

Catlett knew his way around the music and the musicians. Furnishing a lively pulse and tying all the elements together, Catlett helped make the band a happy band. Tradition was in the forefront, but the music never sounded old. The players, with Catlett as the primary stimulus, kept it alive and interesting.

ARVELL SHAW: One of the key things I picked up from Sid was the importance of the drummer and the bass player working as one man. I came to realize that if the drummer's bass drum—his foot—and the bass sound didn't blend, the band was in trouble. Sid was a master at tying in with the bass. He had strength and steadiness; it was easy to connect up with him.

His drumming was melodic. He carefully tuned his snare, tom-toms, and bass drum a third apart. When he would get on those tom-toms with the mallets, he played melodies. He knew enough about rudiments to do what he wanted—to build a climax in his solos.

Did you know that Sid kept his fingernails long? Each one was an inch or an inch and a half long. He'd play on the drums with his fingernails, in combination with a brush. And he'd get

Big Sid circa 1948, again with Louis Armstrong, his frequent employer.
Courtesy of Modern Drummer Publications, Inc.

things going that were unbelievably interesting. I've never seen anyone do that since.

As a storyteller, Sid had few parallels. Bigard was good; Earl Hines could be hilarious. But Sid developed storytelling into an art. He was always breaking up Louis. Sid loved Louis. He called him "Dip," short for "Dippermouth." There was a lot of mutual respect and strong feeling between them.

Did you know flying was not Sid's thing? When we went to France for the first Nice Festival, he and Earl Hines walked the aisle of the plane from New York to Paris. Sid told the stewardess, "Every time I walk by, I want a double scotch, going and coming." When we landed, he was stone sober. That's how frightened he was.

I got so used to playing with Sid that when he left in 1949, the whole bottom dropped out. His time was so good; it was *there*. He had a completely different conception of drums—so melodic and creative. Sid made my job with Louis a pleasure and he added more than a little to Pops' music.

A front-page story in *Down Beat*'s May 20, 1949, issue noted that Catlett had left the Armstrong All-Stars on doctor's orders. He had become seriously ill with heart and kidney trouble just before the band opened at Chicago's Blue Note. Catlett convalesced at his father's home in Chicago. He hoped that he could return to the band.

This never happened. The band's travel schedule would have been too taxing for him. Replaced by Red Saunders, then by former Lionel Hampton drummer George Jenkins, and finally by Cozy Cole, Catlett spent the rest of his life playing, hanging out, and trying to take care of himself.

GEORGE HOEFER: He was determined not to let his ailments break his spirit. In a little more than a month after his collapse, he was in New York City playing with Eddie Condon's NBC-TV orchestra and recording with them for Atlantic.[48]

With the exception of a regular job at Chicago's Jazz Limited, lasting over two years, Catlett free-lanced after leaving Armstrong, often in New York or Boston.

RUBY BRAFF: I worked with him in Boston. Listen to the records he made with Louis. Then compare them to the things Louis cut with other drummers. You can hear a tremendous difference. Sid understood music and musicians.

GEORGE WEIN: Until the end, Sid was one of the great personalities of the drums. Like Jo Jones, he had the ability to hit *anything* and swing. When he worked Storyville, my club in Boston, with Bob Wilber in 1950, I really came to love his solos. As a climax to a solo, he'd get into the press roll on the snare drum and bring the volume way up, uplifting the whole room, and then bring it down until you could hear a pin drop. We'd stand on the chairs to see him. Slowly but surely he would bring the volume down. It was uncanny. The tension, the feeling of excitement in the room, it built until Sid brought the solo to its climax.

When you sat in, as I love to do, you never had to think of the rhythm when Sid was at the drums. He'd size you up in a minute and know what to do with you. The engagement with Wilber [soprano saxophone and clarinet], Red Richards [piano], Sidney De Paris [trumpet], John Field [bass], and Sid on drums was memorable. Sid was totally natural, warm, a master at picking tempos. He had to be the most supportive drummer I've ever heard.

BOB WILBER: I had an eight-week education in jazz rhythm in 1950 at Storyville. I was fortunate enough to be able to hire Sid Catlett. It was a great experience because Sid was such a great accompanist. He had the ability to play personally and very knowingly and sensitively behind each player.

JACK EGAN: I saw him just a few weeks before he died at Jazz Limited in Chicago. The Krupa band was playing on the South Side; I was working for Gene in those days. Gene wanted to go down to Jazz Limited to dig Sid but couldn't get away from a bunch of friends. He really was broken up when he heard about Sid's death. It was so unexpected; Gene and I thought there would be so many other opportunities to spend time listening to and talking to Sid.

Sid always seemed to be around. When I was Tommy Dorsey's advance man in the early 1940s, Sid used to come down to the Astor Hotel here in New York and sit in with the Dorsey band during the afternoon sessions. He always turned up where there was good music. When Jay McShann opened at the Savoy uptown in 1941, with Charlie Parker on alto, and word got out how terrific Parker was, who do you think was one of the first to sit in with McShann? Sid Catlett, of course.

For all the praise he received, Sid Catlett was both underrated and somewhat misunderstood by all but the cognoscenti. Not a virtuoso who could execute ideas and patterns with the speed and ease and flair of Webb, Rich, and Krupa, he emphasized musicality while making the most of his technical resources. He made you *think* and *feel* and ultimately *realize* something important was being said. He played simply, directly, often quite subtly, wasting little or no time on rhetoric.

Listen to "Steak Face" and "Boff, Boff" (better known as "Mop, Mop") on MCA's *Satchmo At Symphony Hall,* a live concert by Louis Armstrong and his All-Stars from 1947. Catlett, in his solos, is deeply musical, compressing and linking his ideas so that they relate directly to the rest of the music.

In a band, large or small, he functions as a soloist much as he does as an ensemble player, reminding one of a fine horn player who strengthens the composition as a whole. Catlett on record is the selfless drummer helping colleagues to get their thoughts out, while bringing to the music his own identity and point of view. When these two elements—selflessness and individuality—meld and are in balance, the best jazz music is made.

For a clear view of Catlett and the creative process, try the two takes of "46 West 52" on *Chu Berry—A Giant of the Tenor Sax*, a Commodore collection from 1938 with tenor saxophonist Chu Berry and trumpeter Roy Eldridge. The alternate take, never released before being placed in this LP, obviously was the first to be recorded. It reveals Catlett developing a set of ideas during a half-chorus solo. The released take, initially marketed by Commodore so many years ago, contains the final product of this thinking—a well-articulated, seamless flow of musical thoughts that connect directly to the music. Surprisingly, considering the period in which it was recorded, there is little that is military about the solo; it unfolds much as good conversation does, staying close to the basic subject, developing sufficiently to provoke your interest and remains in mind long after it's over.

Sid's death at forty-one on March 25, 1951, in Chicago was a major blow to the music community.

BUDDY RICH:　When Sid Catlett split, there was nobody to take his place.

BARRY ULANOV:　Whether he was playing with a trio or a big band, he held it together magnificently with a strong, firm beat. People argue that a man's personality has little to do with his musical ability, but it must be true that Big Sidney's huge frame and his forceful personality helped immeasurably in his task of making a whole group of men sound like one rhythmically. Jazz has known few drummers, and probably will not get to know many more drummers as great as Big Sid Catlett.[49]

The funeral took place on March 30 in the Brown Undertaking Chapel at 3834 Indiana in Chicago. Muggsy Spanier, Miff Mole, Truck Parham, Darnell Howard, Stuff Smith, all players from Catlett's generation, were there to say goodbye. Louis Armstrong and the All-Stars sent a massive floral piece in the shape of a drum. Cab Calloway was represented by flowers and a papier-mâché drum. Flowers also came from Miff Mole, Don Redman, and the Reinhardts, owners of Jazz Limited. There were twenty floral wreaths in all.

HERMAN KOGAN: The preacher said, "Sid Catlett had the impulse of music in him," but Muggsy Spanier, the horn man, put it neater and softer: "Big Sid was a real sensitive guy, had a lot of feelin' about things."

This was a solemn affair with a lady singer offering "When I Come to the End of My Way" and "Shelter Me, Savior in the Heaven of Rest," and Joe Williams singing "My Buddy."

And then the organist played "Goin' Home" and the people walked past the casket and a few murmured, "Well, so long, son," and in the drizzling rain everyone got into the black cars and drove out to Burr Oaks Cemetery.[50]

ARVELL SHAW: No one had in mind that Sid would die. I'll never forget: we left the hotel and got on the bus to go to the job. Louis said, "Big Sid died." He didn't say another word; he really was feeling it. The gig that night was the quietest we ever made. Losing Sid was a shock to everybody.

Decades later, the loss of Sidney Catlett is still felt deeply by those who knew him or admired his way of playing drums. When someone truly important to the music goes, the space cannot be filled.

Dave Tough
(1908-1948)

"In my view, he was a Louis Armstrong, a Bix Beiderbecke, a James P. Johnson. A true giant!"

—*BUD FREEMAN*

Dave Tough practicing between sets in the basement of Eddie Condon's club in New York City. The year: 1946. © William P. Gottlieb.

Dave Tough celebrated the pulse of life, bringing to it the dimensions and flexibility, the flow and inner animation of *music*. A pure, thoroughly unselfish band player, whether in a small or large ensemble, he was supportive in the best sense of the word.

But Tough's talents could be deceptive, particularly if one wasn't attuned to a rhythm player who gave of himself for the ultimate benefit of all. With the selflessness of a deeply dedicated clergyman, Tough made his point through others. Avoiding center stage, rarely if ever soloing or intruding himself on his musical colleagues, he followed this course his entire career.

A drummer who plays this sort of role is admired but not completely understood. Since the emergence of the Godlike Louis Armstrong in the 1920s and the increasing emphasis on the soloist, almost everyone in jazz has wanted a share of the spotlight. Because of this, because jazz is at least partially show business, and because people by their very nature are often concerned with "me, me, me," Tough was a notable exception to the rule.

For a long time, he was the treasure of musicians and music-business insiders. Ultimately, however, he had it both ways. He was admired by musicians and those outside the inner circle. A poll-winner and drum star in the latter years of his short life, he made his approach work most potently with the Woody Herman First Herd of 1944–45. Tough drove the assemblage to previously unattainable heights. After years as an underground celebrity, the drummer finally found his way to the public.

Tough made no compromises. An unconventional player almost entirely lacking in technique, he had no interest in showmanship. Musicality, pulsation, and the beauty of highly integrated ensemble performance were his concerns. Fans found it easier to cement a link with drummers like Webb, Krupa, Rich, Jones, and Sidney Catlett, whose showmanship and technical gifts were very appealing. Things haven't changed too radically since then.

Tough transcended convention. That a drummer could generate such force and do everything right without the benefit of any sort of real facility bordered on the incomprehensible. A drummer with rare gifts for understanding and expressing rhythm and executing what was essential, Tough went to the root of the music. He did so in a manner particular to him alone.

"If a musician, spinning daydreams, conjured up a perfect drummer, the vision undoubtedly would look very much like Dave Tough."[1]

—FRANK STACY

"A giant rhythm player! With the least amount of "chops," Dave inspired a whole, big screamin' band with his subtleties and strong feeling for time. And he was probably one of the most gentle, the kindest, one of the grooviest cats you'd ever want to know."

—WOODY HERMAN

"Dave was the single most musical drummer that I've ever known. When I say musical, I'm talking about sensibilities—his musical sensibilities—which of course were honed by his literary and aesthetic sense of everything in general. My thesis is the more you know about everything, the better you will be."

—ARTIE SHAW

"He was the most imaginative drummer we ever had in the business. Everything the man hit was musical. If he tapped on the floor, it was musical.[2]

—LIONEL HAMPTON

"Dave would lay down such a beat you'd go out of your mind."

—JIMMY MCPARTLAND

"He never made an irritating sound."

—JOHNNY MINCE

"Dave's time was so perfect that your fingers flowed over your horn. He did it for you."

—MAX KAMINSKY

"He was a natural musician who did things effortlessly, and that always made you comfortable.[3]

—JOE BUSHKIN

"His energy force was so strong that you'd think there was a 400-pound guy sitting up there."

—BUDDY RICH

"Dave Tough didn't look as if he was doing anything. But that was very deluding."

—ART FARMER

"It's a shame that Dave Tough wasn't born the son of a sanctified preacher; there's a kind of soulfulness within him."[4]

—DIZZY GILLESPIE

"Tough was the gentlest, the subtlest of men and musicians. Like Dodds, never loud, like Webb never well, Dave was tough only in the demands he made on himself."[5]

—JOHN LUCAS

"Don't forget Dave Tough. Tough was like a clock. Stick him under a band and he'd make everybody play."[6]

—BABY DODDS

"One of the two or three greatest drummers of all time. A sad guy, such a sad little guy."

—DAVE DEXTER

MEMORIES

Saturday afternoon at the Paramount Theater in New York City. The year: 1945. The place was crowded for that time of day. The word was out about Woody Herman's First Herd. George Simon's review of the band in Metronome *was an exclamation point. Frank Stacy was equally enthusiastic in* Down Beat. *The other trades and local papers sensed Woody had a winner.*

A friend and I slid into seats in the orchestra section of the theater as the stage show was about to begin. The theater grew dark. A bluish light hit the rising stage as the Herman band rose out of the pit, playing Woody's familiar theme, "Blue Flame." When the sixteen-piecer hit stage level, it exploded into "Apple Honey" and immediately displayed great

*ensemble power as it dashed through this up-tempo "head" arrange-
ment. My eyes were on the little drummer.*

*Musicians around town insisted he was the heartbeat, the energy be-
hind the band. He went about his business with little of the grace of Krupa
and Jones, and none of the fireworks of Rich. But the excitement built as
Tough, without physically giving the impression of strength, manipulated
the band much as an animal trainer would a beautiful, hard-to-control
beast, making it respond to him. He cracked the whip under the ensemble
and brass passages, adding juice and muscle to the pulse and accents.
Each soloist got individual treatment—a stroke here, an accent there, a fill
further on, all perfectly placed. He moved the band from one plateau to
another, higher and higher. By the time the band was about to go into the
final segment, the audience had been totally captured. There was a point
during the last section when it felt as if the band would take us through
the roof. Trumpeter Pete Candoli was screaming above this nuclear musical explosion—the band in full voice and the pulse making the theater
feel like the inside of a drum. Tough added his little closing signature—
four rapid strokes on the bass drum—and it was over.*

*I couldn't figure out what he had done. He had been in the fore-
ground only during a four-bar break—accompaniment and a capper to
the Candoli exclamations, at the top of the excitement. Otherwise his
was the least self-serving performance I had ever witnessed. I turned to
my friend. "He has no chops. How'd he do it? What happened?" He
smiled, not quite as puzzled as I. "It might not have seemed like much,"
he said. "But whatever he did sure lit a fire under that band!"*

*The show went on. There were a number of acts—a comedian, a
dancer. Woody sang a few things; the band played another instrumental.
But that opener remained with me, as did the questions it provoked.
Could a drummer do all that while seeming to do very little? How could
he dominate a band with that kind of power? The questions seem to
answer themselves as I walked out of the theater and encountered the
early-evening Broadway cacophony: This little guy had his own way.*

ARTHUR TAYLOR: I think Dave Tough played more than any white
drummer I ever heard. I admired him very much. He was one of
my favorites. Every time Woody came to the Paramount, I used
to come downtown and see him. I was lucky that my father
started taking me out when I was young. It was a great thing to
see those performers. They weren't bullshitting. These people
really were doing their stuff. They knew how. They were show
business people. When I look at the business now, compared to
then, it's like baby stuff, you know. A bunch of little girls trying
to do it. They're still in the playground, you dig? Yeah! Dave
Tough. He could *play!*

Tough came in the game early and instinctively realized—with some help from idols like Baby Dodds—what had to be done to make jazz music a living thing. He understood that styles may change, but the elements central to the music's strength and identity remain relatively unaffected. He learned that a little can be a lot—and it ain't what you do, it's the way that you do it. All the technique in the world is no substitute for *taste* and *talent*.

JIM CHAPIN: Some of the most revered players in history could hardly execute at all in the scholastic rudimental sense. What they did to an extraordinary degree was relate intimately to the musical situation at hand, and to comment with their instruments in a unique and individual manner. This is a far more effective means of becoming indispensable than just striving to be a drum athlete.

Who was Dave Tough? It is truly difficult to say. Even he never really knew. He had flashes of self-understanding. Just as frequently, however, he was exasperated with his life and inability to be everything he envisioned for himself. The Dave Tough story is sad and often depressing, for although he found self-realization as a musician, he never resolved his difficulties.

His story is somewhat analogous to that of Bix Beiderbecke. They both came from the same generation, had some of the same problems, and died comparatively young. Tough's intimates hoped he could conquer his demons. He was so bright, they all say, so well read, so knowledgeable.

At the beginning it all seemed quite promising for Dave Tough. Jazz was new in the 1920s. It reached out and caught hold of him and his friends in and around Chicago, offering boundless possibilities. Jazz was a highly appropriate answer for these young people and, indeed, for a whole generation searching for identity in a suddenly liberated decade.

Like many of the early white devotees of jazz, Tough came from a financially comfortable family. He was born in 1908 and raised in Oak Park, Illinois, an affluent suburb of Chicago. Like the Beiderbeckes of Davenport, Iowa, the Toughs in Oak Park never really understood or accepted their son's interest in jazz.

Young Dave was completely fascinated with the music, and drumming seemed the best means of being a central part of this marvelous new thing. Bud Freeman, Jimmy and Dick McPartland, Frank Teschmaker, Jim Lanigan, and Dave North—the "Austin High Gang"—and other aspiring musicians Dave knew well—including Eddie Condon, Gene Krupa, Benny Goodman, Mezz Mezzrow, George

Wettling, Joe Sullivan, Floyd O'Brien, and Muggsy Spanier—became captives of this exotic import from New Orleans, and its best and most influential players.

The climate of the period had much to do with the attraction of young musicians to jazz. Prohibition, the new freedom in several areas (behavior, attitudes, dress, sex, art), the turning away from the horrors of war and America's inhibited past, all had more than a little to do with it. Jazz itself was a key factor in the 1920s. It boldly defined and clearly underlined what was being felt and thought about. Almost more than anything else, it set the feeling of the period. The music's relevant tone and pulse spoke to these young men and changed their lives.

BUD FREEMAN: Dave started playing drums as a Boy Scout. He was an Eagle Scout and a fantastic drummer at twelve. Three years later, in 1923, he began playing professionally. When we were quite young, we had a little intellectual cult, if you'll forgive the rather smug descriptive. All of us were somewhat ambivalent; we didn't know if we wanted to be writers, poets, or musicians. We went into jazz because it was a new sound and because it really got to us. As for being professional players: we didn't think about that much at first. Jazz was a labor of love. Money didn't enter into it.

Most of the Austin High group didn't have to work. We all lived at home and went to school. We dressed well and were deeply into our artistic interests. Our parents thought we were nuts.

There is a wonderful story about that. We lived in a very nice community in Austin out near Oak Park. Dave was almost a neighbor; he lived about a mile away. Anyway, my brother Arnie, who has enjoyed great success as an actor, was readying himself for the profession. He was sixteen. I had musical aspirations and was in the process of preparing myself to be a jazz performer. This was in 1924. I remember because I had recently turned eighteen.

People in the suburb had meetings about us. They called my father and said: "Mr. Freeman, why don't you have your boys *do something!* Why don't they go to school? Why don't they work? My father would say: "You don't understand. My boys are different. They're crazy, but you'll hear of them someday."

After my father had been brainwashed by the community for several months, he dared to come into our bedroom one morning about 7:30. That was a cardinal sin because my brother and I and Dave and a few others had been out all night listening to King Oliver and Louis Armstrong at the Lincoln Gardens in Chicago.

We had gotten home at 6:30 A.M. I pretended to be asleep when my father came into the room. He shook my brother and got him up. "You're going out into the world and get jobs. You're going to live as normal people do," he said, angrily. Whereupon my brother responded, "Sir, how dare you wake us up before the weekend?"

I must admit we were crazy as hell and rebellious. But we didn't have a pernicious bone in our bodies. We were just guys who were crazy about art and jazz music. Dave was our intellectual leader. He brought us to the black man and to the black man's music. He got around town and saw and heard everyone, even though he was just a kid.

You've got to remember the situation in those years. There was terrible prejudice and separation of the races. Blacks, particularly poor blacks, could live only in this one section of Chicago, on the South Side. And they were allowed none of the privileges that we whites had. We crossed the line and went out and became friends with black people, particularly the musicians, and found them to be beautiful.

Dave was the first to assimilate the music and make it his own. Dave and Bix taught us so much. They introduced us to King Oliver and Louis Armstrong and Bessie Smith and Ethel Waters and Jimmie Noone and Earl Hines. I can't tell you how much I was influenced by Dave.

We were into everything black people did. The most creative black musicians and entertainers inspired us: the black horn players, the black pianists, the black drummers, the black singers, the black dancers. Dancing was a very, very big thing. To this day, there have been few drummers, other than Dave and one or two or three other gifted rhythm men, who had the wonderful beat that the great black dancers had.

JO JONES: Without Dave Tough, you would never have heard none of the musicians that have got these reputations out here that were supposed to have been so great in Chicago. Davey Tough dared to go over to the South Side and go back and show the guys what he had learned from the black musicians.[7]

BUD FREEMAN: Even as a young kid, Dave had something very special. He made it easy for those who worked with him. He practically played your instrument for you. When I performed with other drummers, my fingers would lock up because these guys didn't keep good time. Dave's beat was so powerful that my fingers flew over the horn.

Dave was a little beyond being a drummer. That was a hell

of a deep mind working there. I don't think an ordinary man could play that well. He was just incredible. So strong yet so subtle. He sounded like another note in the band.

Eddie Condon, one of Tough's oldest friends, vividly remembered the first time he played with the little drummer.

EDDIE CONDON: I worked on a date at Northwestern University in Evanston, just over the line from Chicago. A gaunt, hollow-looking kid came in, dragging drums. He said his name was Dave Tough; he set up the drums and I wondered where he would find the strength to hit them. He was behind me when we started our first number; what he did to the drums nearly drove me through the opposite wall. He was possessed.[8]

At the very outset of Tough's journey into jazz, there was difficulty at home. As he and Condon were having a bit of refreshment between sets that first time they worked together, the drummer agonized: "My family doesn't understand what I'm doing. I can't get a job with a big band because they don't play this stuff. I must be crazy to keep playing it, but I do."

Condon acknowledged Tough's family problems and attributed them to his background, the drummer having been brought up in Oak Park, "the richest village in the world."

Tough's difficulties making peace with his family had no effect on his playing. His drumming made fans of many of his friends and colleagues. Gene Krupa frequently told me how much he looked up to Tough, insisting Tough knew what had to be done on the instrument, accomplished it in an original, nonintrusive manner, and probed the soul of the music.

MEZZ MEZZROW: Dave Tough was my boy. He was a little bit of a guy, no chubbier than a dime and lean as hard times, with a mop of dark hair, high cheekbones, and a nose ground fine as a razor blade, and he popped with spirit till he couldn't sit still. It always hit me to see that keyed-up peanut crawl behind the drums, looking like a mouse huddled behind an elephant, and cut loose with the solid rhythms he had picked up from the great colored drummers.[9]

JIMMY MCPARTLAND: Davey just loved to play. We all did. We couldn't wait to get to work. The reason they called us the Austin High Gang? We played a fraternity dance one night and some guys said we stank. So I started punchin'; my brother, too. So after that happened a few times, they'd say you don't fool with those guys, man; they're a *gang*. We got respect that way. They didn't know what we were playing', anyway.

We all hung out together and spent a lot of time listening to the black musicians and singers. The group included Dave, my brother Rich, Jim Lanigan (my brother-in-law), Bud Freeman, and Tesch [Frank Teschmaker]. Generally we'd go to the Lincoln Gardens, later the Sunset, both on the South Side of Chicago. Just kids, in 1923 and 1924. We thought Oliver and Louis and Lil Hardin and Baby and Johnny Dodds were just wonderful. My God! How could you help but love 'em? And they liked us. They'd spend time at our table and talk because they could see we were so enthused about them and their music.

Man, Louis loved Dave. Louis used to come over a couple of times a week when the gang had a gig for a period of time, like at the White City Ballroom on the South Side, and just stand in back of the bandstand and listen.

How did Dave play? How did he sound? Well, he had a relentless beat. He'd start off nice and smooth and easy and he would build. He'd never get unnecessarily loud. And the beats he played were so swinging and fitting. The man had such drive. We all played with drive back then in Chicago. But Davey was our foundation. His talent, his beats, his concern for the band swinging overshadowed any personal flamboyance. You know what I mean?

You know Davey could read! When we would rehearse classical things with our band, there were ritards, different time signatures. And Davey cut his parts without much trouble. He had studied with Ed Straight, I believe it was, and learned a variety of "legit" things from him.

Instinctively Davey knew what his job was. The great black drummers like Baby Dodds and Jimmy Bertrand and others made it unmistakably clear what had to happen when a drummer performed. Keeping time was the thing. That's just what Davey did. He kept things the way they should be; he didn't go off on tangents like some guys do. They play solos while you're trying to create something. Davey knew you had to lay down a good solid beat so the guys up front could improvise.

Over the years, he just got better and better. He was great except when he started to drink. I guess we all drank; it was part of the lifestyle. It was very hip back in the Twenties to have a bottle of bathtub gin on your hip. But Davey couldn't really take it. He'd get sick as hell and knocked out and we'd have to carry him home.

But when Davey was sober, forget it. There was nobody like him. I've felt that way since we first worked together at socials and things at the Columbia Park Refectory in Chicago.

Music and the artist's life took precedence over school: Tough never graduated from Oak Park High School. He went to Lewis Institute, a prep school in the Chicago area, which he described as a place "for two kinds of people—those who can't go to the best schools and those who get thrown out of them."

WHITNEY BALLIETT: Tough was already, as Art Hodes put it, "a runner-around;" he was also two people—the hard-drinking drummer and bohemian, who read voraciously, did some painting and drawing, took language and literature courses at the Lewis Institute, and hung out at a night club called The Green Mask, where he accompanied readings by such as Max Bodenheim, Langston Hughes, and Kenneth Rexroth.[10]

Tough listened and evaluated what he heard from others. Then he translated these ideas into terms relative to the then-emerging Chicago jazz style.

Tough based his conception on what he derived from the best of the black drummers, Baby Dodds in particular. On his early recordings with Red Nichols and others, and even later in the mid-1930s with Tommy Dorsey, you hear suggestions of Dodds in his work. His syncopated playing on the rims of the snare drum and bass drum, the bits of color he extracted by using one element of the set against another, his marvelously creative cymbal playing, were all reminiscent of Dodds. But somehow it was always Dave Tough.

BUD FREEMAN: Baby Dodds was the key influence on Dave because he was so far ahead. None of the New Orleans drummers had Baby's talent. Later, you know, Dave went far beyond Baby Dodds, eventually getting into modern music after World War II.

How Dave was as a person affected his playing and made it more complete. Generous, kind, very intelligent, he never was sentimental. If he did something for you, he wouldn't let you know about it. He couldn't bear obvious things or stupidity or bad humor. But he wasn't unkind about any of these things unless he was drunk. If he was, he might make a nasty remark to the stupid person who told the tasteless joke.

But what I always remember about Dave has little to do with his drinking. He was a very literary person, with expansive interests. That's what had the impact on me. He had a way of looking at things that was helpful to many of us. An example? Dave and I went to take in a Cézanne exhibit in Chicago—we were just kids. And I said to Dave, "Gee, I wish I could say something about this magnificent work." And Dave looked directly at me and said, "That's the best thing you'll ever say about it." In other words, all this bullshit that critics have been getting away with for years has nothing to do with how an artist thinks.

We concluded that had Cézanne known that he was going to be categorized—called a French Impressionist, an Abstract Impressionist—he would have hated the idea. It's the same thing with really good jazz musicians. You can't say to a jazz performer, whose talent is worth anything, that he plays avant-garde, or that he plays Dixieland, or that he is modern or a proponent of the Chicago style. A substantial musician will say, "I just play."

Because of his wide-ranging cultural interests and need for new experiences, nineteen-year-old Tough accepted an offer to play in Europe in the summer of 1927. Banjo player George Carhart, a jazz promoter, assembled a seven-piece band, including Tough, clarinetist Danny Polo, and pianist Jack O'Brien. The band played in Belgium and Germany, where it recorded on the Tri-Ergon label. Tough also free-lanced in France, mostly in Nice and Paris.

His playing had a strong effect on musicians in Europe, particularly drummers trying to find their way into the new music.

LEO VAUCHANT: I never heard a drummer as good as Dave. Tough was way ahead of all the other drummers. He wasn't the first to play four to the bar. I was. I was doing it in 1918. . . . But Dave was the first to complement the soloist's rhythmic ideas. He kept a marvelous beat and he had this wonderful ear so he'd pick up the rhythmic ideas in a solo and complement them on the drums.[11]

BERT MARSHALL: I wanted to get the swing of jazz on the drums, but although I could feel it, I couldn't play it. So after [the E. E. Thompson band] left the Abbaye Thélème, there was a white band which came to Paris—I can't remember their name. They used to go to a café after playing. And this boy used to get on the drums [most probably Dave Tough]. So I used to watch this guy doing this, and slowly I began to get it.[12]

But the propulsion of Tough's work, the strength of his beat didn't always have a positive effect. When he played in Nice for a tea dance at the Negresco Hotel, he and the band were fired on the spot. Saxophonist Spencer Clark remembers:

SPENCER CLARK: Dave was really driving the band along, the gigolos were swinging the old ladies around and everybody was tapping their feet. Less than halfway through the number, the manager came down and fired us.[13]

Four beats to the bar, briskly and potently played, obviously was not what the international set wanted.

Whatever the response to his drumming, Tough was very much in his element in the Paris of the 1920s. The cultural center of the world, Paris drew many of America's leading writers and musicians. The city's intensely creative atmosphere and the respect artists of all kinds received made it the place to be.

Tough associated with the leading lights in the arts like F. Scott Fitzgerald and Fujita, the highly-esteemed Japanese artist. Dave also became involved with England's Prince of Wales, who fancied himself a drummer.

BUD FREEMAN: F. Scott Fitzgerald was fascinated with Dave's brilliant mind, and on many occasions he invited Dave to meet his literary friends and Dave always declined. . . . I hadn't seen him in a few years and upon seeing him in Paris for the first time [1929], he asked me how I liked Ernest Hemingway. When I confessed that I had not read the book [*The Sun Also Rises*], he was shocked, and didn't speak to me for about ten minutes. How could I, his best friend, not have read Hemingway?[14]

Tough returned to America in March 1929, playing on the S.S. Ile De France. He went back to Paris almost immediately, only to turn around and come back in May. Working briefly with Red Nichols and Benny Goodman, he ultimately made his way back to Chicago and entered a period dominated by alcohol. Music became secondary; he played infrequently for several years. Until he joined Tommy Dorsey in 1936, his life was enveloped in darkness.

RICHARD HARRISON: Poor man had to fight the bottle all the time. The situation was ruinous. But sometimes there was humor in it. In Chicago, Dave went to his favorite barbershop. He had a small bottle of whiskey in his pocket. He and the barber got to talking and drinking. About an hour later, Dave emerged from the shop with his hair cut on one side but not on the other.

By 1935, Tough was back in New York. He dropped by clubs on 52nd Street and sometimes sat in. Those who knew him during this period say he was not terribly confident about himself and his playing. His drinking remained a problem.

CARMEN MASTREN: When I went with Tommy Dorsey, Dave had just joined the band. He traveled with us on the band bus for a couple of months without playing. He looked pretty haggard, his hair hanging over his collar; he was a bit of a wreck. Dave had to prove to Tommy that he could stay sober. And he did. That's the way he got on the band.

I think it was Bud Freeman who got Dave the job. Tommy didn't like the drummers he was using and Bud probably said, "Look, this guy is fantastic. Give him a try!" As it turned out, Tommy loved Dave; it's too bad he's not around to tell you. But one thing is for sure, it was a difficult thing for Dave to stay off the sauce.

You have to understand that Dave really was two people. Drunk—he generally was a mess, completely out of it. Sober—he was one of the most intelligent, witty guys; he had that dry sense of humor. And he was always reading. The only times he wasn't trying to learn things through books was when we were on the stand playing or when he drank.

All it took in Dave's case was a few beers. And the bender would start. You know, he couldn't really tolerate drink the way a number of other guys could. He would get sick and pass out. But he kept on anyway. He had some problems. I never got to the bottom of his difficulties, but I feel they stemmed from an early period in his life. From the Chicago days. He seldom got into it, though we spent a lot of time together. For a while, Bud, Davey, and I shared a suite of rooms in the Forrest Hotel, off Broadway. Cost us each seven bucks a week.

We had one really hellish experience with Dave. The band had a vacation; this was in 1937 or 1938, probably '38. Most of the guys went to Havana. My wife and I, Davey, and Casey [Majors, Tough's girlfriend] decided to take a trip to Bermuda. Because Casey was black and there was so much prejudice, we got her on board by saying she was my wife's nurse. Well, two days out, forget it! Dave began drinking. He disappeared. We thought he had fallen overboard. We called in the captain and the ship was searched. After a while, we found him. Dave was in a spot on a distant part of the vessel where he could quietly get very loaded.

I had promised Tommy that I'd get Dave back to New York in good shape for our opening at the Paramount. When we did return for the engagement, Dave didn't last too long. His drinking had become constant. Of course he returned to the band a couple of times. But as I said, it was touch and go.

When in control, Dave was an unbelievable player; he had great time; he knew how to shape an arrangement, how to back soloists and remain out of the way. *He made you play!* But he was very quiet about it all. Even when we complimented him, he seldom said anything. He didn't play drums to impress anyone, you know what I mean? As for solos, he hated them. But that didn't matter. When he played with the band; he had power and taste and the ability to do the right thing in the right spot. But when he got down and into his problems and started drinking, all that was lost.

JOHNNY MINCE: He had problems with his folks. They didn't want him to be a drummer; they hoped he'd be something special. They didn't realize he *was* very special. They almost disowned him because he continued in the music business. Davey, himself, had split feelings about being a drummer. It could well have been the result of the family situation—the fact that he got no encouragement whatever from them. I don't think they ever came to hear him play.

As Carmen said, he didn't communicate much. As intelligent as he was, Dave never was one for sitting down and just having a nice, comfortable conversation. Not at all. In fact, when I first met him—Gene Krupa introduced me; we both were with the Buddy Rogers band—Dave was stoned out of his mind. He just sat there, looking down, and said nothing beyond "How do you do."

But when he stayed away from drinking, he was the best of all the drummers who played with the Dorsey band. What he did for the band was just wonderful. He was very swinging and never made an irritating sound. Dave was an inspiration when he was alright and very pleasant and polite as well.

PEE WEE ERWIN: I first met Dave in about 1935 when I was in the Ray Noble band. This little man came up to me in Hurley's Bar in Rockefeller Center in New York and confronted me with something and then walked away. Then Bud Freeman said to me, "You know, that's the greatest drummer in the world." Of course I took that with a grain of salt. But I realized, after being in the Dorsey band with Dave for a while, that Bud was right.

His playing was so uplifting. I know one thing. Dave could make me play in a way that was impossible when any other drummer was back there. I don't know why; I never really analyzed it. I never knew what he was doing, not being a drummer; I couldn't identify any particular pattern that got to me; it was the whole thing. Dave was just thrilling.

You never had the idea you were playing with a rhythm section, or a set of drums. When he drummed and you played, it was like sitting on someone's hands that were carrying you right along. Most of the time when you work with drummers, they sound like drummers—guys trying to keep time and play the instrument. With Davey, you never were aware of all that. He just kept helping the band and inspiring you. He wasn't concerned about filling every hole in an arrangement. Time was his thing; he made his time your time.

BOB HAGGART: When I first played with Dave in the 1930s, I thought I was really draggin' ass, because he seemed ahead of everybody. When he played, it was as if he was saying, "Go with me or else!" Finally I got off my butt and started going with him and it was thrilling to play with the guy.

PEE WEE ERWIN: When not performing with the band and just fooling around on his set, Dave sounded awful—like a kid playing on pots and pans. He couldn't get the instrument to have a pleasant sound. But when he became part of the band, you'd be on cloud nine. Other than Dave, there are very few people who have given me that feeling. Cliff Leeman was another one. I've thought a lot about how Dave created that feeling and concluded that his technical limitations had a lot to do with how he played. The only thing he could do was keep creative time.

A lot of us had trouble with alcohol back then. We'd drink a good part of the time. We became alcoholics. Some of us stopped drinking and lived; others didn't stop and they died.

STANLEY DANCE: What I remember about Dave in the Dorsey days was his love of Shakespeare. During one of my trips here from England in the late 1930s, the Dorsey band was at the Commodore Hotel in New York City. I went to listen and got to know Dave and Bud Freeman. All they wanted to talk about—because I was English—was Shakespeare. In England, Shakespeare is a big part of your education; it's sort of compulsory and becomes irritating and boring. But here were these two guys absolutely in love with Shakespeare and they knew far more about him, really, than I did. And it struck me as very funny at the time.

Tough loved language. He "tipped delicately over his words like they were thin ice," Mezz Mezzrow remembered, adding that the drummer "always used to lecture me on how important it was to keep your speech pure, pointing out that the French and people like that formed their vowels lovingly, shaping their lips just right when they spoke, while Americans spoke tough out of the corners of their mouths, clipping and crunching all the sounds."[15]

But whenever people remember Dave Tough, it all comes back to his drumming.

DANNY BURGAUER: The Dorsey band was playing a New York theater sometime in 1938. I guess it was the Paramount; that's usually where the band worked. The guys were feeling very good and it was the second show of the day. They came up with a funny little game and made a bet they could have an effect on Dave's time. They set a metronome at the side of the orchestra. Dorsey was watching; he was the judge. The sax section dragged like crazy, the brass raced, and Davey played with the metronome, keeping great time without wavering through the whole number.

AL MERCURI: I remember seeing and hearing him with Dorsey early in 1939. His equipment was in bad condition. Popsicle sticks held together his bass drum pedal—a Heyn Pedal made by the St. Louis Duplex Company. His set and cymbals, though relatively new, didn't look too hot, particularly a large Chinese cymbal, which looked as if he had been nibbling pieces out of it.

But once he got behind the band it didn't matter. He brought to the band an unusual, original, pulsating quality. Tough had a way of enhancing the pulse, elaborating, expanding on it, building, building. He played unusual patterns on the bass drum. They were subtle and suggested what started to happen with the advent of the boppers several years later.

Tough's recordings and air shots with the Dorsey band reveal two basic things. He had a great deal of natural talent and an original mind. Stylistically, he mingled techniques and the general rhythmic feeling stemming from New Orleans, particularly from Baby Dodds, with an inclination to level the beat out and play in 4/4. Unlike a number of others during that period, Tough instinctively knew how to shape and pace arrangements and bring to them the pulsation, sense of development, and rhythmic security, plus the light and shade that, in sum, made them work.

The Dorsey band of the middle and late 1930s was an ensemble seeking its image. It tried instrumental and vocal novelties, classical-cum-swing items, e.g., "Liebestraum" and Mendelssohn's "Spring

Song," romantic numbers, and straight-ahead swing pieces, eventually defining itself within a 4/4 idiom. To what was essentially a relatively commercial repertoire, Tough instilled a strong jazz feeling.

A number of fine soloists, including trumpeters Bunny Berigan and Pee Wee Erwin, saxophonists Bud Freeman and Babe Russin, clarinetists Joe Dixon and Johnny Mince, enhanced the jazz flavoring. Along with the fine rhythm section of guitarist Carmen Mastren, bassist Gene Traxler, and pianist Dick Jones (later Howard Smith), they gave the drummer good material with which to work.

The Dorsey band was basically an assemblage of Dixieland-oriented players breaking into the swing idiom. The band often sounded somewhat like the ensemble led by Bob Crosby, which was responsible for popularizing the big-band Dixieland style. But because of Dorsey's need to experiment, the band kept trying new approaches and new types of arrangements—experiments that culminated in the Dorsey swing machine of the 1940s.

Traditional at its foundation, the 1930s Dorsey organization was an outgrowth, though a bit larger, of the bands Tough had worked with in Chicago. The drummer provided a firm, rock steady, inspiring rhythmic foundation as he adjusted to the many styles Dorsey was trying at the time. He brought his personality to bear both in the ensemble, and during his simplistic but musically relevant breaks.

One gets a very good idea of how Tough and the men of Dorsey performed and *felt* on a head arrangement called "Stop, Look and Listen," recorded for Victor in April 1937. Over a traditional rhythmic foundation, the band is loose and relaxed. Tough is firm and his effects are charming. He plays foil to clarinetist Johnny Mince and responds to his friend Bud Freeman with charming ideas that are not so much techniques as consonant, appropriate bursts of energy. The beat is there, moving things along; Tough and the band create an affable, pulsating impression.

The commercially successful recordings by the Dorsey band— "Song of India" and "Marie," cut for Victor in January, 1937 and released on the same 78—are excellent examples of how Tough operated during that period. In the 4/4 mode, both pieces are built upon a most danceable medium tempo. The little drummer uses "Tough-isms" to good effect during each performance. He makes his small cymbals speak in crucial spots. The cymbal exclamations function as accents and spots of brightness, all the while melding with the band sonorities. On "Song of India," Tough drives hard behind trumpeter Bunny Berigan, pushing the pulse on his Chinese cymbal, a crucial center of rhythm. He allows the cymbal to ring and throb to its fullest effect. "Marie"—a direct steal from a chart played by the Sunset

Royal Entertainers, a black band—demonstrates Tough's ability to play a minimum of strokes in just the right place, with perfect timing. His three-stroke exclamation leading into Berigan's solo is particularly potent.

Like most drummers of the period, Tough emphasizes the bass drum, using it as his primary time source. But how he coordinates the bass drum with what he plays with his hands makes the difference. The effect may not immediately be apparent. For example, the way he plays the high-hat has a progressive impact. The pulse gets stronger as he goes along. When he wants to enliven the band, he allows the cymbals to remain partially open and plays the dotted eighth and sixteenth rhythm with unusual clarity, making sure the cymbals really splash when he is trying to extract a feeling of interior swing from his colleagues. For someone who has so little facility, he is indeed surprising. As Bud Freeman says, "He could do what he had to do."

His performances on recordings from the late 1930s indicate that he cared little how he would be viewed as an individual. He performed to please the musicians in the band and himself. It became apparent as time passed that he wanted to be an ensemble player only. His solos on the Dorsey sides had no ego about them; they could easily be dismissed as the work of a deficient player in the area of technique. But somehow they work as *music*.

When Tough deals with excellent material, as he does on the May 1, 1939, Victor recording session by the Dorsey band, he brings his playing to the brink of true art. The centerpiece of that date, the Bill Finegan two-part arrangement of "Lonesome Road," comes alive because of imaginative touches by the arranger and marvelous orchestral and sectional performances. Finegan aptly combines the simple and straightforward with segments that are difficult to play. The chart is also memorable for its contrasts, sonorous textures, and the ease with which the ensemble plays. More than anything, the performance suggests the precise Jimmie Lunceford band. Ultimately the recording points in the direction that Dorsey was taking toward well-coordinated 4/4 swing. Through it all, Dave Tough gives a strong, graceful, well-controlled performance.

The drummer helps the score evolve by supporting its rhythm with quiet assurance. He defines its outlines and flow, accenting in climactic spots; he structures and colors passages, building and connecting elements of the chart as it moves along. One is conscious of Tough, but he is never too loud or pushy; he's there to keep things rolling and to encourage the music to live.

Before you know it, things are really swinging in the straight-ahead yet restrained manner that the arranger called for. Your spirits are uplifted; you have an urge to dance and to tap on whatever is available.

Tough's recordings reveal a drummer encouraging a band to sing in its most rhythmic and communicative voice. Like an extraordinary supporting actor, he adds to the overall performance without making you too conscious of his presence. Without him, the band and the arrangement would lose much of its character, strength, and rhythmic edge.

Tough's drinking and demons drove him out of the Dorsey band in January 1938. He returned to the band in 1939 and Dorsey took care of him over the years, giving aid and encouragement whenever things were going bad for him. He dried out sufficiently after leaving Dorsey to work briefly with Red Norvo, and to join Bunny Berigan for a few months in early 1938.

GRAHAM FORBES: We roomed together when I became the piano player on the Berigan band. At the time, Dave was on very good behavior, not hitting the bottle at all and playing great. We were on tour about two months.

It was a fun type band. Certain guys hung together. Georgie Auld, who played most of the tenor sax solos, and trumpeter Steve Lipkins were buddy-buddy. The other reed players—Joe Dixon, Clyde Rounds, and Mike Doty—were very friendly. Davey and I would practice together, each one working out his own needs. But he wasn't too close with anyone. He was pretty quiet, seemed educated—a higher type guy, a private man.

It was just a matter of going from job to job on the road, as far as he was concerned. The only time we all would get together away from the stand was when we went out after-hours to hear some music and get something to eat. And that was usually when we were in New York.

I'll tell you something: Dave carried that band. He had the ability to integrate all the elements in a big band. No one else could do it quite that well. And he seemed completely confident about doing the job. He had a kind of wry smile going. Yes, he knew how to pull everything together.

JOHNNY BLOWERS: I replaced Dave in the Berigan band when he went over to take Gene Krupa's place with Benny Goodman. Dave was wonderful to me—very, very friendly. "I'm so glad you're coming in this band," he told me. "You're going to like it and it will do you worlds of good." I was just a nervous wreck about it. I was jumping out of a little pond into a big thing. And Dave sensed this and was so helpful. We got to know one another real well. I came to care about him a great deal and, along the way, got the feeling he was not very happy being a musician.

He was living with Casey when I met him. Musicians never thought a thing about it. I guess people did. An interracial relationship was a very unusual situation for the time. Because of this, they stayed very close to the apartment down on MacDougal Street in the Village. Dave never left except to go to work. He and Casey didn't go anywhere. Casey would go out and shop and cook, take care of Dave. It was a difficult situation for him.

On March 19, 1938, Dave Tough replaced Gene Krupa in Benny Goodman's band.

D. RUSSELL CONNOR and WARREN HICKS: When Goodman approached him, Tough made it clear that "I'm no Krupa." He was not, but he was a very fine band drummer, one with that indefinable quality called "lift," a kind of buoyancy underneath the band that raised, rather than propelled it, to superior play. His style was less powerful, less technical than Gene's; his solos had a "melodic structure," a style seldom heard today. Audiences accustomed to Gene's pyrotechnics were perplexed, sometimes puzzled, often disappointed in Dave's work.[16]

Goodman pianist Jess Stacy, who had suggested to the leader that he get Tough and Bud Freeman, noted in an interview with *The New Yorker*'s Whitney Balliett that Goodman never was really satisfied with either of these musicians. The clarinetist had problems with drummers, generally, but after Krupa left he was particularly difficult, making Tough's job almost impossible.

CHRIS GRIFFIN: When Dave joined the band, Benny was completely turned off by drummers. Gene had been central to the band's personality for so many years. Benny was looking for anything that was *not* percussive. Soon after Dave came with us, Benny cut off almost all the instruments that he played. First came the cymbals. Then the high-hat went. Not long after that, Benny said, "Don't play the bass drum." Finally Dave was limited to the snare drum, playing what Benny called the "fly swatters." He didn't even formalize things by using the regular descriptive: wire brushes.

There we were with a big, loud band and poor Davey sitting there using brushes, just the way Benny wanted. It was a very difficult thing to see, knowing what a great, great player he was.

I don't believe the period he spent with the band was one of his happiest. He was dry at the time—never touched liquor of any sort. He seemed sad. If you knew Dave at all he *always* looked the part anyway. He had kind of a sad face.

But somehow, Tough transcended what was a negative situation. His work on Goodman air shots is particularly effective, much more so, generally, than his studio recordings. He swings forcefully, making his cymbals sing and swing. In the Goodman small-group setting, in particular, he is an indisputable master, the beat becoming more and more convincing and communicative as the group takes hold. A quartet air check (radio broadcast) of "Benny Sent Me" from August 30, 1938, makes the point very well. The up-tempo item takes off soon after the first statement of theme, with Dave generating extraordinary swing.

LIONEL HAMPTON: Each night I could hardly wait to play with the quartet because Davey swung me so. You know, he didn't care much about playing the big-band feature numbers like "Sing, Sing, Sing." I did those. He was very comfortable in the small band and was nothing short of wonderful. He had a great way of playing cymbals. You'd be performing on a certain level. When all at once we had to get louder, he had a way of making the sound of the cymbals swell and he'd be swinging like mad. We made one record with the quartet, "Opus One Half" (1938 Victor), that really tells the Dave Tough story. Boy, I get a thrill every time I play that recording. His time is so great. He's swinging us. We played so good on that because of Dave.

JOHNNY BLOWERS: Hamp told me, "When you work with Dave, it's like being on a magic carpet after the first chorus. Everything becomes so easy."

Critics agreed that Tough was doing a very good job with the Goodman band. Though he wasn't as free as he had been with Dorsey, and played so unlike Krupa, he made the band looser and more pulsating and allowed it to express its personality more completely. Not being in the Krupa groove was a benefit, according to certain reviewers.

DAVE DEXTER: Dave Tough's style on the hides—despite prejudiced and unfounded statements by diehards—blends with the "new" [Goodman] band in a manner which Krupa never was able to approach. Even Benny himself is carried away by Dave's rock-

ribbed beat, a steady solid staccato attack which on every offering inspires the boys magnanimously and results in terrific
deliverance of pop, evergreen, and standard tunes such as was
not possible previous to the Tough entrance.[17]

But his difficulties with drink persisted. Certain record produc-
ers found him "unreliable."

MILT GABLER: I always wanted to get Dave Tough on Commodore. But
the two times I booked him, he was stone drunk and very unreliable. I had to have Lionel Hampton sub for him on one session;
on the other, Dave showed up but couldn't produce. Marty
Marsala did two sides and Dave two. He just couldn't complete
the session.
   Dave wasn't easy to control in the studio either. But, of
course, that wasn't his fault. He loved to play the big cymbals.
And we couldn't contain the shimmer in the small studios; in
those days we didn't even use flats to isolate the rhythm section,
so there was leakage from one mike to another.
   Did you know that Dave was Eddie Condon's favorite drummer? The reason is not difficult to find. Dave had a way of exciting players—the way he used his foot and played on the drums
and cymbals. He had a feeling for what the other guys were
doing. I loved to watch and to listen to him. But I just wasn't
lucky. I was dying to use him on certain dates. It just didn't work
out.

People always were trying to save Dave Tough from himself.
Even Dave Tough made a major effort. One of the things he always
wanted to be was a writer. He had the background; most of his friends
felt he had rare insight when it came to literature and writing. In the
late 1930s, a few months before he went with Goodman, he wrote
several drum columns for *Metronome*, temporarily replacing Gene
Krupa. Some are good; others are amusing. Collectively, they indicate that he could have pursued writing as a career, if he had had the
time, patience, and proper motivation.
   The August 1937 column in which he comments on the effect of
chewing gum on swing drumming is very much worth reading because it is so dryly humorous and good-natured. His little satiric
take-off on Hemingway is very much on the mark, with his language,
meter, and images strongly resembling those of the great author:

Ah, the joy of wine when it is red! Those lovely summer nights in the
Bois with the swift, inner uptake of the Pernod. It turning milky in your

glass and the taste of wine, hard, clear, and tannic, in your mouth, volatile all through you—and you would go to Birch Tops in the Rue Pigalle and hear her sing "The Boy In The Boat," and hope you don't meet Ernest. Those dear dead days![18]

When Gene Krupa resumed the drum column, *Metronome*'s editors, including Tough's advocate George Simon, wanted Tough to continue writing for the magazine. They offered him carte blanche, including the opportunity to write on subjects outside of music.

But Tough never submitted any more copy to the magazine. Whatever his reasons, he allowed the opportunity to slip away. For the rest of his life, he talked about writing, and did little. In 1947, he published a piece titled "Three Ways To Smoke a Pipe" in the *Esquire 1947 Jazz Book*. Chubby Jackson speaks of some articles printed in *The New Yorker*, but the publication has no record of them. Despite his inability to produce as a writer, and his frustration thereof, Tough continued to give every indication of great ability and evolution as a player.

The drummer was with the Goodman band until November 1938; then he moved from job to job. Before rejoining the clarinetist for an important stint in 1941, he appeared with Mezz Mezzrow, the Jack Teagarden band, and the Joe Marsala group at New York's Hickory House (to which he subsequently returned), played very briefly with Goodman in California, and was in the Dorsey band for a bit, as noted.

In addition, he worked with Bud Freeman, with whom he recorded "Prince of Wails" on Columbia in 1940. An up-tempo, straight-ahead 4/4 item, with traditional stylistic overtones, it features excellent performances by all—trumpeter Max Kaminsky, trombonist Jack Teagarden, clarinetist Pee Wee Russell, guitarist Eddie Condon, pianist Dave Bowman, and bassist Mort Stuhlmaker. It is one of Tough's best small-band performances and certainly one of his most free-wheeling.

MAX KAMINSKY: The feeling on the record is just wonderful. And the primary reason for it is Davey. He's so uplifting and swinging. I'm proud to have been on the thing. It's that good.

RAY MCKINLEY: I heard Dave with Goodman after Gene left and he played quite well. Of course, later on with Woody he was simply great. Yet he didn't have any effect on me personally during his stays with either band. But the records he made with Bud Freeman—Jack Teagarden, Pee Wee Russell, and Dave Bowman were on the sessions—had a major influence on my playing, for some reason.

Tough was in the Goodman band again for a short while, beginning in October 1940, when the clarinetist returned to work after a
back operation. The band played in and around New York. After
joining the band in January 1941 as a regular member, the little
drummer made some extremely important records that emphasize
his growth as a player.

The best of the big-band Goodman recordings, according to
Tough, was "Scarecrow," a brisk Buster Harding original, recorded
for Columbia in February 1941. Essentially an ensemble performance, with solos from Goodman, tenorist Georgie Auld, and trombonist Lou McGarity, the recording documents Tough's ability to
play almost perfect time that feeds on itself and progressively makes
the performance more exciting. The record also emphasizes how well
a drummer can play with a compatible rhythm section (Mike Bryan,
guitar; Artie Bernstein, bass; and Johnny Guarnieri, piano) while
carrying and supporting one and all in a strong and highly tasteful
manner.

The way Tough uses the high-hat—partially open, producing a
pulsating sizzle, or closed, with the addition of counter-rhythms
played on the high-hat stand—blends particularly well with the dom-

Tough recording with Benny Goodman in 1941.   Columbia Records/George T. Simon Collection.

inant sound of the bass drum. Like many of the recordings on which Tough is the motor in the orchestral machine, he simultaneously provokes the ensemble and soloists and gives them an undeniable feeling of security. He controls the band and literally makes it move. To appreciate his sense of time on this effort, listen to how he catches and supports a figure comprised of four eighth notes and a quarter note toward the end of the performance. He is right at the center of the beats in the figure, and the feeling couldn't be more appropriate.

However, the best of his Goodman big-band records is not "Scarecrow," but "Perfidia" (Columbia 1941), an Eddie Sauter chart for Goodman, featuring vocalist Helen Forrest. Set in a medium dance tempo, "Perfidia" builds excitement. Tough adds color and the necessary accents to an undeniable pulse. His bass drum work, in combination with his efforts on the high-hat (open and closed), and the way his cymbals swish, splash, and sing in appropriate spots all add dimension to the rhythm *and* the melody.

In the closing segment of the performance, as Ms. Forrest is concluding her vocal, she sings, "And now I know my love is not for you." Tough gives the bass drum a double shot, shifts gears, and opens up the band with his strength and enthusiasm, leaning on open high-hats, which he uses like a top cymbal. All the while he tolls the time on the bass drum. Near the coda, he takes the band down in volume and manages it as few can. He is as effective playing softly as he is when performing with all stops out. His high-hat facility and finesse in the last section, when he combines time-keeping with accenting band figures, is surprising indeed.

Dave Tough with the Goodman sextet is just a scaled-down version of the big-band drummer. With Goodman, guitarist Charlie Christian, trumpeter Cootie Williams, tenor saxophonist Georgie Auld, bassist Artie Bernstein, and pianist Johnny Guarnieri, he produces enviable pulsation on two memorable records from the period: "Smooth One" and "Air Mail Special" (both Columbia, 1941). Because it is a small group, Tough plays more compactly and makes the feel a bit tighter. He varies the brush pattern on the snare, giving the beat more fluidity. The drums are tuned for crispness, very much in keeping with the Goodman conception and this sort of small-group environment.

Tough combines exterior time and the inner pulse in a meaningful way. Exterior time is firm, somewhat automatic, straightforward, and obvious; what comes from inside is more subtle. Interior time depends on instinct and ability, particularly the capacity to adjust to the differences among players, while creatively blending and controlling them. A drummer's positive inner time impulses make possible performances that are flexible, human, and communicative.

The affiliation with Goodman, which lasted from January to April 1941, was an evolutionary one. Tough got better, stronger, and more creative as the months went by. In the big band, he made major strides, utilizing his cymbals with a greater degree of intensity to fill openings and support accents. His high-hat work was looser and set a precedent for drummers who would later adopt the open high-hat sound, particularly behind ensemble playing. Tough gave the high-hat the feeling later associated with the top cymbal. He leaned on it in shout choruses, and gave it a variety of other roles. Like the great man of the high-hat, Jo Jones, he played it in a manner fitting the occasion—splashy-bashy behind ensembles, closed and with precision behind section work or soloists, open and closed in combination to stir up ensembles and soloists. Tough, in short, was an artist of the high-hat.

His bass drum habits were changing. He established the pulse on the big drum but often threw in double and single accents to change the feeling and the course of the music. Though he seldom dropped bombs, combining the left hand with accents in the bass drum foot, he altered the way the bass drum was played, and established a new foundation for the future.

JIMMY MAXWELL: Dave and I were together in that 1941 Goodman band. He had a very small ego, almost nonexistent. I don't mean he was wishy-washy. What I'm trying to say is that his ego never got in the way of his playing. He never tried to show off. He was sure of what he was doing and didn't feel he had to push himself. He let his playing speak for him.

I suspect Dave would have liked to have been better known and maybe a bit flashier. I think he desired the acknowledgement of the public that other people got—not just the praise of musicians. The lack of recognition could have been one of the reasons he drank more than he should.

We talked a lot about books and music when we were together. I didn't look for any message and special understanding when it came to novels. But Davey would find all kinds of meanings in them.

Dave was interested in black music and black drummers—that's certainly true. But not exclusively. He also liked white musicians. In fact, in that area we sometimes disagreed. I didn't know much about white players and white music. Almost all my favorites were black. So we'd talk a lot about that and he'd try to educate me about people like Muggsy Spanier—people that I thought were terrible.

Playing with Dave in the band was great. He always took the

beat where I thought it should be. Dave and Big Sid were drummers who made it easy; Dave said he liked working with me
because he didn't have to *pull* me. He didn't play that way. Gene
and Buddy did. Dave just played in the same way the band did.

Aside from his fantastic time, Dave made more "sounds"
than any drummer I ever heard. He was fascinated with sounds.
I did a radio show with him later—I think it was "The Eddie
Duchin Show." I used to talk to him a lot at intermissions because he always was filling his bass drum with little slips of
paper. He'd touch everything up until he got the right sound. If it
wasn't right, he'd open the drum up and take out some of the
paper. He was very conscious of the sound of everything he
played.

Dave wanted a duller sound than was usual. He would tune
his drums to pitches—the bass drum and snare drum and the
tom-toms as well. He didn't want a pitch exactly like that of the
band. He wanted a pitch that was kind of no pitch, you know, an
indeterminate kind of sound.

Subtlety was Dave Tough's calling card. Because he couldn't do
too many technical things, he sought simple, powerful means to make
the music interesting. He broke up the basic dotted eighth and sixteenth rhythm—the means of keeping jazz time—and sometimes
changed it entirely, using four quarter notes or strokes to the bar,
bringing into play various elements of the drum set. This way, he
could make the time more powerful without resorting to flash.

JIMMY MAXWELL: Dave sometimes sounded like one of those African
    drum ensembles. He would use different sounds and come in in
    unexpected places. Sometimes he gave me the feeling that there
    were three drummers playing at the same time.

Always, however, he lived on the edge, and his employers and
friends watched and waited, hoping he wouldn't fall off the wagon or
move out of sight.

MAX KAMINSKY: Benny kept an eye on Davey because he was so afraid
    he'd start drinking. All Dave had to do was find a bar and he just
    wouldn't come back to work. Anyway, after this record date at
    Liederkranz Hall here in New York, Benny and Dave were walk-
    ing down Park Avenue. As they passed Sulka, the haberdashers,
    Benny said, "Dave, come on in. I'll buy you a tie." But Dave was
    on to him and answered, "No, Benny, I've got a tie."

JOHN HAMMOND: Davey never took care of himself. I have so many ghastly memories of Dave Tough. One night—the Goodman band was playing one of the New York hotels—I recall bringing Davey home after one of the evening sessions with Benny. He was living with Casey on 111th Street and Seventh Avenue. It was a six-floor walkup and I had to *carry* him up. He only weighed about 105. But it was dead weight. You can imagine how difficult it was carrying him. Casey was there—what a marvelous woman! God, she took care of him. But she couldn't do anything *with* him.

You know, one of Dave's great sorrows, I believe, was that he wasn't born black and that he had to play with so many callous and nonunderstanding musicians. Dave rarely was able to play with black musicians and it bugged him to death. He'd sit in uptown whenever he could. But that wasn't the same as playing regularly with black musicians.

Before I really *heard* him, people used to tell me how wonderful he was and imply he was better than all of the black drummers I loved. Until I got Dave's message, I would deny that vociferously. But I had been wrong about drummers before. I made a mistake about Walter Johnson, the wonderful drummer with Fletcher [Henderson]. I think Walter really was the Dave Tough of black drummers. He was just incredibly subtle. Marvelous. And he played such smooth brushes.

Tough moved from clarinetist to clarinetist—from Goodman, back to Joe Marsala, then to Artie Shaw for an important experience. The 32-piece Shaw Orchestra took form in August 1941. An ambitious undertaking, the orchestra featured standard dance band instrumentation—seven brass, five reeds, four rhythm—plus fifteen strings. Its library included standards, riff-based instrumentals, Tin Pan Alley concoctions featuring vocals, and what are now known as third-stream works, which combined elements of jazz and classical music.

Shaw fans, like most people who follow a band, soloist, or singer, were somewhat discomforted by the fact that the clarinetist was trying new things. They wanted "more of the same"—swing-rooted instrumentals, like "Begin the Beguine" and "Back Bay Shuffle," which brought the band fame. But Shaw was moving into experimentation, which satisfied the intensely musical side of him. Because of this uncommercial attitude it was generally difficult to keep the orchestra afloat.

The orchestra derived its essential character and much of its energy from jazz. Even when the Shaw ensemble was interpreting the compositions that incorporated classical elements, it brought to them the looseness basic to jazz. Shaw had great sympathy and feeling for what he describes as "the Afro-American contribution."[19]

ARTIE SHAW: Davey Tough was probably the most underestimated drummer of all and . . . so musical. When I say musical, I'm talking about his sensibilities, which of course were honed by his literary and esthetic sense of everything in general. My thesis is the more you know about everything, the better anything you do will be. The more enriched and subtle it will be as well. Your reference points are greater because there are more of them.

Davey had a pretty well-stocked mind. As a result, he could never take cheap shots. He hated taking solos, as I'm sure his other friends and colleagues have mentioned. He would just shrug and look embarrassed when I asked him to take four, eight, or sixteen bars. There was something exhibitionistic about it he didn't like.

Another thing about Davey. He tuned his drums beautifully. He realized drums are a musical instrument, and if they're not musical they're terrible. Most people don't know what tuning means. They think a drum is just something you bang on.

One other point about Davey: It was astounding that he could muster up such a great rhythmic pulse. He had a tremendous number of physical problems, being such a frail guy. But he was remarkable. I think he was working on nervous energy. It's part of the reason he died so early.

The Shaw recordings from 1941–1942 made for Victor during the life of the thirty-two piece orchestra—i.e., Ray Conniff's "Just Kiddin' Around" and "Needlenose," Paul Jordan's "Suite No. 8" and "Carnival," Margie Gibson's "Deuces Wild," and Fred Norman's "Solid Sam"—reveal a musically muscular Tough. He continued to color and accent with his cymbals during arrangements, to push and place emphasis in a provocative way with his bass drum, and to lift the entire ensemble with a minimum amount of strokes and tricks.

Tough's ability to give substance to charts was enhanced during the Shaw period. He breathed and moved with the band. Though a directorial influence, he never overwhelmed soloists, sections or the ensemble, no matter what the degree of excitement. His playing always seemed to be saying, "The beat is here; follow me!" His drumming was persuasive, a natural phenomenon; his Zildjian cymbals hummed and slashed through the orchestra's sound, giving the music a variety of hues and a terrific beat.

The recipe was the same as it had been with Goodman. But Tough played with a new vitality and even greater solidity. He was unobtrusive when he had to be, but he smashed through when the orchestra began to shout. The drummer knew when to let the ensemble take off and when to rein it in. His secret was his ability to make large and small bands do his bidding.

A review by George Frazier in *Down Beat*, with a subhead, "Tough Is Stupendous," is typical of the critical response to Tough in the Shaw band:

> For my money, the star of Artie's band—the only really indispensable man in it—is Dave Tough. His drumming is nothing short of stupendous and without it the band would be a considerably less exciting affair than it is at the moment. There is never any exhibitionism to anything that Tough does, never any of the juvenile delinquency of Buddy Rich's playing, for example—just enormous competence, impeccable taste, and one of the most miraculous beats in jazz.[20]

The Shaw experience lasted only a few months, until December 1941. The leader felt that fronting a band for civilians no longer made sense and after Pearl Harbor, gave the band notice. Tough is reported to have said, "Just when you get a good job and are making some money, they start a war."

Before enlisting in the Navy during the summer of 1942 to play with the Artie Shaw service band, Tough worked briefly with Woody Herman and the band that sweet trumpeter Charlie Spivak led. The drummer must have been in pretty good shape with Spivak; he made another positive impression, on Barry Ulanov, who wrote in *Metronome:*

> It's the jazz that a new listener to this band will find astonishing. . . . A lot of credit for the fine quality of the hot must go to the brilliant rhythm section, and to a comparative newcomer, Davey Tough. Davey's drumming has given the whole band a wonderful lift, which is noticeable in the ballads as well as the up-tempo instrumentals, but which makes more of a difference in the shaping of the latter. For Mr. Tough is drumming at his very best, which means that tempos have an unerring steadiness, that the band has a solid beat behind it and a steady inspiration for jazz kicks.[21]

Tough's stint in the Navy with the Shaw band, including an extended stay in the South Pacific area of operations, was draining, to say the very least. It was difficult from the beginning. He almost didn't get in the service, being too small and a poor physical specimen. Casey fed him spaghetti for several weeks so he could make the weight. The doctor who examined Tough asked Shaw whether this musician really was necessary to his band. The clarinetist insisted Tough was crucial, describing him as "the greatest drummer in the world." So Tough found himself in uniform.

ARTIE SHAW: He was an alcoholic, and like all alcoholics, he always
found things to drink. I'd assign a man to him if we had an
important concert coming up—say for the crew of an aircraft
carrier—and that man would keep an eye on him all day. This
was so he wouldn't fall off the bandstand, which he had done a
couple of times.[22]

Tough's military experience came to an end in February 1944
when he was given a discharge. Two months later, after a recovery
period, the drummer rejoined the Woody Herman band, the First
Herd, and embarked on a wondrous period for him as an artist.

WOODY HERMAN: What happened when Davey joined was an explosion. The band really started to make some sense. The rhythm
section got us off the ground. Bassist Chubby Jackson worked
closely with Davey and we got a very good result.
      Ours was the "blackest" band in which Dave had ever
worked. That's why he was so inspired. Does that make sense to
you? The band made a change in his playing.
      You know, his rudiments were nil. His roll sounded like
something else because it wasn't played in the correct way. But
it didn't matter. As soon as he got under the music, it was something else. At a certain point in an ensemble or a "head" thing, he
had a unique way of playing on the high-hat and the cymbals.
When the band got really charging, it sounded to me like there
was a shuffle [beat] happening, except he wasn't playing a shuffle. All I can say is that during a charging ensemble, there was
something *more* there. The feeling was transmitted to the whole
band and the public. It's really difficult to describe.
      The guys in the band were in love with his playing because
of what he did for them. He got them to play a hell of a lot more
than any of the other drummers who had been in the band. When
Davey was with us, the band was at its best, its very best.

JOHN VON OHLEN: He [Woody] loved Dave Tough. He wouldn't down-
trod anybody else because he had some great drummers, but
Dave Tough was always the magic in his eyes.[23]

MEL LEWIS: One thing about Dave Tough: he always was Dave Tough,
just as Buddy Rich always was what he was. Tough realized we
are what we are. The important thing is to be put into a musical
situation where what you are can "happen." Tough found his
place with Woody Herman.

The First Herd touched many people. It was Herman's most successful band because the recipe was near perfect. This Herd had ex-

traordinary potency; its beat was undeniable; the soloists—trumpeters Pete Candoli and Sonny Berman, trombonist Bill Harris, and tenor saxophonist Flip Phillips, among others—all had individuality.

Young musicians, myself included, were particularly fascinated with the band because it mirrored many of the new ideas that Dizzy Gillespie and Charlie Parker had developed. Herman combined contemporary and traditional ideas in a just right ratio.

Here was a true jazz band that interpreted popular songs and original jazz material, much of it based on Gershwin's "I Got Rhythm," commenting cogently on contemporary musical trends, while picking up the pulse of the times. Basie, Ellington, Goodman, Lunceford, and Shaw had also done this a few years earlier. The only difference was that the Herman Herd did it more explosively.

Pretty soon, the band was no longer the exclusive possession of devotees of jazz and the musicians. When the Columbia records came out, the whole country got a chance to hear a band on fire.

WOODY HERMAN: Davey was at the heart of it all. He played what was necessary for us to make our point. The band brought out his very best and impelled him to do what might have been impossible in other circumstances. He fooled a lot of people. You know how musicians put down cats who can't play their axes [instruments]. They say unless you're able to do *everything* on the instrument, you're nothing. Well, Davey really convinced even the most cynical, critical guys.

Davey had that droll sense of humor and it extended into his playing. He was very together, a meticulous little man who was so very bright and intelligent. By meticulous, I don't mean tight or inflexible. Meticulous is arriving an hour before the gig to water down your drum heads and tune them for the feeling you want. Because of this, when Dave hit a drum, particularly the bass drum, it was a *musical* sound.

And remember: he never played a tune with us without putting a capper [a small bass drum comment] on the end; it was like a signature. That was the black element, the black influence. What went through his mind, I believe, was what happened at the Apollo Theater and the Regal in Chicago—all the black theaters where the kids hung out to catch the shows and the music. The drummer's gig in those days was to cover everything. By that I mean, if a guy took a bow on stage, the drummer played a budda-budda-boom. Like a punch line on a joke. If you wanted to get added punch, you added still another sound. Dave was incorporating the *black* version of that in our music.

I can't say enough about him. He gave the band so much. He was a gentleman, a hell of a player, and a bright man. Now how many guys do you know who have all those assets? Did he stay sober? Yes, for quite a while. Something important should be brought out here, if you think it's good judgment. I found out just before he was wheeled out of the band that he was a victim of epilepsy.

People never understood. He always was worrying he'd get an attack. The thing would work on him and build the pressure to the breaking point. And that's when he had his first drink. All it took was one or two and he'd disappear for a week. Casey would find him, clean him up, and bring him back.

Yeah, his brightness probably made him unhappy. He saw and knew too many things. There were a lot of morose moments in his life. But there also was a kind of ironic kind of humor, always there right on the top.

Tough was deeply challenged by the rhythmic changes basic to bebop. He loved what was happening and had great affection and respect for what Max Roach and the others were doing. But he couldn't *really* deal with it.

LEONARD FEATHER: Bop had arisen. Dixieland was on the defensive, and Dave found himself in the position of the liberal who is at home with neither the communists nor the fascists.[24]

ARTIE SHAW: Dave couldn't quite get over bop. He was too rooted in other things. It might well have been a great source of frustration for him because he prided himself on being aware of everything. But he couldn't quite get up to it. I remember hearing some of the recordings Woody sent me. Dave was struggling a little bit with the stuff. But then, what the hell, he couldn't go where Max Roach went.

The records on Columbia and broadcasts on Hindsight show Tough the swing master trying to move into modernism. He began incorporating into his drumming things he heard Roach, Kenny Clarke, and Stan Levey doing; he started playing little "bombs" and further modernizing his bass-drum playing. But he remained Dave Tough. Listen to "Caldonia" (1945), "Apple Honey" (1944), and "Northwest Passage" (1945) on Columbia, and "Is You Is or Is You Ain't My Baby" (1944) on Hindsight.

The first impression is that of enormous power. The bass drum remained his primary weapon. His cymbal playing, always a presence, a shimmer, a wave of sound that enlivened the orchestra, combined with the bass drum to form an aural painting. Often he seemed to achieve a level of superhuman vitality. The sounds, patterns, and accents emanating from his loosely-tuned, low-pitched drums and breathing, cutting, splashing cymbals, notably his huge Chinese cymbal, kept *time* central to everything. The band leaped out and grabbed hold of your emotions.

ED SHAUGHNESSY: Dave's rhythmic approach in a big band was much the same as Sid Catlett's in a small band. He was unrelenting, remarkably steady; he had great simpatico with the other players and, of course, he was so musical.

CHUBBY JACKSON: One experience remains embedded in my mind. We were at the Paramount Theater in New York. I was doing my bass feature up front. As we were moving into the last two choruses when Pete Candoli came out to play some high notes and the band went into some riffs, I took my hand off the bass, for a breath, a theatrical gesture. And the band came back in *slower*. I felt a little desperate about it because I felt I had done it—dropped time.

But it seemed to work so well. As I began playing again, the band seemed larger and more powerful than I could ever have imagined. It felt like there were twenty trumpets behind me. I remember thinking, "Listen to this thing! Listen to it move!"

When the show was over, I went over to Dave as the band was moving into the pit and said, "I'm sorry, man. I didn't mean to drop. . . ." He smiled and said, "Wait a minute, Snuggy"—that's what he called me—"didn't you like that?" He explained he had slowed the band down purposely to make the beat sound wider and to give the band a more solid feeling.

Dave was a believer in nonmetronomic time. He adapted to what he felt was happening, to the orchestra and the soloist. He used to say we should complement and go with the player, the section, the orchestra. He would maneuver the whole band while allowing it to express itself. He didn't think the beat had to be inflexible. He thought it was absolutely wrong for a band to finish where it started. Dave insisted there had to be *dynamics in time*. He'd say: if you rush and don't know you are rushing the tempo— uh, uh, wrong. Or if you lose time and aren't conscious of it—that also is a no-no. But if you know where you are going and the way the arrangement is developing and *control* the situation and make things more expressive—well, okay!

Dave never let the band get lazy. He was the general. If he

felt we weren't doing what had to be done, he would play five quarter notes on the cymbal as a warning to straighten up. Dave was our guide. And I learned so much from the man about playing and music and the bass.

He wanted me in a spot close to the drums so we could easily communicate. I'd watch his arms and legs and face. He'd give me a look, you know, and I'd hear a little ripple of a fill, and I'd know where to go and what to do.

All the guys in the band, particularly the writers—Neal [Hefti] and Ralph [Burns]—would take advice from Dave. We respected him, not only for his talent and the way he motivated the band, but because of his experience. He was the "old man" among us, the sage who knew how to do things.

When he finally left the band in September 1945 in Birmingham, it was like there had been a death in the family. He was sick and couldn't go on. There had been problems for a while. But he always would come back to us and do it, playing as only he could.

Dave had the *intensity*. He kept telling us, "There should be intensity at any level, from soft to loud," and show us how it was done. I remember him saying to me, "You tell your woman, 'I love you,' it should make the same impression, regardless of the volume. It's no different with the playing."

There is so much about Davey that lingers in mind. When he played, he took off his Florsheims and put on a little pair of black shoes, heavy in the rubber department underneath. The shoes had no laces—nothing to inhibit the foot. He was very stiff-backed. Never bent over. And constantly he was tuning his drums, so they wouldn't resound, have echoes.

As Dizzy Gillespie said to me recently, "Dave never got in the way; he didn't overplay. What we need today are a few Dave Toughs."

The fight went on to stay straight, to be sober and ready to play. It was a constant contest to determine what side of his personality would win. At times he would be late or not show up at all for work with the Herman band, particularly later in the association.

STAN LEVEY: The first time I met Dave Tough, I was playing with Dizzy at the Three Deuces on New York's 52nd Street with that first bebop band—Charlie Parker (alto sax), Curly Russell (bass), Al Haig (piano). Some people loved what we were doing; others hated the music. Dave was at the Deuces because he had scope. He was crazy about the modern movement and was excited about what was happening. He moved along sequentially with what the modern

Dave Tough during his peak period, with Woody Herman's First Herd, 1944–45.   Photo provided by The Avedis Zildjian Company.

people were doing. As new things came along he got right into them. He came in the club a lot, sometimes with Woody.

I respected him a lot and kept my distance and waited for him to open up and starting talking. After a while, we got some warmth going and I was invited down to the Hotel Pennsylvania to hear Woody's band. At that point, I had no idea I would be asked to sub for Dave. The band was a great experience. I knew most of the guys—Sonny Berman, Pete Candoli, Conte Candoli, Ray Linn, Flip Phillips, Sam Marowitz, Chubby, Ralph Burns.

That first night in the Cafe Rouge, I heard this little guy take the band and turn it upside down and inside out; he did whatever he wanted with it. I couldn't figure out where the power and energy were coming from. I kept looking for a second drummer. Davey had more drive than anyone!

This was a strong, big, loud band. And he just took complete control of it. It was amazing how he worked the cymbals and bass drum and locked the band in. One thing is certain: he had the strongest foot I've ever heard.

He was just as effective in The Woodchoppers, Woody's small group. He would just shift gears and bring it down into the softer reaches of the sound spectrum and make things fit the dimensions of the unit. His drums were perfectly tuned for his manner of playing. And the set itself seemed a part of him: the bass drum was small for the time—twenty-two-inch—and everything else was in scale.

But he had to deal with alcoholism. And the problem was becoming severe in 1945. He became more and more unreliable. He'd show up late or not come to work at all, leaving a gigantic hole in the band. Lo and behold, who did they call but Little Stan Levey. Oh boy, was I in trouble! I had never played with a big band. But I was eighteen and said yes.

When I got to the Pennsylvania for my first night, I had to rearrange Dave's drums because I'm left-handed. That felt sacrilegious. But I had no choice. The guys were very supportive. And that's half the battle when you're new on a job. I told you about Dave driving the band. Well, the band drove me. It opened me up and made possible the production of the right sounds. I literally was flying without a plane.

I would come down to the hotel and play two, three, maybe four nights a week. Dave missed more and more of the job. I felt very badly for him. But there was nothing I could do but take care of business. This went on for several weeks.

Then the band closed and went on to the Meadowbrook on Pompton Turnpike in New Jersey. Dave was not able to be there on a steady basis either. So I ran out to play, usually riding in a cab with dancer Baby Laurence. Woody had just hired him for the show. I was getting used to playing in a big band and was of more help to the guys.

When the band finished its engagement at the Meadowbrook, Dave rejoined it for a road trip. I went back with Dizzy at the Deuces. A few weeks later, I suddenly got a call from Woody's manager. He told me Davey had fallen off the bandstand in Minneapolis and really hurt himself. Because he was in bad shape, I was asked to fly out immediately and fill in. I stayed on the road with Woody for a while. Progressively I came to the realization that when someone like Dave drops out of a band, he leaves a hole that cannot be fully filled by anybody. I'm sad to say I never saw him again. I loved his talent. He was a great teacher.

BILLY BAUER: It started to come apart in New York. Dave was drinking and worried Woody a lot. Woody figured everyone was going to be coming into the Hotel Pennsylvania and he wanted to make a good impression.

Deep down, Dave didn't believe his drumming was that good. He had some sort of hang-up about it. And the drinking did him in. In California we had to send for Lou Fromm because Dave got bombed out in the middle of the tour.

Maybe it was the pressure. He might have had to prove something to himself. After all, he had been around for a long time and had a reputation for putting things together in bands. And *this* band could be overwhelming.

One night in Detroit, it got going so much, the hair on my arms stood up. We just looked at one another. It really got into a power thing. Davey was so little; he could hardly keep up. It wasn't that he couldn't hold it together. But he had to use all of his energy to get up there. Sometimes when we were playing a theater, after a big evening like the one in Detroit, he had difficulty getting himself together for the first show. He couldn't seem to get his body going. It was not easy in Woody's band. Those fast tempos took a lot out of a person.

I never got to know what his *real* problems were. Maybe he never attained that certain prestige or something.

Tough was tortured by feelings of inadequacy. He told both Leonard Feather and George Simon that he didn't feel he was contemporary enough, that people didn't really like his playing, that something was lacking in his performances. Max Roach became a role model, and frequently Tough said that he couldn't possibly do what Roach did.

Not only was he insecure as a drummer, he was torn about what he would ultimately do with his life. On the one hand, he wanted to play and remain in the vanguard; on the other, he spoke increasingly of tossing over the drums and becoming a full-time writer. His stress level was high; the only relief he found was in drink and the respite, however temporary, it provided.

Tough wore down like a watch. Carmen Mastren, his old friend from the Dorsey band, had warned him about going with Woody

Herman. He said, "Davey, I don't know. That kind of band is going to be a labor for you." As it turned out, it was the glory moment of the drummer's life. He won *Down Beat* and *Metronome* polls, and was cited for the excellence of his drumming in *Esquire* and other general interest magazines.

At last everyone knew Dave Tough, not just musicians. He was on the cutting edge of jazz. Though not exactly a modernist, he had become a factor in the modern movement because he played so well in a very up-to-date band. In *Down Beat* (September 23, 1945) he spoke out against reactionary Dixieland, calling it "just Straight-Republican Ticket kind of music." People listened to Tough and openly admired him. Yet it was too little, too late.

Some say he left Woody Herman because he had become non-functional and ill; others insist he suffered a fit, probably due to his epilepsy, and then disappeared. Still others indicate he no longer was sufficiently responsible to hold the job. Whatever the reasons, his terminating this affiliation marked the beginning of the end.

JOHN HAMMOND: Because he was drunk all the time, Davey was fired from Woody's band. I got a pass from Fort Benning in Georgia, where I was stationed with the Army and drove up to Birmingham with Davey and an Army buddy in my little Hudson convertible. It was a long way—several hundred miles. Fortunately I had gas coupons; as you recall, fuel was rationed. When we got to the Armory in Birmingham, there was a new drummer in Woody's band. It was Don Lamond. I tried to plead with Woody to take Dave. He said, "No John. I've got a reliable guy now and I'm not going to take any more chances." I must confess I couldn't blame him.

WOODY HERMAN: He never wanted to be anywhere but in our band. I think he felt most comfortable and lasted the longest with us.

BUD FREEMAN: His happiest period was with Woody. The band followed him, you know. And of course Woody is a wonderful guy. Dave loved him.

WOODY HERMAN: Those last two years before his death were very trying for Dave.

They were unhappy, frustrating, and largely unfulfilling years. He worried about his playing and his place in jazz. Though a supporter of the bop revolution, he continued to wonder what would become of him as the music progressed. He drank, and his health became increasingly fragile.

Tough's résumé at this point reflects his split musical personality. He worked briefly with Benny Goodman, with his traditional friends at Eddie Condon's, on 52nd Street with Bill Harris and Charlie Ventura and other modern players. For a time he traveled with Norman Granz's Jazz At the Philharmonic, his last steady job.

When sober, Tough was as many remember him—quietly intelligent, dryly humorous, helpful, a gentlemen who played as well or better than anyone.

LOU STEIN: Dave and I were together in the Bill Harris Quartet at the Three Deuces on 52nd Street in 1947. We played opposite Charlie Parker's group. The gig was for six weeks. I was still finding my way. I had left the Ray McKinley band and was free-lancing around town. In his way, Dave was extremely helpful to me. We had some really good conversations. He didn't give me any specific direction. But he was complimentary and encouraging and made me feel that my ideas were honest and good and compatible with the way he played. That made for the sort of excitement that I had never experienced before. Dave knew how to blend, how to play in the rhythm section and fill the role of the *accompanist*. You could lay back on his beat and feel as secure as it is possible to be.

More and more, however, Tough's desperation about music and himself permeated his day-to-day life. With the intensity of a man near the end of his rope, he sought something that would be fully satisfying to him. He spoke of giving up drums for writing, of teaching drums, of studying percussion.

HENRY ADLER: Dave came to my teaching studio/store on 45th Street three months before he died. "I've got a problem," he said. "I have a chance to go to Chicago with Muggsy Spanier for three bills [$300] a week. But I can teach in Newark, where I live, at a school for GIs. The guy at the school guarantees me $150 a week, with the possibility for more. Every student after ten, I get an additional $15. What should I do?" "Stay in town, if that's what you want," I told him. Even though he had studied and could read, he insisted, "I don't know anything." He started to cry. "What am I going to teach a guy—the way I play? How could I do that? I can't teach them how to *feel*." He seemed so down. "Help me teach. Show me how to teach," he said. He had seen some of my students and figured I had the answer.

Dave was a challenge. How he could play! I would tell kids to go out and buy his records. They were a lesson in how to play in bands. He was a talent, a real talent. But he was so dissatisfied with his own work. Can you believe that?

Whether or not Tough ever pursued teaching has not been documented. However, he did go to Chicago with Muggsy Spanier in November of 1947 to play at the Blue Note, a recently-opened jazz club. He then came back home to Newark and returned to a Veterans Hospital in Lyons, New Jersey, where he spent four months.

LOUIE BELLSON: Dave lived with me for two weeks before he died. We were at the Hotel Schuyler in Manhattan. A couple of us out of the Tommy Dorsey band had the penthouse. At the time, Davey was in the hospital and came in town on the weekends. One day I asked him, "Dave, what do you want to do more than anything in the world?" He said, "I want to study tympani and develop my technique, so I can have good hands." He wanted to do those things so badly. We talked about it a lot.

But he continued to drink, though always promising to quit.

JIMMY MCPARTLAND: I told him about Alcoholics Anonymous in Chicago in 1947. I explained I had stopped drinking and that I felt great and was playing real good. I asked him to join my band and give AA a try. He was very interested in staying sober. He said he would go back home, talk things over with Casey, and come out and play with my band. Marian [McPartland, the pianist, his wife at the time] was with me and we had a lot of work lined up.

But Tough couldn't stop.

STANLEY KAY: I saw Dave shortly before he died. He certainly wasn't in very good shape. He came in pretty juiced to a New York club where we, the Buddy Rich band, were playing. Buddy wanted to help him and asked what he needed. "Money" was Dave's response. Buddy gave him all he had—a hundred dollars. He asked if that was enough. Dave said it wasn't, took it, turned, and walked away.

DANNY BURGAUER: One morning I got to the store [Manny's in New York City] bright and early. There was Dave, lying in front of the door, bleeding and dirty. He had been rolled. I took him in, locked all the doors, and carried him up the staircase and put him on our shipping table. I washed him up and let him sleep. About noon-time, I saw that he was very bad and paid a cab driver to take him to Bellevue Hospital. That was shortly before he died. It was the last time I saw him.

Some days later, in the late afternoon of a cold day in December 1948, Dave Tough slipped on a Newark street and cracked his skull. Some say he had been drinking; others say he had an epileptic attack. He died the next morning, and his body lay in the morgue for three days until it was identified and claimed by his wife.

When the news broke that the great jazz drummer had passed away at age forty, there were accolades and expressions of love, respect, and admiration from musicians, jazz devotees, and the press.

"Dave was going home, going home to Casey. But he just never got there," said his old friend Bud Freeman. Dave Tough tried to find his way home through his entire life. Let us hope the last trip was successful, and that this gifted, tormented man sleeps in peace.

Buddy Rich
(1917–1987)

"Who will fill his shoes? No one can, but if we just heed his example and fill our own shoes, maybe we will work wonders."

—*JIM CHAPIN*

Buddy Rich at New York's Paramount Theater with the Tommy Dorsey band in 1941. Ziggy Elman, TD trumpet star, is blowing up a storm on the left.
Courtesy of Alvin Stoller.

During his career in jazz, Buddy Rich was a much-admired yet controversial figure. Some rather knowledgeable people, a few of them drummers, contend that he broke little new ground as a drummer. They say he mingled previously created ideas and techniques in a highly provocative manner, executing them with unbelievable speed and flair, bringing to bear *only* his strong musical personality. They insist that *other* drummers were the true innovators.

The late Shelly Manne, an unusually sensitive and expressive percussionist, took another position: "Buddy Rich is a tremendous drummer, and I have utmost respect for him," he declared in *Down Beat*. "But I don't retain anything Buddy plays. I walk out thrilled for the moment and I say to myself, 'My God, how did he do that with his foot . . . what did he do with his left hand?' It amazes me but only reaches my head. He doesn't reach my heart and soul."[1]

Those who say Rich introduced little to the art of jazz drumming certainly have every right to that opinion. Yet if Rich had not done anything innovative, there would not be a school of drummers, spanning several generations, who endeavor to do what he did. And I'm not talking only about speed. Because of a unique relationship between his hands and feet, and a natural connection to the music, Rich continually created ideas, patterns, and a time feeling that were his alone. With drum history as his foundation, he evolved an approach to music that links jazz drumming's beginnings to what's happening today.

Rich's drumming continued to be valid almost fifty years after he started because he took his cues from what the music unleashed within him. Not limited to any particular style, he was an overwhelming amalgam of everything you've heard. *And* he offered something new every time he played. Rich changed the view and conception of drums as had other great players of the instrument, like Baby Dodds, Chick Webb, Kenny Clarke, Max Roach, Tony Williams, Elvin Jones, and Gene Krupa. At a party given in Krupa's honor shortly before his death, the ailing Krupa spoke with deep feeling to the community of drummers and entertainers who had come to pay him homage. Speaking of drums, he pointed to Rich and said, "There's only one genius on this instrument. And he's sitting over there."

"I think Buddy Rich is far and away the greatest drummer who ever lived."

—*RAY MCKINLEY*

"He was put on earth to play drums."

—*STANLEY KAY*

"Rich is a superb drummer. He has the kind of technique on drums that Art Tatum had on piano. He can play anything he can think of with all the speed and dexterity and flexibility necessary."[2]

—*RALPH J. GLEASON*

"Buddy Rich is just incredible. He's a great, fantastic player. If it can be done on a drum, he can do it. . . . I've heard people say he doesn't swing. I think he swings. I used to practice with the things he does. I've heard it said he's not subtle. I've heard him be so subtle, so gentle. This man can play."[3]

—*ED THIGPEN*

"That damn fool knows the instrument!"

—*JO JONES*

"I don't know if he learned anything from me, but I certainly learned a lot from him."[4]

—*GENE KRUPA*

"I remember Gene Krupa once said that Buddy was 'outside of it.' By this he meant, there were drummers and then there was Buddy."

—*BOBBY SCOTT*

"I've heard him in every circumstance. And of all the drummers I've been around over the years, Buddy Rich is the consummate genius of the drums. He's like Tazio Nuvolari was with the racing car. He has complete control."

—*MEL TORMÉ*

"Buddy has something that no other drummer had, or will ever have. I don't know how it came about and I don't think he does either. It doesn't matter."

—*MEL LEWIS*

"Buddy summarizes all that has happened on drums throughout the history of jazz and popular music."

—JIM CHAPIN

"Buddy, Max, and Blakey—these people are Godlike to me. . . . Buddy's the kind of cat that I would pay to listen to and watch. Just solos, you know. I don't necessarily want to hear him with a band. I've heard him with a band a thousand times. But just to dig his solos, I'd pay money and sit down. He's something else."

—GRADY TATE

"I stood next to Buddy Rich night after night, week after week, month after month, under good conditions and bad—on theater stages, in airplane hangars, school gymnasiums, and nightclubs— and heard this guy play. He never ceased to amaze me, particularly those solos."

—PHIL LESHIN

"Give him a long drum solo and he'll just blow the place up."

—JOE MORELLO

"The more I hear him play, the harder it is to believe. . . . It is my feeling that when jazz history is set down, this tremendously inspiring, swinging drummer will go down, along with Davey Tough, as the man on his instrument."[5]

—GEORGE SIMON

MEMORIES

Buddy Rich has been a part of my life since the Tommy Dorsey days. My first encounter with him certainly had an effect on me. In 1942, I was all of twelve and in New York's Paramount Theater before noon one Saturday morning. With an uncle in tow, I had got there before the prices went up in the afternoon. That was a big thing in those days: the price. What was it? Thoroughly unbelievable by today's standards: thirty-five cents, or was it half a buck? You could see a movie, a stage show, the news, and a cartoon and have lunch for less than two dollars.

I had already seen and heard Krupa. As far as I was concerned, Rich was just another photograph in a Sixth Avenue store, a block away, among the glamor shots of musicians. In this case, it was the movie that drew me into the theater. That Tommy Dorsey and his Orchestra—featuring such stalwarts as Frank Sinatra, Connie Haines, the Pied Pipers, trumpet ace Ziggy Elman, pianist Joe Bushkin, and this guy Buddy Rich—were onstage was a secondary matter.

At a little after 10:30 in the morning, following a newsreel, a lighthearted cartoon, and some flashy organ playing, the lights went out. The Tommy Dorsey band rose majestically out of the pit, playing its theme, "I'm Getting Sentimental Over You," with the spotlight remaining on Dorsey in a white suit.

With surprising suddenness, the band cut away to a brisk Sy Oliver arrangement of "Deep River," an up-tempo item that immediately nailed you to the chair.

The curly-haired pixy-faced drummer, behind a white Pearl set exactly like Krupa's, became the focal point of the number. At the top of the stand, seated right next to the trumpets, Rich lifted the band with a strutting time feeling, the facility of his hands and feet bringing unusual strength to the brass and ensemble figures. Rich was at the center of everything. He heightened the snap and crackle of accents and punctuations. He explosively enhanced the flow and impact of groups of notes and phrases within the arrangement. Each stroke he played on the snare drum coordinated with what he added on the bass drum, and helped define the character of each pattern and the chart as a whole.

The wiry kid—he was twenty-five but looked a good deal younger—was precise, colorful, and very much in control. He blended elements of show biz flamboyance with pure jazz art. The beat was a constant, building phenomenon, and Rich kept adding to the surge of the performance. The auditorium echoed with his tart, crisp, vital snare. He worked the set, including the high-hat cymbals, as if it were an extension of himself. When he took a solo toward the end of the piece, Rich commented on the whole arrangement, compressing some of Sy Oliver's ideas, and expanding on others.

I really didn't know exactly what he was doing as he went about his task that morning. But as I learned about drums in the years following that experience, I remembered how easy he made everything look. Initially, he seemed the ideal, sleek drum machine, who seldom made mistakes. But it was the humanity of his playing—the way he shaped time and expressed ideas—that jolted listeners upright.

The Dorsey band was smoking by the time it reached the climactic spot when Rich soloed. As the curly-haired devil opened up, he developed a little bit of a story while moving across the drums and cymbals. There was a beginning, a middle, and an end. The conclusion, however, remains very much in my mind because I had never seen or heard anything like it before. He uncorked a single stroke roll, so fast and furious that his sticks became an absolute blur. Then, very suddenly, as he hit the sixteen-inch cymbal on his far right, it was over. There was a pause, then the audience erupted, calming down only when Dorsey came to the microphone to announce the first act.

After that vivid opening, the show streaked by. I couldn't get enough of everything. I persuaded my uncle, who was quite surprised by my intensity, to stay on for another stage show. Rich was dynamite on the rhythm tunes, and good but a little bored on the ballads by Sinatra and the Pipers. He was amazing with the acts—the dancers, the comedians; he caught every accent and nuance, adding dimension to what they did.

I walked out of the theater in mid-afternoon, hungry and wondering how I could play drums like Buddy. I thought back then that it was possible, with hard work, to achieve that level of excellence. It was a few years before I realized how impossible a goal that was. My oldest friend, who later played in Rich's band and sat in for him when he was up front, declared in no uncertain terms the impossibility of the quest. My few remaining delusions were fast eradicated by Gene Krupa who, long after I had stopped playing, laid it out for me in his characteristically good-natured way: "There's only one like him. I don't think there will be another drummer with talent like his. It's as simple as that."

Another time, Rich really turned me around. It was during an engagement by one of his early big bands at the Apollo Theater in Harlem. He had broken his left arm in several places, playing handball. When the curtain opened and the band began playing its opening number, it wasn't immediately apparent that anything unusual had occurred. The drum set and the comparative darkness of the stage obscured the fact he had his left arm in a sling. Musically there didn't seem to be any difference; his feet and right hand did all the work.

When Rich came down front after the opening to make an announcement, there was a collective gasp heard in the theater, followed by the buzz of whispers. The broken arm was hidden in a stylish sling, the same color as his jacket. Rich made nothing of his disability and went about his business, ultimately causing a riot uptown, then downtown. Drummers, indeed all sorts of musicians, came to Harlem and later visited the Paramount Theater on Broadway to witness still another aspect of Rich's freakish ability.

Describing the Harlem performance, Down Beat *was as awestruck as the rest of the music industry: "He danced around the stage and sang; sang a blues; drummed for dancer Steve Condos and then danced with him—first putting Condos' arm in a sling so they'd be evenly matched. The show came to a climax with Rich doing his famous 'Not So Quiet Please' number with one hand and his feet. Legend has it that Basie drummer Jo Jones, after seeing the performance quipped, 'If that arm heals, it ought to be broken again.' "[6]*

BUDDY RICH: I don't want to be America's swell guy in music. I just want to play and tell the truth. Every time I sit down at the drums, I have enough ego to say that what I did last night was good. But not good enough for tonight.

I don't play as well as I want to play. And I'm a bitch! I have never achieved the level of complete satisfaction. It's really impossible. That's what I mean when I say, "Set a goal." But you never reach it because it's always changing; you want more and more from yourself. Smugness is your enemy. It's over for you as an artist if you think, "Hey, I'm so good I don't have to try too hard."

Art Tatum didn't play as well as he wanted to. Oscar Peterson, "the man" on piano, is still working to create and execute something that doesn't seem possible. And he'll never stop. He'll keep trying to be the most complete, the best artist possible. I'm sure that he, too, says, "I'm not as good as I want to be."

There's too much control of our day-to-day lives. We're told what to read, what films are good for us, what music we should listen to, how fast we should travel on the highways. We're programmed by pressure groups and critics when it should be left to the individual to make up his own mind about things.

You gotta be what you are. You can't be what somebody else would like you to be. I'm myself, and what I am I think I like. The nicest part about it is that I know who I am, and so I don't have to grope for identity.[7]

As Bird said, "Now's the Time." What really is the key to this whole thing is whether you can play *now*, and relate to what's *now*, and use your past experience to communicate with the people who are listening to music *now*. That's what it's all about!

Every night is new, a challenge. As I said many times, I don't go to work at night. I go to *play!*

One of the leading lights of the major vaudeville circuits, "Traps, the Drum Wonder," "The Biggest 'Little' Act in Vaudeville" (as he was known back then) was in a Broadway show at age four in 1921. Two years later, Rich did a drum specialty called Village Toyshop in "Greenwich Village Follies," which added to his reputation. He had tutors when it came time for schooling; in 1931, at fourteen, he finally entered public school for the first time. Being one of the top child stars of the era, giving Jackie Coogan some heavy competition, made it impossible for him to live as other kids did. He dismissed that from his mind and just did his job as an entertainer. He did it so well that in a competition held by the Keith Theatre in New York, for the most popular vaudeville program, Traps finished second. Such stars of the period as Ruby Norton, the Duncan Sisters, Eddie Cantor, and Gallagher and Shean came after Rich.

When he began touring internationally as a solo act—he had begun as the finale to the act of Wilson and Rich, his mother and father—the reaction was as enthusiastic as it had been in the States. During a 1925 tour of the theaters in Australia, he was warmly received. One review typifies the general response of the critics. The added flavor of British reserve brings to it a suggestion of humor:

"Traps made his drums a decided medium for imparting pleasure to his interested audience. He was recalled several times."

Drummer, singer, dancer, and comic, Rich continued making appearances in theaters and other venues into the 1930s, as vaudeville faltered and ultimately died. By then, he had begun to find other interests.

BUDDY RICH: I've been playing drums since I was eighteen months old. But playing drums on a stage, with a band in the pit, is something I've put behind me. I have no recall of those years because I don't want to remember them. To reflect on what I did as a kid is of no interest to me. I hate being reminded that I was a star as a child. That was another lifetime.

In the early years of the 1930s, I decided to be a jazz drummer. I didn't want to be in vaudeville, have an act, or be an actor. I wanted to play a certain kind of drums. I sat down with my Dad and explained my feelings about it. He gave me the $54 to join the union, even though I had no job at the time.

GEORGE SIMON: I remember meeting Buddy a few years before he joined Joe Marsala at the Hickory House on New York's 52nd Street. My brother and I, for some reason or another, took a boat ride up to Playland in Rye, New York. We had no idea there was going to be any entertainment. This kid was master of ceremonies. I had to go to the bathroom so I passed the backstage area. There I saw a kid with a pair of drum sticks, playing all sorts of fabulous things on a chair. Because of my interest in drums, I struck up a conversation with him. He told me he really was a drummer and what he wanted to do was work with bands. What he was doing was just to make money, he insisted.

GRAHAM FORBES: My mother and dad took me to some company function at one of the hotels in mid-Manhattan. Buddy was one of the acts. It was in the early 1930s. He danced and drummed on the back of a chair. He was a hell of a dancer. And what he did with the sticks was beautiful. We met later on, when I was briefly with Tommy Dorsey during the war.

JIM CHAPIN: I'm certain Buddy learned a great deal during the years
he spent in vaudeville and right after that as well. The best drummers of the time were in pit bands. Because he came into constant contact with them, I'm sure he must have gotten all kinds
of free lessons and watched these drummers very closely.

Having had such a variety of experience as a youngster, it
was inevitable that a whole lot of show business and music filtered into him. He's forgotten more about drums than most of us
will ever know. When did I first come across him? In the mid-
1930s. I heard him at Dickie Wells' club in Harlem. Boy, what he
could do with his hands and feet—the way he combined them
when playing time and in solos. From the start, his bass drum
foot was his greatest strength.

Rich knew exactly what he wanted from life by the time he was
sixteen. Show business was the past; music—the future. With typical
Richian determination, the youngster did all he could to ready himself for a career as a jazz drummer. "Buddy had to learn to play *with*
people rather than *for* them," Jo Jones said on a number of occasions.
Rich sought the company of musicians; he sat in around town whenever possible.

With friends from his Brooklyn neighborhood, Rich started traveling around to hear jazz. He visited Harlem and saw a Chick Webb
show at the Apollo shortly before his eighteenth birthday. Webb's
performance made him realize there were a number of possibilities
for a jazz drummer. That Webb played so well and was a *band leader*
excited him.

RICH: I really began listening to jazz at sixteen. The Casa Loma
[band] gave me the first inkling of what jazz was all about. The
band's drummer, Tony Briglia, impressed me. He had a beautiful
press roll. If you recall, very few guys played high-hat cymbals in
those days. The ride cymbal was incidental; no one played it.
Most drummers concentrated on press rolls. Tony played a closed
roll with an accent—a regular roll with an accent on two and
four of each bar. His roll was comparable in sound and execution
to what Billy Gladstone, the great drummer at New York's Radio
City Music Hall, played. Billy was peerless; every chance I got, I
would sit in the back row of the theater and just listen. Both Tony
and Billy played a concert roll. Very closed. Very clean. When
Tony got it going, it cut right through the sound of Casa Loma's
brass section.

I used to sit with my family in the living room of our house
in Brooklyn, listening to the Casa Loma late evening broadcasts

from the Colonnades, a rather elegant dance and dining room at the Essex House in Manhattan. We're talking 1936. It was almost unheard of in those days for a band with a jazz foundation to be booked in a spot like that. Only "sweet" bands, like Lombardo, were hired for elegant hotels. I was quite impressed that Casa Loma made jazz acceptable in an unlikely situation. The band's versatility was its secret—the basis of its success in the room. Casa Loma dance sets were wonderful. All the people that came to the Colonnades were pleased because the ensemble had range. Not only that, that band dressed for its role—in tails. Even the setup on the bandstand—huge, gold music stands—fit the feeling of the room. Casa Loma played good jazz and made it painless for the patrons who came to dance. Smart. . . .

The Goodman band, with Gene Krupa, Harry James, and all the guys, also had a lot to do with my getting deeply involved in jazz. Here was a group of musicians that could be wild *and* subtle.

Gene covered all the bases. He could come down front and play with the trio and quartet or blow the band out, without having to make radical adjustments. He knew what to do. With the small groups, he used brushes and kept things soft and swinging. Gene was crafty with the small units. Yet when it was time to go back there with the band and get into "Sing, Sing, Sing," he just shifted gears, opened up and played like a monster. That's a great drummer!

Gene did a lot to call attention to the drummer. Until things began to change in the late 1930s, drummers were not considered part of the band. It wasn't unusual for a leader to say, "We have thirteen musicians and a drummer." The drummer had no stature; he was just a guy who sat in the back and played. Then along came these three impressive players: Chick Webb (the ultimate in hipness), Tony Briglia, and Gene Krupa—all outstanding players who made a great impression. They made me feel great about what I was doing.

Listening to these fellows was part of my education. You must understand I never had been any place where jazz was played before I made up my mind to involve myself in the music. I was from another world, a world that didn't have anything to do with music. I had a lot of catching up to do.

When I really got into it, I made it a point to check out every drummer who ever lived. I wanted to know exactly what each one did, how one differed from another. The guys I admired had concepts of their own: Briglia, Jo Jones (so subtle, so great on the high-hat), Chick, Gene, Sid Catlett (how he could play cymbals!),

Davey Tough. Davey was the only drummer I ever heard who could play behind an ensemble shout chorus with brushes and make a big band wail. Pretty hard thing to do. Tough was so skinny and small. But his energy force really was strong!

The more I came to understand others, the easier it became to shape my own concept. You don't steal or copy, just assimilate and change ideas and make things work your own way. If you stay honest, you can give *identifiable*, interesting performances, have something of your own.

Rich's fantastic technique, the ability that made him a child star, captivated those who heard them. But because he was young and lacking in experience with other players, he could be a bit overbearing and deficient when it came to shaping performances and bringing to them character and the subtleties that charm players and discerning listeners. Yet young musicians who heard him felt compelled to do whatever they could to get Rich exposure. His presence soon was felt on the jazz scene.

WOODY HERMAN: Shortly after we started at Roseland in 1936, pianist Joe Bushkin came in one night with a very young man. He took me aside and insisted, "This kid is the greatest drummer in the world. You gotta take him for your band!" It was Buddy. "I can't take him," I told him. "We have a cooperative band. It may carry my name. But the drummer and each guy in the group have as much to say as I do." Joe was a little impatient. Then he shrugged and smiled and said, "Well, then, I'll take him over to 52nd Street and talk to somebody."

Rich's friends in Brooklyn were equally vocal on his behalf. One of his biggest champions at that time, drummer-teacher Henry Adler, was mildly cynical until he heard Buddy play.

HENRY ADLER: I was working at a place called the Crystal Cafe on Church Avenue, near Rogers Avenue, in Brooklyn. It was a nice band, with George Berg on tenor and pianist Joe Springer. We had a real good time. Every night we started with a trio and ended up with ten or eleven guys on the stand. Everybody used to sit in—bassist Sandy Block, who later played with Buddy in the Dorsey band, Irv Cottler, the drummer who worked with Sinatra. So many drummers, trumpet and saxophone players—I forget. It was so many years ago.

One night, Barney Salad, a kid I used to teach, came in. He had Buddy Rich with him. He said, "This kid says he plays better than Gene Krupa." So I thought, *big man!* During the next set, I played all my tricks. I figured that I ought to straighten this Buddy Rich cat out. I let him play the next set. "Play soft," I said, because the first thing he did was pick up the sticks. "You better play with brushes." He looked at me and answered, "I'll try." I weakened and let him do what he wanted, "Okay, you can play with sticks. But keep it down."

Well, to say the least, he knocked me out. I became the happiest guy in the world because I realized it was possible to do what I'd been trying to do for so long. Admittedly, he had had no experience with bands yet. But the sheer control of his playing was unbelievable. It was not how great he played but the way he performed and turned his wrists.

I had studied with so many guys and practiced and practiced. And along comes this kid and does what I was trying to do, as if it were nothing at all! He had developed his muscles in a way that made playing easy. The first thing I asked him was "who taught you?" He looked at me in a puzzled way and said, "What are you talking about?" I told him I wanted to go to the guy who gave him lessons. Then I questioned him about how he came to hold the sticks the way he did and turn his hands that way. I scared the hell out of him.

Buddy gave it to me straight: "Nobody ever gave me lessons; I never studied." I grabbed George Berg and said, "See, that's the way it should be done." Buddy had come upon the right way of playing, *naturally.* He was wonderful to behold. Unlike a lot of guys, I wasn't intimidated by him, just happy to have found the guy who really knew how to play and had all the mechanics down.

Around that time, Joe Marsala asked me to come back into the Hickory House with him. I was too happy on my Brooklyn gig to make the change. But I had an idea. I told Joe, "This kid—he's been sitting in with us every night; he has so much goddamn talent. I'd like to bring him in for you to hear."

One thing you have to know. At this point, the guys in the little band in Brooklyn weren't too happy with Buddy. He didn't know exactly what to do with a band. But I sensed he would come along. All he had to do was *listen* and in two seconds his instincts would tell him what to do. He didn't read music. I began working on it with him. I felt that if he played charts in bands, he should know how to read. There was some doubt about this whole reading thing. His dad came to me and asked, "Do you think learning to read will hurt him?" I told Mr. Rich, if anything, reading would help him make more money. As it turned out, he was the exception to the rule; he could do everything we do instinctively and get to the heart of the arrangement and what should be done faster than guys who read.

RICH: I didn't get to play the first three Sundays I went to the Hickory House.

ADLER: Joe kept putting me off. He said things like "There are too many important people here, big stars." I said: "Joe, if you don't let him play, you can forget about our friendship. This is ridiculous. You gotta let the kid play. He has to be heard. It's as simple as that."

RICH: At ten to six on the fourth Sunday, Marsala motioned to me to come to the stand. We played a medium-tempo thing and it went okay; I played time. Then he asked me if I could play "up" Well, I lived "up" in those days. So we took off on a thing called "Jim Jam Stomp."

ADLER: Joe looked over at me at the bar and asked if the kid could play fast. "Fast as you can play that damn clarinet," I said. Joe was knocked out because Buddy played such good time and didn't get in anybody's way. Then Joe gave him a solo. And the place went wild. Never had they heard anything like it. I remember Lionel Hampton was signing autographs in the back and he was *smiling*. He had looked up because he couldn't believe what he had heard.

RICH: Everybody started walking out of the joint when I sat down. Then I got going on the fast tune and took a solo and they all filed back. Right after we finished, Marsala asked me if I'd ever played regularly in a band. And I said, "No." Then he put it right to me, "Can you come back tonight? The band starts about 10." I remember saying, "I have to call home first." I spoke with my mother and then my dad and said, "Look, I'll be home very late. Mr. Marsala asked me to come back and play." I was a kid. In those days, if you were a kid, you still asked for permission to stay out. They gave the okay. I don't think I'd ever stayed out till four in the morning before.

When I returned to the Hickory House that evening, I remember getting a real bad brush from Marsala's drummer, Danny Alvin. I played the second set. After it was over, Marsala asked me if I wanted the job. I said "yes." I took the gig without asking Dad's permission. I can't tell you how good it made me feel. He asked me if I could start in two weeks. I nodded. I never mentioned money. All I knew was I had the job. The $66 a week was secondary.

JOE MARSALA: I actually had [Buddy] on salary and kept two drummers for a while, because I didn't have the nerve to tell Danny Alvin I hired somebody else . . . he [Buddy] was a great jazz drummer right from the start. It didn't matter that he couldn't read, because he had a phenomenal ear even then.

Buddy was with me for about seven months. . . . We always got along fine—no personality problems. He was cocky all right, but with me this was more of an advantage than a handicap, because his self-confidence became contagious. Like at one time we played one of those concerts run by someone like Martin Block [a prominent New York DJ]. Our group had to follow the Benny Goodman Quartet.

You can imagine what it was like having to follow Goodman, Wilson, Krupa, and Hampton. But Buddy said to me, "Are you worried?" And I said, "Well, this isn't any easy spot for us, you know. That's Benny Goodman up there." He simply said, "Don't worry, we're gonna wrap it up!" That's how cocky he was. I always used to announce him as the greatest drummer in America, even in the presence of Krupa, who was one of my close friends.[8]

There is another version of how Rich came to be hired by Joe Marsala. The co-founder of the Hickory House, who booked musicians for the popular steak house, insists that he discovered Rich in Brooklyn, at a club facing Ocean Parkway, on the edge of Washington Cemetery. Impressed with the young drummer, John Popkin offered him a job at the Hickory House during intermission. Rich didn't believe him, so the club owner drove Rich home at four in the morning and woke up Pop Rich. Pop Rich believed him, says Popkin. Then it took a week for Popkin to persuade Marsala to hire Rich. The Rich and Henry Adler version seems more likely.

A caring family in the Sheepshead Bay area of Brooklyn gave Rich warmth in what can be an impossibly cold business. Years after death had claimed his mother and later his Dad, he and his two sisters and brother remained close. Buddy's father, "his greatest fan," says Illinois Jacquet, was very special to him. A veteran of vaudeville, a dancer, and comedian, "he was a wonderful man, a liberal and understanding father," said Rich.

RICH: When I got the job with Marsala, my pop couldn't understand my enthusiasm. He thought I was giving up my whole career "to be what? A drummer in a band?" And I said, "But that's what I want." To a vaudevillian who didn't know that jazz musicians are pretty swell people, it didn't seem plausible.

Yeah, my dad thought I was taking a step back. But, see, I was wise enough in those days to realize that vaudeville was dead and there wasn't really anything too special about a sixteen- or seventeen-year-old cat dancing and singing and MC-ing. Besides, I didn't want to do that anymore. Jazz was my thing. Eventually my pop came to understand how I felt, particularly when he saw how much I enjoyed myself and that I was becoming a success.

One thing you have to realize: my father always had my well-being in mind. A week or two after I started at the Hickory House, he said he wanted to talk to me. I went home every night. I took the BMT at four in the morning and arrived at the house about 5:30. Today, I'd have to carry an automatic weapon. Pop and I got together one afternoon. He talked about drugs. He made me promise that I would steer clear of hard drugs and bad people and alcohol. That I would keep our name unblemished.

You know, I went through my whole youth without ever smoking a cigarette. Never drank. I didn't start smoking until a little over twenty years ago. I kept my promise to him. I never got involved with anything. This was important to him. It's equally important to me, my daughter, my wife, and family.

While Rich was becoming established at the Hickory House, he began making the rounds of spots on "The Street" and in Harlem. He caused something of a furor at Dickie Wells' uptown, and even filled in briefly for Chick Webb at the Savoy.

TEDDY MCRAE: Chick brought Buddy Rich up to the Savoy from some place downtown. "Yeah, yeah, I got a guy I went to hear," he said. "He got two fast feet, wrists good. You gonna hear a lot from him." He let Buddy come up in the band. I think the band scared Buddy to death, you know. I don't think he had ever played in a band that heavy. Chick called the set; he threw a good set on Buddy, man. And he played. He played good. Chick told us: "If I'm not around, keep this guy in mind. Remember this name: Buddy Rich. He's gonna be a great drummer one day."[9]

TEDDY REIG: I used to go to the Hickory House and sit in the corner because I couldn't afford it. I'd listen to Buddy there and then watch him go up and down 52nd Street and cut everybody on the block. He'd get more drummers fired than anybody. After a club owner heard Buddy, he'd get the idea that *his* drummer sounded like nothing at all.

GENE KRUPA: I [first] heard Buddy play when he joined Tommy Dorsey's orchestra at the Palmer House in Chicago. The *only* reason I didn't hear him *before* then . . . I was scared to death. The guys in the Goodman band—like Harry James and all the chaps—used to come by and say, "Man, this kid over at the Hickory House is going to scare you to death. Wait till you hear him."[10]

HENRY ADLER: The guy had everything right away. How? Who the hell knows? Some guys called him a freak. I knew what he had and used to bring people in to see him. It used to aggravate Buddy when I said to my friends, "Watch his wrists; watch his foot!"

Adler wasn't alone. Musicians and jazz fans flocked to the Hickory to pick up on the phenom. Later, Sinatra, fascinated by Rich's technique, took associates and friends to Buddy's gigs and urged them to observe him close up.

STANLEY KAY: I played in Buddy's band for an extended period of time—sat in on drums when he was up front. Later I managed him. I had a lot of opportunity to dig the guy's playing. I go back with him to the Hickory House. My sister knew Buddy even earlier. They were both child performers. She had an act and worked on the bill with him.

I was there the Sunday afternoon he finally got to sit in at the Hickory. O'Neil Spencer played. A guy from Eddie Mallory's band sat in. Another drummer, from Andy Kirk's band, got his chance. When Buddy finally played "Jim Jam Stomp," I just said, *"he's the one."* I had never heard anything like that. I became a fan of his. That was it. I was totally dedicated to him from that point on.

It was during his stay at the Hickory House that Buddy got to know Basie. Did he ever tell you the story? Well, Buddy went over to the Famous Door and Basie came over to him and said, "I hear you're pretty *bad!*" Buddy was humble. He answered, "Well, you know . . ." Basie urged him to play in the band. I think Buddy was one of the few white guys who sat in who could really do what had to be done. He played the style perfectly. And the guys—Sweets, Pres, Buck Clayton, Jack Washington, Earle Warren, Walter Page, Freddie [Green]—loved what he did.

Buddy could play anybody's drums at any time—morning, night, noon. That's it; he could do it all. I always said to him that somebody put you here to play drums, that God said he was going to put a man on earth that can do this thing better than anybody else and he chose you.

At the heart of his great talent was uncanny rhythmical co-ordination. And the funny thing is that he didn't know what he did. He couldn't really tell you how he developed something. I'm convinced he didn't know. It just flowed, came out. It was a bit of a miracle.

Like everyone else, however, Buddy had certain insecurities. Not reading music for most of his career was one of them. In the early years, he thought guys put him down because he wasn't the complete musician. But what he always did was *total*. You can't play charts any better than he did. Case in point: shortly after he became a band drummer, he worked on a CBS radio show called "The Saturday Night Swing Club." It featured a studio orchestra directed by Leith Stevens. No one knew he couldn't read. The music was put on his stand; of course he couldn't tell the difference between a whole note and a quarter note. But he could *hear*. He listened to the arrangement once or twice and that's all that was necessary. He played it down as if he had written it himself.

RICH: I was at the Hickory for about a year. I did a radio show on CBS, had a band of my own for a short while at the Piccadilly Hotel Roof and then went out on the road with the Bunny Berigan band. We had a lot of fun. There were some good cats. George [Auld] was on the band; Bunny [Berigan] could really play but he fell down a lot. He could really drink. It seemed all we did were one-nighters. A lot of times you'd wonder what town you were playing. It became a blur. That went on for six months.

When I returned to New York, I got a call from Georgie [Auld] to come over to the Hotel Lincoln to sit in with Artie Shaw. I played that night and two weeks later, in January 1939, I went to work for Artie Shaw.

ARTIE SHAW: I was looking for individualists who would add character to the organization. Georgie Auld, the tenor saxophonist, was one of the people who had the qualities I was seeking. He brought a new sound and a wealth of jazz feeling to the band. Trumpeter Bernie Privin had his own thing. And Buddy provided the fire we never had before.

RICH: Yeah, I feel I changed things around, somewhat. There were a bunch of great cats on the band. Artie played fantastically well and he had vision as band leader. Then, of course, there were Georgie, Privin, trombonists George Arus and Les Jenkins, trum-

peters Johnny Best and Chuck Peterson. These guys could spark
the whole band and keep it inspired.

That's what I tried to do after I joined. I was full of steam. I
loved to play hard and loud. I felt a great sense of responsibility
when it came to the band's performance. The heart of any group
is the drummer. If a big band is going to be right, he certainly has
to do his job.

Rich was in some ways misunderstood. He knew what he wanted
to do, but he got flack from band leaders and fellow musicians who
weren't crazy about being told by a kid how an arrangement should
be played. Rich was unstintingly blunt when it came to his feelings
about music and just about everything else. He didn't make a lot of
friends.

HELEN FORREST: The band was a hard-driving collection of excellent
musicians, especially after Buddy Rich got behind the drums. . . .

After Buddy Rich joined us, I talked to him because no one
else would. And I liked him. If you've seen him guesting on the
Johnny Carson show in recent years, you know Buddy to be a
wisecracking smart aleck. He hasn't changed a bit, except maybe
to get worse. But I got along with him. Buddy was my age when
he joined the band, but he seemed younger. He was a cocky kid
who was afraid of being in the wrong. If someone told him how
to do something, he'd tell them off. He threw his drum sticks at
the sidemen who messed up during a number on stage and threw
his fists at some offstage.

Artie put up with Buddy because he was a great natural
drummer, maybe the best that ever lived, one of the few white
musicians that black musicians really have admired. He's been
the best technically, and maybe the best at giving a band a driving beat. But he had the worst temper of any person I ever met.[11]

BERNIE PRIVIN: Buddy wasn't chummy; he didn't hang out and frat-
ernize with all the guys. Georgie and I were close to him. The
reason—we were the only guys on the Shaw band that he knew
before coming aboard. I had been a member of the group he
headed at the Piccadilly Roof in 1938. It was Adrian Rollini's job
until Buddy took it over. Georgie, of course, played with him on
the Berigan band and helped get him the job with Artie.

Yeah, Buddy might have been a little uppity. He would get
cute once in a while. But it was nothing serious. He knew he was
good. Even then, I wished I could play trumpet as well as he
played drums. I was spoiled working with Buddy. Other drum-

mers never really sounded right after I had been with him on the Shaw band.

BOB KITSIS: Buddy liked to have fun. On this one occasion, it was at my expense. The Shaw band was playing the Golden Gate Theater in San Francisco. During one of the stage shows, Shaw announced he would play "St. Louis Blues," on which I had a long piano solo. But when I tried to get into it, I found all the keys of the piano were stuck together with gum. It was pretty embarrassing not being able to play. Everyone, outside of Shaw and me, thought it was a scream, particularly Buddy, the culprit.

RICH: I was a pretty wild guy. I was considered a rebel in my youth. When I was eighteen or twenty, I had very strict ideas about how I wanted to present myself. But I had two choices to make; I could do my own thing, and be out of work, or I could almost do my own thing, and work. So I compromised—never to the extent where I was unhappy, but if I wanted to work for somebody, and [he] said, "This is the way I think it should be done," and if there was an area for agreement, I *did* it that way. If I didn't, I had the option to quit.[12]

SHAW: When Buddy first came with me, he was wild—totally undisciplined. I have certain records of mine, made at that time— radio air checks where he actually got going and sped up the tempo to beat hell. He had not yet developed full control. And he was difficult to curb. Sometimes it was him against the band.

Another thing about Buddy: When I first gave him a long, long drum solo, he threw everything, including the kitchen sink, at the audience. So, one evening, I talked to him about it. "Buddy," I said, "what are you doing up there? Do you realize that when you start where you do, there's no place to go but down?" Well, he hadn't quite thought of that. That's how naive he was. I told him: "Start easy and build, build, build! Save your best shots till the end. You're delivering the knockout blow in the first round, for Christ's sake!"

But when he did develop the technique that provided control, he became a revelation. I mean he really uplifted the band. But I had problems with him until the end of our playing relationship. In fact, just before I left for Mexico in November 1939, we had a really major confrontation.

I said to Buddy: "You know, it's just not working. You don't play with the band anymore. It's getting to the point now where's it's like a drum solo accompanied by the band. You're going to have to tone it down." He said, "Man, I don't know how I can do that." I pointed out: "You've got to learn, Buddy! You know, loud doesn't mean good. Sometimes a tremendous amount of energy can be propelled through a quiet, understated thing. . . ."

RICH: I was quite clear about what my job was by the time I went with Shaw. I knew I had to embellish each arrangement, tie it together, keep the time thing going, inspire the players always to be better. My way was to keep the energy level up and push hard. This concept was strictly from Harlem. I learned from black drummers like Chick Webb, Jo Jones, Sid Catlett, and O'Neil Spencer. I was never a fan of white drummers, with the exception of Gene Krupa and Tony Briglia; they were just too bland. I loved excitement, fast tempos, lots of color.

In the old days, the only reason you were hired was to keep the band together. It was up to you to swing the band, add impetus and drive. And it certainly helped if you had a feeling for what the arranger wanted when he brought a new chart in. The function of the drummer is to play *for* the band. If you're good enough, you'll be noticed. You don't have to sit up there and be a focal point, because if you are, what's the point of having a band?

But what Rich was trying to do annoyed leaders. Though they liked the energy, intensity, and pulsation he brought to a band, they were offended by the means he used. In essence, he tried to enhance charts. To give them new dimensions, he played accents and fills that moved the music forward. By introducing cross-rhythms, he also provided a sense of surprise. By dramatically underlining brass and ensemble figures and spotlighting crucial spots within the music, while keeping the time firm and buoyant, Rich added a flow and continuity and vitality that was lacking in the work of most drummers.

As far as he was concerned, what he did was quite natural and much needed. A few years later, most discerning musicians would accept his ideas and praise his playing. Obviously his concept was musically valid.

RICH: I'm *physical* when I play. One of the reasons for the physicality of my work, particularly in big bands, is the tendency of lead trumpeters to lay back. I like everything *aggressive!* The reason I started using the bass drum to accent figures with the brass and the ensemble: very simple. What was being done just wasn't sharp enough! Other drummers didn't shape arrangements with the muscle that was called for. By simply adding the bass drum to a figure, you bring to it importance, new power. You add energy to the sound.

On breaks and fills, if you do what is necessary, you can make the music *live*. Let's say you have one bar to do the job. You don't use the fill as a solo opportunity to show speed; you play some kind of jazz feeling that gives rise to the entrance of the band.

About incorporating the bass drum into things: when I joined Artie's band it used to drive him crazy, because instead of accenting things with the brass on the snare drum, I would accent on the bass drum, simply keeping the time on the cymbal and using the bass drum to accent. Artie was used to hearing four and not having the drummers make the accents with the brass. Drummers were time-keepers. . . . So I used to augment my sound with my left hand and by using the bass drum to accent things. It used to drive him crazy, but when I didn't do it he missed it, because the bottom wasn't there, and it was all highs. I started to develop the foot by playing not only accents. . . . I began to incorporate it into solos, by simply leaving two or three beats out with either hand, and using my foot.[13]

Leaders don't want drummers who overpower either the leader or the band. They want to know you are there; they want to *feel* you. But they don't want to *hear* you. Understand? If I did something that was not written in the chart, say at a rehearsal, leaders and some of the guys would say, "What was *that?* Where does it say *that?*"

I had so many problems because I felt what I was doing was right. And I continued to follow my instincts. Leaders and some of the critics weren't ready for a punk kid to set the pace in a band. But I felt what I did was okay as long as it didn't interfere with the chart. If I could add a bar or two of excitement, it was worth the problems. For the most part, Artie and later Tommy Dorsey came to understand that it had little to do with showing off. I was trying to do things that would clarify and energize a chart. I guess it stems from a feeling, a sensitivity that I have for charts.

George Simon, an aficionado and leading critic of the big bands, at first had the same difficulties with Rich as some leaders and musicians did. Even though, he, too, is a drummer, with an understanding of drummers' motivations, Simon found it hard to go along with Rich's concept until later. In a review of the Shaw band, he made his position clear:

GEORGE SIMON: The rhythm section is apt to play too much. The recent advent of Buddy Rich is probably the main cause. Buddy is a brilliant percussionist; he has tremendous technique, he's steady, and he gets a fine swing. But like so many drummers who have grown up in the Krupa era, he's cursed with the misconception that a drummer's supposed to do much more than supply good background. As a result Buddy, in his enthusiasm, plays too much drums, consequently breaking up the general rhythmic effect. . . . With Rich building garages, beautiful as they are, a lot is taken from the style and swing too.[14]

In a reevaluation of Rich years later, Simon readjusted his position just a bit:

SIMON: I was reviewing the band right after Buddy joined it, and it's quite conceivable that he hadn't yet achieved the simplicity that Artie admits is so difficult to achieve. Certainly, Buddy soon did settle into a tremendous groove and the Shaw band began to swing as it never had with any of its previous drummers.[15]

GUS JOHNSON: The first time I met Buddy was in Kansas City. I was playing with Jay [McShann] when he had seven pieces. And he was with Artie Shaw's band.

The manager of the restaurant where we played, see—it was a club restaurant—on the Plaza . . . came over and said, "We have a young drummer out here. See if you can get him to sit in." One of those things.

And he came over . . . and sat in with the band, and he was something else. Right then and there, I knew he could outplay Krupa.

We used to have a lot of battles in Kansas City. Jesse Price—he was one of the main drummers. I told him about Buddy Rich, and he said, "Oh, he can't play no drums. I'll take my wire brushes and tear him up." I said, "Now, just a minute, Jesse. You cannot play wire brushes like this guy plays wire brushes."

He said, "I'll show you. I'm going to meet him downtown tomorrow, and we're going to have a battle down there." So they met down there. . . . at a little club right next to the College Inn. Musicians came down with their horns and Jesse Price brought his snare drum and sock cymbal. No bass drum. He figured Buddy couldn't play without a bass drum.

Buddy came there and just tore him up. Jesse said, "You know, he can play drums, can't he?" I said, "I told you: he just whupped you all over the place."[16]

When Mel Tormé heard Rich during the Shaw period, he sensed what the drummer was trying to do and appreciated his efforts fully.

MEL TORMÉ: From the moment I was exposed to his talent via Artie
Shaw's record of "Carioca" [Bluebird, 1939], I instinctively knew
I had heard drums played at their optimum, and that this blind-
ingly gifted performer's technique, taste, sense of dynamics, and
his uncanny grasp of what syncopation was all about, began
where every other drummer's ended.[17]

The Shaw band was utterly different with Rich in the drum
chair. He sparked the band with both his drumming and exclamations. He'd yell in key spots in an arrangement, adding to it an
infectious sense of enthusiasm. I remember a variety of other
things as well. His high-hat work, for one. Buddy used a very
interesting semiclosed, just barely open choke cymbal sound
with Shaw that is almost indescribable. He choked the high-hat
just enough so he wouldn't cover up the figures the band played.

His drum breaks were marvelous—I'll tell you that. The little gem he played on Shaw's recording of "Prosschai" [Bluebird,
1939] lingers with me. There actually are four two-bar breaks; on
the last, he plays a terribly fast single-stroke roll, culminating
with four shots on the bass drum, socking it under the brass.
Nobody had ever used the foot that way before. Chick Webb—
none of them. One of the most incredible characteristics of Buddy
Rich's playing, then and now, is the fantastic correlation between his hands and feet.

RICH: The [Shaw] band was a hell of an experience. I think Artie was
a very dedicated guy. He taught me a lot about music, behavior
on the stand, things in general. I liked what we did—the good
tunes, the show music, even the pop tunes. The band always
sounded good. Even the ballads had a pulse. The simplicity and
naturalness of the scores were a big plus. There always was melody and a strong feeling of swing.

There was only one minor problem when it came to playing
the music. Because it was natural, it took a great deal of concentration to keep it that way.

I had a marvelous time that whole year, and for one simple
reason. I was young and didn't know any better! Sitting in the
bus in a snow storm, putting newspapers in the windows to keep
warm, was one of the realities. Freezing in the cold months, fighting off bugs and sweating your butt off in the summer, while
traveling from town to town, are not the kind of experiences that
make for a feeling of nostalgia.

I must admit, though, the large, appreciative audiences
made you forget a lot of the inconveniences. I remember many a
night getting off the band bus, after coming God knows how far,

in unbelievable weather. And there it was: another ballroom, club, or auditorium. But the people, who patiently waited for us, got the juices going in me. Because they were so devoted, enthusiastic, you wanted to be great for them. You wanted to live up to their expectations.[18]

In the eleven months with the clarinetist, Rich rapidly matured from a green, impetuous, terribly talented young drummer to a musician whose concept was beginning to bear consistent fruit. The live recordings of the Shaw band reveal Rich's inclination to push the bass drum too hard and play it too loud. But the swing he motivated in the ensemble and his adroit inventive solos more than compensate the listener.

On an RCA set (*Artie Shaw in the Blue Room/in the Cafe Rouge*), comprised of 1938 and 1939 broadcasts from the Hotel Lincoln and Hotel Pennsylvania in New York, he offers a picture of a drummer absolutely bursting with talent and enthusiasm. The integration of the bass drum with ideas expressed by his hands make what he does simultaneously provocative, interesting, and surprisingly functional within the big band context. Yes, he is loud. But the volume serves to enhance the energy of the band. And always, as on the appropriately titled "Everything's Jumpin'," the pulsation is utterly irresistible.

Buddy uses all his equipment in service of the beat, everything from the high-hat stand—getting a pinging sound that cuts right through—to the cowbell. He is not the completely mature swinger he would be in later years. But he gives every indication that he has the wherewithal to become the premier drummer of the big band generation.

RICH: After Artie split for Mexico, I decided to relax for a while before getting back to work. The Shaw band continued without Artie up front. But I wasn't terribly interested in being a part of that. It seemed to me it was a time for me to think about a few things. I began to realize where I stood in the music business. It was clear that I had value to band leaders.

I hung around the house in Brooklyn with my family. We talked a lot. I slept late, ate my favorite food (many times at Nathan's, the great hot dog and hamburger place in Brooklyn), and generally cooled out. Nights you generally could find me at the Pick-A-Rib on 52nd Street and Sixth Avenue in Manhattan. It was a great spot that had marvelous ribs and swinging music on the juke box. The place had a very special feeling. All the cats who meant anything on the music scene would drop by.

One evening my Dad got a call from a guy named Bobby

Burns, the manager of the Tommy Dorsey band. He told Burns that I probably could be contacted at the Pick-A-Rib. To make a long story short, Burns told me that Dorsey had heard and liked my playing and wanted me to join the band. Because I didn't want to play with a band that was so deeply into Dixieland and ballads, I turned the cat down. Burns kept calling me. He offered some pretty good money and sent me an airline ticket to Chicago, where the band was appearing at the Palmer House. No commitment was made; I made the trip to hear what was going on, musically, and to meet Dorsey. I sat in with the band and again was offered the job. If I decided to make the move, I would be replacing Cliff Leeman once more. As you know, I followed him into the Shaw band. But the band didn't appeal to me. It just wasn't my style, so I turned down the offer and flew home.

But the calls kept coming from Burns. He asked me to fly out to Chicago again. He said Tommy had told him that Sy Oliver was coming over from the Jimmie Lunceford band to change things around on the Dorsey band. When I heard that, I was excited about the possibilities. The band could easily become heavy in the swing department with a guy like Sy writing for it.

I returned to Chicago and made arrangements to join Dorsey. The money was good; I got billing. All in all, it looked okay.

From the start Rich had his difficulties with Dorsey and with a few of the guys in the band.

RICH: Dorsey was the greatest melodic trombonist in the business, but he was a drag to work for. We never really got along. He was another heavyweight in the juice department. Leaders like to have their own way, but I knew what I wanted to do and did it. He always resented when I talked back to him, but he respected what I played and knew it was good for the band.[19]

CARMEN MASTREN: Buddy joined the Dorsey band at about the same time [1939] as Sinatra did. I remember Tommy was sick and I was leading the band—in the Empire Room of the Palmer House in Chicago. I'd already been in the band for three years. Every night, Buddy would come in and say, "Let's do this, let's play that." He wanted to swing. Most of the early evening we concentrated on dinner music—quiet stuff with the brass playing softly, generally with mutes. Buddy didn't go for that and made it very clear. I said, "Look, if you don't like it, pick up the phone and call the 'old man' upstairs."

For a few years, I kept Rich out of the Dorsey band, unbeknownst to him. Tommy had heard a lot about him, see? He said, "There's this kid drummer, Buddy Rich, with Joe Marsala at the Hickory House. Everyone says he can really play!" I told Tommy, "He's still a young kid. You ought to wait before you talk to him." Buddy was cocky. You know that, don't you? He was that way back then, not just when he became known.

So two years passed; Tommy heard Buddy play and hired him. Rich gave Tommy a lot of headaches. He would quit and Tommy would give him a raise. The guy left the band a couple of times on the road and Dorsey was put in a spot. The way I look at it, if you ask for the top figure and get it, I believe you owe the man paying you some loyalty.

I must admit I didn't hit it off with Buddy when he first came into the band. But I *never* put down his talent. I don't know anybody who's as fast. His bass drum work is unbelievable—so forceful and quick. And Buddy has a fantastic memory. When he was with the Dorsey band, he couldn't read. We offered to teach him. He said okay. But nothing ever happened. Why? He'd hear an arrangement once and the next time we played it, he knew it.

But he overplayed. He backed brass and ensemble figures; he would get into a soloist's style and do things during a solo. He'd anticipate what the guy was going to do. All that drives me crazy. What I want to hear is good *time*. That's what Dave Tough and Cliff Leeman did—gave the band a good foundation. As far as I'm concerned, good music is *time*, not all the embellishments.

Another thing: Buddy hated to play for the acts in a night-club or theater, though he did it quite well. I used to lead the band when the entertainers came on in theaters and clubs. Tommy would just step away for a break and throw it to me. Each time Buddy had to do that part of the drummer's job, he'd make it clear how much he disliked it.

Buddy and Sinatra were buddies because they joined the band at about the same time. When some of the guys talked about Buddy, Frank would say, "Maybe they're jealous of Buddy." I told him, "What the hell have we got to be jealous about? This is a number one band. We're not a bunch of ama-teurs!" You know what I mean?

When Buddy was hired by Tommy he was young and full of piss and vinegar, raring to go all the time. That probably both-ered a couple of the guys. If he had his way, we would have played Sy Oliver arrangements all night, which was great for *him*. He really could play those charts. But ours was an all-around band. We played ballads and had a diversified book. Tommy didn't play one style.

Buddy didn't like to play brushes either. Yet when he used them, he was sensational. On those records he made with Art Tatum [*The Tatum Group Masterpieces;* Pablo, 1955], he played brushes almost all the way. I wonder how the hell he held himself down in order to play that way? I was so surprised. He just played great time. I said to the guy who listened to the records with me, "It can't be Buddy Rich!" He reassured me it was. It only goes to prove what the guy could do if he had the motivation.

On his first night with Dorsey, Hymie Schertzer, one of the building blocks of the great Benny Goodman orchestra, became aware of Buddy Rich's love for swinging music, and a bit of the drummer's humor.

HYMIE SCHERTZER: I had spent all that time with Krupa and those last few weeks when Dave Tough was breaking in [with Goodman]. I knew Tommy as a ballad player. The night I joined him, naturally the first thing we played was his theme, then immediately went into a loud up-tempo number. Buddy Rich was the drummer. And he swung. A ballad was the next piece in the set. As we began to play I couldn't hear any drums. I looked around and there was Buddy sitting behind us with his arms folded across his chest. "What about some rhythm, Buddy?" I asked. He looked at me as though I was nuts. "Sorry, Hymie, I don't play ballads, only swing numbers."[20]

JOHNNY MINCE: Buddy was a friend of mine. So I didn't have the nerve to tell him not to play so damn loud on my solos. But I did open up about this friend of mine back in Chicago Heights—that's where I'm from—who had played in a little group with me. He wrote me that he didn't have any drums to take to work. And he didn't have money to buy new equipment. When Buddy heard about this guy's predicament, he said: "Listen, Johnny, every year Slingerland gives me a new set of drums. When I get my new drums, these are yours. Send them to your friend." That's how good he was about that. I never did get to collect the set, though; I was inducted into the Army and couldn't be around when Buddy received his new drums.

There are so many Buddy Rich stories. One of the best concerns this dance act. We were booked to play a theater in Pittsburgh. We got there early in the morning to rehearse the show before the theater opened. The male half of the act passed out the music to the band. Buddy got his part and put it aside, saying, "I don't need that." The dancer walked over to Tommy, a little bit panicked, he said, "Your drummer won't play the music; there are a lot of cues. He's got to catch the cues. Tommy said, "Oh, don't worry about it. Just go ahead and do your show."

Buddy sat, watching the dancers do their act. He didn't make a move or give them a bit of assurance. As we went through the show, I thought: "Isn't this awful. Those people are really sweating it out. They're going on thinking they might be ruined." Well, the dancers shouldn't have worried; everything couldn't have turned out better. The dancers went to Buddy and told him they had never had a performance go so well. He not only played every one of their cues but added a lot to their presentation with little subtleties. That was his kind of trick; Buddy could do things like that. It's instinct and memory. He just seemed to know where everything fell, where the stops are, how many bars are allotted for solos. The whole thing.

GEORGE HOEFER: The Dorsey band was a group loaded with temperament. Tommy himself, never reluctant to say it as he saw it, was involved in his intermittent fights with brother Jimmy. And when Frank Sinatra joined the band, the combination became really explosive. Sinatra, capable of being as salty as Rich, didn't always enjoy the drummer's sense of humor.

On one occasion, Rich talked a girl into approaching Sinatra for his autograph as he was coming off the stand on New York's Astor Roof. Sinatra gave it to her. And the girl, carefully coached by Rich said, "Gee thanks. Now if I can get two more of these, I can trade them for one Bob Eberly." Sinatra, seeing Rich laughing on the sidelines, was furious.[21]

Though Sinatra and Rich were roommates and quite close for periods of time, there was an increasing sense of competition between them.

RICH: Oh, I've had falling-outs with everyone. Frank and I were roommates when we were with Dorsey and when you have two strong personalities, you always have conflicts. Each one wants to be top man. That causes friction, arguments, and fights. But then it's over. As intelligent people, it's over and you shake hands. It's like being married.[22]

JACK EGAN: The competition between Buddy and Frank really was something. An incident in Indianapolis makes clear what was going on between them. Tommy called me one night—I was the band's advance man. I made preparations and did publicity for

Tommy on the road. He wanted me to have a blowup [photo] made of Frank. He was plugging the hell out of Frank because of his anger about Jack Leonard, his star vocalist, walking out on him. It was a strange move for Tommy because he never built up singers or anybody else in the band. Really, it was an unusual thing for a leader to do and leaders generally didn't push anyone in those days.

After the first show in Indianapolis, TD called me again and asked how long it would take to have another blowup made. I said I could possibly get it done overnight. He said, "Have one made of Buddy. Get one right away!" It seems when Buddy saw Frank's picture in the lobby of the theater or on the outside, wherever it was, he wanted the same treatment.

As you know, Buddy grew up in show business. He had enough ham in him to want the attention and billing. This happened right after Frank joined us. The Lyric Theater in Indianapolis was one of his first dates with the band.

One other thing: don't forget Tommy was crazy about Buddy's playing. He had Sy Oliver writing special stuff for Buddy as soon as he came to work for the band.

SY OLIVER: Buddy came on the band shortly after I did. Dorsey called me one afternoon about five o'clock and said, "Buddy Rich has been hired, he's arriving in Chicago tomorrow. Can you do a number for him that we can rehearse tomorrow?" I said, "Tommy, it's five o'clock in the afternoon; I'm in New York." He said, "You can do it!" So I wrote the damn number on the plane. It was called "Quiet Please." I landed in Chicago; Tommy picked me up and we went to the Palmer House. The piece was copied, rehearsed by the band, and Buddy played it on the job that night.

Now there's a case in point. The ending on "Quiet Please" was one of those double F figures—you've heard it—you know what it's like. Buddy was playing it before the band. He picked up on it the first time down. He was the first to play the ending right.

The figure kept doubling up. It was a pattern, of course. He was playing a solo and catching those accents. Fantastic. . . .

I never told Buddy how to do anything. I'd put an arrangement up. And by the time the band was beginning to get into it, he was doing just the right sort of playing and catching everything. Buddy was the only guy I ever worked with who could successfully do what I call playing lead trumpet, while keeping the rhythm going too. You know some drummers catch figures the band is playing and sacrifice a certain amount of impetus when they do that. They don't have the taste and discrimination to know when to do it and when to hold back. Buddy's musical sensibility told him just when to apply the pressure and when to sit back and play time.

Did you ever notice that as much as Rich played, he was never intrusive? He never overdid or played in the wrong places, even back then. Jimmy Crawford, of course, was the perfect example of this. He swung with the Lunceford band without making a noise. I mean, you felt him!

As far as my relationship with Buddy Rich: I never had a moment's difficulty with him. In all the years I've been in this business I've never had any trouble with anyone who could *play*.

Remember one thing: if you come along with new ideas, they're not going to be accepted right away. You're going to have trouble being understood. That's what guys like Rich and Dorsey had to face—they never really could come into their own until they had their own bands.

Rich, as a drum soloist—let's put it this way: when I wrote an extended piece for drums, Buddy made it interesting. He was exciting, while most drummers are just dull—*bombs*! And he knew that you can't swing a band with just your hands. I tell drummers all the time, "Put your god damn hands in your pocket and play the bass drum and foot cymbals. You can't swing a band without playing those very well!"

PHIL LESHIN: I joined the Tommy Dorsey band at the King Edward Theater in Toronto in the early 1950s. It was a kick playing the Sy Oliver arrangements. We did two weeks up there and then got on a train for New York. I was sitting in the club car the night we left with Sam Donahue, Charlie Shavers, and a few other guys. Tommy walked in. It was the first time I had a conversation with him. He sat with us for a while and shot the breeze. He turned to me at one point and said, "So you came off the Buddy Rich Band, huh, kid?" "I sure did," I answered. "How's he playing?" Dorsey asked. "Great," I responded. "You're right!" he said. Tommy paused for a few seconds and then went on, "Hey, how did God ever give so much talent to such a terrible guy?" "That's funny," I told him. "That's exactly what Buddy said to me when I gave him the news I was joining you!"

Tommy's feeling about Buddy's playing really was put in perspective a bit later during a rehearsal. Our drummer wasn't really making it. And Tommy shouted, "For God's sake, why can't you play like Buddy Rich?"

Rich not only made a major impression on musicians in the first five years of the 1940s, with Dorsey; he had a highly discernible effect on fans. They strongly supported him, making possible victories in the drum category in the 1941, 1942, and 1944 *Down Beat* polls. Rich was a showman, particularly in theaters, yet his combination of ease, musicality, imagination, pulsation, and blinding facility was what won everyone over.

The drum wonder had taken what in essence was the Chick Webb/Gene Krupa style and remade it in his own image. Impossibly well coordinated, truly ambidextrous, he was able to play equally well with his left hand what he articulated in the right. With this expressive pair of hands and his dancing feet, he could provide a creative foundation for either a big- or small-band performance, while artfully adding an unexpected subtlety or two that made everything work.

For many who watched and listened to him during this period—myself included—Rich seemed a magical maker of sounds and inventor of ideas. I vividly remember walking down the stairs of the 400 Restaurant, a large New York spot that booked top bands in 1944 and 1945, and picking up the sound of the Dorsey band. It seemed to me that no one could make the snare drum whisper and shout, and the bass drum explode, the way Rich did. And the way he kept time! He gave every evidence in 1945 of being the only drummer who could make the Dorsey band come alive in a very special way.

How did Buddy feel about playing with Dorsey? He was never completely forthcoming on the subject. But Rich remained in the band from 1939 until 1945, with time out for the service. Certainly the money must have been right, and the music more than okay.

RICH: People think of the Dorsey band as playing sentimental music; but when you remember "Well, Git It" and "I'll Take Tallullah" and all the things that were popular in the Forties, that was a hard-driving band for the particular era.[23]

On the other hand:

RICH: When I was with Dorsey, I always was looking to go with a band that was hipper. I was never satisfied.

A lot of drummers were listening to what Rich was doing with Tommy Dorsey.

ALVIN STOLLER: He just caught my ear, like Chick Webb did. I loved what I heard. Buddy had that spark; his enthusiasm, the feeling of his playing were just right for my taste at that time. Buddy became a giant influence on me.

I knew Buddy from Brooklyn. I spent a lot of time getting to know him, living at the house with Mom and Pop Rich, Buddy, and the rest of the family. Very often I'd ride into Manhattan with Buddy and Pop Rich to spots like the Astor Roof where Buddy was appearing. I'd sit backstage and listen and observe this guy. It was amazing. I don't know whether we'll ever have another like Buddy again, in our era or in the next 100 years. . . . I don't believe anyone can actually replace Buddy. I was fortunate to be the one to *follow* him [in the Dorsey band]. He was just something else!

MEL LEWIS: I didn't hear Buddy until he became involved with the Dorsey band. I was quite young at the time and felt "here is this very fast, flashy kid who knocks me out!" He sounded and acted very much like Gene Krupa. I didn't hear anything I hadn't heard before. But I couldn't believe his speed.

In those days, I know that Buddy dug Gene. I think he was influenced by Krupa. But all along, he had this special thing about his playing. He was impossible to imitate. I have no respect for drummers who have tried to turn themselves into Buddy Rich. They're fools to try. These imitations remind me of women who try to look and sound like other women. So many tried to transform themselves into Marilyn Monroe, for example. They can't do it; there's no way. There's so much more to it than what's on the surface. Imitators only can copy the most obvious characteristics of Buddy Rich.

You couldn't capture him. He just had something no other drummer ever has had or will ever have. I don't know how it came about. No one does. Not even Buddy knew.

ALLEN PALEY: I remember him with Dorsey. The way he played off the snare. The continuity. It was unbelievable. How he got around the set. Back then, a lot of guys had good hands but they couldn't get around the set the way he did. In other words, he could go from the snare to a cymbal to the tom-tom to something else, and it was as though he was still playing on the snare drum. It was that easy for him.

LOUIE BELLSON: Anyone with great technique can be made to suffer because of it. Certain people stigmatize you. Buddy and I talked about this. For a long time, Buddy was put down for being able to play whatever he had in mind. Cats would say, "Man, he's a great technical player. But I'd rather have someone else in the rhythm section." Because he was such a vital force as a soloist, his other talents were ignored. These people I'm talking about never stopped to listen to what Buddy could do in a band. I heard him on so many occasions play great with bands. Really he never sounded bad. His work with the Basie band was just so fine. I understand this thing about technique. I've been put through a few changes of the same kind, myself.

ED SHAUGHNESSY: If Buddy hadn't been so creative and tried to play fresh all the time back in the Dorsey days, his remarkable technique wouldn't have meant anything. He worked so hard to be good. I've always respected his integrity and spirit.

But his humanity is seldom discussed. There is so much concentration on Buddy's volatility and bad moods. When he was with the Dorsey band, he did something for me I've never forgotten. I was seventeen and had begun playing on New York's 52nd Street. I had some great *musical* gigs—with Bud Powell and Jack Teagarden and a few other cats. But I was broke. I literally didn't have another drumstick. I didn't want to use the other drummer's sticks at the place where I was working. It wouldn't have looked right. So I told a friend about my predicament. He said, "Walk over and see Buddy Rich. He's with the Dorsey band at the Paramount Theater." My pal said, "Say hello to Buddy for me; I'm old friend of his." So, feeling I had a bit of entrée—though I had never met Buddy—I went over to the stage door and asked for him. He invited me up and I told him my story. "I'm embarrassed by this," I said, "but your man told me to say hello. He thought you might be able to loan me a couple of sticks." Buddy smiled and answered, "Hey, man, are you kidding? We've all been there." He called the band boy and told him to "get me that package in my dressing room upstairs." The guy came down and there were something like two dozen pairs of sticks in the package. Buddy said, "This will cool you for a while."

Dorsey used Rich's flair and experience as an entertainer to his advantage. Aside from having drum features written for Rich, which fans increasingly demanded after the drummer became one of the stars of the band, Dorsey often put Rich to work as a dancer.

RICH: Every time we played a theater and we would have a dance act on the bill with us, like the Nicholas Brothers or Tip, Tap and Toe, Tommy would call me down from the drums as a sort of finale thing and I'd . . . dance with the various acts. It was kind of fun, every now and then to be able to dance and get away from the drums.[24]

Rich had a particular rapport with dancers. He not only combined his background as a dancer and his drum style, he had a way of playing for dancers that almost everyone remembers with unusual clarity.

PHIL LESHIN: Timing was Buddy's thing. Coming out of a show business background, it was ingrained in him. It was clear to him when still a kid that timing was everything, no matter what you did in the business.

I used to run into dancers who worked with Buddy when he was with Berigan or Shaw or Dorsey. Some of them were major stars and far bigger in the business than Buddy was at the time. But he was special to all of them. They agreed that working with him for the first time was a unique experience. It made them realize what it was like to truly dance in *time*.

The service was inevitable during the war years for any able-bodied young man. Rich chose the Marines; he wanted to fight, not play in a band while others were in combat. He left Dorsey, played briefly with Benny Carter, and reported for duty in late 1942. He served for almost two years; there were run-ins with officers and non-commissioned officers. Rich became a judo instructor at California's Camp Pendleton. At one point, however, he was injured during training, hospitalized, and ultimately given a medical discharge.

MEL TORMÉ: A freshly discharged BR sauntered into the Palladium Ballroom in Hollywood one evening . . . still wearing his marine "greens" and sporting the shortest haircut in tonsorial memory. He had not had a pair of drumsticks in his hands for over six months. The resident bandleader, Charlie Spivak, spotted Rich, introduced him to the audience, and invited him to "sit in" with the band on "Hawaiian War Chant." Spivak's drummer, Bobby Rickey, handed Buddy the sticks somewhat reluctantly and the erstwhile judo instructor proceeded to stun the crowd with an incredible tour de force. He had never heard the arrangement before; yet, with that amazing, built-in radar unit he was born with, he caught brass punctuations and sax nuances as though he had personally authored the chart.

When the ovation he received finally subsided, he stood, bowed mockingly, one arm behind his back, one across his stomach, like a six-year-old reciting a poem, and handed the sticks back to Rickey with an offhand "Here, kid." Bobby, at that precise moment, looked as though he would like to pursue another line of work.[25]

After the service, Rich had eyes for a band of his own. But he returned to Dorsey and remained for about a year. What did he remember about it? Very little.

RICH: The past is not something to dwell on. I have no real recall when it comes to yesterdays. I don't want to think too much about them. But there is an experience that stands out in my memory. The year: 1944. Jo [Jones] was being drafted into the Army. Basie called me. I was with Tommy's band in Hollywood making a movie. Basie was opening in a joint called the Plantation on Central Avenue in Los Angeles. He said, "Can you come down and help me out?" I was so honored, so proud that Count Basie asked me to play with the band, I still get goose bumps when I think about it.

I'd get up about 6 A.M. and drive out to Metro to do the picture with Dorsey—I think it was *DuBarry Was A Lady*—shoot out from MGM at 6 P.M., go back to my Beverly Hills apartment, change clothes, and then drive down to the Plantation and work with Basie until 2 A.M. I'd get back to my place about four, wake up at six, and start the whole thing over again.

That went on for three weeks. I look back on the stand at the Plantation with Basie as one of the monumental things in my life. It had nothing to do with my playing. Just the memory of performing with that band is important to me. That's all.

GEORGE HOEFER: For some reason, Basie and Rich never got around to discussing money. After [three] weeks, a regular substitute for Jones arrived. Basie handed Buddy a signed blank check and told him to fill in as he saw fit. "My pleasure," Buddy said—and gave the check back. So Basie bought Buddy an expensive watch. Later, Basie said the musicians in the band had been so appreciative of Rich's drumming that they came to work early for the first and last time during his stint.[26]

TEDDY REIG: One time Buddy was in Reno with the Harry James band. Basie was in Vegas. We called him because Basie's drummer, Sonny Payne, had taken sick and we needed a drummer very quickly. He said "okay" and drove all the way from Reno. Buddy lived in Vegas at the time. When he got to the club, the first thing he said was, "When Sonny gets well, you send him to Harry James, and I'll stay here with Basie."

Well, Buddy did terrific that night. But there's more to this little story. He was playing so well that Basie gave him a long solo. I tell you, man, the bass drum pedal was moving so fast that I thought I was seeing double. When he climaxed this exhibition, he hit three cymbals in one fast sweep around the set. Then he fell off the drums and passed out. His wife got him a little brandy and he started to come around. When he sat up, he looked me in the eye and said, "Do I get the fuckin' job?"

Whenever Basie called, Buddy was ready. On one occasion, Rich flew to Chicago on a moment's notice to sub for an ailing Basie drummer, ignoring the inconvenience and the intense lower back pain he was feeling at the time. "I would have done anything for the man," Rich said. "I was honored he thought of me in his times of need."

Rich's love affair with Basie and his music began while the drummer was appearing at the Hickory House on New York's 52nd Street. The Basie band was working a block away at the Famous Door, building an enthusiastic following, particularly among musicians. In fact, Basie and his musicians rapidly were becoming the talk of the town.

Rich often came by to listen and visit with Basie and the men in the band, sitting in on several occasions. Basie was very encouraging to him, as was Basie's drummer, Jo Jones. Their music—straight-ahead, rhythmic at its very core—came to lie close to Rich's soul. That he performed so well in the fluid circumstances that only Basie could devise was no surprise to anyone who knew him.

CHARLIE PERRY: Basie loved Buddy. Basie frequently came to hear Buddy play and unfailingly showed his appreciation. Just as often Buddy would appear where Basie was working, sit in and excite everyone. One night, I was sitting in Birdland with Marshall Brown, that great teacher of young musicians who has since passed. There was a break, a bit of an intermission. Our attention strayed; the focus became conversation rather than music. The band quietly came back to the stand. The music began. The drums sounded so different, so good, so right, we stopped talking and turned to face the bandstand. Buddy had taken over the drum chair. The musical climate had changed entirely. Everything became sharper, more colorful, and pulsating.

By 1945, the year he left Tommy Dorsey to form his first big band, Rich personified the great swing drummer. He generally locked in with the bass player; the flow went in a straight line. The pulse was built by repetition, which was the cause of its intensity. Pulsation was rarely broken, except by occasional bass drum accents. Rich was more flexible than most swing drummers because of the size of his talent and what he heard in the music. Though lighter and more conversational in small groups—refer to recordings he made during this period with Lester Young and Nat Cole—he remained the classic

big-band stylist. The bass drum was the center around which his
hands evolved patterns. When one heard him play breaks and solos,
the picture emerged of a highly inventive tap dancer. The picture
constantly reappeared as Rich created hand and foot patterns behind
the ensemble and individual sections. He had cleverly translated
what he had learned from dancers to the drums.

Listen to some of the Victor recordings made in 1945, such as Sy
Oliver's "That's It" and "The Minor Goes a-Muggin' " (the latter fea-
turing Duke Ellington at the piano) with Dorsey. Also try "Rattle and
Roll" with Benny Goodman; and "Your Father's Mustache" with
Woody Herman (both Columbia, 1945).

The Dorsey sides are notable for their forceful forward motion,
with a strong "bottom" provided by Rich's foot; on the Goodman
recording, Rich pushes the band with the straight-ahead strength
and buoyancy basic to the swing idiom.

"Your Father's Mustache," however, is a bit different in character. It reflects some of the turbulence and the changes in mid-1940s
jazz. Woody Herman's First Herd provocatively combined the traditional and the new while Dorsey and Goodman were content to linger
in the past and play polished, jazz-oriented dance music in the swing
style.

Herman's nurturing and understanding attitude and adventurous charts by Ralph Burns and Neal Hefti offered a fertile environment for a jazz drummer. On "Your Father's Mustache," written by
trombonist Bill Harris and Hefti, Rich mixes tension with a sense of
liberation. He contributes a great deal to the success of the recording
by emphasizing key rhythmic patterns in the arrangement. He supports these patterns with his left hand and foot, while defining the
outline of the tune and laying down the time in an uninhibited, confident manner. A team player, he brings all the rhythm and color
necessary to this striking number.

Because Woody Herman conducted such a great school for jazz
players, one wonders what might have happened if Rich had replaced
Davey Tough full-time instead of just filling in when Tough was ill.
Would Rich then have played differently when he moved on to lead
his own big band?

ED SHAUGHNESSY: I think it's significant that the only drummer who
    successfully subbed for Davey when he was ill was Buddy Rich—
    this was before Don Lamond permanently succeeded [Tough].
    During Davey's tenure, and he was sick quite often, a number of
    good men filled in, but the only one who could come in and
    match that intensity and team spirit was Buddy. Some people
    aren't aware of how much a team player Buddy could be. I think

with his own band everybody knew he was dynamite within the band as well as being the greatest soloist. But in those days, the 1940s, a lot of people didn't know that. When he subbed with Woody, guys in the band would tell me how great he was; that he was the only one who could match Davey's fire.[27]

At this juncture, in 1945, it is important to remember that Rich was still performing within the swing idiom. While he was forming his first big band, which made its debut at the Terrace Room in Newark in 1945, the music of Charlie Parker and Dizzy Gillespie began to gain increasing currency within the jazz community. The concept of jazz rhythm, and the role of the drummer in small and large bands, was undergoing some alterations. Rich had to deal with a new set of ideas.

Until that time, the drum wonder had gone virtually unchallenged. Because he was unique and completely outdistanced others on the instrument, Rich was always treated with great deference by musicians and entertainment industry people—almost like a mini-divinity. He was "the one," as Stanley Kay and Terry Gibbs aptly named him, and seemed untouchable. Certain leaders and players disagreed with his approach to music, and commented on his temperament and black moods. But his ability was never in doubt on any level.

The advent of bop brought conflict. Rich moved ahead, playing adventurous, modern arrangements with his band. But he didn't favor the type of drumming some of the charts demanded. He disliked the way bop drummers broke rhythm; their concept of time annoyed him—it wasn't aggressive enough. Rich disagreed with the manner in which the younger players used the bass drum—not as a time center, but only for accents. He found little that was appealing in the new concept of swing. This linear, almost melodic sort of playing didn't have enough weight for him.

GEORGE HOEFER: During the early days of bebop, he expressed disdain for the new drummers, saying they had no right to break the rhythmic flow of a band with constant explosions and extraneous back beats. To him, drums constituted a complete instrument, designed to set and hold the beat, and even when throwing in explosions, he would never sacrifice rhythmic continuity. He felt the modernists were sacrificing the essential reason for drums in order to get a new sound.[28]

Despite major reservations about what modern drummers were doing, Rich appropriated what worked for him, making certain contemporary modifications within his basic style. The changes are not immediately discernible on his records or remote radio broadcasts from the 1940s, but things were beginning to happen.

Rich lightened up on the bass drum; and experimented with ideas employing his left hand and foot. His approach, though still intensely rhythmic and rooted in the swing manner, took on a more melodic emphasis as he moved from drum to drum. He turned to larger cymbals for time-keeping, and away from the snare drum.

Ultimately, he offered listeners his own view of what had been happening on drums. It was a process of assimilation—slow and measured. Rich remained Rich. His contention was that to copy others was to die as an artist.

STAN LEVEY: When I first saw Buddy with Artie Shaw, I wasn't impressed—not thrilled in the least. And you know, he was good. But later he seemed to change, to listen, to become more conscious of his surroundings. Okay? Of course he had this fabulous technique that had always been his calling card. But he matured, musically; I guess that was what it was.

TERRY GIBBS: Buddy became a better and better drummer—greater than he ever was—because he opened his mind to what other drummers were doing. At one time, he turned away from the new people. That was in the bebop days. But once he let the contemporary music into his system, he just grew and grew.

PHIL BROWN: For almost two years [1951 and 1952], I sat next to Buddy, playing bongos, or filled in for him on drums when he led [his] band down front. When he was playing, I literally was as close to him as anyone can get. I was so near him that his perspiration would fall on me. That's pretty close!

It wasn't any easy job. He'd listen to me and come around and say: "Why are you paying so much attention to those guys at Birdland? Why do you think those modern drummers are so important?"

He didn't pull his punches when it came to his feelings about things. But I didn't let all that bother me because being around him was like going to a fantastic school. Being in the band with great musicians and having the opportunity to be on intimate terms with his playing was more than compensation for whatever difficulties I had with him.

Buddy was a lot tougher in those days. He wasn't easy to get close to or to fully understand. But if he respected and liked you, a relationship could be established. As a player, there's nothing to say about him because everybody knows what he could do.

PHIL LESHIN: When you worked for him, you had to do it *his way!* He was that good, that dominant. As for the bop thing: Buddy, unlike Tommy Dorsey who put down the music, wanted to get with what we were doing. He knew we all loved Diz and Bird and Max Roach and Bud Powell. Of course he fired whole bands. But it wasn't because they were boppers. It had to do with attitude and one essential problem: *bad time.* In the early days of the bop movement, there were a number of players who thought they were doing terrific things. Not so. A bunch of them had bad time. Buddy couldn't take that. He never felt negative about Bird or Phil Woods or Davey Schildkraut. He loved those guys. How he behaved toward a player depended on whether the guy's time was good, whether he swung and moved him. Buddy didn't care if you took figures and phrases across the bar line and brought them down and forward again.

It came down to *talent.* If a musician had it together—that's all that mattered to Buddy. When I was on the band and in his small groups, I saw him strongly react to so many players. It didn't matter where they stood, stylistically. He dug Allen Eager, Harry "Sweets" Edison, Kenny Drew, Wynton Kelly, Sonny Criss, Al Cohn, John Bunch, Zoot Sims. . . . He played in a way that he thought would bring out the best in them.

When Zoot first joined the band in the late 1940s, we were doing a lot of theaters. One day between shows, Zoot told me how he felt about Buddy's playing, "No matter where I am in my solos, I always feel that guy pushing me. He makes you play!

TERRY GIBBS: For a while when I was on Buddy's band in the 1940s, I traveled with him from date to date in his Cadillac. I thought I'd make a few suggestions. One night after the gig, while on the road, I said, "You know, Buddy, the guys in the band love Johnny Mandel. You never let him play. You really ought to give him some solo time." He said, "Really?" The next night we get on the bandstand and he lets Johnny play. The guys didn't believe it. Now, the next night, Buddy and I are together again in his car, speeding along. I said: "You know something, the guys want to be encouraged to play. They need that so badly. Why don't you say to them: 'Let's play tonight!' " He looked at me and answered, "Really?" So we're on the bandstand the next night and he says, "Let's play!" The cats in the band couldn't believe what was happening.

This went on for a week. On the eighth night, we were going through the Arizona desert on our way to L.A.; it was about four in the morning. Again, I started telling him what changes needed to be made. He stopped the car and said, "I don't want to hear any more of this shit. Get out of my car!" I tumbled out. "Come on, you're out of your mind," I said. He sped away. Here I am standing in the dark; I was frightened to death. I kept hearing these night sounds. I thought every sound was a snake. I'm deathly afraid of snakes. I thought he was putting me on and would come back. No such luck. I waited for four hours until the band bus—which only went about thirty miles an hour—picked me up. Buddy knew the bus would eventually come along and pick me up. But he had to make his point. I've never forgotten that experience.

PHIL LESHIN: I joined the band late in 1949 at the Apollo Theater. I was young, scared, and thrilled about this job, my first really top, professional gig. I guess I thought I was pretty hip. I idolized Ray Brown and tried to play the bass just like him. Though I didn't think so at the time, Buddy was helpful to me. He took whatever talent I had and made me go with it.

My first show with the band was something. We had this instrumental to do. Buddy started playing very heavily on the bass drum. I couldn't hear myself. He said: "Get up on the neck; let me hear you!" We were cooking on "Sweet Georgia Brown" or "Swingtime in the Rockies"—I'm not sure which one it was— and he kept playing the bass drum louder and louder. The stronger I got, the louder he pounded. Though I resented what he was doing, I kept up with him. Instead of plucking the notes, I was reaching over and pulling the strings real hard. This was before most bass players used amplifiers. Buddy forced me to play out! He liked a dominant bass line on the bottom of the band. I took the stamina from somewhere and kept getting more and more forceful. My hands and fingers hurt! But the pain meant nothing, considering what I had found out about myself.

GEORGE HOEFER: [Rich] had grown up in a world of clawing, scratching, and fighting for survival, where those that fought the hardest sometimes won. . . . He had learned that a good offense was often the best defense. He was to use much of what he learned in later hassles with band employers, booking agents, and managers."[29]

And sidemen . . .

EDDIE BERT: We were at the Apollo. Buddy hired Philly Joe Jones to play for the acts. On opening day, most of us came in a little before the first show at 10 A.M. Buddy played the opening number. Then he waited for Philly to come out and play for the acts.

Philly wasn't around. Buddy had to do the whole show: dancers, comedians, singers, the whole thing. You could almost see smoke coming out of the top of his head. He was that angry!

Philly made it for the next show. Buddy didn't say anything. But after some of the acts had done their thing, Buddy came to the microphone and announced, "Ladies and gentlemen, we're going to have a drum battle." I'm sure the Apollo management was quite surprised by this move. Buddy sat at one drum set and Philly at the other. You could see Philly was nervous. He played his cute, subtle ideas and got some applause. Then Buddy just blew him away with fireworks. It was no contest. After he had torn him up, Buddy went over to Philly and said, "Now make sure you're here and ready to play every damn show!" During the rest of the engagement, Philly Joe was on hand and played every show.

Being a band leader at the tail end of the big band era was no picnic, particularly if you wanted to play good music. Rich got off to a good start. Frank Sinatra backed him to the tune of $50,000, a lot of money in 1945. The Rich band had a good sound, good charts, good players. And needless to say, rhythmic appeal. It was a sharp, appealing mixture of Goodman, Basie, and modern jazz.

RICH: The first year I had my band, I grossed almost three hundred thousand dollars.... Then the band business really started sliding....[30]

It was a difficult, transitional time in American music. Bop took jazz out of the mainstream; singers were predominant in the popular realm. Commercial material—novelties—increasingly found its way onto records. Bands lost their place in the hearts of the public. There were final manifestations of interest early in the 1950s when Glenn Miller–style bands, led by Ralph Flanagan and Jerry Gray, temporarily caught on. The Billy May organization was successful; fans liked the sound of its saxophone section, which played in what veteran commentator Leonard Feather describes as a "novel glissando unison style." But these were the last gasps of a noble era.

Buddy Rich kept trying to keep his band going for approximately four years. He quietly disbanded his first big band in 1949. He held on as long as he could, making minor concessions to popular taste; but a jazz orchestra dedicated to swinging, contemporary music had appeal only to musicians in the late 1940s.

Many young musicians in the big cities, particularly New York, made a point of listening to the band when it came through. It had the fire and modern approach that had brought Woody Herman fame and a stable financial position. The Rich band's records for Mercury in the mid-1940s merely suggest what many of us heard in person. Johnny Mandel's arrangement of Dizzy Gillespie's "Oop Bop Sh'Bam," though badly recorded, is the best of the releases. Very much in the modern idiom, it features Rich reacting to the modish feeling of the band and has an excellent trumpet solo by Red Rodney.

Broadcasts preserved on the Joyce and Golden Era labels give the listener a better idea of what Rich and company could do. Players like Mandel (bass trombone); Allen Eager, Zoot Sims, Jimmy Giuffre, and Al Cohn (tenor saxophones); Terry Gibbs (vibes); Jerry Thirlkeld (alto saxophone); Charlie Walp, Carl "Bama" Warwick, and Bitsy Mullins (trumpets); Earl and Rob Swope (trombones); and Harvey Leonard (piano)—the list goes on and on—gave the band unusual substance. Arrangers Mandel, Tadd Dameron, Tiny Kahn, Eddie Finckel, Billy Byers, and Jimmy Giuffre, among others, developed a library that inspired musicians and people close to the band.

While most people remember, above all, the band's musical value, Buddy's friends and associates have different memories:

MEL TORMÉ: Frank Sinatra came around to one of the band's first rehearsals and heard Buddy sing an arrangement of "Aren't You Glad You're You." Frank suggested to his old friend that he sing with the band. Fortunately Rich took his advice. One of the things that lingers with me from that period is his singing. In 1946, he made one really memorable vocal record with the band for Mercury: "Baby, Baby All The Time."

I had been aware of Buddy's interest in singing and songs for a while. He hadn't sung in public before he formed his band. But I recall, right before he left Dorsey to go out on his own, we used to drive to Casino Gardens, not far from Hollywood, where he was working. We'd talk about songs on the way. He loved Jerome Kern's "The Touch Of Your Hand," a poignant, delicate, little waltz. That was his favorite song of that time. There was another song, "Some Other Time," a beautiful Sammy Cahn/Jule Styne thing. Buddy would sing it a lot when we drove to the Gardens. You wouldn't think that a heavy swinger like Buddy would like songs of that kind. But he loved ballads. He loved Kern.

STANLEY KAY: I remember two great engagements—one at the Apollo when he had the broken arm. The other was at the Paramount, two years later, in 1949. We shared billing with Mel Tormé. Buddy decided to perform with just two bass drums on a feature number.

Ray McKinley had introduced the two bass drum thing in 1940 with Will Bradley. Then, seven or eight years later, Louie Bellson got a lot of publicity by performing with two bass drums. Other drummers, like Ed Shaughnessy, picked up on the idea.

Buddy had the Slingerland Drum Company send him two bass drums. They were mounted on a platform. His vehicle was an arrangement of "Ol' Man River" that Basie gave us that year. Well, Buddy just folded his arms and played two bass drums in front of the band. He didn't practice, woodshed, or study. He just played those two bass drums, as if it was the most natural thing in the world.

RICH: I got tired of hearing about Louie Bellson and his two bass drums. Let me preface this by saying Louie and I are . . . great friends. But I got tired of hearing how difficult . . . it was to play two bass drums. I decided that if you're going to play two bass drums, you should play two bass drums. . . .[31]

Rich played the opening section of the "Ol' Man River" chart and the first drum solo on the set. During a band interlude he walked down to the bass drums, stage front, and went into the second solo with just his feet.

MEL TORMÉ: Do I remember Buddy's double bass drum solos? I should say so! I came on to close the show, right after he broke the place up with his feet. It took what seemed like an eternity to get hold of the audience after Buddy did his thing.

For the next decade, Rich continued to play well and evolve as an artist. He traveled and recorded with Norman Granz's "Jazz At the Philharmonic" troupe, performing with some of the best jazzmen ever, ranging from Lester Young and Roy Eldridge to Illinois Jacquet, Charlie Parker, and Gene Krupa. He worked as star sideman for periods of time with the Harry James band, and appeared with the "Big 4" in the company of saxophonist Charlie Ventura, bassist Chubby Jackson, and pianist Marty Napoleon. Rich returned briefly to Tommy Dorsey, who was co-leading a band with brother Jimmy, and spent several months with Les Brown's Band of Renown, with which he recorded a memorable version of "The Carioca" for Columbia in 1949.

During this segment of his life, there were also several Buddy Rich small groups and a few reincarnations of the big band for specific engagements, featuring players who stimulated him. The years preceding the rebirth of the Buddy Rich Big Band in 1966 were also notable for the drummer's recording activity. He made a number of recordings that are still in print, including some with Charlie Parker, Harry James, Lionel Hampton, and Art Tatum. He also went into the studio with Basie and made albums of his own with large and small groups and as a singer.

Some of them are quite striking. "The Golden Bullet," a Columbia single with the transitional Basie small band, vintage 1950, is Rich at his best—forceful, limber, buoyant.

An album tribute to his friend and mentor, *This One's For Basie* (Norgran, 1956), finds Rich in the groove in which he seems most comfortable. The band is relatively small (eleven including Buddy), compact, and light-footed. It swings in a manner reminiscent of the Basie organization of the late 1930s. Unpretentious arrangements of familiar Basie material by Marty Paich provide excellent frameworks for the musicians. All the players are on intimate terms with the meaning of the early Basie band and know how to play its music. Buddy is persuasive in the role of the supportive band member; he has a number of solos, but for the most part he leaves his ego outside the studio. Buddy, Paich, pianist Jimmy Rowles, tenor saxophonist Bob Cooper (in a Lester Young mode), trombonist Frank Rosolino, and trumpeter Harry "Sweets" Edison make this LP a most communicative, valid musical experience.

An intense and swinging Rich at Birdland, New York City, in 1960. Charles Stewart.

Buddy Rich Just Sings (Verve, 1957) reveals a surprisingly musical singer, very much at home in the jazz milieu created by Harry Edison, the great tenor saxophonist Ben Webster, pianist Paul Smith, bassist Joe Mondragon, and drummer Alvin Stoller. Buddy's work as a singer goes way beyond the mere competence of a hobbyist. His ability to interpret standards makes me wonder what might have happened if Rich had not thrust this aspect of his talent in a closet after an abortive attempt or two to launch a singing career.

According to Rich, all this activity just filled time until he took it upon himself to go into the band business again—against all advice. Between big bands he seemed to lack a real center of interest in his musical life; he seemed at odds with himself. Periodically he announced he was through with drums; he talked about singing, dancing, having an act. Reports in music magazines further reinforced the impression that Rich was not satisfied with his life. There *were* forays into show business—He played dates as an entertainer—but audiences were generally unaccepting of Rich the singer/buck-and-winger. To people around the world he was a drum champ. When he tried other things, the change of image seemed to disturb them.

Lack of stability and inner peace lead to stress, so it was not entirely surprising when he had a major heart attack in 1959. Afterward, the doctors suggested he take it easy, seek a quiet life. Rich examined the options while recuperating. It was clear that inactivity would kill him, and he felt very strongly about providing for his wife and daughter. So he returned to work.

Rich continued with small bands for a while. Then he began touring with the big band he felt the country needed, one that would epitomize *today* in jazz and popular music. Though deeply involved with the history and traditions of his instrument and jazz itself, Rich could never tolerate nostalgia; to him, the revival of the music of the past was nothing more than a cardboard replica, lacking the depth, power, and true effect of the originals.

The Rich band's library covered a wide range. Its leader was not afraid to take chances when it came to material and new writers, "as long as it sounds good and swings." He relied on arrangers and composers he favored like Bill Holman and John LaBarbera, but remained open. The only thing he was really against was over-stylization. "The sense of freedom is lost when you stick to a certain sound or way of playing, as Glenn Miller did," he said.

"I have a concert band," he insisted. Embellishing on this theme, Rich told writer Eliot Tiegel, "I'm trying to establish an art form without all the gimmicks, without all the bullshit, without having broads come out and dance and jiggle. I'm selling music . . ."[32]

Rich was a tough employer, giving 110 percent on the bandstand

and demanding that his sidemen do the same. He expected them not only to perform well but also to look good and behave like adults. "I want the guys clean, straight, dignified, totally involved," he said.

Rich shouted at his players, keeping after them. Admittedly, the Rich band could be a pressure cooker. But the leader got results, and if he didn't, the musicians in question didn't stay around long.

PAT LABARBERA: Buddy's band could be tense at times. He got upset when the guys didn't perform on a certain level. But if you only knew Rich the intense, demanding musician, you'd only have one side of the man. Very quietly, he took care of people. When Art Pepper was on the band, he was sick, really sick. Buddy would take him to the hospital in his own car and pay for everything. When I had problems in Chicago (my wife had a miscarriage), Buddy was marvelous to us, just unbelievable.

It was all a matter of how he responded to someone. If he respected a person, and certainly if a relationship had been established, there was little he wouldn't do. Sure he was an argumentative cat. I saw him really get into it with heavy players in the band, like saxophonist Joe Romano. But when they got up on the stand, everything was said and worked out in the *music*. That's the ultimate testing ground.

JOHN LABARBERA: We were at a high school in Westchester County, not far from New York City. I was traveling with the band, trying to get some new ideas that I could develop into charts for Buddy. The band was nearing the close of the concert. Standing in the wings, I happened to turn around—something took my attention from the music. And there was Gene Krupa, sitting quietly where he could get a good visual shot at Buddy. Obviously he was quite ill. Buddy took his bows, did his usual shtick with the audience, and came offstage, at first not noticing Gene. When he saw him, the show-business mask dropped and there, for a moment, was BR with his guard down. His expression communicated a whole lot of feeling. It almost was as if he said, "Sorry I made you wait; I didn't know you were here!" It was a touching moment that is hard to talk about. It showed how much feeling Buddy had for Gene, how much he cared about him. For a moment, the gruff, funny, cutting Buddy I knew disappeared, and you got a look at something terribly real.

RUBY BRAFF: I'll tell you what he did for me. One year in Newport, I arrived at the Viking Motel very sick. It was the beginning of my trouble with allergies. I had chills and fever, felt terrible. Buddy was upstairs with his family. When he found out I was sick, he came to my room. Recently out of the hospital himself, he laughed and said, "I'll fix you up, man. I'm taking the key to the room and taking charge of everything." And he did. He was up and down for the entire night, telling jokes, keeping my spirits up. How could I do anything but love him?

Rich had always had a pretty good idea who he was. It remained for him to find a vehicle for conveying to the fullest *what* he was. Putting together his own ensemble over twenty years ago was the key move of his career. Like Duke Ellington, Rich needed a large band to make definitive contact with people, to wholly fulfill himself. He never functioned well in situations where he didn't have much to say about the music and its presentation. The success of the Buddy Rich Big Band was the direct result of three things: its contemporary quality, the talent and proficiency of its players, and Buddy's masterly ability to play any kind of music well.

One person also played a major role in Rich's success: Johnny Carson. On his *Tonight Show*, Carson introduced Rich and the band to millions who otherwise might never have known about them. Buddy was allowed to be himself—a wisecracking, quick-witted personality who happened to play drums better than anyone else. An amateur drummer who really cares about music, Carson continues to showcase jazz and jazz people, naturally and realistically.

For most of the year, the band was Rich's family. The drummer traveled around the country and abroad; he loved going from place to place, meeting people, playing for new audiences. He never practiced, but spent his days thinking, reading, watching TV and movies, going to ball games, playing golf, and focusing on *business*. By staying away from the drums, he built within himself an edge of anticipation.

His life since the formation of the band was not without complications. For one, there was the scourge of drummers: serious back problems.

MEL LEWIS: I took time off from my commitments to go with him to Atlantic City a few years ago. He was going through hell. The pain was almost incapacitating; he could hardly stand up. But he got up on the bandstand and played his butt off. I couldn't believe it.

He told me, "Your being here made it possible for me to play. If you hadn't come down and been around, I wouldn't have been able to do it." "I don't understand," I said. He pointed out: "I couldn't go up there and give them half of what I can do. Despite the pain, I went all out because you were here to pick up the

Rich in a thoughtful mood at the Newport Jazz Festival in 1965.   Charles Stewart.

pieces, if things didn't work out. If I blew it in the middle of a set, the audience would be disappointed. They don't care if I'm dying up there; they want me to *play*. So having you on the scene was a safety thing. No matter what happened, the performance could be saved; I could live up to my obligation."

When I went back to New York after hanging around for two days, he hugged and kissed me and said, "Thanks, man." He felt good. I felt good. It worked out well all the way around.

MEMORIES

In 1980, I suggested to Kool Jazz Festival producer George Wein that we do a Buddy Rich evening. He greeted the suggestion with enthusiasm. But for one reason or another, we didn't bring it to reality until 1982, June 27, to be exact, at Carnegie Hall. It was six months in the making— this retrospective on the drummer's life and time. I consulted Rich regarding almost everything. After all, it was his evening. He had to be happy. But he never was overbearing; he let me do what I thought was necessary. There was a sense of trust.

We featured the Buddy Rich band. It took several guises. Early in the program, it played Artie Shaw and Tommy Dorsey material; then it became the Buddy Rich band of the 1940s, ultimately showing its own contemporary face.

Buddy protested loudly about going back into the past. He had misgivings about what it might do to his image and didn't want the audience to think he was mired in yesterdays. Three days before the concert, he called me to his apartment. He was very upset. "The band can't play those older charts the way they should. I want to scrap them." He was angry. I wasn't exactly elated. We stared at one another. My hands shook a bit. He spotted the nervousness. "Why are you so uptight?" "That's obvious," I responded. "You can't do a retrospective concert and ignore the past." He leaned back in his chair, looked out of the window and, in a resigned manner, said: "Okay. We'll do them."

The older charts, mildly updated by Rich arranger John LaBarbera, were a hit. The capacity crowd was glad to hear Shaw's "Carioca;" Sy Oliver's steamer for the Dorsey band, "Well Git It;" and Rich's Dorsey feature, "Not So Quiet Please." A balance was struck between yesterday and today. Dizzy Gillespie played Johnny Mandel's chart of his "Oop Bop Sh'Bam" out of the 1946 Rich library. He followed with the Rich band's contemporary arrangement of Thelonious Monk's " 'Round Midnight."

The evening just worked. It was fun and very musical. Mel Tormé hosted the program. An admirer of Rich like myself, he was very pleased to be part of the project. A jam session sequence showcased some of the Brooklyn drummer's favorite players, all of whom had worked with him: Zoot Sims (tenor saxophone), Harry "Sweets" Edison (trumpet), Phil Woods (alto saxophone), Eddie Bert (trombone), John Bunch (piano), and Bob Cranshaw (bass). His young band was "up" for the occasion.

A biographical script I wrote for Mel gave the evening a theme. The music provided the substance. Films and slides from various segments of Rich's career provided another dimension. And there was a great deal of humor. Mel and Buddy threw amusing lines at one another during much of the show, each kidding the other about age, ability, and childhood prowess as entertainers.

One of the most humorous incidents came as the first half was drawing to a close. Mel ushered on Armand Zildjian, "owner of the greatest cymbal-producing company in the world." What followed was a comedy of errors. In a rather halting manner, Zildjian endeavored to make a presentation to Buddy of a specially crafted, ten-inch cymbal. He fumbled through the segment, excusing himself as he tried to read the citation, which spoke of Rich's artistry and spirit and contribution to the music world. While Zildjian faltered because of nervousness or too much of the grape, Buddy added to the comic flavor, making snide, cutting, humorous remarks. The audience joined in the fun, laughing more and more. After the situation had been milked for all it was worth, Zildjian finally got himself together and made the presentation, and everyone filed backstage for intermission.

There is an awful lot to remember. Tormé sang inventively and well. Rich tap-danced with the great Honi Coles as the band swung softly behind them. I had a marvelous time opening the show onstage and seeing that it all ran as planned. George Wein's people were perfect, really professional. And Rich played his patootie off. Because it was his night, he felt an extra bit of pressure. And he responded, as expected. His "West Side Story" solo was a history of jazz drumming coupled with the sort of facility and showmanship that one rarely witnesses.

Gary Giddins, jazz critic for the Village Voice, *was quite surprised at what he had seen and heard. "I didn't realize Buddy could do so many things so well," Giddins said, speaking for the audience, which exploded in exhilarated appreciation at the end. It was a memorable night for Buddy Rich. For me, one of the best.*

Not long after the Carnegie Hall concert, Rich underwent open-heart surgery—a quadruple bypass. He resumed his schedule eight and a half weeks after getting out of the hospital, with a tour of Britain.

FREDDIE GRUBER: He was up and around long before he really should have been. That tour was on his mind. He didn't want to cancel. Every day, he'd call and ask me to walk with him, to play on pillows, drums, whatever was around, so he'd be ready. As you well know, he was a *stubborn* cat.

RICH: I came back to work at least six months earlier than was prescribed for me. When I got out of the hospital, people were saying to me I should carry another drummer and just front the band— and do certain things that are totally against what I believe in.[33]

Buddy went full steam, playing as he always had. Difficult? Certainly. He was hard pressed and tired during much of the tour and for a while thereafter. Bravado or bravery? It was a little bit of both.

But he had a great deal of support. Family and friends gathered around. Sinatra was on the case, from the time he heard Buddy had been stricken.

RICH: Sinatra was the first one to call at the hospital when they announced on the air that I had become ill. He was one of the true inspirations of my recovery. Since we were practically neighbors in Palm Springs, he came around frequently. He was the first one to come to the house, take me for a walk, and make sure I was doing alright. Frank's the most genuine guy; he's a man; he's lovely.

Sinatra called Rich in England before the first gig, warning him to take it easy: "No sixteen-minute drum solos!" When Sinatra heard that Rich was telling his audiences what a great person he was, the singer sent the drummer a telegram: "If you don't stop saying all those nice things about me, you're going to ruin my entire image. Much love and take care of yourself, Frank."

The drummer was deeply touched by the concern of the music and entertainment community. Particularly attentive were Johnny Carson, Basie, Tony Bennett, and a number of drummers. When Rich returned to work at the Bottom Line in New York, he expressed his feelings openly to the audience.

JOHN S. WILSON: His drumming was as polished, precise, and emphatic as ever. The only indication of any variation in the Rich style came in his traditional "rap" with the audience as he toweled away the perspiration brought on by his big solo. There was a bit of sentiment and mellowness in his expression of appreciation for the support and sympathy he received during his recuperation.[34]

On January 26, 1987, long after resuming his performance schedule, Rich had a seizure.

FREDDIE GRUBER: The first time it happened, he was lying in bed in New York; leaning against the headboard, hands folded behind his head. He was watching TV and it was relatively early in the day. All of a sudden, his left arm began to do some strange stuff; it jumped uncontrollably. Then it stopped. He couldn't figure out what had happened. It scared him something terrible. Steve Marcus, the featured tenor in the band and an old friend, came by. It gave Buddy the opportunity to get out of his apartment; he was edgy, to say the least. Marcus and Buddy walked up to this little joint on 72nd Street, near the apartment, and got hot dogs. On the way back, Buddy fell and hit himself hard on the curb. He insisted he was alright. Being with Marcus gave him a chance to talk about what had happened to him.

Rich checked into Mt. Sinai, where, two days later, doctors told him that he had a brain tumor. They recommended an immediate operation. The family, however, decided that Buddy should be near them. He flew out to L.A., checking into UCLA Medical Center.

MARIE RICH: He stayed in the hospital for two and a half weeks, getting all kinds of tests. Then he was released. Despite the seizures, there didn't *seem* to be any sign of the tumor. The people at UCLA couldn't understand why the New York doctors thought it was a brain tumor. He was home for ten days. At one point, he had eight seizures in one day, then eight more, and was rushed back to the hospital. Buddy remained in the hospital until ten days before he died.

STAN LEVEY: Buddy was fighting hard every day. The left side of his body was affected by the tumor; his speech was a little slurred. But he tried to get up and walk. He was uplifted by the fact that so many people came to see him. His close friend Freddie Gruber was a great help to him.

   Mel Tormé came by. So did Jerry Lewis, Martha Raye, and Nick Condos. Many drummers kept Buddy company; Irv Cottler, Alvin Stoller, and I were just a few of the drummers who showed up frequently. Annie Ross was there a lot. Jack Jones came, Johnny Carson visited on Saturdays. Terry Gibbs was there several times. And the family—Marie, Cathy, his sisters and brother always were around, doing whatever they could.

FREDDIE GRUBER: Buddy made it easy for everyone. By joking around and keeping it light, he took his mind off the problem and did the same for his friends.

STAN LEVEY: Unfortunately, it was hopeless from the outset. Buddy demanded the operation. "Don't send me home half done," he said. "If I make it—fine; if not, okay." It was a matter of a man going downhill day by day. But he was a good one, no doubt about that.

FREDDIE GRUBER: Just before the operation—we were going down in the elevator—the doctors asked him if he was allergic to anything. Buddy said, "country and western music." He kept going, he fought and screamed bloody murder. By the time he was diagnosed at UCLA he had three tumors. Fear? When all the people were around, he danced around it. At night, we got into his life—from the time he was a kid and toured Australia. It was nitty-gritty time; he was frightened and he talked himself through it. He would say, "we're gonna beat this thing, give it hell," or he would do a turnaround and bawl me out, shouting, "Will you listen to me and get here at a decent hour so I can tell you the things that have to be done just in case this thing works out badly!"

After the operation, he was laid up. Both times he stayed at Sam Nassi's place in Bel Air. Sam's an old and dear friend. He wasn't in the mood for visitors. And he didn't have too many.

The day before he passed away, I picked up Lennie Di Muzio of the Zildjian Company and Armand Zildjian. They finally got together with Buddy after trying for several months. Armand and Buddy reminisced about the many years they'd known one another. Suddenly Armand started to cry, saying, "I want you to know, pal, you've given me the greatest musical experiences of my life." Buddy cried. And I was so affected I had to leave the room.

LENNIE DI MUZIO: [After the operation Rich went] through fourteen days of chemotherapy and cobalt treatment, which was really very hard on him. He was paralyzed on his left side, but there was a very slow gradual increase in strength that was coming daily. He was in a lot of pain, but . . . the fight was still there at the end. That's what intrigued me so much. Most people would never have lasted that long after what he had been through. . . . Right up to the very last moment, he was talking about going back on the road. . . . I admired his attitude and his inspiration. He showed us how to live as musicians, and he showed us how to die. He went out with a lot of dignity and with a lot of pride.[35]

FREDDIE GRUBER: The last day he was thinking of the young people and what he could leave behind. We had talked about doing an educational video together on the history of the trap set. He brought it up, and insisted I go ahead with it. "Never tell them what to play," he said, "only how to approach the instrument!" I assured him it would be done. He kept on, "Make sure you've heard what I said! Leave something for the young people!" That was his bottom line. The tape would be a part of his legacy.

MARIE RICH: His heart just stopped. He couldn't stay in that crippled body anymore.

STAN LEVEY: The funeral took place at Pierce Brothers Mortuary in Westwood [California]. The setting was beautiful. Flowers were placed on either side of the closed casket. In front—one of Buddy's drum sets. Really very tasteful.

Everyone was there—Frank Sinatra, Mel Brooks, Angie Dickinson, Artie Shaw, Jerry Lewis, Mel Tormé, Robert Blake, Milton Berle—on and on. I was a pallbearer—Irv Cottler, myself, and a couple of other drummers paid our respects that way. There was a little group playing—Terry Gibbs on vibes, Al Viola on guitar, a good bass player, doing tunes like "My Buddy" and others apropos to the occasion. Really quite touching.

Sinatra gave the eulogy. He talked of the days when he and Buddy were roommates on the Tommy Dorsey band. Carson came to the microphone and completely broke up crying. Jerry Lewis was impressive. Artie Shaw recalled Buddy's early days with his band and how he had committed to memory the whole Shaw library in two or three nights, sitting in front of the band in the Blue Room of New York's Hotel Lincoln. Quite a feat. But he had to do it that way. Buddy couldn't read music at the time.

One of the most memorable speakers was Robert Blake, the actor. A street-wise guy like Buddy, he cracked everybody up. The things he said were so beautiful and so touching. There wasn't a dry eye in the house. Just lovely. After the funeral, Joanna Carson, a friend of both Marie and Buddy, gave a party at her home in Bel Air. Good food and drink, music and singing. An upbeat ending for a sad day.

LOUIE BELLSON: I can't get it into my mind that he's gone. Of course, to me he's always going to be there, because every time I sit down to play, I'm going to be thinking about him, Jo Jones, Chick Webb, and all these beautiful guys.[36]

JIM CHAPIN: Who will fill his shoes? No one can, but if we just heed his example and fill our own shoes, maybe we will work wonders.[37]

Other Major Figures

Sonny Greer
(1903 – 1982)

"On the ground floor when jazz was being put together, Sonny was there to witness its development and be a key part of it.

—*MERCER ELLINGTON*

Sonny Greer in action with the Duke Ellington band at the Trianon Ballroom, Southgate, California, in 1942. The shot reveals that Sonny used much more equipment than other drummers of the period.   © 1942 Harry Tate.

William Alexander "Sonny" Greer, singer, entertainer, bon vivant, drummer of distinction, was integral to the sound and rhythmic feeling of the Duke Ellington Orchestra. He was there at its inception in 1923 and remained until 1951. An intimate of Ellington, Greer and

307

the great man of American music were professionally associated from 1920, when they played their first job together in Washington, D.C. The relationship with Ellington and his family lasted all of Greer's life, even beyond Ellington's death in 1974. The bond between the drummer and the world of his piano-playing friend was strong indeed.

Greer was born in Long Branch, New Jersey in 1896, 1902, 1903, or 1904, depending on your reference source. He was private about his birth date because he tried to hold tight to a youthful image.

He lived in Asbury Park, New Jersey, until he went out into the world. An essentially self-taught, "natural" drummer, he had one teacher: vaudeville drummer Eugene "Peggy" Holland, who gave him musical pointers and served as a prime example of how a man should carry himself. Also a dancer, singer, and sartorially splendid man, Holland set the pace for Greer, but life truly began when the drummer and Ellington got together in Washington.

LAWRENCE BROWN: When I joined the Ellington band in 1932, it soon became clear just how important Sonny was. He was almost as popular as Ellington. Not only did he have excellent musical instincts and natural ability as a player, he was very genial and served as contact man for Duke. Sonny wasn't a schooled musician. But he could pick up things very readily. He was so much a part of what we did; he fit perfectly.

Sonny got to know music and his instrument by playing and being out there performing and absorbing what was happening around him. Adept as a rhythm man and as a colorist, Sonny also was a great "flash," an incredible showman. He had one of the most lavish drum sets in the world. Many drummers and other musicians came to see and hear Sonny because of his splendid equipment.

MERCER ELLINGTON: Sonny knew what audiences liked. He was one of the few people from whom Ellington readily took advice. A great reactor to material, he needed only a skeleton of an idea. With that as a base, he would contribute a great deal to the glory of a work. Sonny had a great ear and unusual reflexes. Ellington often referred to him as the real leader of the band. On the ground floor when jazz was being put together, Sonny was there to witness its development and be a key part of it.

Most important, no one played with such a sense of relevancy in the Ellington band. His recordings with the Ellington orchestra and with small groups out of the organization make the point for him.

Listen to "Cotton Tail" (Victor, 1940), "Main Stem" (Victor, 1942), and "Jumpin' Punkins" (Victor, 1941) with the Ellington Orchestra. Also recommended are "Chasin' Chippies" (Vocalion, 1938) and "Downtown Uproar" (Variety, 1937)—both with Cootie Williams and his Rug Cutters. These records reveal Greer's capacity to respond buoyantly and creatively to his colleagues, to swing, and to give the musicians and the music what they needed.

An imposing artist, someone to be *seen* and *heard*, Sonny Greer lived up to the description given to him by Jo Jones: he was indeed "Mr. Empire State Building."

George Wettling
(1907 – 1968)

"George Wettling had great enthusiasm for life and for music. And, undoubtedly, he was the most important drummer in the Chicago style of jazz."

—JEFF ATTERTON

"A good band is based on good drums and good piano. Give me a good piano and George Wettling and I'll give you a good band any time."[1]

—EDDIE CONDON

George Wettling had his own way of doing things. But his roots were quite apparent. Like a number of his contemporaries, he was genuinely inspired by the music of the New Orleans jazz pioneers. His love for jazz in general—the New Orleans style and its Chicago offshoot in particular—was so intense that he built a life around them. Even in his last days, the fire burned brightly. "Some guys get old and tired and get out of jazz," he noted. "I'll never do that. Hell, man, jazz's been my whole life."[2]

His favorite drummers were Baby Dodds, the classically inventive New Orleanian who also influenced Gene Krupa and Dave Tough; Zutty Singleton, another marvelous New Orleans drummer; and others, including Harlem's George Stafford, Benny Washington (who played with Earl Hines), Tubby Hall, Ben Pollack, Chick Webb, and Krupa. But Dodds was his man; you could hear it in his playing.

Wettling began in the manner of most drummers—he heard the drums and was captivated. This happened in Topeka, where he was born in 1907 and remained until 1921. George Rake, his maternal grandfather and something of a musician, encouraged his interest. Wettling got drums, after working hard to earn the money to buy them. He moved to Chicago with his family and began to play in earnest. By 1924, he had had his first professional job. He ignored school somewhat; drums and music predominated.

310

George Wettling working out in a friend's apartment in Hollywood in 1942.
© 1942 Harry Tate.

Wettling's credits varied in quality and musical style. They included bands led by Louis Panico, Elmo Mack, Floyd Towne, Wingy Manone, Joe Kayser, Art Jarrett, and Eddie Neibaur. To make a living, he played with the essentially commercial bands and shows. For pure joy he jammed with jazz people like Bix Beiderbecke, Bud Freeman, and Eddie Condon.

In 1926, he took Dave Tough's chair in the Wolverines, a historically significant jazz group that first featured Beiderbecke and then Jimmy McPartland on trumpet. A year later, he made his first record with the Jungle Kings on Paramount. Two of his associates on the session were Muggsy Spanier and Frank Teschmaker.

Wettling came to New York with British leader Jack Hylton and his band in 1935 and settled in Gotham the following year, entering a key phase of his career. He worked with the Artie Shaw, Bunny Berigan, and Red Norvo bands, then the Paul Whiteman organization for an extended period. When Benny Goodman was changing drummers, he often sat in with his band.

Wettling's records with the Shaw and Berigan bands indicate his base in four-beat Chicago jazz. He used the whole drum set and his cymbals as sources of color and rhythm, much as Baby Dodds did, but brought a very personal aspect to the style. Wettling performances worked well in big bands, and over the years Charlie Barnet, Woody Herman, Johnny Long, Chico Marx, and Muggsy Spanier also hired him for their ensembles.

He made recordings for Milt Gabler's Commodore label in the late 1930s and early 1940s with musicians who shared his conception of jazz: Condon, Wild Bill Davison, Jess Stacy, Freeman, George Brunies. These recordings helped him make his name. He played the often all-stops-out Chicago style with great abandon and understanding. His time was firm; it bubbled and danced. His breaks had an inner life and logic. His solos were well-crafted bursts of energy. Often he brought together the snare and bass drums and played one against the other in an infectious manner. Try the four-bar close on "Strut Miss Lizzie" (Commodore, 1939) for a taste of this provocative juxtaposition.

Wettling had a fine touch, ample technique, and a distinctive sound on the snare drum. He was a good listener and responded inventively to ensembles and solos. He would change the background behind each soloist, adapting, giving and taking, building, serving as the time center and as another interesting voice in the ensemble. The 1938 trio records on Commodore with Freeman and Stacy provide some excellent examples of his ability as an improviser.

MILT GABLER: He was the perfect guy to play on the Commodore dates. He had lived with the traditional Chicago style since he was a kid. And he knew just what to do and how to do it.

Because he was a fine reader of music, a very flexible drummer, and an excellent tympanist, Wettling held a variety of jobs, including several in radio and TV. For approximately ten years, 1943–1952, he was a staff man at ABC Radio. But he devoted the major portion of his time to bringing fire and intensity to small bands, most of which were traditional.

Wettling died in 1968 at age sixty, of lung cancer. Those who knew him well say he was a colorful yet regular guy, a many-faceted person who painted and wrote well, took excellent photographs, and could converse with authority and humor on a variety of subjects. But for the essence of Wettling, refer to the records, specifically the many sessions he did for Commodore. They tell you what he was all about in very basic terms.

Cozy Cole
(1909 – 1981)

"Cozy really did his job. He fed and inspired his fellow musicians, provided a solid rhythmic foundation, and *swung*. And he was such a dedicated drummer—always studying, always learning."

—*HELEN OAKLEY DANCE*

"The more you study, the more you find out you don't know, but the more you study, the closer you come."[1]

—*COZY COLE*

"He always keeps by himself . . . practicing all the time . . . tick-tacking with his sticks."[2]

—*MARIO BAUZA*

"Cozy Cole—he had the greatest feeling for the instrument of all the drummers I worked with over the years."

—*LAWRENCE LUCIE*

Cozy Cole's whole life was the drums. He began banging on the furniture in his New Jersey home when he was only five. A few years later, he played in the school band and gave every indication that drums were his future. His interest was so intense that he became Sonny Greer's band boy, just so he could hang around and watch and listen to him. Frequently he transported Greer's drums from the job—this was before Sonny joined Duke Ellington—to the drummer's home in Asbury Park. Cole lived nearby in Atlantic Highlands.

But Cole had to sacrifice his ambitions to support his family. The close-knit Cole family—three brothers plus Cozy and a sister, headed by the paternal grandmother—worked hard to put Cole's sister through Wilberforce University. For a few years after the high school, Cole worked at a number of jobs ranging from domestic to dancer. Dancing kept him occupied and employed, but when he realized he

Cozy Cole cheerfully keeping the time moving. The year: 1958.   Charles Stewart.

would never dance as well as Bill Robinson, he followed his instincts and began studying drums with Charlie Brooks, the pit drummer at Harlem's Lafayette Theater, for a dollar a lesson.

Natural talent carried him through the first several years as a professional. His live and recorded work reveals a drummer with a strong feeling for rhythm and a sense of invention. Listen to "Load of Coal" (Victor, 1930, available on *Mr. Jelly Lord*), one of his few recordings with Jelly Roll Morton. The breaks just flow out of him.

Band leaders and other musicians in the 1930s liked Cole's work, so he was seldom unemployed. He drummed with the Blanche Calloway band, which included saxophonist Ben Webster and trumpeter-arranger Edgar Battle. Later he played with the Benny Carter band, the first attraction at Harlem's Apollo Theater when it turned to stage shows. From the Willie Bryant band, he moved into Stuff Smith's little band on New York's 52nd Street and became more widely known.

All the while, Cole studied and practiced constantly. He worked to make himself the complete musician under the direction of a variety of leading teachers, including Radio City drum virtuoso Billy Gladstone and vibraphonists Freddie Albright and Milton Schlesinger. He learned tympani from Saul Goodman of the New York Philharmonic.

Cole became internationally famous with the Cab Calloway band, in which he was a featured artist from 1939 to 1942. His ability to keep good time, to integrate key elements of the Calloway arrangements, and to play well-developed solos captured the attention of audiences and musicians. His solo showcases with Calloway included "Paradiddle," "Ratamacue," and "Crescendo in Drums"—the first two based on two drum rudiments and their variations, the third an expansion of an idea from his work with Stuff Smith's band. All three, well orchestrated and colorful, were recorded for Columbia—the latter two in 1939, "Paradiddle" in 1940.

Earlier recordings with Lionel Hampton small groups, Coleman Hawkins and Roy Eldridge ("Bean at the Met," Keynote, 1944), Roy Eldridge's Trumpet Ensemble ("St. Louis Blues," Keynote, 1944), and his own group ("Smiles," Keynote, 1945) all offer evidence of the sort of versatility that kept him recording almost constantly. Cole could swing like a tap dancer, particularly in his solos; he had intensity and drive, if not the light buoyancy of Jo Jones. But his concern for rudimentary excellence sometimes negatively affected his basic talent and feel for music.

His continuing formal training, however, had positive effects. He became a good teacher; the late Philly Joe Jones, one of his students, credits Cole as central to his development. For several years, from the 1950s into the 1960s, he co-headed a drum school with Gene Krupa. His ability to read and interpret music very well also permitted him to play in Broadway shows like "Carmen Jones." Cole became one of the first blacks to perform on staff at CBS Radio, to play on film soundtracks, and to work for bandleaders like Benny Goodman.

Cole played and recorded with everyone, from Louis Armstrong to Dizzy Gillespie to Frank Sinatra to his old Smith and Calloway colleague Jonah Jones. He even earned a gold record for his version of "Topsy" in the 1950s.

Well liked and respected, Cozy Cole spent his life doing what he loved, always trying to be better. Influenced by drummers like Chick Webb, Sonny Greer, Gene Krupa, Jo Jones, Dave Tough, Jimmy Crawford, and George Stafford, Cole assimilated what they did while building his own identity. Though he never became a "modern" drummer, at the time of his death in 1981, William R. "Cozy" Cole was still learning about all aspects of music as a student and lecturer at Ohio's Capital University.

Jimmy Crawford
(1910 – 1980)

"He never was intrusive. Craw swung a band
without making a noise . . . you felt him."

—*SY OLIVER*

Jimmy Crawford was a drummer who instinctively knew what had to
be done, regardless of the style or size of the band. He created a
warm, positive, musical feeling whenever he performed. Amiable,
personable, sincere, always smiling, he was well liked on and off the
bandstand.

Craw, as he was known to his friends and musical associates,
learned on the job. He did not need or seek out formal training on
drums until late in his career, when he began playing Broadway
shows.

Jimmie Lunceford, a Memphis instrumentalist, teacher, and ultimately band leader, took on eighteen-year-old Crawford as his
drummer in the summer of 1928. Crawford grew with the band,
which became one of the truly great jazz and show ensembles of the
1930s and 1940s. After fourteen years of almost constant traveling,
Crawford left Lunceford in 1942.

SY OLIVER: When Lunceford was a teacher at Manassas High School
in Memphis, he came across Crawford dancing in the school yard.
He was impressed with what he saw and told Crawford he was
going to make a drummer out of him. Jimmie wanted to train
Craw and put him in the band.

What Lunceford didn't know was that the young string bean had
been fascinated with drums since the age of fourteen. After seeing and
hearing drummer Booker Washington at the Old Palace Theater in
Memphis, his hometown, Crawford knew what he wanted to do.

JIMMY CRAWFORD: He [Washington] just thrilled the whole audience.
When the overture hit, the man would do things—throwing
sticks, twirling [them] in the air, shooting pistols, blowing horns,
and everything. He was a nice-looking fellow with a beautiful

318

Jimmy Crawford, the rhythmic foundation of the great Jimmie Lunceford band, goes about his business with Lunceford. Like a number of other pictures in this book, this one was taken by Harry Tate at the Trianon Ballroom in Southgate, California, in 1942.   © 1942 Harry Tate.

    smile, and, when you saw him on the street in a derby, he was quite a dude.[1]

SY OLIVER: Craw was the personality kid of the Jimmie Lunceford band. All of his traits and talent came out in his drumming. He played like he was.

He never was intrusive. Craw swung a band without making a noise. I mean, you *felt* him. Most people who came to hear the band would walk away impressed with Craw. But it wasn't so much his technique that got their attention. The man's charm as a person and as a player reached them.

TRUMMY YOUNG: Craw had great spirit. He consistently picked the band up. He was the driving force. I enjoyed playing with him because he was so supportive. When you're a horn player, you really need someone behind you. I'll never forget Craw. I hope a drummer comes along some day and moves everyone the way he did.

Crawford brought something special to music both in the Lunceford band and over the course of his career. He was fresh yet controlled; he carefully developed each performance. In the swing mode, his drumming had a strongly pulsating quality; the beat was central to all of his work. A solid, adaptable, and exciting drummer, he tied a band together as few can. The Lunceford recordings on Decca (now MCA) and Columbia reveal Crawford could be open and very swinging, yet run down the scale to quiet and subtle. He was convincing and comfortable in any time signature, but became most widely known as the foundation of the famed Lunceford two-beat.

When his Lunceford days were over in 1942, Crawford played in an Army band with Sy Oliver, Buck Clayton, and other leading swing players. Before and after his stint in the Army, Crawford performed with various small bands, including those led by Ben Webster and Edmond Hall. He worked briefly with Harry James, Stan Kenton, and Fletcher Henderson before embarking on his Broadway show and recording years in 1950.

If anything, Crawford became even more well known during his years on Broadway. One show followed another, beginning with *Alive and Kicking* with Jackie Gleason. He seemed to have a flair for this kind of work. Until he retired in 1972, he piled up numerous Broadway credits—*Pal Joey, Jamaica, Mr. Wonderful, Golden Boy, Bye Bye Birdie, How to Succeed in Business,* and others.

The drummer also filled his schedule with countless recording dates. He provided the pulse for so many people: Frank Sinatra, Count Basie, Bing Crosby, Sy Oliver, Ella Fitzgerald, Quincy Jones—the list goes on and on. Like Tommy Henrich, the great hitting outfielder for the old New York Yankees, Crawford was "old reliable." A band leader knew there was little to worry about if he saw Crawford's smiling face in the pit of a show, in a recording studio, or on a job of any kind.

James Strickland Crawford died in 1980 at seventy. A fastidious performer and a real gentleman, he never missed a performance, showed up late, or did anything that would demean him in the eyes of other musicians or the public. We need more like him.

O'Neil Spencer
(1909 – 1944)

"He had his own style. A bit heavier than Jo Jones, he could be compared to Sid Catlett— powerful in a big band, subtle in a small band . . . a terrific show drummer."

—LAWRENCE LUCIE

O'Neil Spencer is a legendary figure of Swing Era drums. Though he didn't appear with too many bands and died young, he is vividly recalled by those who played with him and those who heard him.

LAWRENCE LUCIE: We were together in the Mills Blue Rhythm Band in the 1930s. O'Neil was a wonderful person, jovial, always smiling, telling jokes. And he could really play those drums. He had his own style. A bit heavier than Jo Jones, he could be compared to Sid Catlett—powerful in a big band, subtle in a small band. He was a terrific show drummer. When the Blue Rhythm Band played the Cotton Club, he did some marvelous things behind the acts.

JOHN WILLIAMS: If a drummer was needed to fill in at the Cotton Club, the call would go out for O'Neil Spencer. He was a marvelous player of shows. Like many of the greats of the 1930s, he tuned his drums. The tuning made the drums sound like an *instrument*. Using wood shell drums helped as well. It made for a warm sound.

Born in Cedarville, Ohio, in 1909, Spencer grew up in Springfield, Ohio, and began playing drums professionally in Buffalo in 1926. He was with the Mills Blue Rhythm Band for six years (1931–1936), first under the direction of Baron Lee, later with Lucky Millinder at the helm. But it was with the softly persuasive John Kirby Band, an enormously popular sextet for several years (1937–1943), that he became established. His brush style with Kirby impressed fans and musicians, and influenced a number of drummers.

BUDDY RICH: I first met Spence when I was at the Hickory House on 52nd Street with Joe Marsala. He was down the street at the

322

O'Neil Spencer at a recording session, circa 1939.   Courtesy of the Institute of Jazz Studies at Rutgers University.

Onyx Club with the Kirby band. I learned about playing brushes from him. With those brushes he caught the feeling and pulse of a hip tap dancer; his sound was clean and perfect. I haven't heard too many guys play with the kind of depth and technique and the sound that Spence had. He could really make the little band move. He was great.

DANNY BURGAUER: I don't think there was a finer brush man than O'Neil Spencer.

ALLEN PALEY: I came across a guy on 52nd Street who really was great when it came to laying down rhythm. His name was O'Neil Spencer.

Spencer's drumming is cogently illustrated on a number of Kirby recordings. On "Royal Garden Blues" and "It Feels So Good" (Vocalion, 1939), Spencer's brush- and stick-playing is unobtrusive yet powerful and assured. His drumming strongly defines the beat; his solos are succinct, not flashy or in any way rhetorical. His brush work uses diverse accents and patterns to create a sense of swing. At his most heated, Spencer with brushes often approximates a shuffle rhythm that further enhances the intensity of the pulse.

After successful years with Kirby, Spencer contracted tuberculosis; by 1942, it was clear that his health was on the decline. He worked briefly with Louis Armstrong in 1941, after leaving Kirby temporarily, and returned to the little band early in 1942. During a Kirby engagement at Harlem's Apollo Theater in June of 1943, he collapsed and was forced to stop playing. A little over a year later, O'Neil Spencer passed away, leaving behind a legacy of recordings.

Cliff Leeman
(1913 – 1986)

"What made his drumming distinctive was his involvement in the music, how much he brought to each performance."

—*PEE WEE ERWIN*

Cliff Leeman with Artie Shaw, 1938. He later used several more tom-toms.
Photo provided by The Avedis Zildjian Company.

"Cliff Leeman was one of the best drummers during the Swing years. He played well until he passed. Cliff performed for others, for the band. We neglect drummers of that kind. We don't seem to know

what a drummer really is. He's not the showman—the guy who sits the highest or has his cymbals on backwards. He's the guy who makes the band sound good. That was Cliff Leeman."

—BUDDY RICH

"Cliff was a great band backer. He seldom came forward and played very technical things on his breaks or behind the band. He could do stuff like that. But he preferred to make the men he worked with feel good. Cliff knew exactly what to do in small or big bands."

—CHRIS GRIFFIN

"It wasn't a matter of technique or the kind of drums and cymbals he had. What made his drumming distinctive was his involvement in the music, how much of himself he brought to each performance."

—PEE WEE ERWIN

Cliff Leeman was a well-kept secret. Musicians knew and admired him; devotees of jazz acknowledged his gifts. The public, however, was only peripherally aware of Cliff Leeman, giving its attention and affection to more colorful members of the jazz fraternity.

That didn't seem to bother Cliff. Ever since he was a child in Portland, Maine, he found his greatest happiness in the act of playing. He studied music locally, learning about the xylophone as well as drums. His practice habits were poor; only when he began traveling on the road years later did he apply himself and fully develop his native ability for expressive performance on drums.

After he was stranded at twenty-one in Kansas City in 1934 with Dan Murphy's Musical Skippers, a novelty band, his taste for jazz developed and really took hold. He heard and fell in love with the Count Basie band at the Reno Club. Jo Jones became his idol; Jones' unfettered and elegant playing affected how Leeman would ultimately develop.

Artie Shaw hired Leeman in 1936. For almost three years, during which he played drums on the band's key records—i.e., "Begin the Beguine" and "Back Bay Shuffle" (both Bluebird, 1938)—Leeman learned his craft. Shaw and Chick Webb were very helpful, Leeman said. They spent a lot of time with the young drummer and became his mentors.

Black drummers were a primary source of inspiration for Leeman. He admired, in addition to Jones and Webb, Sid Catlett for his technical skill and ability to make music sound fresh and surprising.

As time passed, Leeman developed his own manner of playing, notable for a subtle, telling use of cymbals. After playing with Tommy Dorsey in the late 1930s and joining Charlie Barnet in 1939, he established himself as a drummer who could uplift a band in a consistently persuasive manner. Economical, thoughtful, and explosive, Leeman also tuned his drums in a distinctive way. Leeman remained with Barnet until 1942, making some excellent records with the band: "Afternoon of a Moax," "Leapin' at the Lincoln," "Tappin' at the Tappa," (all Bluebird, 1940), "Harlem Speaks," "Blue Juice," and "Murder at Peyton Hall" (Bluebird, 1941), among many others.

Playing in the modern, Ellington-influenced 1942–1944 Woody Herman band, Leeman began to sense that the big band era was winding down. He turned to small jazz groups by the mid-1940s; his playing became quieter and more fluid working with John Kirby, Ben Webster, Don Byas, and Bobby Hackett. Leeman also began devoting part of his time to radio (and later TV) and commercial recordings.

He had a brief flirtation with bebop in the Charlie Barnet "modern" band of the late 1940s, but for Leeman, bebop didn't have the sort of feel and movement he loved. From the mid-1940s until the end of his life, the drummer remained an important player of mainstream jazz, active on the studio and recording scenes. When he died in 1986 at seventy-three, Leeman was still full of ideas and enthusiasm about his main concerns in life.

An excellent time-keeper, Cliff Leeman "left little to be desired when he played behind you," said Pee Wee Erwin. "He never did too little or too much. Just enough."

Ray Bauduc
(1906 – 1988)

"Ray was a swinging, very flexible drummer with a great sense of humor. When this guy got behind you, you had to play good . . . or else."

—EDDIE MILLER

"Ray Bauduc wasn't a banger; he made music on his instrument. I've never forgotten how good he was in the Bob Crosby band. He got this funky, chunky, warm, and resonant sound from his snare drum. He was a very distinctive player."

—MEL TORMÉ

"Ray had his own thing. Chick Webb thought an awful lot of him. He always said Ray was a natural drummer."

—HELEN OAKLEY DANCE

Born and raised in New Orleans, Ray Bauduc was the product of the city's wide-ranging musical tradition. His playing contained elements of march music, ragtime, vaudeville, eccentric tap dancing, and "legit" influences stemming from European music. Predominant in this mixture were the feelings, inflections, syncopations, and down-home qualities of the emerging New Orleans jazz style that was so much a part of his early life. Over the years, he tempered his style with more current ingredients, but the Bauduc style, at the core, was based on the rhythmic language of traditional Crescent City jazz.

RAY BAUDUC: When I was twelve or thirteen, my brother Jules got me started on drums. He took me to see and hear as many good drummers around New Orleans as he could. Some of the guys who had an influence on me were Baby Dodds (he worked with Fate Marable on the Riverboat Sidney), Emil Stein (I got to dig him at the Palace Theater), Chinee Foster, and Zutty Singleton. I took my first lesson from Kid Peterson, the best teacher in New Orleans at the time. Later I learned a lot from Paul Dedroit—who

Ray Bauduc, circa 1945, in what looks like Frank Dailey's Meadowbrook, Cedar Grove, NJ. During this period, Bauduc headed his own big band. Courtesy of the Institute of Jazz Studies at Rutgers University.

was with his brother Johnny's band and also played in the pit at the Orpheum Theater—and from Adrian Gosley who was with the Tony Parenti Orchestra in the pit of the Strand Theater.

JOHN CHILTON: [Ray] was making a living at music by the time he was fifteen, at eighteen he toured all over the states, at twenty he made his recording debut, [with the Original Memphis Five on Pathe] and at 21 he worked in Europe [with Freddie Rich's band] as a drummer and specialty dancer. For six years, from 1928–34, Bauduc drummed in Ben Pollack's band whilst the leader conducted up front, and it was during this period that he perfected his own style of drumming, which became an inimitable part of the Bob Crosby band.[1]

Bauduc learned a lot from Pollack, an often-underrated groundbreaker on drums. However, contrary to what John Chilton says, I believe that Bauduc evolved progressively in the years preceding the Crosby stint and during the years with the band.

BOB HAGGART: Ray often played on the bass drum, same as Pollack. Ben would use a brush; Ray did his thing with sticks. With the Crosby band, an extension of the Pollack group, Ray developed his own technique. After a while, it became easy to recognize him. He used all the paraphernalia—traps, cymbals, snare drum, bass drum, tom-toms. Ray didn't play a high-hat until later. He had a way of playing on the wooden rims of the snare and bass drum, using them as additional "sounds." And if the music interested him and it swung, he could *really* lay it down. Ray hated ballads and commercial tunes. The opposite of Krupa, Ray was loose, more like Zutty Singleton than anyone else.

All through the Crosby years (1935–1942), which we shared, Ray not only was creative on drums, he was an idea man when it came to inventing things for the drum set. He created a great new pedal, the Speed King, that Ludwig sold and later came up with a pedal tom-tom that could be operated like a tympani. One other thing. He and Cliff Leeman were among the first to use two small tom-toms attached to the left side of the bass drum.

And he was a great showman. Sometimes during solos, he'd shake his body back and forth like a seal. It was something!

Bauduc gave the Crosby band rhythmic character, style, and more than a little flash. His crowd-pleasing solos and breaks were inventive, developmental, and musical. There were Bauduc solo vehicles that fans expected him to perform, including "Big Crash From China," "Big Noise From Winnetka" (both Decca, 1938)—on which he played a duet with Haggart and drummed on the bass strings—and a marvelous number, particularly effective in theaters, called "Smokey Mary." (Decca, 1939) At his best, Bauduc was visually arresting, musically interesting, and seldom boring.

The drummer brought a variety of Crescent City experiences to the Crosby band. He had worked in theaters and with various bands, notably that of trumpeter Johnny Bayersdorffer. Subsequently, Bauduc garnered knowledge and musical values in the company of Tommy and Jimmy Dorsey, Joe Venuti, Red Nichols, Eddie Lang, Ben Pollack, Benny Goodman, Jack Teagarden, and Jimmy McPartland.

After the Crosby years and a stint in the Army, Bauduc led a big band of his own for a short while. He played with Jimmy Dorsey's band from 1948 to 1950, at a time when the ensemble took its identity from Dixieland arrangements. After that, small, traditional jazz bands remained his primary means of expression. A resident of Houston for a number of years before his death in 1988, he continued to play frequently, fix, and invent things, and live a good musical life.

Epilogue : Into the 1940s

As the 1940s began, there was little evidence of the changes that were to dominate the next ten years. Popular music did not seem all that different from what had preceded it in the 1930s. The music business was still built around the big bands. They continued to make money; the demand for them remained.

However, singers like Frank Sinatra with Tommy Dorsey, Bob Eberly with Jimmy Dorsey, Ray Eberle with Glenn Miller, Billy Eckstine with Earl Hines, Pha Terrell with Andy Kirk, Ella Fitzgerald with her own orchestra, Helen Forrest with Artie Shaw, Benny Goodman, and later with Harry James were on the rise. With the advent of World War II, music began to turn increasingly romantic.

The increasing importance of singers did not affect the swing band formula in a major way, at least at first. Leaders mingled pulsating instrumentals with ballads. People continued to dance and flock to hotels and ballrooms to participate in popular music. But that was on the surface; underneath there was turbulence.

Musicians, almost all of them black, had been seeking to make music more meaningful and expressive. Even while the big bands were at their height, these players tired of the patterns and repetition basic to band arrangements. What they thought was possible and what their talents made plausible moved them out of the mainstream.

In the area of drums, Kenny Clarke, as early as 1935, began involving himself in rhythmic counterpoint in the Lonnie Simmons band in New York's Greenwich Village. He played rhythmic patterns against the basic time, whether it was two or four beats to the bar. He continued to experiment through the 1930s, ultimately getting fired from the Teddy Hill band in 1940 for his unusual ideas. While Krupa and Webb reigned as kings of the drums, Clarke was developing a new concept that would soon dominate jazz rhythm.

Jo Jones, who was the heart of the Count Basie rhythm section and Basie's close friend and ally, and tenor saxophonist Lester Young, jazz's most potent solo voice until the advent of Charlie Parker, also were bringing change. They helped redefine how the music was conceived and performed.

Jones loosened up jazz rhythm, making it more fluid. He was among the first to drop "bombs"—to buoy up ensembles and to fill openings left by the band or a soloist. One of the most subtle drummers of his time, he combined time and decoration to achieve a perfect balance of the two and a most affirmative musical feeling.

In a manner that his numerous disciples have only approximated, Young brought to jazz a style totally different from that of Coleman Hawkins—the music's premier tenor until the coming of the great Lester, or "Pres." Young modified the sound of the instrument, introducing a new beauty and cool suggestiveness. Where Hawkins was rhapsodic, Pres was succinct, economical yet thoughtful; he created and traveled up and down a longer melodic line, lengthening and shortening it, diversifying his accents, using repetitions to create shapely solos that grabbed hold of your emotions. Though seemingly not a "hot" player, Young performed with an inner heat that could be searing. Most important, what he did with rhythm and harmony and the general structure of solos made musicians think in new ways. Not only that, he paved the way for Charlie Parker.

Others were much involved with innovation. Trumpeter Roy Eldridge increased the impact of his music—its depth and value—by enhancing its harmonic adventure and rhythmic interest, building a bridge to bop. Guitarist Charlie Christian with the Benny Goodman band and small groups in the first years of the 1940s and bassist Jimmy Blanton with Duke Ellington at the same time, made significant contributions during the short period they were on the scene. They freed their instruments and helped define a path to more interesting jazz improvisation.

Blanton took bass out of the dark ages; he made it into a far more viable rhythm and solo instrument by bringing to bear a great natural musical intelligence. He enunciated clearly on the instrument, plucking and pulling the strings rather than slapping the instrument. His solos grew from the music and were relevant statements. What he did made possible bassists like Ray Brown, Charles Mingus, and Red Mitchell.

Blanton and Christian rearranged phrase lengths and patterns so they swung more easily; both were technically gifted and knew music, and their solos mirrored horn-like feeling and harmonic and rhythmic adventure. They broke away from convention, as did Clarke, Jones, Young, and Eldridge.

Art Tatum, perhaps the greatest of all jazz pianists (with the possible exception of Bud Powell), also broke away from what he had heard others do. His unbelievable technique and ability to structure breathtaking comments reflected his enormous gifts and restless nature. A product of his time (the 1930s and 1940s), Tatum was linked stylistically to Earl Hines, Fats Waller, and the Harlem stride pianists. Yet Tatum's talent and motivation to play what he heard in his head moved him into harmonic and rhythmic areas that even the modernists of the mid-1940s found inspiring.

As the war progressed, singers took an increasingly prominent role in popular music. Servicemen, their girl friends, and their families had a propensity for sentiment. Frank Sinatra filled this need, first with Tommy Dorsey and then in a truly major way on his own. Americans—indeed, people through the English-speaking world—wanted to hear the *words*.

A record strike called in 1942 by the American Federation of Musicians made this possible. The AFM, better known as the Musicians' Union, forbade instrumental musicians to go into the studios and cut records. The strike lasted until 1944. James Petrillo, AFM's president, wanted a larger share of the money made by recordings for his musicians. But his musicians were the losers; singers recorded with vocal backgrounds and their efforts were released on a regular basis. "The time was ripe for singers, with personalized messages," said George Simon, chronicler of the Swing years, "and the strike helped them blossom by leaving the entire recording field open to them."[1]

The war had an effect on the situation in still other ways. Musicians were drafted in increasing numbers. The bands, both the large and the small, were not as uniform in quality as a few years earlier. Gas rationing made it difficult to reach clubs, ballrooms, and hotels. The government's 20 percent amusement tax compounded the situation, making it more expensive for people at places where live music was made.

By the time the guys and gals began coming home from the war in 1945, music and the music business were quite different. Small record labels had sprung up and began to record jazz, much of it the modern variety. Bop had become a factor in big and small bands; Charlie Parker and Dizzy Gillespie were having a great influence on musicians, particularly the young ones. And the public, even though not immediately responsive to modern jazz, was becoming conscious of its existence.

Singers were all over the radio dial, and the record industry catered to them. Bands were not dead, but after the great success of the Woody Herman First Herd in 1944 and 1945, it was clear that the public was moving away from the music and the musicians of the 1930s. Bands, some shaped by modern jazz, continued to travel, enjoying occasional spurts of success. Glenn Miller's music continued to be appreciated. But for all intents and purposes, the Swing years came to a close at the conclusion of the war, for a variety of reasons.

Much of the music of the middle and late 1940s was not really appropriate for *dancing*. Certainly the jazz and experimental bands—i.e., Stan Kenton, Woody Herman, Boyd Raeburn, and even Claude Thornhill, Charlie Barnet, and Artie Shaw—did not focus on dance music. People could no longer get involved in the musical experience by getting out on the floor and moving around.

And there was a domino effect. One ballroom closed, then another; one hotel room or club shuttered, then another. The choice in 1945, and for a few years thereafter, was between two polar opposites: the modern-jazz movement, and the pop singers. There were peripheral dance bands, hotel bands that continued to exist and draw some people. But it was a new world in which swing bands and musicians had increasingly minimal roles.

Soon there would be television, the LP record, rock and roll, and the emergence of other musical means of expression, such as country music and rhythm and blues.

The drummers who built the foundation for those that followed in the Swing years—Baby Dodds, Zutty Singleton, Ben Pollack, George Stafford, Vic Berton, Kaiser Marshall, Walter Johnson—gave way to Webb, Krupa, Catlett, Jones, Rich, McKinley, Tough, and others. And they in turn were superseded by a generation spearheaded by Kenny Clarke, Max Roach, Shelly Manne, Stan Levey, Shadow Wilson, Art Blakey, Roy Haynes, Ed Shaughnessy, Don Lamond, and Irv Kluger.

The process continues.

Notes

INTRODUCTION

1. Russell Sanjek, *From Print to Plastic: Publishing and Promoting America's Popular Music (1900–1980)* (New York: Institute for Studies in American Music, Brooklyn College of the City University of New York, 1983), 17.
2. Lans Lamont, quoted in "Swing As a Way of Life" in *The Swing Era 1941–42* (New York: Time-Life Records, 1970), 17.

CHICK WEBB

1. Barry Ulanov, "The Ideal Jazz Musician," *Jazz 1955—The Metronome Yearbook*, 40.
2. Dave Tough, "Hide-Hitters' Hangout," *Metronome*, July 1937, 46.
3. Teddy McRae, Oral History Files, Institute of Jazz Studies, Rutgers University, Newark, N.J.
4. Jo Jones quoted in Chip Stern, "Papa Jo," *Modern Drummer*, January 1984, 46.
5. Richard Gehman, "The Chick Webb Legend," *Saga*, April 1962, 79–80.
6. Stanley Dance, liner essay, *Chick Webb: A Legend (Volume I: 1929–36)*, Decca DL 9222.
7. Gehman, *op. cit.*, 80.
8. Helen Oakley Dance, "Drum Mad and Lightning Fast," *Saturday Review*, June 15, 1963, 52.
9. Otis Ferguson, "Breakfast Dance, in Harlem," *The Otis Ferguson Reader*, edited by Dorothy Chamberlin and Robert Wilson (Highland Park, IL: December Press, 1982), 58–59.
10. Artie Shaw, *The Trouble With Cinderella* (New York: Da Capo Paperback, 1979; originally published by New York: Farrar, Straus and Young, 1952), 230.
11. Jervis Anderson, "That Was New York, Harlem, IV—Hard Times and Beyond," *The New Yorker*, July 20, 1981, 71.
12. Mario Bauza, Oral History Files, Institute of Jazz Studies, Rutgers University.
13. John Hammond, extracted from the George Hoefer Collection, Oral History Files, Institute of Jazz Studies, Rutgers University.
14. "The Rise of a Crippled Genius," *Down Beat*, February 1938, 31.
15. Gehman, *op. cit.*, 80.
16. Dance, "Drum Mad and Lightning Fast," 52.

17. Jones quoted in Chip Stern, *op. cit.*, 48.

18. Dicky Wells as told to Stanley Dance, *The Night People* (Boston: Crescendo Publishing Company, 1971), 14.

19. Bauza, *op. cit.*

20. Sandy Williams quoted in liner essay by Stanley Dance, *Chick Webb: King of the Savoy* (Volume Two, 1937–39), Decca DL 9223.

21. McRae, *op. cit.*

22. *Ibid.*

GENE KRUPA

1. Benny Goodman interviewed in *Melody Maker* (London), December 22, 1973, 43.

2. Whitney Balliett, "Drummin' Man," in *Such Sweet Thunder* (Indianapolis: Bobbs-Merrill, 1966), 166.

3. George Frazier, "Gene Krupa: Creator of a Culture," *Boston Globe*, October 1973.

4. John Lissner, "Goodbye Mr. Drums," *The Village Voice*, October 25, 1973, 52.

5. Rudi Blesh, *Combo: U.S.A.* (Philadelphia: Chilton Book Company, 1971), 135–136.

6. Mezz Mezzrow with Bernard Wolfe, *Really The Blues* (New York: Random House, 1946), 146.

7. Eddie Condon with Thomas Sugrue, *We Called It Music* (New York: Henry Holt, 1947), 155.

8. Richard Hadlock, *Jazz Masters of the 20s* (New York: Macmillan, 1965), 124–125.

9. Max Kaminsky and V. E. Hughes, *Jazz Band: My Life in Jazz* (New York: Da Capo Press), 47.

10. Gene Krupa quoted in *Metronome*, March 1938, 48.

11. Harry Francis, "As I Heard It," *Crescendo*, March and June 1981, 16, 14.

12. John Hammond, liner notes for *The Complete Benny Goodman, Vol. III*, RCA Bluebird.

13. Hymie Schertzer quoted in Michele Wood "The Men Who Made Music: Gene Krupa," in *The Swing Era Into the '50s* (New York: Time-Life Records, 1971), 33.

14. Lionel Hampton in an interview with Skitch Henderson on "The Music Makers," WNEW-AM New York, October 1984.

15. Benny Goodman quoted in liner notes by Mort Goode for *The Complete Benny Goodman, Vol. VIII*, RCA Bluebird.

16. Francis Perkins quoted in Whitney Balliett, *Night Creature* (New York: Oxford University Press, 1981), 150.

17. D. Russell Connor and Warren W. Hicks, *BG On Record* (New Rochelle: Arlington House, 1970), 220.

18. George Simon, "Krupa Band Kills Cats," *Metronome*, May 1938, 9.

19. John McDonough, "Face Yonkers, Drummers! Gene Krupa Lived There", *High Fidelity*, March 1974, 53.

20. Graham Young quoted in Ian Crosbie, "Let Me Off Uptown," *Coda*, 1975, 9.

21. *Ibid.*, Roy Eldridge quoted.

22. *Down Beat*, December 15, 1941, 1.

23. Anita O'Day with George Eells, *High Times Hard Times* (New York: G. P. Putnam's Sons, 1981), 109, 110, 104.

24. *Down Beat*, May 15, 1943, 16.

25. Bobby Scott, "Gene Krupa: The World Is Not Enough," Gene Lees' *Jazzletter*, January 1984, 2.

26. Don Fagerquist quoted in Crosbie, "Let Me Off Uptown," 13.

RAY MCKINLEY

1. George Simon, *Simon Says: The Sights and Sounds of the Swing Era, 1935–55* (New Rochelle, NY: Arlington House, 1971), 10.

2. No author credited, "Dorsey Brothers Have Fast Climb To Fame," *Down Beat*, January 1935, 1.

3. Gene Krupa, "Drummer's Dope," *Metronome*, January 1937, 51.

4. George Simon, *Glenn Miller and His Orchestra*, (New York: Thomas Y. Crowell, 1974), 63–64.

5. A paraphrase of Ray McKinley, "No Sense of Rhythm, Then Give It Up!," *Metronome*, October 1940, 33.

6. Will Bradley quoted in George Simon, *The Big Bands* (New York: Schirmer Books, 1981), 98.

7. Mike Levin, "McKinley Has a Tuba and Band That Comes On," *Down Beat*, May 15, 1942, 2.

JO JONES

1. Whitney Balliett, "Cootie, Jo and Philly Joe," *The New Yorker*, November 4, 1985, 78.

2. Chip Stern, "Papa Jo's Time Tunnel," *The Village Voice*, December 16–22, 1981.

3. Count Basie from an interview with William B. Williams on "The Make Believe Ballroom," WNEW-AM, April 15, 1981.

4. Bob Blumenthal, "A Beat For All Seasons—Jo Jones Returns To Sandy's," *The Boston Phoenix*, October 3, 1978.

5. Martin Williams, "Count Basie and Lester Young," *The Jazz Tradition* (New York: Oxford University Press, 1970), 111.

6. Jo Jones quoted in Nat Shapiro and Nat Hentoff, *Hear Me Talkin To Ya* (New York: Rinehart and Company, 1955), 377.

7. Jo Jones quoted in Chip Stern, "Papa Jo," *Modern Drummer*, January 1984, 12–13.

8. Combination of Interview with Burt Korall and Oral History Files, Jazz Studies Institute, Rutgers University, Newark, N.J.

9. Stern, *op. cit.*

10. Jo Jones quoted in Stanley Dance, *The World of Count Basie* (New York: Charles Scribner's Sons, 1980), 50.

11. *Ibid.*, 101.

12. Harry Edison, Oral History Files, Institute of Jazz Studies, Rutgers University.

13. Albert Murray, *Good Morning Blues, The Autobiography of Count Basie* (New York: Random House, 1985), 159–160.

14. Bob Brookmeyer, liner essay, *Kansas City Revisited*—Bob Brookmeyer's KC Seven, United Artists Records.

15. Eddie Durham, Oral History Files, Institute of Jazz Studies, Rutgers University.

16. Eddie Durham, quoted in Dance, *The World of Count Basie*, 63.

17. *Ibid.*, Gus Johnson quoted, 287.

18. John Hammond with Irving Townsend, *John Hammond On Record—An Autobiography* (New York: Ridge Press/Summit Books, 1977), 172.

19. Count Basie quoted in Murray, *Good Morning Blues*, 184.

20. Harry Edison, Oral History Files, Institute of Jazz Studies, Rutgers University.

21. Jo Jones quoted in Shapiro/Hentoff, *Hear Me Talkin' To Ya*, 289.

22. Eddie Durham, Oral History Files, Institute of Jazz Studies, Rutgers University.

23. Jo Jones quoted in Dom Cerulli, "Jo Jones," *Down Beat*, June 26, 1958, 42 and 19.

24. Dicky Wells quoted in Stanley Dance, *The Night People* (Boston: Crescendo Publishing Company, 1971), 62.

25. Harry Edison, Oral History Files, Institute of Jazz Studies, Rutgers University.

26. Dan Morgenstern, "Jo Jones: Taking Care of Business," *Down Beat*, March 25, 1965, 15.

27. Jo Jones, Oral History Files, Institute of Jazz Studies, Rutgers University.

28. Ken Emerson, "A Memorial to Lady Day," *The New York Times*, June 30, 1979, 10.

29. Lee Jeske, "On Jazz," *Cash Box*, September 21, 1985, 21.

SID CATLETT

1. Whitney Balliett, *Improvising* (New York: Oxford University Press, 1977), 145.

2. Cliff Leeman, Oral History Files, Institute of Jazz Studies, Rutgers University, Newark, N.J.

3. Bill Esposito, "Big Sid Catlett," *Jazz Journal*, May, 1969, 10–11.

4. Don DeMichael, "Evolution of the Jazz Solo," *Down Beat*, March 30, 1961, 24–25.

5. Mel Powell in an interview with Loren Schoenberg on WKCR-FM in New York, February 8, 1987.

6. Barney Bigard quoted in Whitney Balliett, "Big Sid," *The New Yorker*, March 8, 1976, 109–110.

7. Rex Stewart, "My Man, Big Sid," *Down Beat*, November 17, 1966, 40.

8. *Ibid.*, 20.

9. John Simmons, Oral History Files, Institute of Jazz Studies, Rutgers University.

10. Jo Jones quoted in Chip Stern, "Papa Jo," *Modern Drummer*, January 1984, 46.

11. Ed Shaughnessy quoted in Jim Szantor, "Eddie Shaughnessy: 'Play Like You Mean It,' " *Down Beat*, April 12, 1973, 16.

12. Connie Kay quoted in Jeff Potter, "Connie Kay," *Modern Drummer*, February 1987, 24, 74, 76.

13. Helen Hume quoted in Balliett, *Improvising*, 139.

14. Earl Hines quoted in Stanley Dance, *The World of Earl Hines* (New York: Charles Scribner's Sons, 1977), 103.

15. Stewart, *op. cit.*

16. Gladys Catlett quoted in Balliett, *Improvising*, 142.

17. Louis Armstrong quoted in George Hoefer, "Big Sid," *Down Beat*, March 24, 1966, 27.

18. Stewart, *op. cit.*

19. Milt Hinton quoted in Balliett, "Big Sid," 107.

20. Sid Catlett quoted in Robert Fletcher, "Big Sidney Says He Likes Snare Drum Best," *Music and Rhythm*, April 1941, 74.

21. Tommy Benford quoted in Balliett, *Improvising*, 143.

22. Earl Hines, quoted in Balliett, "Big Sid," 107.

23. Hoefer, *op. cit.*

24. Dicky Wells as told to Stanley Dance, *The Night People* (Boston: Crescendo Publishing Company, 1971), 19.

25. Dizzy Gillespie quoted in Arthur Taylor, *Notes and Tones* (New York: G. P. Putnam's Sons, 1977), 124.

26. Shaughnessy quoted in Szantor, 17.

27. Hoefer, *op. cit.*

28. Last paragraph: Billy Taylor quoted in Nat Shapiro and Nat Hentoff, *Hear Me Talkin' To Ya* (New York: Rinehart and Company), 1955, 363.

29. Balliett, *Improvising*, 141.

30. Whitney Balliett, *The Sound of Surprise* (New York: E. P. Dutton, 1959), 147.

31. Ernie Anderson, "Big Sid (1910–1951) An Appreciation," *Melody Maker*, March 31, 1951, 3.

32. Hoefer, *op. cit.*, p. 26.

33. Max Kaminsky and W. E. Hughes, *Jazz Band: My Life In Jazz* (New York: Da Capo Press), 71–72.

34. Anderson, *op. cit.*

35. John Simmons, Oral History Files.

36. *Ibid.*

37. Sid Catlett quoted in Hoefer, 26.

38. D. Russell Connor and Warren W. Hicks, *BG On The Record* (New Rochelle, N.Y.: Arlington House, 1970), 309.

39. Peggy Lee, quoted in Whitney Balliett, "Still Here," *The New Yorker*, Aug. 5, 1985, p. 67.

40. John McDonough, "Benny," *Down Beat*, August 1986, 39.

41. Simmons, Oral History Files.

42. George Hoefer, "History of the Drum in Jazz," *Jazz*, November 1965, 15.

43. Sid Catlett quoted in Fletcher, 74–75.

44. Max Roach quoted in Chris Kuhl, "Max Roach: Interview," *Cadence*, July 1982, 5.

45. Second paragraph: Shaughnessy quoted in Szantor, 16.

46. Phil Payne, editor, *The Swing Era, 1940–1941, How It Was To Be Young Then* (New York: Time-Life Records, 1970), 31.

47. George T. Simon, *The Big Bands* (New York: Schirmer Books, 1967), 54.

48. Hoefer, "Big Sid," 29.

49. Barry Ulanov, "Sidney Catlett 1910–1951," *Metronome*, June 1951, 8.

50. Herman Kogan, "Friends Bury Big Sid," *Chicago Sun-Times*, March 31, 1951.

DAVE TOUGH

1. Frank Stacy, "Key Men, New Ideas, Set Herman Style," *Down Beat*, April 1, 1945, 3.

2. Lionel Hampton quoted in Mort Goode, liner notes, *The Complete Benny Goodman, Volume V*, Bluebird AXM2-5557.

3. Joe Bushkin quoted in Whitney Balliett, "Little Davey Tough," *The New Yorker*, November 18, 1985, 161.

4. Dizzy Gillespie quoted in Dizzy Gillespie with Al Frazier, *To Be Or Not To Bop* (Garden City, N.Y.: Doubleday, 1979), 162.

5. John Lucas, "Tough Stuff," *Jazz Journal*, June 1959, 5.

6. Baby Dodds quoted in Scott Kevin Fish, "Profile of a Legend: Dave Tough," *Modern Drummer*, January/February 1979, 51.

7. Jo Jones, Oral History Files, Institute of Jazz Studies, Rutgers University, Newark, N.J.

8. Eddie Condon, narration by Thomas Sugrue, *We Called It Music—A Generation of Jazz* (New York: Henry Holt), 1947, 109.

9. Mezz Mezzrow with Bernard Wolfe, *Really the Blues* (New York: Random House, 1946), 109.

10. Whitney Balliett, "Little Davy Tough," *The New Yorker*, November 18, 1985, 160.

11. Leo Vauchant quoted in Chris Goddard, *Jazz Away From Home* (New York: Paddington Press, 1979), 173–174.

12. Bert Marshall quoted in Goddard, 25–26.

13. Spencer Clark quoted in Goddard, 221.

14. Bud Freeman, *You Don't Look Like a Musician* (Detroit: Balamp Publishing, 1974), 59.

15. Mezzrow, 112.

16. D. Russell Connor and Warren Hicks, *BG on Record: A Bio-Discography of Benny Goodman*, 221, 222.

17. Dave Dexter, "Tough Rock-Ribbed Beat Sends New Band," *Down Beat*, July 1938, 2.

18. Dave Tough, "Hide Hitters Hangout," *Metronome*, October 1937, 54.

19. This paragraph paraphrases Burt Korall, liner essay, "Three Chords For Beauty's Sake, and One To Pay the Rent," *The Complete Artie Shaw, Vol. Five, 1941–42*, Bluebird RCA AXM2-5576.

20. George Frazier, "Frazier's Thumbs Go Up For Shaw Band," *Down Beat*, September 15, 1941, 9.

21. Barry Ulanov, "Tommy Dorsey, Spivak Bands Thrill," *Metronome*, July, 1942, 12.

22. Artie Shaw quoted in Balliett, 162.

23. John Von Ohlen quoted in Scott K. Fish, "John Von Ohlen: Natural Style," *Modern Drummer*, March 1955, 70.

24. Leonard Feather, "The Dave Tough Story," *Down Beat*, July 1, 1953, 21.

BUDDY RICH

1. Harvey Siders, "Drum Schticks," *Down Beat*, March 15, 1973, 15.

2. Ralph J. Gleason, "Buddy Rich, a Demon With a Drum," *New York Post*, February 22, 1967, 45.

3. Ed Thigpen quoted in "Boy With A Drum," Gene Lees *Jazzletter*, February 1986, 2.

4. Gene Krupa quoted in Gene Webb, "The Last Interview," *Down Beat*, March 14, 1974, 16.

5. George Simon, "Buddy Rich," *Metronome*, August 1953, 12.

6. George Hoefer, "Buddy Rich—Portrait of a Man In Conflict," Part I, *Down Beat*, June 9, 1960, 19.

7. Buddy Rich quoted in "What I Like To Listen To," *Crescendo*, November 1974, 19 (note for this paragraph only).

8. Joe Marsala quoted in Leonard Feather, "The Joe Marsala Story," *Down Beat Music Yearbook '69*, 24, 60.

9. Teddy McRae, Oral History Files, Institute of Jazz Studies, Rutgers University, Newark, N.J.

10. Gene Krupa quoted in Willis Conover, "Gene Krupa and Buddy Rich," *Metronome*, April 1956, 27.

11. Helen Forrest with Bill Libbey, *I Had the Craziest Dream* (New York: Coward, McCann and Geoghegan, 1982), 78.

12. Buddy Rich quoted in "Rich and Tormé—Wild Repartee," Part II, *Down Beat*, February 23, 1978, 21.

13. Les Tomkins, "Buddy Rich: The Freedom of Discipline," *Crescendo*, June/July 1983, 24.

14. George Simon, "Artie Shaw Kicks with Seabiscuit Gusto," *Simon Says: The Sights and Sounds of the Swing Era 1935–1955* (New Rochelle, N.Y.: Arlington House, 1971), 124.

15. *Ibid.*

16. Gus Johnson, Oral History Files, Institute of Jazz Studies, Rutgers University.

17. Mel Tormé, "Buddy Rich: One of a Kind," *American Way*, December 1974, 19.

18. Buddy Rich quoted in Burt Korall, *The Complete Artie Shaw, Vol. II*, liner essay, Bluebird Records.

19. Whitney Balliett, "Super Drummer," *Improvising* (New York: Oxford University Press, 1977), 163–164.

20. Hymie Schertzer quoted in Mort Goode, "Hey Gate, How Do You Get to Carnegie Hall?", *The Complete Benny Goodman, Vol. 5*, liner essay, Bluebird Records.

21. George Hoefer, *op. cit.*

22. Buddy Rich quoted in Cheech Iero, "Buddy Rich: Revisited," *Modern Drummer*, December 1980/January 1981, 13.

23. Buddy Rich quoted in "Buddy Rich 1973—The Les Tomkins Interview," *Crescendo*, December 1973, 20.

24. Conover, *Metronome*, 27.

25. Tormé, *The American Way*, 20.

26. Hoefer, Part II, *Down Beat*, June 23, 1960, 21.

27. Ed Shaughnessy quoted in Jim Szantor, "Ed Shaughnessy: Play Like You Mean It," *Down Beat*, April 12, 1973, 21.

28. Hoefer, Part I, *Down Beat*, June 9, 1940, 18.

29. *Ibid.*

30. Les Tomkins, "Buddy Rich—On Love, Faith and Honesty," *Crescendo*, July 1981, 12, 13.

31. Buddy Rich, quoted in "Rich and Tormé," 21.

32. Elliot Tiegel, "Rich Raps," *Down Beat*, March 1982, 17.

33. Buddy Rich quoted in "The Unbeatable Buddy Rich," *Crescendo*, May 1983, 6.

34. John S. Wilson, "Jazz: Buddy Rich Band," *The New York Times*, April 24, 1983, 53.

35. Lennie Di Muzio quoted in "Buddy Remembered," *Modern Drummer*, August 1987, 24.

36. Louie Bellson quoted in "Buddy Remembered," *Modern Drummer*, August 1987, 23.

37. Jim Chapin quoted in "Buddy Remembered," *Modern Drummer*, 24.

GEORGE WETTLING

1. Max Jones, "George Wettling," *Melody Maker*, February 16, 1957.

2. Richard Gehman, "George, The Legendary Wettling," *Jazz*, October 1965, 19.

COZY COLE

1. Cozy Cole quoted in Dan Morgenstern, "Keep It Swinging: Cozy Cole," *Down Beat*, March 20, 1969, 22.

2. Mario Bauza, Oral History Files, Institute of Jazz Studies, Rutgers University, Newark, N.J.

JIMMY CRAWFORD

1. Jimmy Crawford quoted in Stanley Dance, *The World of Swing* (New York: Charles Scribner's Sons, 1974), 119.

RAY BAUDUC

1. John Chilton, *Stomp Off, Let's Go—The Story of Bob Crosby's Bob Cats and Big Band* (London: Jazz Book Service, 1983), 181.

EPILOGUE

1. George Simon, "The Rise, the Glory and the Decline," *The Big Bands* (New York: Schirmer Books, 1981), 31.

Discography

The selections in this discography are not intended as a complete accounting of the recorded output of these artists. In all cases they are selected key recordings that represent notable examples of the performer's work.

CHICK WEBB

Chick Webb: A Legend, Volume I, 1929–1936 (Decca—Jazz Heritage Series).

The Immortal Chick Webb/Stompin' At the Savoy (Columbia—Jazz Archive Series).

Chick Webb & His Orchestra Featuring Ella Fitzgerald (Folkways).

Big Band Bounce & Boogie, In the Groove, Chick Webb, 1934–1939 (Affinity—Great Britain).

Chick Webb and his Orchestra, 1937–1939 (First Time Records)

Chick Webb: King Of the Savoy, Vol. II, 1937–1939 (Decca—Jazz Heritage Series).

Chick Webb & His Orchestra 1939 (Alamac).

The Golden Swing Years, 1935–1939, Chick Webb and his orchestra (Polydor International).

Bronzeville Stomp, Chick Webb and his orchestra (Jazz Archives).

Princess of the Savoy, Chick Webb with Ella Fitzgerald, Vol. II (Decca-France).

Ella Swings The Band, Chick Webb with Ella Fitzgerald, Vol. IV (Decca-France).

GENE KRUPA

EARLY PERIOD

The Sound of Chicago, 1923–1940, Jazz Odyssey, Vol. II (Columbia).

The Chicagoans, "The Austin High Gang," 1928–1930 (Decca).

SWING PERIOD

Swing, Vol. I (RCA). An anthology of recordings made in 1936, with Benny Goodman, Roy Eldridge, Jess Stacy, Chu Berry, Allen Reuss, Israel Crosby, and Helen Ward.

BENNY GOODMAN (1934–1938)

The Complete Benny Goodman, Vols. 1–5 and 8 (Bluebird).

Roll 'Em, Volume 1, Benny Goodman (Columbia Jazz Masterpieces).

Benny Goodman Live At Carnegie Hall (Columbia Jazz Masterpieces).

The King of Swing, Benny Goodman, Complete 1937–1938 Jazz Concert No. 2 broadcasts (Columbia).

The Benny Goodman Treasure Chest broadcasts (Vols. 1–3) (MGM).

THE GENE KRUPA ORCHESTRA (1938–1942), (1945–1949).

Drummin' Man/Gene Krupa, early and later bands (Columbia).

Wire Brush Stomp, 1938–1941, early band (Bandstand Records).

Gene Krupa, early band (Top Classic Historia—Germany).

That Drummer's Band, band between 1940 and 1942 (Epic Encore Series).

Gene Krupa, His Orchestra and Anita O'Day Featuring Roy Eldridge, including material from early and later bands (Columbia).

What's This?, the modern band (Hep—Great Britain).

1940s The Small Groups: New Directions, includes five tracks by the Krupa Jazz Trio, all recorded in 1945 (Columbia Jazz Masterpieces).

THE 1950s, 1960s, 1970s

Norman Granz' Jazz At the Philharmonic, Hartford 1953 (Pablo).

Jazz at the Philharmonic: Gene Krupa & Buddy Rich, The Drum Battle (Verve).

Krupa, Hampton, Wilson (Verve).

The Gene Krupa Quartet (Clef).

Gene Krupa Plays Gerry Mulligan Arrangements (Verve).

Chicago And All That Jazz (Verve).

Together Again, with Benny Goodman, Lionel Hampton, and Teddy Wilson (RCA).

Percussion King, with orchestra conducted by George Williams (Verve).

Burnin' Beat, Buddy Rich/Gene Krupa (Verve).

Jazz At the New School, Krupa with Eddie Condon, Wild Bill Davison, Kenny Davern, and Dick Wellstood (Chiaroscuro).

RAY MCKINLEY

EARLY PERIOD (1934–1939)

The Fabulous Dorseys Play Dixieland Jazz 1934–1935, The Dorsey Brothers Orchestra (Decca).

The Dorsey Brothers Orchestra 1935 (Circle).

Dixieland Jazz Battle, Volume 2, Ray McKinley's Jazz Band (Decca).

Jimmy Dorsey's Greatest Hits, Jimmy Dorsey and his orchestra (Decca).

George Gershwin Music Played By Jimmy Dorsey and His Orchestra (Coral).

MIDDLE PERIOD (1939–1945)

Boogie Woogie, Will Bradley Orchestra with Ray McKinley (Epic).

On The Air, Will Bradley Orchestra with Ray McKinley (Airchecks).

Will Bradley and his Orchestra 1939–1941 (Bandstand).

Ray McKinley Orchestra 1942, singles, i.e., "Rock a Bye Bay," "That Russian Winter," "Hard Hearted Hannah," "Big Boy" (Capitol).

Glenn Miller Army Air Force Band, five-record set (RCA Victor).

LATE PERIOD (1946–1960s)

Ray McKinley Orchestra, The Most Versatile Band in the Land Featuring Compositions & Arrangements by Eddie Sauter (All 28 sides in this two-record set originally appeared on Majestic Records. They were cut in 1946 and 1947) (Savoy Jazz).

One Night Stand with Ray McKinley, 1948 and 1949 airshots with the McKinley Orchestra (Joyce).

Hi-Fi Dixie, Ray McKinley Dixie Six, 1955 (Grand Award).

The New Glenn Miller Orchestra under the direction of Ray McKinley (RCA Victor).

The Glenn Miller Sound, Glenn Miller Orchestra under the direction of Ray McKinley (RCA Victor).

Dance Anyone, Glenn Miller Orchestra under the direction of Ray McKinley (RCA Victor).

Glenn Miller Time, Glenn Miller Orchestra under the direction of Ray McKinley (RCA Victor).

Echoes of Glenn Miller, Glenn Miller Orchestra under the direction of Ray McKinley (RCA Victor).

One Band Two Styles, Ray McKinley and his orchestra, six Eddie Sauter originals and six Rodgers and Hart tunes, arranged by Sauter (RCA Camden).

Ray McKinley's Greatest Hits, Ray McKinley and his orchestra, small and large bands (Dot).

JO JONES

The Best of Count Basie, Count Basie and his orchestra (Decca).

Good Morning Blues, Count Basie and his orchestra, featuring Jimmy Rushing, Helen Humes (Decca).

Basie Live! Count Basie and his orchestra broadcasts (Trip).

Count Basie At the Savoy Ballroom, Count Basie and his orchestra broadcast (Everest).

Count Basie and His Orchestra, 1937 broadcasts (Alamac).

The Complete Count Basie, Vols. 1–10, 1936–1941, Count Basie and his orchestra (French CBS).

The Complete Count Basie, Vols. 11–20, 1941–1951, Count Basie and his orchestra (French CBS).

Swingmusic From The Southland Cafe, Boston, Count Basie and his orchestra broadcast (Collector's Classics).

Lester Young & Charlie Christian, 1939–1940, broadcasts with Count Basie Band (Jazz Archives).

Charlie Christian, Lester Young Together 1940, members of the Count Basie and Benny Goodman Bands (Jazz Archives).

The Lester Young Story Vol. 1, *Jones-Smith & Wilson-Holiday Inc.*, (Columbia—John Hammond Collection).

The Lester Young Story, Vol. 2, *A Musical Romance*, with Billie Holiday (Columbia—Contemporary Masters Series).

The Lester Young Story, Vol. 3, *Enter the Count* (Columbia—Contemporary Masters Series).

The Lester Young Story, Vol. 4, *Lester Leaps In* (Columbia—Contemporary Masters Series).

The Lester Young Story, Vol. 5, *Evening of a Basie-ite* (Columbia—Contemporary Masters Series).

Billie Holiday, The Golden Years (Columbia).

Billie Holiday, The Golden Years Volume II (Columbia).

The Complete Commodore, Vol. I (Mosiac).

Lester Young, Kansas City Six and Five (Commodore).

Lester Young, The Kansas City Six (Commodore).

The Commodore Years, The Tenor Sax: Lester Young, Chu Berry & Ben Webster (Commodore sides on Atlantic).

Historical Prez, Lester Young 1940–1944, including broadcasts with the Count Basie band (Everybodys).

The Basie Special, Count Basie and his orchestra 1944–1946 broadcasts (Everybodys).

Count Basie—V Discs, 1944–1945, Count Basie and his orchestra (Jazz Society).

Lester Young, including "Jammin' The Blues" soundtrack (Jazz Anthology—Musicdisc).

Lester Young, Pres, The Complete Savoy Recordings (Savoy).

Count Basie With Illinois Jacquet, Count Basie and his orchestra (Saga).

The Count, Count Basie and his orchestra (RCA Camden).

Basie's Basement, Count Basie and his orchestra, featuring Jimmy Rushing (RCA Camden).

The Essential Buck Clayton (Vanguard).

Count Basie At Newport, Count Basie and his orchestra (Verve).

The Tatum Group Masterpieces in eight volumes (one of the volumes features Jones, Red Callendar, and Tatum) (Pablo).

Lester Young, Pres And Teddy And Oscar (Verve).

The Impeccable Teddy Wilson (Verve).

Basie Reunions, (featuring former Basie sidemen (Prestige).

Jo Jones Trio (Everest).

Percussion And Bass, Jo Jones and Milt Hinton (Everest).

The Essential Jo Jones (Vanguard).

The Main Man, Jo Jones (Pablo).

The Drums, Jo Jones (Jazz Odyssey).

The Lion and the Tiger, Willie "The Lion" Smith and Jo Jones (Jazz Odyssey).

SID CATLETT

Sammy Stewart and Orchestra singles: "Cause I Feel Low Down," "Old Man River," Crazy Rhythm," "Wob-a-ly Walk," 1928 (Vocalion).

Benny Carter 1933 (Prestige).

A Study in Frustration, Fletcher Henderson and his orchestra, (Columbia).

Teddy Wilson and His All-Stars (Columbia).

Benny and Sid "Roll Em," Benny Goodman and his orchestra airshots (Honeysuckle Rose).

Clarinet À La King, Benny Goodman and his sextet/orchestra (Epic).

Benny Goodman at the Hotel Sherman (Fanfare).

The Alternate Goodman, Vol. 5, Benny Goodman and his orchestra (Phontastic).

Benny Goodman presents Arrangements by Eddie Sauter, Benny Goodman and his orchestra (Columbia).

Benny Goodman, Volume II: Clarinet A La King (Columbia Masterpieces).

Satchmo Forever, Louis Armstrong (MCA).

The First Esquire All-American Jazz Concert (Radiola).

In the Beginning, Dizzy Gillespie (Prestige).

Duke Ellington, Vols. 26–27 (Dets).

Carnegie Hall Jazz (Verve).

Satchmo At Symphony Hall, Louis Armstrong (Decca).

Louis Armstrong and the All-Stars (SwingHouse).

The Complete Keynote Sessions, including sessions with Lester Young, Coleman Hawkins, Benny Morton (Keynote).

The Complete Commodore Recordings, Vol. 1 (Mosaic).

Swing Exercise (Capitol Jazz Classics Vol. 10).

DAVE TOUGH

Red Nichols Featuring Benny Goodman (Sunbeam).

The Complete Tommy Dorsey, Vol. II, 1936 (Bluebird).

Vol. III, 1936–1937 (Bluebird).

Vol. IV, 1937 (Bluebird).

Vol. V, 1937 (Bluebird).

Vol. VI, 1937–1938 (Bluebird).

Bunny Berigan, the 1936 Sessions, Vol. I (Jazz Information).

The Complete Benny Goodman, Vol. V, 1937–1938 (Bluebird).

Vol. VI, 1938 (Bluebird).

Vol. VII, 1938–1939 (Bluebird).

Vol. VIII, 1936–1939 (Bluebird).

Easy Does It, Tommy Dorsey and his orchestra, 1937–1950 (Swing Era Records).

Bud Freeman All-Star Jazz (Harmony).

The Greatest of Small Band Swing (Riverside).

Benny Goodman Dance Parade, Vol. II (Columbia).

Charlie Christian With Benny Goodman Sextet and Orchestra (Columbia).

Clarinet A La King, Benny Goodman and his sextet/orchestra (Epic).

Benny Goodman Presents Arrangements By Eddie Sauter, Benny Goodman and his orchestra (Columbia).

Benny Goodman, Vol. II: Clarinet A La King (Columbia Masterpieces).

The Complete Artie Shaw, Vol. V, 1941–1942 (Bluebird).

The Complete Artie Shaw, Vol. VI, 1942–1945 (Bluebird).

The Thundering Herds, Woody Herman and his orchestra (Columbia).

Woody Herman and His First Herd 1944, Vol. II (Hindsight).

Woody Herman 1945 (Fanfare).

The Complete Keynote Sessions, (Keynote).

Euphoria, Charlie Ventura (Savoy).

A Melody From The Sky, Flip Phillips (Doctor Jazz).

BUDDY RICH

EARLY PERIOD (1937–1939)

"Bei Mir Bist Du Schön," 1937 single, The Andrews Sisters with Vic Schoen and his orchestra (Decca).

"Jim Jam Stomp," 1938 single, Joe Marsala's Chicagoans (Vocalion).

Bunny Berigan, His Trumpet & His Orchestra, Volume I, Vintage Series of original 1937–1939 recordings (RCA).

The Great Dance Bands of the 30s and 40s, Bunny Berigan and his orchestra (RCA Victor).

The Complete Artie Shaw, Vol. I, 1938–1939 (Bluebird).

The Complete Artie Shaw, Vol. II, 1939 (Bluebird).

The Complete Artie Shaw, Vol. III, 1939–1940 (Bluebird).

MIDDLE PERIOD (1940–1949)

"Bugle Call Rag" and "One O'Clock Jump," a 1941 single, The Metronome All-Stars (RCA Victor).

The Incomparable Tommy Dorsey, Sentimental Gentleman Of Swing (Reader's Digest).

Swing High, Tommy Dorsey and his orchestra (Sounds of Swing).

Easy Does It, Tommy Dorsey and his orchestra (Swing Era Records).

The Sentimental Gentleman, Tommy Dorsey, broadcasts (RCA Victor).

A series of singles, Herbie Haymer Quintet, 1945 (Sunset).

Woody Herman—The Thundering Herds, including "Gee, It's Good To Hold You" and "Your Father's Mustache," 1945 (Columbia).

Benny Goodman, Volume III, All the Cats Join In, including "Rattle and Roll," 1945 (Columbia Jazz Masterpieces).

Giants Three, Lester Young, Nat King Cole, and Buddy Rich (Clef).

"Sweet Lorraine" and "Nat Meets June," 1946 single, The Metronome All-Stars (Columbia).

Buddy Rich, Both Sides, EmArcy Jazz Series (Mercury).

One Night Stand With Buddy Rich 1946, broadcasts (Joyce).

One Night Stand With Buddy Rich, Vol. 2, broadcasts (Joyce).

"Leap Here" and "Metronome Riff," 1947 single, The Metronome All-Stars with the Stan Kenton Orchestra (Capitol).

LATE PERIOD (1950–1986)

Charlie Parker With Strings, two 10" sets (Mercury).

Jazz At The Philharmonic, Norgran Blues 1950 (Verve).

Jazz At the Philharmonic, The Trumpet Battle 1952 (Verve).

Jazz At the Philharmonic, Gene Krupa & Buddy Rich, The Drum Battle (Verve).

The Orchestra and the Octet, Volume VI—1946, 1950/1951, Count Basie (French CBS).

The Tatum Group Masterpieces (Pablo).

Buddy and Sweets, Buddy Rich and Harry "Sweets" Edison (Norgran).

Buddy Rich Just Sings (Verve).

This One's For Basie, Buddy Rich and his orchestra (Norgran).

Rich Versus Roach, Buddy Rich and Max Roach (Mercury).

Playtime, Buddy Rich and his buddies (Argo).

New Versions of "Down Beat" Favorites, Harry James and his orchestra (MGM).

Buddy Rich: Swingin' New Big Band, recorded live at The Chez in Hollywood (Pacific Jazz).

Big Swing Face, the Buddy Rich Big Band, recorded live at The Chez in Hollywood (Pacific Jazz).

Keep The Customer Satisfied, the Buddy Rich Big Band, recorded live at the Tropicana in Las Vegas (Liberty).

Mercy, Mercy, the Buddy Rich Big Band, recorded live at Caesars Palace in Las Vegas (World Pacific Jazz).

Class of '78, the Buddy Rich Big Band (The Great American Gramophone Company).

Rich in London, the Buddy Rich Big Band, recorded live at Ronnie Scott's (RCA).

Transition, Buddy Rich/Lionel Hampton (Groove Merchant).

Mr. Drums, the Buddy Rich Big Band, recorded live on King Street, San Francisco (Cafe Records).

SONNY GREER

Duke Ellington 1938, Duke Ellington and his orchestra (The Smithsonian Collection).

Duke Ellington, 1939, Duke Ellington and his orchestra (The Smithsonian Collection).

Duke Ellington 1940, Duke Ellington and his orchestra (The Smithsonian Collection).

Duke Ellington 1941, Duke Ellington and his orchestra (The Smithsonian Collection).

GEORGE WETTLING

Ballin' The Jack, Eddie Condon and his jazz band (Commodore).

Jazz A-Plenty, Wild Bill Davison and his Commodores and George Brunis and his jazz band (Commodore).

Three's No Crowd, the Bud Freeman Trio (Commodore).

COZY COLE

The Complete Lionel Hampton 1937–1941 (Bluebird).

16 Cab Calloway Classics, Cab Calloway and his orchestra (French CBS).

The Complete Keynote Collection.

JIMMY CRAWFORD

Rhythm Is Our Business, Vol. I, 1934–1935, Jimmie Lunceford and his orchestra (Decca—Jazz Heritage Series).

Harlem Shout, Vol. II, 1935–1936, Jimmie Lunceford and his orchestra (Decca—Jazz Heritage Series).

For Dancers Only, Vol. III, 1936–1937, Jimmie Lunceford and his orchestra (Decca—Jazz Heritage Series).

Blues In The Night, Vol. IV, 1938–1942, Jimmie Lunceford and his orchestra (Decca—Jazz Heritage Series).

Lunceford Special, Jimmie Lunceford and his orchestra (Columbia Hall of Fame Series).

O'NEIL SPENCER

Boss Of The Bass, John Kirby (Columbia).
The Biggest Little Band, John Kirby, 1937–1941 (The Smithsonian Collection).

CLIFF LEEMAN

The Complete Artie Shaw, Vol. I (1938–1939) (Bluebird).
The Complete Charlie Barnet, Vol. III (1939–1940) (Bluebird).
The Complete Charlie Barnet, Vol IV (1940) (Bluebird).
The Complete Charlie Barnet, Vol. V (1940–1941) (Bluebird).
The Complete Charlie Barnet, Vol. VI (1941–1942) (Bluebird).

RAY BAUDUC

The Best of Bob Crosby, Bob Crosby and his orchestra (MCA).
Bob Crosby 1936–1956, Bob Crosby and his orchestra (Coral).
Bob Crosby and his Orchestra 1938–1940, broadcasts (Sunbeam).

The Interviewees

HENRY ADLER is the innovative veteran New York drum teacher.

VAN ALEXANDER, arranger and bandleader, first gained a reputation as a member of the arranging staff of the Chick Webb band.

ERNIE ANDERSON is a concert producer and publicist.

JERVIS ANDERSON is a staff writer at *The New Yorker*.

LOUIS ARMSTRONG, who made a giant contribution as a trumpeter and vocalist, increased the sophistication and impact of jazz improvisation, particularly in his breakthrough years, the 1920s.

JEFF ATTERTON, a lifelong music fan and a journalist, has been employed for many years as a jazz expert in major retail record outlets.

WHITNEY BALLIETT is jazz critic for *The New Yorker*.

EDDIE BAREFIELD, saxophonist, clarinetist, and arranger became a professional in 1926 and has played with Bennie Moten, Cab Calloway, Les Hite, Fletcher Henderson, Duke Ellington, Benny Carter, Sy Oliver, and others.

DANNY BARKER, guitarist, singer, composer, educator, and author, has been associated with such top-level musicians as Sidney Bechet, Bunk Johnson, Wilbur DeParis, James P. Johnson, Lucky Millinder, Benny Carter, and Cab Calloway.

COUNT BASIE, a name synonymous with swing, was a leader of great bands from 1935 until his death in 1984.

MARIO BAUZA, a trumpeter in the bands of Chick Webb and Cab Calloway, helped organize Machito and his Afro Cubans in the early 1940s and was musical director of that organization.

BILLY BAUER, a guitarist who came to fame with the Woody Herman First Herd in the 1940s, has been associated with Lennie Tristano, Lee Konitz, Jack Teagarden, Benny Goodman, and a number of other top-level jazz people.

LOUIE BELLSON, drummer, composer, and bandleader, is a veteran of many musical experiences, including the bands of Benny Goodman, Tommy Dorsey, Duke Ellington, Harry James, and Count Basie, and all-star small groups and his own big and small bands.

TOMMY BENFORD, a pioneer on drums, has worked and/or recorded with such leading lights of jazz as Jelly Roll Morton, Coleman Hawkins, Elmer Snowden, Rex Stewart, Bob Wilber, Eddie South, Dick Wellstood, and the Harlem Blues and Jazz Band.

EDDIE BERT, a trombonist, has performed with musicians of every stripe, i.e., Sam Donahue, Red Norvo, Woody Herman, Charlie Barnet, Stan Kenton, Benny Goodman, Thelonious Monk, Charles Mingus, Buddy Rich, Thad Jones and Mel Lewis, and worked in Broadway shows as well.

BARNEY BIGARD, a distinctive New Orleans clarinetist, worked with King Oliver but gained a worldwide reputation as a featured player with the Duke Ellington Orchestra and the Louis Armstrong All-Stars.

JOHNNY BLOWERS, a drummer who has been associated with traditional jazz, broke in in the 1930s with Bobby Hackett and Bunny Berigan and subsequently has functioned as a New York studio man and free-lance jazz performer.

BOB BLUMENTHAL, the well-known jazz writer and critic, writes regularly for the *Boston Phoenix*.

WILL BRADLEY was a facile, highly individual trombonist who led a successful band in the 1940s and later turned to free-lance performing and studio work in New York.

RUBY BRAFF is a leading jazz trumpet stylist who has worked with a variety of musicians.

BOB BROOKMEYER, valve trombonist, pianist, educator, and composer-arranger who concerns himself with exploratory projects, has performed and/or written for several European radio bands, Gerry Mulligan, Jimmy Giuffre, the Terry Gibbs Dream Band, the Mel Lewis Jazz Orchestra, and his own unit, co-led by Clark Terry.

LAWRENCE BROWN, a facile and distinctive trombone stylist, spent much of working life (1932–51, 1960–70) as one of the key members of the Duke Ellington Orchestra.

PHIL BROWN, a drummer who played with Charlie Parker, Stan Getz, and the Claude Thornhill and Buddy Rich Orchestras, is now a New York businessman.

DANNY BURGAUER, who began as a drummer, later became a top executive at Manny's, the famed New York musical instrument store.

JOE BUSHKIN, a piano stylist who first became active with major jazz musicians in the 1930s, has had a diversified career working with Tommy Dorsey, Benny Goodman, Bing Crosby, and his own groups.

AL CASEY, a guitarist with the Harlem Blues and Jazz Band, has had a distinguished career playing with such memorable musicians as Fats Waller, Chu Berry, Teddy Wilson, Earl Hines, Big Sid Catlett, and King Curtis.

GLADYS CATLETT was married to the famed drummer Sid Catlett.

SID CATLETT, JR., is the son of the great jazz drummer.

JIM CHAPIN is a drummer, drum teacher, and scholar whose accomplishments, particularly as a teacher, are admired in the world music community.,

DOC CHEATHAM, both a lead and jazz trumpeter, has played with many bands and groups, including those fronted by Chick Webb, Cab

Calloway, Sam Wooding, Teddy Wilson, Eddie Heywood, and Benny Goodman.

JOHN CHILTON, a British trumpeter-flugelhorn player and composer, is also a noted jazz writer with several books to his credit, including *Salute To Satchmo* (with Max Jones) and *Who's Who In Jazz—Storyville to Swing Street*.

SPENCER CLARK was a bass saxophone player who played with drummer Dave Tough in Europe in the late 1920s.

BUCK CLAYTON, trumpeter, arranger-composer, bandleader, teacher, and author, was a member of the late 1930s/early 1940s Count Basie Orchestra that many critics feel was Basie's best.

EDDIE CONDON, guitarist, banjo player, group leader, author, and impresario, moved from Chicago, where he performed with other significant players of his generation (i.e., Dave Tough, Gene Krupa, Bud Freeman, Jimmy McPartland, and Frank Teschmaker), to New York, where he blossomed as a player, recording artist, group leader, concert producer, and nightclub owner.

D. RUSSELL CONNOR is co-author of *BG—On Record, A Bio-Discography of Benny Goodman*.

HELEN OAKLEY DANCE, who has done very meaningful work as a jazz record and concert producer, is a respected jazz critic.

STANLEY DANCE is a jazz critic and authority on the Swing period.

DON DEMICHAEL, a drummer and vibraphone player from Louisville, Ky., became widely known as a critic and editor of *Down Beat* in the 1960s.

DAVE DEXTER, journalist and former recording executive for Capitol Records, wrote many informative reviews and articles during the Swing years.

LENNIE DI MUZIO is the director of artist relations with the Avedis Zildjian Cymbal Company.

BABY DODDS, the late New Orleans drummer who became a model for many drummers in the 1920s and 1930s, long has been widely admired for the creativity, drive, and precision of his work with such important jazz practitioners as Bunk Johnson, King Oliver, Louis Armstrong, Jelly Roll Morton, Jimmie Noone, and Sidney Bechet.

FRANK DRIGGS, a noted jazz authority, is a record producer, writer, and collector of rare jazz photographs.

WILSON DRIVER, a drummer from Birmingham, Ala., taught Jo Jones and was an important influence on him during his early years.

EDDIE DURHAM, trombonist, guitarist, composer, and arranger, performed and wrote for Swing era bands headed by Bennie Moten, Willie Bryant, Count Basie, Jimmie Lunceford, Glenn Miller, Artie Shaw, and the International Sweethearts of Rhythm.

HARRY "SWEETS" EDISON, trumpeter, a longtime member of the

Count Basie band, is an immediately identifiable stylist who has worked with Jazz At the Philharmonic, as a free-lance and studio musician, and as a leader of his own groups.

JACK EGAN, journalist, PR man, band manager, and advance man, was the intimate of many of the most significant musicians and band leaders of the Swing years.

ROY ELDRIDGE, a highly influential trumpeter, particularly during the Swing years, was featured with Fletcher Henderson, Teddy Hill, Gene Krupa, Benny Goodman, Artie Shaw, and a variety of small bands.

MERCER ELLINGTON, son of Duke Ellington, composer-arranger, trumpeter, now leader of the Ellington Orchestra, worked closely with his father and has written for bands (i.e., "Things Ain't What They Used To Be") and led them since the 1940s.

NESUHI ERTEGUN was an esteemed record producer, executive and jazz authority.

PEE WEE ERWIN, featured trumpeter with Joe Haynes, Ray Noble, Benny Goodman, and Tommy Dorsey during the 1930s, led his own bands and was a prominent New York studio musician.

BILL ESPOSITO is a writer on jazz.

DON FAGERQUIST was a modern trumpeter who functioned well in various contexts: with bands (Gene Krupa, Artie Shaw, Woody Herman, Les Brown, Pete Rugolo), small groups (Dave Pell, Shelly Manne, Laurindo Almeida), and singers (Mel Tormé and Anita O'Day).

ART FARMER, a distinctive modern trumpet/flugelhorn player, is a product of a number of bands (Lionel Hampton, Gerald Wilson, Benny Carter), small units (Charles Mingus, Horace Silver, Gerry Mulligan), and his own groups—some of which he co-led with saxophonist-composer Benny Golson.

LEONARD FEATHER, a leading jazz critic, writes regularly for *The Los Angeles Times* and a variety of newspapers and magazines here and abroad.

GRAHAM FORBES, a pianist who played with the bands of Bunny Berigan and Tommy Dorsey, was also Frank Sinatra's accompanist.

HELEN FORREST, one of the best of the big band singers during the Swing years, was featured with Artie Shaw, Benny Goodman, and Harry James and is still active.

VERNEL FOURNIER, a drummer from New Orleans who has performed with many jazz musicians, ranging from Lester Young to George Shearing, made his reputation with the Ahmad Jamal Trio in the late 1950s and 1960s.

GEORGE FRAZIER, one of the most provocative jazz writers of the late 1930s/early 1940s, went on to write for top publications, including *Life* and *Esquire,* closing his career as a columnist for the *Boston Globe.*

BUD FREEMAN, a pioneer jazz musician and a key influence on tenor saxophone, has been a factor in bands led by Ben Pollack, Red Nichols, Tommy Dorsey, Benny Goodman, Paul Whiteman, and countless smaller units featuring leading musicians.

MILT GABLER, the internationally known record producer, formed his own jazz label, Commodore, in the 1930s.

STEVE GADD, one of the most in-demand drummers in New York, has recorded with most of the biggest names in popular music, from James Brown and Aretha Franklin to Stevie Wonder and Paul Simon.

SHELTON GARY is a New York drummer who was a protégé of the late Jo Jones.

RICHARD GEHMAN was a popular free-lance writer who had a great interest in jazz.

TERRY GIBBS, a modern counterpart to Swing vibraphonists Lionel Hampton and Red Norvo, became a familiar name in the 1940s as a member of the Buddy Rich and Woody Herman bands, later working with Benny Goodman, Buddy DeFranco (as a co-leader), and with his own big bands and small units.

DIZZY GILLESPIE, the trumpeter-composer-arranger-bandleader who co-led the bebop revolution of the 1940s, continues to be innovative.

RALPH J. GLEASON, the respected jazz and pop music critic, started out as founder of the periodical *Jazz Information,* moved on to write a syndicated column for the *San Francisco Chronicle* while contributing to a variety of magazines, and concluded his career as an executive with Fantasy Records.

BENNY GOODMAN, clarinetist and bandleader, was one of the most prominent figures of the Swing years who retained his influence until his passing in 1986.

GORDON "CHRIS" GRIFFIN, trumpeter, a member of the great Benny Goodman band of the mid and late 1930s, has spent much of his career as a New York studio man and free-lance musician.

FREDDIE GRUBER is an important drum teacher in Los Angeles.

RICHARD HADLOCK, a well-known jazz authority, is the author of *Jazz Masters of the 20s* (Macmillan).

BOB HAGGART, bassist, bandleader, and studio player, became internationally known as a member of the Bob Crosby band (1935–42).

LENNY HAMBRO, saxophonist and clarinetist, has headed jazz groups, made records as a leader, played with bands (Gene Krupa, Ray McKinley, Billy Butterfield, Machito), and worked on the business side of music, running a company that produces music for films and commercials.

CHICO HAMILTON, drummer and group leader, played with Lester Young, Count Basie, Charlie Barnet, Lionel Hampton, and Gerry Mulligan before heading his own groups, which have featured several excellent players, i.e., Eric Dolphy, Buddy Collette, Jim Hall, and Charles Lloyd.

JOHN HAMMOND, legendary talent scout and recording man, brought Count Basie out of Kansas City and discovered and/or recorded many key artists, including Billie Holiday, Aretha Franklin, Bob Dylan, and Bruce Springsteen.

LIONEL HAMPTON, pianist, drummer, singer, and a great vibraphone player, has led bands of his own since leaving Benny Goodman in 1940.

RICHARD HARRISON, a long-time devotee of jazz, gained a great reputation as a cartographer for *Time Inc.*

CARL HAVERLIN, a devotee of many kinds of music, was president of BMI for over two decades.

HAYWOOD HENRY, a saxophonist-clarinetist who worked with the Erskine Hawkins band from 1935 until the mid-1950s, continues to be associated with Swing Era musicians.

NAT HENTOFF is the internationally known jazz authority and social commentator.

WOODY HERMAN was a much admired bandleader from 1936 until his death in 1988.

WARREN W. HICKS is a co-author of *BG—On Record, A Bio-Discography of Benny Goodman.*

EARL HINES, a pianist and bandleader who had an influence on several generations of musicians, performed with most of the great jazz creators, ranging from Louis Armstrong to Charlie Parker.

MILT HINTON, the jazz bassist, educator, and photographer who spent many years with the Cab Calloway band, subsequently became one of the busiest musicians on the New York studio and record session scenes.

GEORGE HOEFER, one of the pioneer jazz critics, wrote a column, "The Hot Box," on recordings, for *Down Beat* from the mid-1930s until the 1960s.

HELEN HUMES, the singer who replaced Billie Holiday in the Count Basie band in 1938, had notable success as a jazz and rhythm and blues singer before passing away in 1981.

CHUBBY JACKSON, who established his reputation as a bassist and personality with Woody Herman's First Herd (1943–1946), has led his own bands and been featured with Charlie Barnet, Charlie Ventura, and Lionel Hampton, among others.

ILLINOIS JACQUET, saxophonist, bassoonist, and bandleader, played with Lionel Hampton and Count Basie in the 1940s before going on his own and appearing as a soloist in and leader of small and large bands.

LEE JESKE, a former *Down Beat* staff member, is jazz critic for the *New York Post* and New York Bureau Chief for *Cash Box*, the music trade publication.

GUS JOHNSON, a drummer who first became known with the Jay McShann band featuring Charlie Parker, has performed with an interesting set of leaders, including Count Basie, Earl Hines, Cootie Williams, Buck Clayton, Al Cohn, Zoot Sims, Woody Herman, Gerry Mulligan, Stan Getz, and Yank Lawson and Bob Haggart (The World's Greatest Jazz Band).

TAFT JORDAN, trumpeter, performed with bands led by Chick Webb, Duke Ellington, Don Redman, Benny Goodman and in the pit band for the Broadway show, *Hello Dolly!*

MAX KAMINSKY, who played trumpet with Tommy Dorsey and Artie Shaw during the Swing years, has spent much of his career appearing and recording with traditional jazz musicians like Eddie Condon, Bud Freeman, Georg Brunis, Art Hodes, Sidney Bechet, Mezz Mezzrow, and Jack Teagarden.

CONNIE KAY, the drummer with the Modern Jazz Quartet from 1955 to 1974, and from 1981 to the present, is an adaptable musician whose multiple credits, ranging from Benny Goodman to Charlie Parker, testify to his ability.

STANLEY KAY, a drummer who worked with Buddy Rich, Patti Page, Frankie Laine, and Josephine Baker, has been in personal management in the entertainment business for many years.

ANDY KIRK is a well-known Swing era bandleader, who featured a number of fine musicians in his organization.

BOB KITSIS (CURTIS), a pianist during the Swing years with bands led by Artie Shaw, Tommy Dorsey, Gene Krupa, Red Norvo, and Eddy Duchin, has spent much of his career as a New York studio musician and free-lancer.

IRV KLUGER, one of the early bop drummers in the 1940s, applied his talent in the bands of Georgie Auld, Boyd Raeburn, Artie Shaw, Benny Goodman, Stan Kenton, Tex Beneke, and Woody Herman, in a variety of Broadway shows, and in Hollywood and Las Vegas.

HERMAN KOGAN was a writer for *The Chicago Sun-Times.*

JOHN LA BARBERA, a trumpeter-composer-arranger who made his name writing for the Buddy Rich Big Band, also has contributed original compositions and arrangements to the libraries of the Count Basie, Glenn Miller, Doc Severinsen and Woody Herman bands.

PAT LA BARBERA, a tenor saxophone soloist who came to prominence via his association with the Buddy Rich Big Band, has been featured with Elvin Jones and records albums under his own name.

PHIL LESHIN, long-time bassist with Buddy Rich's large and small bands, is a New York PR man, personal manager, and concert producer.

STAN LEVEY, now successfully involved in his own photography business in Los Angeles, is a drummer who helped modernize jazz in the 1940s and 1950s in the company of such pathfinders as Dizzy Gillespie, Charlie Parker, Woody Herman, Stan Kenton, and others.

MIKE LEVIN is a writer and critic who did some of his most important writing on jazz in the 1940s.

JOHN LEWIS, who became firmly established in the 1950s as the Modern Jazz Quartet's pianist and musical director, has enhanced his reputation over the years as a pianist, composer, and all round musical influence.

MEL LEWIS, one of the most important modern drummers, was a highly respected band leader.

HARRY LIM was the noted record producer and jazz authority.

JOHN LISSNER is an advertising agency executive who often writes reviews and articles on jazz.

MUNDELL LOWE, a guitarist who has played with both small and large bands, notably the Ray McKinley big band in the mid-1940s, now composes and arranges for TV and films and teaches.

JOHN LUCAS, known as "Jax," was a record reviewer and writer for *Down Beat* in the 1940s.

LAWRENCE LUCIE, guitar, has been working regularly since the 1930s with fine musicians like Fletcher Henderson, Lucky Millinder, Duke Ellington (as a sub), Coleman Hawkins, Cozy Cole, and Louis Armstrong.

NELLIE LUTCHER, a distinctive singer-pianist who had a series of hit Capitol recordings in the 1940s (i.e., "Hurry On Down" and "He's A Real Gone Guy") has continued to perform while also functioning in executive capacities in the music business.

JOE MARSALA, a clarinetist, emerged in the 1930s as a New York leader of traditional, small jazz bands that featured such top drummers as Buddy Rich, Dave Tough, and Shelly Manne.

BERT MARSHALL, a drummer and singer active in Paris clubs—Bricktop's and the Folies Bergères—in the 1920s, recorded as a vocalist with Django Reinhardt and Stéphane Grappelli in 1934.

CARMEN MASTREN, guitarist, played with Tommy Dorsey (in mid-1930s to early 1940s) and the Glenn Miller Army Air Force Band during World War II, and also was active as a New York studio and free-lance musician.

JIMMY MAXWELL is a trumpeter whose ability has been clearly defined in the bands of Benny Goodman, Count Basie, Raymond

Scott, Quincy Jones, Duke Ellington, and Gerry Mulligan, in the NBC Symphony, and as a CBS staff musician.

JOHN MCDONOUGH is a free-lance jazz journalist whose work most frequently appears in *Down Beat.*

JIMMY MCPARTLAND, an important musician who emerged in Chicago in the 1920s, is a cornetist who admired and was admired by Bix Beiderbecke and, over the years, has played with like-thinking traditional jazz musicians.

TEDDY MCRAE, saxophonist and arranger, has performed and/or written for Chick Webb, Lil Armstrong, Cab Calloway, Artie Shaw, Lionel Hampton, Jimmie Lunceford, and Louis Armstrong.

JAY MCSHANN, most widely known for his 1940s band out of Kansas City that featured Charlie Parker, now works as a soloist and leader of small groups.

AL MERCURI is a drummer who has played with local bands in the Greater Boston area.

MEZZ MEZZROW, who first came to the foreground as a clarinetist in the 1920s, later was responsible for some important jazz recordings and a book, *Really The Blues,* a discussion of his life.

EDDIE MILLER, clarinet and tenor saxophone soloist with the Ben Pollack band (1930–34) and the Bob Crosby organization (1935–42), has been a studio musician and free-lancer in Hollywood since the breakup of the Crosby band during World War II.

JOHNNY MINCE, a clarinetist who rose to fame with Tommy Dorsey in the 1930s, remains an extremely active free-lance player.

JOE MORELLO, the drummer and teacher who first became internationally prominent with the Dave Brubeck Quartet (1956–1967), also has played with Gil Melle, Marian McPartland, Stan Kenton, Tal Farlow, Phil Woods, Sal Salvador, Jackie Cain and Roy Kral, and with his own groups.

DAN MORGENSTERN, critic and jazz authority, is director of the Institute of Jazz Studies at Rutgers University, Newark, N.J.

GERRY MULLIGAN, a baritone saxophonist and composer-arranger who came to the fore with the Gene Krupa, Claude Thornhill, and Miles Davis' "Birth of the Cool" bands in the 1940s, has developed into a major instrumentalist, composer and bandleader.

JOE NEWMAN, trumpeter and educator, made his reputation as a featured soloist with the Count Basie band.

ANITA O'DAY, a highly original jazz singer who first received recognition in the 1940s with the Gene Krupa and Stan Kenton bands, has worked and recorded on her own ever since, retaining her audience and enhancing her reputation for innovation.

SY OLIVER, composer and arranger with the Jimmie Lunceford and

Tommy Dorsey Orchestras during the Swing years, also was a trumpeter, singer, recording director, and bandleader.

ALLEN PALEY, a very promising drummer in the 1930s, became a drum teacher in the 1940s and later a businessman in the Washington, D.C. area.

BEVERLY PEER, bassist with the Chick Webb band (1936–1939), has been a member of the Bobby Short trio for many years.

CHARLIE PERRY, drummer, a veteran of numerous small and big band jazz experiences, is a well-known drum scholar and teacher.

CHARLI PERSIP, a drummer, bandleader, and teacher, is a veteran of stints with Dizzy Gillespie, Harry James, Tadd Dameron, Billy Eckstine, Gil Evans, Roland Kirk, and many others.

MEL POWELL, who first became known as a pianist and arranger-composer with Benny Goodman in the 1940s, later pursued a career as a classical composer and educator, only occasionally involving himself with jazz.

BERNIE PRIVIN, a trumpeter with various top bands during the Swing years—Artie Shaw, Charlie Barnet, Benny Goodman, the Glenn Miller Army Air Force Band—essentially has been a studio musician since the mid-1940s.

RAM RAMIREZ, composer of the standard "Lover Man," is a pianist who has worked alone, with his own trio, and in the company of such major jazzmen as Rex Stewart, Sid Catlett, Charlie Barnet, and John Kirby.

TEDDY REIG, a highly respected jazz record producer, is remembered in particular for supervising the Charlie Parker Savoy recordings and many latter-day Count Basie albums and singles.

JOAN SWALLOW REITER was an assistant editor on the staff of Time-Life Records' "The Swing Era 1940–41."

MARIE RICH is drummer Buddy Rich's widow.

MAX ROACH, drummer, composer, educator, and group leader, who has been associated with musicians of all kinds, from Red Allen to Charlie Parker to Cecil Taylor, is generally credited with bringing a variety of new concepts to drumming.

RED RODNEY, a significant bop trumpeter in the 1940s and 1950s who became prominent with the Gene Krupa, Claude Thornhill, and Woody Herman bands and the Charlie Parker Quintet, returned to high-level visibility and creativity in the 1970s and 1980s after a period away from music.

PHIL SCHAAP, a jazz authority and well-known New York disc jockey, is identified in the Metropolitan area as "the voice of WKCR-FM."

HYMIE SCHERTZER, one of the great lead alto saxophonists of the Swing years, worked with Benny Goodman and Tommy Dorsey, and, as a New York studio musician, with many top pop and jazz artists.

BOBBY SCOTT is admired for his work as a jazz pianist, for his songs ("A Taste of Honey"), for his singing, arranging, and activity as a recording supervisor, and for his fiction and nonfiction writing.

TONY SCOTT, one of the truly distinctive modern jazz clarinetists, initially worked on New York's 52nd Street with Ben Webster and Sid Catlett, and later appeared with Buddy Rich, Claude Thornhill, Duke Ellington, Billie Holiday, and Harry Belafonte before devoting himself to his own groups and concepts here and abroad.

ED SHAUGHNESSY, the drummer on TV's "Tonight Show" (hosted by Johnny Carson) since 1964, is a deeply experienced musician, having worked with big bands (Randy Brooks, Count Basie, Benny Goodman, Lucky Millinder, and Duke Ellington), small groups (Charles Mingus, Teddy Charles), and his own units.

ARTIE SHAW, top clarinetist and writer of fiction, and nonfiction, was one of the great bandleaders of the Swing era.

ARVELL SHAW, the bassist with the Louis Armstrong All Stars from 1945 to 1953, intermittently until 1957, and again in the 1960s, also has made his presence known via stints with Benny Goodman, Teddy Wilson, and others.

JOHN SIMMONS, a versatile bassist, worked and/or recorded with such leading jazz people as Benny Goodman, Roy Eldridge, Louis Armstrong, Duke Ellington, Sid Catlett, Thelonious Monk, Erroll Garner, and Tadd Dameron.

GEORGE SIMON, an editor of *Metronome* Magazine (1935–55), is a world-famous jazz critic whose primary interest is the Swing years.

FRANK STACY was New York Editor of *Down Beat* in the 1940s.

LOU STEIN, who played piano with the Ray McKinley and Charlie Ventura bands in the 1940s, later diversified, working in a variety of contexts with all kinds of musicians.

CHIP STERN, the jazz writer, critic, and drummer, is published regularly in *Musician* magazine.

REX STEWART, a trumpeter known for his half-value effects, initially made his reputation in the Fletcher Henderson band and became world famous as a member of the Duke Ellington Orchestra.

ALVIN STOLLER, a drummer with several important bands, (i.e., Tommy Dorsey and Benny Goodman), has worked in Hollywood for several decades in TV, films, radio, and recordings.

GRADY TATE, an extraordinarily flexible drummer and a singer, has been associated with the best people in jazz and popular music, ranging from Duke Ellington, Stan Getz, and Count Basie to Lena Horne, Peggy Lee, and Sarah Vaughan.

ARTHUR TAYLOR, modern drummer, author, jazz group leader, has appeared and recorded with many of the most influential jazz musicians, including Coleman Hawkins, Miles Davis, John Coltrane, Bud Powell, and Art Farmer.

BILLY TAYLOR is the famed jazz pianist, educator, and TV and radio personality.

ED THIGPEN, a drummer-educator who splits his time between America and Europe, has played with Oscar Peterson, Ella Fitzgerald, Johnny Hodges, Bud Powell, and Lennie Tristano, among others.

MEL TORMÉ, a great singer with an affinity for jazz, is also an arranger, composer, songwriter, and author.

BARRY ULANOV, long-time editor of *Metronome* Magazine, now defunct, is a leading American jazz critic and author.

DICK VANCE, a trumpeter and arranger-composer, helped bring character to the Chick Webb, Fletcher Henderson, Charlie Barnet, Don Redman, Cab Calloway, Glen Gray, and Earl Hines bands.

LEO VAUCHANT, a French drummer who showed unusual understanding for jazz in the 1920s, later came to this country and worked as an arranger in Hollywood under the name Arnaud.

JOHN VON OHLEN, a drummer who has headed has own big band and recorded as a leader, also has been in the employ of Billy Maxted, Woody Herman, and Stan Kenton.

EARLE WARREN, who played lead alto saxophone and sang with the Count Basie band from 1937 to 1945 and intermittently after that, also has been a bandleader and jazz soloist.

GEORGE WEIN, the inventor of the jazz festival, is an internationally successful concert and festival producer.

DICKY WELLS, one of the most distinctive trombone soloists of the Swing years, joined Count Basie in 1938 and rose to fame with the band.

BOB WILBER, an accomplished clarinetist, soprano and alto saxophonist, arranger, composer, and bandleader, has been associated with Sidney Bechet (his mentor), Benny Goodman, Bobby Hackett, Jack Teagarden, Eddie Condon, and The World's Greatest Jazz Band.

JOHN WILLIAMS, a bassist equally skilled in large and small bands, recorded with Billie Holiday and has appeared with the Mills Blue Rhythm Band, Benny Carter, Teddy Wilson, Frankie Newton, Coleman Hawkins, Edmond Hall, and Buddy Tate.

MARTIN WILLIAMS, the veteran jazz critic, is the author of such books as "The Art Of Jazz," "The Jazz Tradition," and "Jazz Masters of New Orleans," and countless articles for music and general interest publications.

SANDY WILLIAMS, trombonist, is known for his performances with Chick Webb, Fletcher Henderson, Benny Carter, Coleman Hawkins, and Duke Ellington, among many others.

JOHN S. WILSON is the long-time jazz and cabaret music critic of *The New York Times.*

SAM WOODING, an international figure who brought a band to Europe in the 1920s, subsequently led orchestras here and abroad and worked as an educator.

TRUMMY YOUNG, who became world-famous as a trombonist and singer with the Jimmie Lunceford band (1937–43), also was featured with Earl Hines, Charlie Barnet, Louis Armstrong, Benny Goodman, Claude Hopkins, Roy Eldridge, and Jazz at the Philharmonic.

Index